Frontier
Scouts

The Frontier Scouts

Charles Chenevix Trench

OXFORD UNIVERSITY PRESS

1986

Oxford University Press, Walton Street, Oxford OX2 6DP

Oxford New York Toronto
Delhi Bombay Calcutta Madras Karachi
Kuala Lumpur Singapore Hong Kong Tokyo
Nairobi Dar es Salaam Cape Town
Melbourne Auckland

and associated companies in
Beirut Berlin Ibadan Nicosia

Oxford is a trade mark of Oxford University Press

First published 1985 by Jonathan Cape Ltd.
First issued as an Oxford University Press paperback 1986

British Library Cataloguing in Publication Data

Trench, Charles Chenevix
The frontier scouts.
1. Great Britain. Army. Indian Army. Frontier Corps—History
2. North-West Frontier Province (Pakistan)—History, Military
I. Title
954.9'12035   DS392.N67
ISBN 0-19-285164-0

Printed in Great Britain by
Richard Clay (The Chaucer Press) Ltd.
Bungay, Suffolk

Contents

Illustrations

Maps

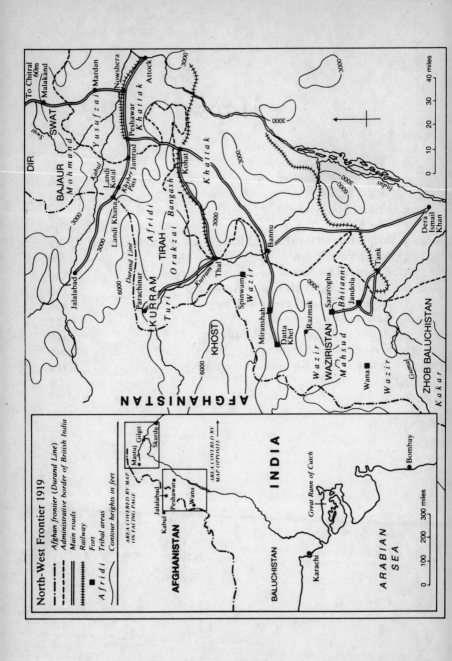

North-West Frontier 1919

- Afghan frontier (Durand Line)
- Administrative border of British India
- Main roads
- Railway
- ■ Fort
- Tribal areas
- *Afridi*
- Contour heights in feet

AFGHANISTAN

To Chitral 60m
Malakand
SWAT
DIR
Swat
BAJAUR
Mardan
Nowshera
Attock
Mohmand
Yusufzai
Kabul
Peshawar
Khattak
Landi Kotal
Jamrud
Khyber Pass
Landi Khana
Afridi
Durand Line
Jalalabad
TIRAH
Orakzai
Bangash
Kohat
Khattak
Parachinar
KURRAM
Turi
Kurram
Thal
Bannu
Spinwam
Wazir
Miranshah
Datta Khel
KHOST
Razmak
Sararogha
WAZIRISTAN
Bhitanni
Jandola
Mahsud
Wazir
Wazir
Wana
Dera Ismail Khan
Tank
Gumal
Kakar
ZHOB BALUCHISTAN
Indus

3000
6000

N ← 0 10 20 30 40 miles

AFGHANISTAN
Kabul
Jalalabad
Peshawar
Wana
Mastuj
Gilgit
Skardu
INDIA
AREA COVERED BY MAP ON FACING PAGE
AREA COVERED BY MAP OPPOSITE
BALUCHISTAN
Karachi
Great Rann of Cuch
Bombay
ARABIAN SEA

0 100 200 300 miles

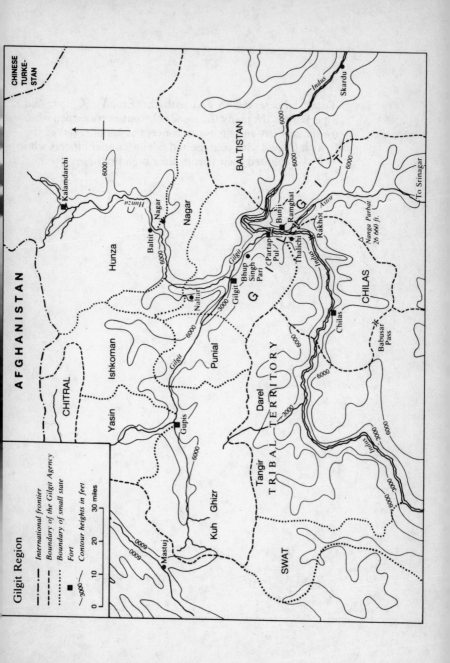

Gilgit Region

- ---- International frontier
- -·-·- Boundary of the Gilgit Agency
- ········· Boundary of small state
- ■ Fort
- —3000— Contour heights in feet

0 10 20 30 miles

CHINESE TURKE-STAN

AFGHANISTAN

Kalamdarchi

Hunza

Nagar

Baltit

Nagar

BALTISTAN

Indus

Skardu

6000

Gilgit

Naltar

CHITRAL

Ishkoman

Yasin

Kuh Ghizr

Mastuj

Gupis

Punial

Darel

Tangir

TRIBAL TERRITORY

SWAT

Bhup Singh Pari

Gilgit

Partap Pul

Thalichi

Bunji

Ramghat

Astor

Rakhot

Nanga Parbat 26,660 ft.

CHILAS

Chilas

Babusar Pass

Indus

To Srinagar

6000

3000

To all who served in and with the Frontier Corps, and especially to the many thousands of frontier tribesmen who, for modest pay and their own concept of honour, served the British Crown with courage and fidelity, under officers who counted their friendship a high privilege.

Foreword
by Philip Mason

This book has two purposes. In the first place, it is meant to provide some record of their life for those who took part in that strange series of adventures – that Homeric alternation of battles and feasts – service with the Scouts on the North-West Frontier of India. But it has also a much wider purpose – to fill one of the gaps of history and let a larger public know how this frontier was guarded, how these men lived – the discomforts and dangers they faced, the compensations they enjoyed – and how they looked on the strange task they had been allotted.

This dual purpose of course is a difficulty for the author. A man who took part in the enterprise will search eagerly for an account of some exploit which made a high point in his own life – but a succession of such incidents would be wearisome to the general reader, who wants only a few examples. The writer has to steer a difficult middle course between too much detail and too little. This Charles Chenevix Trench has skilfully done.

The Scouts were the solution to an insoluble problem. The Pathan tribes of the North-West Frontier presented to the British in India in its most extreme form a difficulty that occurs wherever a central power that governs by law and values peaceful agriculture is confronted by tribal peoples who rely on pillage for their luxuries. The country of the Pathans is much of it craggy and inhospitable, freezing in winter and scorching in summer. It has been called a gigantic slag-heap. It will barely support human life at the simplest level and the Pathan must get the price of a wife or a rifle from somewhere else, whether by force or fraud, by raiding or trading, or simply by blackmail – such as a subsidy from the government in the plains. The people are as craggy as the country, unswerving in the most fundamental forms of Islam, bitter in the blood-feud, reckless of life. They have never called any man master, preserving an obdurate independence from the rulers of the Punjab and of Afghanistan alike. How can such a people be contained?

Some such problem, I suspect, faced Julius Caesar, when he governed the Roman province that became Provence. He seized the opportunity given him by the migration of a powerful and warlike people who were moving into the territory of other tribes who, though they lived beyond the Roman frontier, were comparatively peaceful and outwardly friendly to Rome. The friendly tribes asked for help; Caesar marched in and went on to conquer Gaul. But it was much easier country than the North-West Frontier.

Caesar's solution was called in India the Forward Policy. From the time when the British first succeeded the Sikhs in control of the Punjab, there were advocates of a Forward Policy; some wanted to introduce the rule of law and administer the tribes right up to the frontier with Afghanistan, while a few fire-eaters would have gone on to Kabul. Others, of whom John Lawrence was the first, believed in a Close Border; they wanted no interference with Afghanistan and as little as possible with the mountain tribes on this side of the international frontier. No one knew exactly where this lay until it was demarcated in 1894, when it became known as the Durand Line.

The Frontier Problem had two aspects. Beyond Afghanistan lay Russia, and the Russian Empire had moved nearly a thousand miles closer in the course of the last century. Russia was the enemy. Was it, from a purely military point of view, wise to let the Russians – when they launched their attack – struggle through the mountains and the tribes of Afghanistan and to fight them only when they emerged from the passes? Or would it be better to meet them on a line from Kabul to Kandahar?

That was one aspect of the Frontier question. But it was hardly less important to stop the tribes from coming down from their mountains into administered territory, kidnapping Hindu money-lenders, stealing cattle, and abducting women. The British were sensitive about this. Both the Moguls and the Sikhs had provided an extremely loose administration; so long as the taxes came in and there was no open rebellion, they did not worry much about individual grievances. There were severe penalties for murder and burglary but not much was done to detect or to prevent them. But the British valued the tranquillity of the countryside; they believed that a private person's freedom to go about his business without assault was the justification of their rule. Here again there was controversy; John Lawrence, the supreme advocate of the Close Border, ordered his Deputy Commissioners to keep out of tribal affairs and never to cross the administrative line except to inflict punishment for a raid into administered territory. When punishment had been inflicted, British forces would at once retire. This, said his critics, meant that the tribesmen never saw the representative of the British Government unless he came to burn and kill; it was a policy of 'Butcher and Bolt', and could not possibly lead to anything but growing hostility. In Baluchistan, further south, Robert Sandeman had found it possible to establish some degree of control through tribal leaders. But the Mahsuds and Wazirs are quite different from Baluchi tribes, replied those expert in the ways of the Pathans; they have no tribal leaders in that sense and do no man's bidding.

The controversy never quite died. But eventually a compromise was reached, and it will help to understand the life of the Scouts if this is set out in its essentials, as it existed in the 1930s.

There was the North-West Frontier Province, separated from the Punjab, with a Governor in Peshawar. This consisted of six districts, in charge of six Deputy Commissioners, and was administered not very differently from any other province of British India. Murder was a crime, punishable under the Indian Penal Code; there were magistrates and judges to enforce the Code and they tried criminals under the Code of Criminal Procedure and the Indian Evidence Act. There was the usual hierarchy of officials under the orders of the Deputy Commissioner. Land Revenue was collected, and there was a normal civil police force to prevent or punish crime, as well as the Frontier Constabulary – who were armed police meant to deal with raiders from across the administrative border. In the last resort, there was the regular army.

Beyond the six districts – on the other side of the administrative line – lay tribal territory, a strip of roughly three hundred miles by one hundred, with the Durand Line and Afghanistan to the North-West. In this area there were no taxes and the Indian Penal Code did not apply as between one tribesman and another. But there were six Political Agents, each responsible for keeping in touch with the tribes allotted to him, for knowing something of their plans, reasoning with them when they planned mischief and punishing them when they committed crimes in the administered districts. If a tribesman crossed the line and committed a crime, or if he murdered a British officer in tribal territory, the Political Agent would arrange with his tribe or section that he should be tried by a Jirga, a tribal gathering. If the Jirga found him guilty, the Political Agent would pronounce sentence and hold the entire group responsible for its enforcement. It usually meant a fine of so many rifles. At his back, in support when persuasion was not enough, were the Scouts — under various names, the Tochi Scouts, the Kurram Militia, and so on. They were the Political Agent's striking force if needed; their constant duty was also to show the flag, to proclaim the presence of the Government and its right to go up to the Durand Line.

The Scouts were not regular soldiers, though they were organised like the Indian Army in platoons, commanded by junior officers of their own group. A battalion of the Indian Army had only half as many British officers as a British battalion; the platoons were commanded by Indian officers promoted from the ranks with a Viceroy's Commission. The proportion was about one British officer to fifty men. The Scouts went further and there would as a rule be about one British Officer to two hundred men — three only to a Wing, which was more than the equivalent of an infantry battalion. Further, by the end, quite a few of those who had once been British officers were actually Pathans, holding the King's Commission. The Scouts were lightly armed compared with regular troops; they prided themselves intensely on speed and endurance, on moving fast, sleeping rough and being unhampered by baggage. And when they got to the battle, they were as good as any tribesman at taking cover and marksmanship.

That brings us to the most remarkable aspect of the whole paradoxical situation. Except for the very small number of British officers, the Scouts were all Pathans. They enlisted for a fixed period, which was extended if they were promoted, but in any case they went back to live among the tribes from whom they had come. They fought against Pathans — yet they went back and lived among them in honoured retirement.

The British presence in the Punjab deprived the tribesmen of a field for raids and booty. For this the Government paid them compensation in a number of ways, disguised by various pretences. The Scouts were one form of compensation; their pay and pensions were an asset to the tribes and I suspect that, if the question had been properly put to them and if they had really understood it, most of the tribes would have regarded the disappearance of the Scouts as a loss. Another form of compensation consisted of payments to Khassadars, tribesmen who were supposed to keep the roads open, an even more irregular force, men who, as one new Viceroy remarked, guarded you by day and shot at you by night.

To read an account of the tribal areas when the Faqir of Ipi was at the height of his power might easily suggest that the whole British presence was regarded with unquenchable hate as a foreign army of occupation. This would be to suppose the tribes had a unity and a nationalism which they had not, and also it makes no allowance for their peculiar qualities. They relished danger and to them war was the supreme sport; they had also a strong but distinctly brutal sense of humour. The Scouts provided them with constant opportunities for enjoyable battles and also often appealed to their sense of humour. Tale after tale in Charles Chenevix Trench's book displays their ruthlessness; they showed no mercy and expected none. But when it was over, when the Political Agent had imposed his fine and the kidnapped hostages had gone safely home, they would happily discuss with Scout officers the mistakes either side had made, in the spirit of friendly teams after a football match. They would torture and kill the wounded and mutilate the dead — yet afterwards come to a *tikala* — a feast — and would tell the Political Agent he was their father and mother.

After the South African War, it became possible to buy Martini rifles in the ports of the Persian Gulf. The Afridis round the Khyber Pass invested some of their tribal money in an organisation to buy these rifles and move them secretly across Persia to the Khyber. When the Royal Navy stopped the supply, the Afridis petitioned the Government of India to compensate them for their losses — as though a burglar who had dropped his tools when surprised by the police should ask them to buy him a new set. And after a Scouts battle, the enemy wounded would be brought trustingly into the Civil hospital at Razmak to be stitched up — or even into a Scouts' fort to the Scouts' own hospital.

Among the Scouts themselves, an orderly was expected to stay by his wounded officer and die with him if need be — and he almost always did. What could be more touching than Nat Cosby's story in this book of the boy who would consent to an operation that would save his life only if his Commanding Officer stayed with him? Again and again, personal liking, trust, affection, overcame differences of religion and culture.

Nobody could ever be sure what would happen. A sentry, inflamed by religious zeal, suddenly shot a British officer as he lay sleeping in the open because his feet were disrespectfully turned towards Mecca. Everyone — British and Pathans alike — agreed that the sentry must die. But so that it should not start a blood-feud, there was also agreement that his brother should fire the shot. When it was put to him, the murderer also agreed that this was fitting. So the episode ended decently and in order.

There is paradox upon paradox in any account of this strange situation in which personal relationships so often cut across the Pathan's obstinate determination to keep his hills to himself and his way of life unpolluted. But one overriding element in all that took place was the code of conduct known as Pukhtunwali – what is proper for a Pathan – the code on which Charles Chenevix Trench has, I am sure rightly, laid such emphasis. The essence of it was hospitality and revenge. To allow a guest to be killed was as disgraceful as to leave unavenged the murder of a kinsman. I have heard of a Khassadar who shot his own son in order to protect an English officer whom he was escorting.

In the last half century, we have learnt a great deal not only about human behaviour but about codes of behaviour among animals. Wolves, we are told, are chivalrous to a beaten enemy and to females. In the Maori wars, a truce was observed at sunset so that everyone could fetch water from the river. But in the code of Pukhtunwali, as in everything else, the Pathans seem to have included extremes of ferocity and fidelity to an unusual degree.

The English have generally been successful at getting other people to fight for them and where they have encountered an enemy who was formidable in battle, they have often enlisted the defeated in their own ranks as soon as the war was over. In India, they used Madrassis to conquer Bengal and eventually almost stopped enlisting Madrassis; they used men from Behar and Oudh to conquer the Sikhs – and immediately began to recruit Sikhs. Perhaps their most obviously striking successes were with Highlanders and Gurkhas. But mistakes were made with the Highlanders at first and it was a long time before the Highland regiments were fully accepted as the crack corps that they eventually became. The English have generally been less sensitive to the peculiarities of their Celtic neighbours than to those of Sikhs and Pathans and Arabs, perhaps feeling that it was perverse of anyone so near home to be different at all. There were a number of mutinies in Highland regiments before they settled down into being one of the glories of the British Army.

The Scouts had their troubles too and it may seem to the reader that the early part of this book is a record of failures. There was a problem which could not be avoided. The men had to be trusted; that was the essence of the idea. But it was also necessary to build up a loyalty to the Scout organisation – to the Tochi Scouts or the Kurram Militia or whoever it might be – a loyalty that overrode tribal loyalty. It was eventually decided that, though it was convenient to keep men of one tribe together in a platoon, any combination of platoons must consist of several tribes. That was perhaps the chief lesson of the first period, which ended with 1919.

It had been a period in which there had been many set-backs, and the worst set-back was the retreat of 1919. How slow the British were to learn that everywhere their ascendancy depended on their keeping up the bluff that their power was permanent and they invincible! None the less, in spite of set-backs, the idea of the Scouts had proved a success. In spite of many anomalies, it was on the whole better not to administer up to the Durand Line but confine British ideas of justice to the districts of the Province, and, beyond the administrative line, to keep only the most elementary order, and that in accordance with Pathan standards of conduct. And only Pathans were used to enforce it and as a first line of defence for their own territory.

The policy was Lord Curzon's, and in broad outline it lasted unchanged until Independence. It was a policy of compromise; the tribes were controlled but neither pacified nor cowed. The Scouts were the chief instrument of the policy and they too had to compromise continually, not only in what they did, but in their methods.

Charles Chenevix Trench has a story which illustrates the difficulties. The Scouts intervened in a battle between Mahsuds and Wazirs, which might have been regarded as none of their business. It was highly dangerous and they had insufficient force. But the Political Agent had used his influence to bring the parties to an agreement – and the agreement had been broken. So the Political Agent was involved and he ordered intervention. A battle was already raging but Scout officers rode forward between the battle-lines and the firing stopped; they made peace. At the feast that followed, a tribesman said reproachfully, 'You should not have attempted that with less than a thousand men.' But it had worked. Sometimes, too, the Scouts turned a blind eye and did rather less than they should have done according to the book.

In methods, too, there was continual interplay between British ideas of military discipline and the special qualities needed by irregulars – rapid movement, swift deployment, use of cover and so on. A new commandant might lay more emphasis on one than the other, but everyone recognised that both were essential. Discipline went together with spit-and-polish and in such a force as this – tribesmen keeping tribesmen in order – discipline was a matter of life and death. But the Scouts must also be able to move as well on the hill, to shoot as straight and move as fast and as far in a day as any Pathan – and in all these respects be better than any regular soldier!

This book does not attempt to discuss such questions as control of the Frontier from the air or the value to the British Army, as well as the Indian, of this superb training ground for mountain warfare. What it aims to do, and does, is to set out in vivid colloquial language what the Scouts did and how it seemed from their own point of view. Much of it is told in their own words and they did not as a rule much concern themselves about the wisdom of the policy they were carrying out and whether there was any alternative. It was not their job to ask questions. This surely makes it the more valuable as a record. It is a remarkable record, of courage and devotion to duty, but also of good humour and laughter and affection, between officers and men, between hunters and hunted. Not the least extraordinary part is that so few met such faithful co-operation from so many. Those who took part in it are entitled to remember it with pride.

Acknowledgments

I am indebted firstly to Brigadier J. H. Prendergast, Colonel H. R. C. Pettigrew and Mr Edward Lydall for permission to quote extensively from their excellent books listed in the bibliography.

Apart from printed sources, I have been given access to, and permission to quote from, autobiographical notes by Brigadier R. D. Ambrose, Lieut. Colonel Sir Benjamin Bromhead Bt, Major W. A. Brown, Brigadier R. C. Cosby, Colonel W. H. FitzMaurice, Lieut. Colonel R. J. F. Milanes, Major J. F. S. Ottley, Major T. J. Philips, Brigadier V. L. M. Wainwright, Lieut. Colonel M. W. H. White; and an autobiographical tape-recording by Lieut. Colonel Mohamad Sharif Khan. I have had access to letters contemporary with the events they describe written by Brigadier W. A. Gimson, Mr R. H. D. Lowis and my father, Lieut. Colonel Sir Richard Chenevix Trench. My thanks go to all who made these available – the writers themselves or their families.

Many former officers of the Frontier Corps and the Indian Political Service have contributed photographs, accounts of their experiences, official reports, training instructions, unit standing orders, unit newsletters and much miscellaneous information. A list of all their names would be interminable, and to single out a few would be invidious; but I must mention two who have done so much to organise and facilitate my research – Lieut. Colonel D. R. Venning and Major H. R. Hutchins.

Not having been in Frontier Corps myself, I was entirely dependent on all these officers for detail and atmosphere. Without their help this book could not possibly have been written. Without the help and advice

Acknowledgments

of Mr Philip Mason who read and re-read the manuscript as it developed and who has written the Foreword, it would never have been published.

To all contributors and helpers, whether or not named above, and to the staff of the India Office and Records, I am sincerely grateful.

1984   C.C.T.

Prologue

An Incident, 1920

Sixty Indian soldiers occupied a permanent picquet, a miniature fort built of drystone walls, on a hill overlooking a road which passed along the Tochi Valley in North Waziristan. Day after day they cooked, cleaned their rifles, dozed, chatted desultorily about their villages and their cattle and stared with lacklustre eyes at the bleak hills and the road winding below them. Nothing ever happened, nothing ever moved except a string of camels along the road, a boy herding goats on the hillside, a scavenging raven, a hawk hovering stiff-winged in the cloudless sky.

Every morning at first light ten men were sent for the day to a feature overlooking the picquet. It became a routine move, carelessly carried out. No enemy had been seen for weeks; there was no report of hostiles for miles. Although to reach that feature the ten men had to pass through a few yards of 'dead' ground invisible from the main position, they had only eighty yards to go. For convenience they took the same route every day.

Unseen watchers observed all this, and a gang of Pathans of the Mahsud tribe, camping in a cave nine miles away, determined to ambush those ten men in the few yards of dead ground. On the first night they reached their ambush position in good time, but a shooting star fell in an unlucky direction, so their leader took them home. The second night, a river they had to ford was in spate. On the third night a dog barked as they passed close to a village, so the leader, thinking that the bark might have alarmed a sentry, again took them home. On the fourth night all went well, until just before dawn the youngest squatted to pee. Surely any sentry worthy of the name, less than a hundred yards away, must have heard! Back they went to the cave again. The fifth night every man was provided with a dwarf-palm frond down which to direct, silently, his flow. At first light the ten soldiers left their comrades and strolled into the dead ground. A volley at point-blank range, another blast of fire to keep heads down in the picquet, a rush to knife the wounded and grab the rifles — and the gang was safely away. Truly, as Pathans say, patience is bitter, but its fruit is sweet.

The small disaster passed unnoticed in the Press. But some who heard of it might have wondered why those soldiers were occupying, clearly against the wish of its inhabitants, one of the most useless areas in Asia; what they were supposed to achieve there; and why an army, which two years before had helped demolish the German, Austrian and Turkish Empires, should suffer a defeat, however small, by a few ragged bandits who owned nothing more valuable than their rifles.

The answer to these questions can be found in fifty years' history of what was regarded as the most vital and most vulnerable frontier of the British Empire.

I

The Problem

By their conquest of the Sikhs, completed in 1848, the British acquired
the Punjab, pride and backbone of British India. They acquired also its
insoluble problem, the North-West Frontier.

Seen from India, the Frontier consisted first of the river Indus which
seems to serve it in the office of a moat, but has never proved a very
effective one. Beyond it was an irregular jumble of plains and foothills,
fertile where they could be watered, shaped by the spurs of the great
Suliman Range. Beyond these towered the mountains themselves,
from the eternal snows, alpine pastures and forests in the north,
through the lower, harsher mountains of Waziristan where rocky
outcrops a mere 10,000 feet high petered out in scrub-covered foothills
and ravines, to the desolation of Zhob and Mekran. The mountains
were an effective rampart against invasion, provided the passes were
held.

While the terrain made administration difficult, the characteristics of
the people made government by infidels and foreigners almost impossible. In the extreme north the tribes of the Hindu Kush are hardy
mountaineers but not particularly truculent. In the extreme south the
Baluchis, Brahuis and Pathan tribes of Baluchistan gave little trouble
provided they were left, more or less, to run their own affairs through
their own tribal authorities, which were more or less obeyed. The
problem was how to deal with the Pathan tribes between Chitral and
Baluchistan. By tradition and inclination, in some cases through
economic necessity, they were predators; as Moslem fanatics they
fiercely resisted rule by Sikh or Christian; and as the ultimate demo-

crats, with no man acknowledging another as master, they were difficult to hold to any agreement.

Neither the Amir of Afghanistan, nor the Sikhs, nor the British wanted more than spheres of influence in the mountains. As a safeguard against Russia, the British gained control of the Khyber, Kurram and Bolan Passes, but this did not help them control the Pathan tribes.

The best way of pacifying the Frontier, as has always been obvious and has in fact been proved by the Government of Pakistan, is to provide the tribesmen with education and economic opportunities superior to those gained by raiding. But it is the problem of the chicken and the egg. Which comes first, economic development or some approximation to law and order? To the guardians of the Victorian Empire the answer had to be law and order.

There were two obvious ways of dealing with the tribesmen. The 'Close Border policy', pursued until the end of the nineteenth century, aimed to govern the plains and leave the hills as a sort of human 'nature reserve'. When the denizens of it became too troublesome – killing and kidnapping the dwellers in the plains, driving off their cattle and raping their women – they were subjected to punitive expeditions into a hostile tribe's country which killed a few of the men, blew up the fortified towers, pulled down the terraces of the fields, extracted a fine in cash and firearms, and then withdrew. This procedure was irreverently known as 'Butcher and Bolt'.

Alternatively there was the 'Forward Policy' of occupying and administering the country right up to the Durand Line, the international boundary agreed and demarcated with Afghanistan in 1893. Only in Baluchistan was this successfully carried out by a loose system of indirect rule through the tribal Sardars.

To the lucid mind of Lord Curzon, Viceroy of India from 1899 to 1905, 'Butcher and Bolt' was undignified, unproductive and unacceptable; but half a century's experience, including some thirty punitive expeditions, had proved to most people that the Forward Policy along the whole Frontier was impossible with the resources at India's disposal. Besides, if the tribes on the Indian side of the Durand Line were disarmed and tamed, a large army would have to be permanently employed in protecting them from their unreconstructed neighbours, heavily armed, on the Afghan side. Moreover there was among middle-rank and junior officers a feeling – which did not make policy but contributed to the climate of opinion in which policy was made – that if the Frontier was always at peace, India would be a much duller place;

and that the army benefited immeasurably from annual war-games with the best umpire in the world, who never let a mistake go unpunished.

So there developed a compromise policy. There was an Administered Border of British India, enclosing the fertile plains and lower foothills, to the east of which were all the blessings of civilisation, especially law and order based on the Indian Penal Code and Criminal Procedure Code, while to the west, up to the Durand Line, was an area known as Tribal Territory, or more aptly Yaghistan, the Land of the Outlaws. The Army was held back in cantonments in British India, while in Tribal Territory Political Agents would, without attempting to administer the tribes, do what they could to wean them from their wicked ways.

The Pathan is an individualist whose relations with others are governed by a code of custom and honour known as Pukhtunwali which confers on him certain rights and requires of him certain duties. The most important of the duties is badal, vengeance; he *must* exact vengeance, at any risk and at all cost, for an insult or injury done to himself, his family, his clan or his tribe. If he dies, then they must take up the quarrel. Disputes over women, gold, and land – *zan, zar, zamin* – are at the bottom of most blood-feuds, but the feud continues, with murders and reprisals, long after its origin is forgotten. The Pathan may wait years for his chance, but take it he must, sooner or later, or be utterly shamed.

The duty of badal is modified by the right of Nanawati, which means 'coming in'. A Pathan must extend asylum and protection to anyone who asks for it, even to an enemy. In extreme cases the man seeking Nanawati appears before his foe bare-headed, with the Koran on his head, and a tuft of grass in his mouth indicating that he is his protector's animal; he may bring a sheep as peace-offering, or produce his wife unveiled. Nanawati sought with the Koran is never refused, but to seek it from an enemy is indelible disgrace.

The third element of Pukhtunwali is melmastia, hospitality, which must be offered to any who seek it, invited or uninvited, Pathan or foreigner, Moslem or Unbeliever. It includes food, lodging, entertainment, protection often far beyond what the host can afford. The host is responsible for his guest's safety so long as he remains in the tribal area, to the extent of providing a badragga, escort, who should protect the guests even at the cost of their own lives. There is the case of a Pathan who, to protect his guest, the Political Agent, shot his own son. The saying that a Pathan will do anything for gold except betray a guest is generally, but not always, proved true.

A Pathan is furthermore bound by Pukhtunwali to protect ham-sayas, 'persons sharing the same shade', who may be non-Pathans, or Pathans of another tribe. They include mullahs, barbers, Sikh merchants, Hindu moneylenders, Punjabi artisans, musicians and others whose role is to help maintain the social structure and do the jobs which Pathans are incapable of doing, too proud to do or too involved with tribal affairs.

In Tribal Territory there is not what is generally understood as law and order, nor is there sheer chaos and anarchy – although there would be were it not for the Pukhtunwali code which sets a standard of behaviour to which the Pathan at least aspires. He may not invariably observe the code, when his interests or his passions are too strong, but he will think twice before flagrantly defying it. It was thanks only to Pukhtunwali that a Political Agent could travel with a fair degree of safety through Tribal Territory protected only by a badragga provided by his hosts, the Maliks of the local tribe. If he were shot the murderer would in theory, and often in practice, be exposed to tribal sanctions and the host-Maliks exacting badal. Only the most dedicated Ghazi, burning to kill an infidel, or a man almost out of his mind with some real or fancied grievance, would take the risk of shooting. In 1893 the Political Agent, North Waziristan was attacked while actually eating a meal in a Malik's house; in 1945 the Political Agent, South Waziristan was kidnapped without his badragga firing a shot in his defence. Both cases were thought to have brought shame on the tribe, which took action against the offenders.

In other ways the Pukhtunwali code made the maintenance of law and order very difficult. Thus if a man committed murder in British India and sought asylum across the Border, he *must* be given it, and it would be a gross insult to his host's honour to molest him. But he would be expected, if his sojourn was prolonged, to earn his keep by, say, guiding raids into the country which he knew. An important trans-Border Pathan could, if he were that sort of man, have a dozen hamsayas bound to him by these obligations, combined bodyguards and hit-men. It was reckoned that there were seldom less than a thousand outlaws from British India safely established in Yaghistan. Moreover the blood-feud was a brake on economic progress. How could a man whose life-tenure was as insecure as a trans-Border tribesman's borrow capital for irrigation, drainage, terracing, orchards, improved livestock or any business enterprise? If he could lay hands on any cash, most of it must be spent on weapons and fortified towers.

The problem was aggravated by free coming and going across the Durand Line. About half the Pathans lived west of the Line, in Afghanistan; some troublesome tribes straddled it, others migrated every autumn to the Indus plains and returned every spring to the Uplands of Central Asia. Nothing was easier for a malefactor on one side of the Line than to find refuge on the other.

Since a Pathan's survival depended on shooting first, veracity and fidelity, outside the Pukhtunwali code, and adherence to the principles of fair play, came low in the scale of virtues. It made good sense to shoot an enemy in the back, so he could not get his shot in first, and with a dum-dum* bullet which made a bigger hole. It was common prudence to kill also his women and children, for female snakes produce little snakes, which in time grow into big snakes. (Singularly enough Mahsuds and Wazirs, in other respects the most recalcitrant of Pathans, drew the line at killing women and children.)

In war the Pathan was always crafty, and more formidable in dashing, slashing attack than in dour defence. Discipline was not his strong point. He enjoyed a reputation for Islamic fanaticism, but his adherence to the prophet's teaching was as selective as the average Englishman's to that of Jesus Christ. The Zakka Khel Afridis, for instance, are reputed to have murdered a holy man passing through their country in order to have possession of his shrine and grave as a lucrative centre for pilgrimage in their midst. Only when the Mullahs preached from the fifth verse of the ninth *Sura* of the Koran, 'When the sacred months are past, kill those who join other gods with God wheresoever ye find them', was the Pathan eager to respond.

Theologians might point out that Christians were not idolators like Hindus, Sikhs and Kafirs, but were Ahl-i-Kitab, People of the Book, worshippers of the One God, though lamentably unsound on the vital matter of His One-ness; and that the Prophet had specifically ordered that Moslems respect and protect them. Such hair-splitting was not for the ordinary Pathan.

In war the Pathan generally obeyed approved leaders of his own section and tribe; in peace it was his pride to obey no one. The British, when new to the Frontier, assumed that the tribal Maliks were chiefs 'able to say to one "come" and he cometh, to another "go" and he goeth'.

* Soft-nosed bullets, first manufactured in the Ordnance Factory at Dum-Dum near Calcutta, for use by the British Army *against* Pathans. Banned by the Geneva Convention in the face of strong British protests.

This was not the case outside Baluchistan and the Northern States of Dir and Swat. To the tribes of the Mohmand border, the Tirah and Waziristan a Malik was merely a negotiator with Government and any agreement he made could be challenged and ignored by any adult tribesman. His authority was no more than that conferred by personality and wealth. True authority rested only with the Jirga, an assembly in which every man of the tribe might play an equal part, though of course some were more equal than others.

Pathan characteristics were naturally stronger in the trans-Frontier tribes, that is those resident in Tribal Territory, than in the cis-Frontier tribes who for fifty years had enjoyed or put up with Pax Britannica. Of all Pathans the Mahsuds of central Waziristan were the most difficult, followed closely by their neighbours and cousins the Wazirs, by the Afridis of the Tirah and the Mohmands north of Tirah. No trans-Frontier Pathan, except for the Turi tribe, and very few within British India, felt any real loyalty to a remote and infidel Government, or indeed to any Indian Government, for they never regarded themselves as Indians or their country as part of India. However, there were innumerable individuals and families, especially among cis-Frontier tribesmen, in whom self-interest, some appreciation of the benefits of paternal government, recruitment in the army, *esprit de corps* and, above all, devotion to individual officers, produced attitudes which could easily be mistaken for loyalty to the Raj. This was particularly apparent among cis-Frontier Khattaks, Bangash, and Yusufzais, whom the Army regarded as the most reliable Pathans and first-class soldiers.

'Unarmed', says a Pathan proverb, 'you are my enemy'. To carry out the duties enjoined on them by the Pukhtunwali code, to follow their calling as freebooters and to defend their precious independence, the trans-Frontier tribes were armed to the teeth. Up to the end of the nineteenth century their weapons were the curved sword, a long, straight knife and the jezail, 'a long-barrelled matchlock, better than the musket with which the Army was armed until mid-century, but not as good as the Snider, Martini-Henry or Lee Metford rifles. By the end of the century they had acquired by theft, capture or purchase from Afghan soldiers a fair number of modern rifles, and what they lacked in fire-power, they made up in fieldcraft, cunning and the guerilla warrior's secret weapon, patience.

Such people were not markedly amenable to the Political Agent's admonitions, even when these were reinforced by financial inducements to good behaviour which exasperated soldiers compared to Danegeld. These included contracts for the supply of mutton and firewood, allowances to Maliks which could be stopped if not earned, and good silver rupees paid out for making and repairing roads which opened up Tribal Territory for trade and military expeditions. The Frontier Crime Regulations laid down procedures which could be used to emphasise the Political Agent's wishes. Legal sanction was given to trial by Jirga, according to Shariat, the Islamic law code which lays as much emphasis on compensation to the victim of a crime as on punishment of the criminal, and accepts the principle that if an individual cannot be brought to book, his family, section* or tribe must pay for his offence. When, therefore, a tribe's cup of iniquity was full, the Jirga would be required to hand over the kidnapped Hindus and abducted women, and produce the miscreants responsible for murders, robberies and rapes, or pay compensation for these outrages. Pressure could be applied by the arrest of prominent tribesmen whose friends and relations would use their influence to expedite the Jirga's deliberations; by the seizure of the tribe's livestock; or by a blockade cutting off the tribe from trade with British India and preventing its seasonal migrations.

For all these purposes, to discourage raids and escort caravans, the Political Agent needed an armed and disciplined force composed wholly or partly of local tribesmen. Thus were raised corps collectively known as Frontier Corps, Militias or Scouts. Only if these failed did the Army send in a punitive expedition.

* The clans and septs of which a tribe is composed are known as sections and sub-sections.

2

Poachers Turned Gamekeeper, 1878–1904

Those who, as a result of Lord Curzon's Frontier reforms,* in 1900, formed the Frontier Corps had encouraging precedents. In 1878 an irregular corps had been raised from local tribesmen, mainly Afridis, to protect traffic moving through the Khyber Pass, piqueting the hills on either side, escorting the long strings of camels between the Afghan Frontier and Fort Jamrud at the eastern end of the Pass. They were *very* irregular, unshaven, unkempt, with no uniform but a red tag sewn on to the back of the pagri to distinguish them from those whose principal pleasure and livelihood it was their duty to prohibit. They were armed with the jezail, and were at first known as the Khyber Jezailchis. Their Commandant, Major Sardar Mohamed Aslam, was a man of character and ability; moreover he was an Afghan of the Sadozai section of the royal Durani tribe, and as the Afridis supported the Sadozai claim to the throne, his prestige was enormous. He set about training and disciplining the Jezailchis. Snider rifles replaced the jezails and they were renamed the Khyber Rifles. They were provided with practical, loose-fitting khaki uniforms and a Mounted Infantry troop was added to the original infantry companies.

If it is surprising to find, in the heyday of the Victorian Raj, an Afghan major commanding a celebrated corps, it is surely astonishing that his friend and close collaborator, the Political Agent of the Khyber, Captain of the Empire's very gate, was what would then be termed disparagingly a 'half-caste'. But Robert Warburton, son of an Irish

---

* These reforms included severing the Frontier from the Punjab and setting up a separate North-West Frontier Province (NWFP).

father and an Afghan mother, was an unusual Eurasian. Among his colleagues and superior officers Anglo-Indian colour-prejudice conflicted with Anglo-Indian snobbery, and snobbery won; he was deemed officially and socially acceptable, for his mother was a Princess. He was also a very able man, and since Pushtu, the language of the people, and Persian, a status-symbol among Pathans, were literally his mother-tongues, he was spared the strain and mental fatigue inseparable from conducting all business in a very difficult foreign language. He not merely liked and admired but loved his Afridis, while recording in detail their murders, treacheries and tergiversations. He always went unarmed among them and they never let him down, but gave him countless proofs of friendship. In later years it was considered that no Political Agent could stand the strain of dealing with trans-Frontier tribesmen for more than four or five consecutive years. For Warburton the strain was much less, and he stood – enjoyed – seventeen years as Political Agent, Khyber, acquiring in that time a wonderful knowledge of the Afridis. However, he failed to see that their loyalty was personal to *him*, or in the case of the Khyber Rifles, to Mohamad Aslam and the corps. It was not to the Queen Empress. He himself never doubted that the British Raj was God's greatest gift to mankind.

> Wider still and wider, shall thy bounds be set.
> God who made thee mighty, make thee mightier yet.

That sentiment was accepted by Colonel Warburton, and in his more euphoric moods he convinced himself that it was accepted also by his Afridis.

Early in the corps' history there occurred an event to which those in authority should have paid more attention. In 1882, for purely administrative reasons, it was decided that the fort at Ali Masjid, garrisoned by a company of the Malik Din Khel section of Afridis, should be abandoned and the company moved to Jamrud. Promptly a Subadar and a Jemadar (corps officers) concluded that the Government was on the run and went round, Koran in hand, urging their men to desert with rifles rather than obey the order. A Havildar (sergeant) defied them and managed to get the company back to Jamrud. The lesson should have been plain; an entire company should not be composed of a single section of a tribe like the Afridis; and trans-Frontier Pathans, in their own country, were not reliable when withdrawal was in the wind.

Apart from this incident, the Khyber Rifles seemed to justify

Warburton's and Mohamad Aslam's pride in them. They made the
Khyber far safer than the environs of Peshawar. When the Commander-in-Chief, Lord Roberts, and his Quarter Master General, with
the Political Agent, rode from end to end of what was reputedly the
most dangerous pass in Asia, escorted only by two troopers of the
Khyber Rifles, the Quarter Master General said, 'If this were to be told
in England, or to any officer of the old Punjab school, they would never
believe it.'

Although the terms of their service did not require them to serve
outside the Khyber, the corps volunteered for the Black Mountain
expeditions of 1888 and 1891. They took a prominent part in all major
actions and won half-a-dozen gallantry medals. On their return the
Peshawar Municipality gave them a civic reception and dinner.

The Pathan officers of the corps were notable warriors, many
wearing medals won in wars from China to Egypt. One, Subadar
Mursil, bore on his body the scars of thirty wounds. It was a proud
moment for Warburton and Mohamad Aslam when the Khyber Rifles
marched past the Viceroy as smart as Guardsmen on the parade for the
presentation of the Indian Order of Merit to the Subadar Major. At the
last moment it was discovered, to Warburton's consternation, that no
ribbon had been sent with the medal. What could be done? A Sikh, a
Sikh Orderly Officer to the Viceroy took off his own IOM ribbon for the
Afridi. Such was the spirit of the old Indian Army.

The Khyber Rifles even maintained a sort of precursor of present-
day Boys' Companies. It was quite unofficial, but paraded, saluted and
turned out Guards of Honour for distinguished visitors.

Mohamad Aslam soldiered on until he was quite unfit for active
service, and he insisted on commanding in the Black Mountain expeditions. Somehow the unofficial commander of the unofficial Boys'
Company, an active, handsome twelve-year-old, managed to go too,
and helped the Commandant up the hill in an attack.

'Get away, boy, get away!' the old man panted, 'you'll be killed.'

'Never mind if I am,' said the lad, 'you can throw my body into the
nearest ravine.'

Robert Warburton believed that no other Pathan could command the
Khyber Rifles. Only a Sadozai would have the prestige; with any other,
they would all be quarrelling among themselves. Again and again he
begged the Government to appoint a British second-in-command who
could learn the job from Mohamad Aslam and then take over. This was
done, but far too late, just before the great Afridi War of 1897 which
consisted of a cumbrous, hard-fought invasion of the Tirah, the

mountain-heartland of the Afridis, followed by a somewhat undignified and hasty withdrawal while winter closed in. Warburton believed it need never have happened, and would not have happened had not he and Mohamad Aslam both retired. On 'a day of shame and humiliation for every Englishman in India', the new Commandant, Captain Barton, was given a direct order, allowing him no discretion, to forsake his men and seek safety in Jamrud. Most of the Khyber Rifles posts were over-run and burnt; but the garrison of Landi Kotal, under the much-wounded, much-decorated Subadar Mursil, who had one son with him and two with the enemy, put up an epic defence, killing one hundred and eighteen of their kith-and-kin until, when Mursil was killed, they capitulated.

There followed the Tirah Expedition, a personal tragedy for Warburton who was recalled from retirement to act as Political Officer to the column which fought its way into his friends' country. Four men of the Khyber Rifles, all Afridis, acted as his orderlies,

and also as scouts and guides. All proved faithful and loyal, although working against their own countrymen. When it is remembered that they were literally carrying their lives hourly in their hands, and knew the cruel certain fate which awaited them if they were taken prisoners, I do not think I exaggerate when I say ... that no men better earned the Victoria Cross.

The Khyber Rifles were deployed in numerous small blockhouses, from which they could watch and protect caravan traffic through the Pass. The most unpopular of these blockhouses was that in which, one freezing night, the entire garrison had perished, asphyxiated by the fumes of their charcoal stove. A visitor to another at the turn of the century, Michni Kandao, wrote:

The line of white boulders on the hill across the dip were range-stones. Ten white stones at a thousand yards, nine at nine hundred. They were too big for Khyber marksmen to waste powder on, so there are small white slabs, the size of your hat, laid parallel with them for rifle practice. I saw the men turn out to shoot. The Afridi on his own heath, or scree, is part of the earth, like a markhor or chamois, whether it is fanged-rock or a shelf of sliding shale, it is all the same. Elbow and knee are firm and easy as the rifle comes up and he takes his sight. One feels that the weapon is as much a provision of nature as horn, tooth or claw ...

When they had pounded the small white stone to pieces, we climbed up the iron ladder into the blockhouse. The sweet scent from the wood fire and hot chapattis greeted me from inside. The long low-raftered room with the smooth boards, wooden supports and ladder leading up by a trap-door to another floor, and above all the smell of the flour, reminded me of an old water-mill.

In 1908 this blockhouse was attacked by a horde of Afghans. The night was black as ink, and the besiegers were under the walls and laying a charge of gunpowder when the garrison took off their shirts, soaked them in oil, lit them and threw them over the parapet. In the flare they shot down twenty Afghans.

In the Zakka Khel campaign of 1908, all the Zakka Khel in the Khyber Rifles were paraded by the Political Agent and told that they would not be made to fight against their own people; every man might take six months' leave, and when he came back no questions would be asked. None took advantage of this offer.

The Khyber Rifles were reckoned on all counts to be a success, and if trans-Frontier Afridis could be made into a useful local militia, surely this could be done elsewhere. In Baluchistan Sir Robert Sandeman, the Agent to the Governor General, was, indeed, already doing it. The lynch-pin of his system of indirect rule was at first a force similar to the Khyber Jezailchis. With the annexation of the Zhob in 1889, he formed a much more military force, the Zhob Levy Corps, irregular but uniformed, armed with Government Martinis, trained and more or less disciplined. It was composed of local Pathans, Pathans from further north, and wild Brahui nomads from the desert south-west of Quetta; and it was commanded by an Indian Army major seconded to the Political Department and under Sandeman's orders. Later the corps was renamed the Zhob Militia and, in the somewhat less exacting conditions of Baluchistan where the tribal authorities had some control over their young men, it did very useful work.

In 1892–3 in the Kurram Valley, north of Waziristan and west of the Tirah, an energetic captain, G. O. Roos-Keppel, formed the local Turi tribesmen into a similar force known as the Kurram Militia. But here there was a difference. The Turi tribe are Shiahs, entirely surrounded by Sunnis, and there is no feud more bitter than that between these Moslem sects. The Turis were the trusties of the Sarkar, equivalent to the Campbells in seventeenth-century Scotland. They had besought the British Government to take over their country and protect them, and as a result the Government had introduced a loose administration into the Kurram Valley, based on a Political Agent at Parochinar and the Kurram Militia. The Turis were no less tough than their neighbours (another analogy with the Campbells), no less observant of Pukhtunwali, but they were reliable; so much so that the government kept at Parochinar a reserve of 3,000 rifles for issue to the Turi tribal lashkar, their armed force, in times of trouble.

The advance in 1891 from Gilgit to Hunza and Nagar against very tough opposition, which planted the Union Jack on the Roof of the World, had been a classic example of Victorian empire-building, with the Political Agent shot by a garnet fired from a jezail and many deeds of daring rewarded by three VCs and numerous other decorations. In 1895 the Empire had watched with bated breath the desperate defence, against overwhelming odds, of Chitral Fort and the painfully slow progress through snow-bound passes of the relief columns. Thereafter the Hunza and Nagar tribesmen had reverted to peaceful peasants, their raiding parties no longer the scourge of Central Asia, and the Mehtar (prince) of Chitral had abandoned the amiable practice of securing each succession by the wholesale slaughter of sons, brothers and nephews.

Lord Curzon, something of an expert on the Pamirs and the Hindu Kush (unique among Viceroys and policy-makers, he had actually ridden and walked over them), took very seriously the danger of invasion from Russian Turkestan, through the narrow panhandle of the Afghan Wakhan and over the Hindu Kush. The history of Russian expansion emphasised the danger. It is the task of general staffs to plan for the worst possible eventuality, which here would be Russian and Afghan invasion, assisted by the Pathans of Dir and Swat through which must pass any force moving up from India to Chitral. There were at least three routes – by the Killick pass into Gilgit and the Baroghil and Dorah passes into Chitral – which could be easily defended, but if left undefended were perfectly practicable for trained mountain troops with mule transport.

It was against such a contingency that the local Political Agent suggested in 1900 the formation of a part-time militia of 'trained cragsmen' from the tough mountaineers of Chitral. It was a proposal after Lord Curzon's heart, a loyal militia defending their own country until regular troops could arrive, and it was the genesis of the Chitral Scouts, tribesmen armed with modern rifles, trained for one month a year and providing at a very small cost a tripwire which could at least delay an incursion. In 1913 the Gilgit Scouts were raised on similar lines with a similar role.

The core of the Frontier problem was Waziristan, and in particular its two largest tribes, the Mahsuds* of South Waziristan, and the Wazirs. The Political Agent of North Waziristan, from his headquarters in Bannu, and the Political Agent of South Waziristan, from his headquarters in Tank, employed local levies who were quite useless but retained on the pay roll in the hope that they would thereby be kept out of mischief; the Political Agents had tried to influence them through their Maliks, but several 'loyal' Maliks had been murdered as a warning to others.

Wazirs and Mahsuds are related, but were seldom on good terms except when up to something which had no relish of salvation in it. Wazirs were semi-nomadic, Mahsuds more settled, but neither could make much of a success of cultivating their stony soil; they found it easier to make a living by trading, easier still by raiding. The Wazir has been compared to a leopard, a loner, cunning and dangerous; the Mahsud to a wolf, most to be feared in a pack, with a pack-mentality, single-mindedness and persistence. Even among Pathans the Mahsud is notoriously treacherous, something that he himself will not deny. 'We are a very untrustworthy people,' he will say with a sly grin and not without pride, as though this excused every misdemeanour. In 1900 the Wazir fighting strength was reckoned at 27,000, of whom 15,000 had firearms; the Mahsud at 18,000 of whom 14,000 had firearms.

Both tribes were very difficult to handle. Their rapacity was insatiable, and promoted in their dealings with the Sarkar by a loquaciousness which knew no fatigue and no time-factor, allied to an amazing plausibility in argument. Robert Bruce, a great Frontier officer whose past experience, however, had been mainly in Baluchistan, tried to systematise the *sarishta*, the tribal pecking-order under which duties, subsidies and contracts were distributed among Maliks according to their influence. Try as they would to distribute benefits according to the recipients' deserts, Bruce's successors always came up against the *sarishta* system, a departure from which would cause infinite resentment. Merit often went unrewarded while iniquity prospered, and grievances arising from this were a common cause of murder and rebellion.

It was against this background that the North Waziristan Militia and South Waziristan Militia (also known as Northern and Southern Waziristan Militias) were formed in 1900, poachers engaged as game-

---

* They call themselves Dré Mahsud, Dré Mahsit in their own dialect, 'Three Mahsuds', because they are divided into three sections, Alizai, Bahlolzai and Shaman Khel, each with several sub-sections.

keepers, similar to the Black Watch in eighteenth-century Scotland. Old frontier hands were not lacking who said it was mad to give modern rifles to Mahsuds and Wazirs. But Lord Curzon insisted that trained and disciplined corps, with British officers, would be very different from the 'old salaried loafers and ruffians' of the levies. They would not be part of the army, but would be controlled by the Political Agents and the Chief Commissioner. The officers would be seconded from the Indian Army to the Political Department.

Each corps consisted initially of 850 Pathans, soon increased to 1,850, half trans-Frontier, half cis-Frontier, divided into two Wings of approximately battalion strength, and 150 Mounted Infantry (MI). They were armed with Martini rifles. Each corps had six British officers, two to each Wing, the Commandant, and the Adjutant/ Quartermaster who also commanded the Mounted Infantry – volunteers for what was likely to be 'a short life, if an exciting one'.

They took over from the Army all posts in Waziristan except Jandola. Their duties included: garrisoning posts and piqueting roads; repulse and pursuit of raiders; guarding prisoners and treasure; escorting officers; protection of contractors for road-making; reconnaissance; guide work of all sorts; obtaining political information; arrest of offenders.

The North Waziristan Militia, with its headquarters in Miranshah, was distributed in posts along the east-west road from Bannu to Datta Khel (about sixty miles) and the south-north road linking that with Thal in the Lower Kurram. The nearest army garrison was in Bannu. The South Waziristan Militia with headquarters in Wana had to protect two routes from Murtaza to Wana. The nearest military garrison was in Jandola. Despite warnings that banding together well-armed Pathans outside army control was asking for trouble, in September 1904 the experiment was officially described as 'satisfactory beyond all our expectations'.

Perhaps expectations had not been very high. Even so, within the limitations of their sketchy training, with no time to develop any *esprit de corps* and with many lessons to learn, the Waziristan Militia corps reduced raids across the Administered Border and introduced the shadow, the vague idea, of law and order at least along the roads and in the vicinity of their cramped, unhealthy, flea- and fly-ridden mud forts. But years of modest success for the gamekeeper restraining his friends and relatives from poaching make dull reading; the good stories are provided by the occasions, few but invested with high drama, when the gamekeeper reverted to poacher.

With hindsight one can see that it was unwise to put any trust in Mahsuds. They had a well-established reputation for treachery; the British controlled not a yard of their territory, and so had no hold over them. Wazirs were rather different: quite a lot of their territory was under British control, and the militiamen's families and properties were to some extent hostages for their good behaviour. Many Wazirs served the Sarkar well and with great fidelity, and they were valued for their smartness and local knowledge. Also they bore no love for Afridis. The inclusion of both these difficult tribes in the corps was some safeguard against concerted treachery.

3

Gamekeepers Turned Poacher, 1904–5

British officers particularly liked Mahsuds. There were three Mahsud companies, each about one hundred men strong, in the South Waziristan Militia and one company in the North Waziristan Militia, attracted by the princely pay (ten rupees a month without rations), and the prestige of carrying a modern rifle. Because of their volatile temperament for good and bad, commanding Mahsuds was a challenge for any officer. In September 1904, the very month the experiment was described as 'satisfactory beyond all our expectations', a shot rang out in the middle of the night at the South Waziristan Militia post of Sarwekai. Investigation disclosed that the wall-sentry was missing and the Political Agent, Captain J. B. Bowring, who for coolness had been sleeping on the roof, lay dead on his blood-soaked sheets.

As men milled round in understandable confusion, two shots from the control tower of the keep indicated where the murderer had gone, and that he would not tamely give himself up. He was, it transpired, Sepoy Kabul Khan, of the Abdur Rahman Khel sub-section of the Bahlolzai section of Mahsuds.

Everyone was ordered under cover until daylight, when men of other tribes started sniping at the loopholes in the tower, from which an occasional shot was returned. The British and Pathan officers took counsel. No one questioned that the murderer must die. But how? To storm the keep would cost many lives. To starve him out would be a long-drawn-out business, bad for morale and a considerable strain on the Mahsuds' loyalty. The most awkward question was, who should be put to executing him? There was the gravest danger of the corps being rent with blood-feuds as the Abdur Rahman Khel sepoys took vengeance on the executioner and his tribe took reprisals.

The Post Subadar, an Afridi wise in Pukhtunwali, came up with the only satisfactory answer. Kabul must die by the hand of his brother, a Naik in the garrison. Then there would be no feud, no reprisals. When it was put to him the Naik consented, for the honour of his family, the Abdur Rahman Khel, the Dré Mahsud, and the Militia, to execute by shooting his own brother.

Communication with the man in the keep had hitherto been confined to shouted insults and occasional shots. Now a dialogue was opened by the Post Subadar and the senior Mahsud officer. Kabul's conscience was clear: Bowring, he said, was sleeping with his feet towards Mecca, 'and therefore I shot him'. But Kabul's exaltation had simmered down. There was no way he could escape death, and he did not particularly want the Abdur Rahman Khel to be feuding with everyone else. He accepted the offer of death with dignity.

The time was fixed for five in the afternoon. The garrison was on parade, each man's eyes fixed on the keep. Half-hidden behind a mud-plastered buttress stood a British officer, two Pathan officers and the executioner, all with rifles. A khaki-clad figure climbed on to the keep parapet, rifle in hand. He stretched himself erect and flung down his rifle among the soldiers gazing up at him. '*Allah ho Akbar!*' he cried, 'God is Great.' The executioner raised his rifle, aimed at the erect figure, and fired. Kabul Khan remained for a moment poised still erect, spun round, and fell with a crash into the courtyard below. A prolonged 'Aah-ah-h!' of relief went up.

Kabul's relatives asked for his body to bury, and that request was granted. It should not have been. They buried Kabul in traditional style, with a recess in the grave for the questioning angel to sit. Above the grave they built a shrine to Mahsud patriotism, lit every Friday by flickering lamps. Here the young men came to pray, and resolved to follow Kabul's example.

Had the Commandant, Lieutenant-Colonel R. Harman, been at Sarwekai, the murderer's body might not have been thus honoured. For he was an expert on Mahsuds, speaking fluently their difficult dialect of Pushtu and knowing very well their courage and black treachery. He took on the duties of Political Agent, as well as his own. But even he under-estimated the persistence and loquacity of Mahsuds, whose most innocent amusement is to plague the Political Agent with interminable complaints and petitions, with strident demands for larger subsidies, for road-making and firewood contracts, for intercession in blood-feuds generations old, for honorary titles and distinctions, even for campaign medals earned fighting against the Government forces. Therefore a junior political officer, Evelyn Howell, was sent to take over as Political Agent in order that Harman might concentrate on his military duties.

The ascent of 3,000 feet from the Gomal River to Sarwakai by a rough bridlepath was a taxing one for Howell, for his Militia escort and for the mules and camels carrying his luggage. At the top of the rise were the Mahsud Maliks assembled to meet him, 'Hawk-faced, trim-bearded, hard-bitten ruffians but well mannered and very pleasant-spoken'. One of them, with a charming smile, holding Howell's hands fondly in his, said, 'We are so glad a new Political Agent has come, for when there is no Political Agent, we are as orphans.'

They rode on to Wana where Howell was to live with Harman, the Militia second-in-command Captain Plant, a doctor and a Sapper subaltern responsible for the roads. Wana was a fort, loop-holed and crenellated, constructed mainly of dried mud. It consisted of a perimeter-wall with corner-towers, lined with living-quarters, offices and stores, enclosing a yard of about an acre in the centre of which was a two-storeyed keep containing well, treasury, cells and armoury with spare rifles and ammunition. There were few amenities; there was no ice (except that provided in winter by Nature), no electricity, running water, fresh fruit or vegetables. In summer mosquitoes and sand-flies proliferated, afflicting in turn everyone with malaria and sandfly fever; scorpions lurked in the most inconvenient places such as shoes, or under the seat of the thunderbox; myriads of flies com-muted busily between latrines, kitchens and dining-rooms, jostled each other along the rim of the tea-cup as it was raised to drink, and were only kept out of the (tinned) milk and (tinned) butter by covering jugs and dishes with little beaded nets. Diarrhoea, dysentery and jaundice were rife.

Four thousand feet above sea-level, Wana fort and its attendant bazaar squatted in the middle of a saucer-like plain surrounded by mountains. Scattered acacias, dwarf-palms, berberis and gurgura bushes relieved the monotony of the grey and khaki landscape but (except during the rains) grass was as scanty as hairs in leprosy. (Waziristan in spring could be delightful. As an English-speaking Political Assistant enthused in later days, 'These green, green grasses, these white, white sheeps, these blue, blue skies ... Sir, it is very decent.') The climate varied from scorching heat to snow and blizzards, and there was generally a wind bringing dust-devils and sand-storms in season. For the officers there was moderate partridge-, duck- and snipe-shooting, poker and bridge in the evenings, a phonograph with a few scratched records, and a nine-hole golf course where the 'greens' were of hard dry mud and pebbles on the fairways sent the straightest drive or approach bounding off in unexpected directions. *Age-wallahs*, forward-fellows, preceded the players not, as elsewhere in India, to mark the ball, but to ensure that the bunkers harboured no unfriendly persons.

Harman, having no illusions about Mahsuds, instituted a system whereby would-be recruits were subjected to what would now be called 'positive vetting' by the Maliks of their sections and by Mahsud officers. This was resented by the leading Mahsud personality of the time, the Mullah Powindah, Shabi Khel, an aged, reactionary bigot with meagre sacerdotal qualifications and an unlimited capacity for mischief. He received intermittent funds from Kabul or further north which enabled him to keep at his beck-and-call a gang of accomplished cut-throats. He was, in his way, a patriot, but his patriotism consisted of sticking at nothing to preserve the Mahsud way of life. The construction of roads, Harman's positive vetting and, indeed, the very existence of the Militia were all seen by him as threats to Mahsud integrity. In 1904–5 he was at peace with the Government, busy infiltrating into the Militia his own disciples and at the same time warning Harman, in letters too vaguely worded to be of any use, against treachery in the corps.

On a bitter night in January 1905, when snow lay deep on the parade-ground and roofs, the officers assembled for dinner in their Mess which boasted – and in Wana it was something to boast of – glass panes to windows and door. The doctor had gone early to bed, feeling unwell. The others had, of course, changed for dinner, the soldiers into the 'bum-freezer' mess-jackets of their respective regiments, skin-tight overall trousers, starched shirts and collars, and black bow-ties. Howell, the civilian, wore evening dress with, instead of a dinner-jacket, the dark-blue blazer of the Lions, an Emmanuel College dining club. The worse the conditions, the more important it seemed to preserve standards. They sat round the blazing log-fire, playing liar-dice for pegs of whisky and sherry, and then went into the dining-room to tackle the mulligatawny soup, stringy chicken and caramel custard which was the best that could be expected of any cook willing to put up with Wana. To show confidence in their men, all were unarmed.

It being Saturday night, Harman was about to rise and propose 'Mr Vice, the King!', to which Howell would reply, 'Gentlemen, the King-Emperor!', when there was a tinkle of broken glass and Howell, looking up, saw come through the door a young sepoy in uniform carrying at the port a rifle with bayonet fixed. He halted and stared at Howell; Howell stared back, thinking that he had come from curiosity to see the Sahibs' mysterious tamasha. Then he lowered the muzzle of his rifle, and at that moment Harman and Plant dashed round the table to grapple with him. The others piled in too, and soon the intruder was disarmed and trussed up with his own pagri.

Harman, leaning against the wall, asked, 'Is anyone hurt?'

Howell looked at the others and replied, 'No, are you, Colonel?'

'I think I am,' said Harman, collapsing on his knees to the ground.

A Mess-servant put his head round the door and was sent to fetch the doctor. A Mess Orderly also arrived, and was told to bring an armed guard to take the prisoner to the cells.

The doctor arrived in his dressing-gown, opened Harman's jacket and shirt and examined a bayonet-wound in the left side of his chest. Howell could see from his face that there was no hope.

Harman spoke for the last time. 'They've got me. I knew they would.'

He was carried to his quarters, where he died.

Howell padded off in his evening shoes along the frozen path between piled-up banks of snow back to the Mess, where he wrote a telegram to the Chief Commissioner. As he gave it to a servant to take to the telegraph office, Captain Plant came in.

'The man is a Mahsud,' he said. 'I don't want to force your hand for it's your responsibility. But there is a Mahsud half-company, probably the one to which he belongs, on duty in the keep, and I think they will have to be disarmed.'

'Why?'

'Well, when we reached the big door into the keep and the quarter-guard opened the wicket for us, I saw about a dozen of them standing about, with their rifles and bayonets. It is not a night in which any sane man would loaf about outside when he might be indoors, unless he had some purpose in doing so. I called to them, and when they heard my voice, they all bolted into their barrack. So I stowed my prisoner in the lock-up, warned the quarter-guard and came out.'

The Subadar Major, a grizzled Afridi, then arrived, a rather comic figure in nocturnal deshabillé. 'Is the Colonel Sahib dead?' he asked.

Howell replied that he was. 'A Mahsud killed him. He has been arrested and is in the lock-up. Now what about the Mahsuds in the keep? Do you think they should be disarmed?'

'They should be, but there will be trouble. You should get the Chief Commissioner's sanction.'

'If it is going to be done at all,' retorted Howell, 'it has to be done at once.'

Plant said, 'There are fifty Mahsuds in the keep, and the big door is bolted on the inside. They can overpower the quarter-guard, break open the lock-up, release the prisoner, seize the armoury and treasury without anyone being able to get at them. And there is another full company of Mahsuds in one of the barracks in the outer fort . . . Even if nothing worse happens, when the other classes learn of Harman having been killed by a Mahsud, they will open fire on them. As you know, all the men have their rifles and a hundred rounds at night.'

It was clear that the job had to be done immediately, and the Subadar Major collected as many men as he could from other tribes. They lit several lanterns and walked over to the keep. Howell could not help reflecting that he was somewhat unsuitably dressed. The quarter-guard opened the keep door and they filed through into the empty, silent courtyard. Some men were posted on a roof, others in a line aslant the courtyard, their rifles pointing towards the barrack door. The lanterns were placed to light the doors.

When all was ready, Plant called out, 'Jemadar Salim!' – the Mahsud Jemadar commanding the half-company. There was no reply, so a man was sent to the Jemadar's room which adjoined the barrack. He emerged, looking rather sheepish.

'Go in and tell your men', said Plant, 'that if they obey orders, no harm will come to them. They are to file out and fall in outside the barrack. If they disobey, they will be shot.'

Salim saluted and entered the barrack. There was a confused murmur from inside, but for a long time nothing more happened. Then he emerged, alone.

'They will not listen to me,' he said. 'Perhaps if the Sahibs were to speak to them . . .'

Never did Howell feel so apprehensive as when he advanced through the snow to one door while Plant went to the other. They were in moonlight, the lanterns behind them. In the barrack all was dark and still. Howell became aware of his orderly, who had brought him his revolver, fluttering about him like a hen and then standing so close as almost to shoulder him aside. The orderly, too, was a Mahsud. The Subadar Major and another Pathan officer were with Plant.

'Come out!' they called, and repeated what they had told Salim.

To their enormous relief the doors opened and the men emerged. Under their own Jemadar's orders they fell in, grounded arms, about-turned and took two paces forward. A party detailed for the purpose scooped up the rifles from the snow and carried them to the armoury with commendable celerity. The Mahsuds were shut in their barracks for the night, guarded by the riflemen on the roof. The crisis was over.

As Plant approached the armoury, the Subadar Major said to him, rather loudly, 'The sentry is a Wazir, and Wazirs at bottom are Mahsuds. He should be changed.'

Plant threw the sentry a casual glance. 'A Wazir? So he is. But that's Sarbaz Khan. I'd trust *him* anywhere.'

The sentry threw out his chest and began strutting up and down like a Guardsman.

The Militia practice was for the rifles of all men not actually on duty to be locked in company arms-kots from dawn to dusk. The Mahsuds in Wana and the outposts, about a quarter of the corps, were thus disarmed without drama or disgrace, and sent home on a month's leave from which they did not return.

Howell, the only available magistrate, tried the murderer as dispassionately as he could. The man's name was Shabir Khan, of a Shabi Khel sub-section closely allied to that of the Mullah Powindah. He exulted in what he had done. He had enlisted, he said, with only one aim – to kill all the British officers and 'have a finer song made about me than Kabul'. There could be only one verdict: to be hanged by the neck until dead. He had two requests: for a clean shirt in which to die, and for some collyrium to blacken his eyelids, in the fashion of young Mahsud bucks, so that he would be acceptable to the Houris of Paradise.

But who should hang him? To order any Pathan Militiaman to do this would be trying loyalty too hard. For a civilian 'follower', a sweeper, say, or a shoemaker, to hang the man would be a shame on all Pathans more than they could bear. There was, as in the case of Bowring's murder, only one answer – but a different one. The British officers must carry out the sentence.

The Garrison Engineer constructed the gallows, a beam resting across a corner of the keep courtyard. Shabir Khan, who had spent the previous half-hour smartening himself up, was brought after dark to the place of execution by two Afridi officers. The Engineer positioned the noose round his neck, one British officer pinioned his arms, and two others heaved him over the parapet. It was scarcely what they had joined the Army and the Militia for.

The Subadar Major pronounced Harman's epitaph in a characteristic Pushtu pun: *'Ai ai! Armoon, armoon!** That such a *Bahadur*† should

* *Armoon* means grief.
† *Bahadur* means a hero.

23

die thus! If this Sahib were to be killed [pointing at Howell] or that Sahib were to be killed [pointing at Plant] the Government could send another. But Harman Sahib! *Ai, Ai! Armoon, armoon!*'

It was not possible to prove the Mullah Powindah's complicity, though afterwards he used to boast that he could send out his Sheikhs to slay whomsoever he wanted slain. 'You cannot see, but I can see, Kabul Khan and Shabir Khan in Paradise, lovingly tended by the Houris thereof, masters of the dainty fruit and sweet streams of Heaven.'

Retribution, Pathan-style, was not long in coming. Four months after Harman's murder, ex-Jemadar Kastor, Abdur Rahman Khel (the same section as Kabul Khan), formerly of the South Waziristan Militia but discharged with the other Mahsuds in February, and two of his brothers, were shot dead by a patrol of militiamen, led by Subadar Mohibullah, Jowaki Afridi, in circumstances which suggested that Mohibullah had set them up. However, the official view was that his conduct was as white as snow, and he was awarded the Indian Order of Merit for it. In November, tit-for-tat, Mahsud ex-militiamen shot dead Captain Donaldson, Brigade Major in Bannu. And so it went on.

The murders of Bowring, Harman and Donaldson by Militia sepoys or ex-sepoys seemed to confirm the worst misgivings of those who believed that the formation of the Waziristan Militias was an act of lunacy. In fact only Mahsuds had been responsible; other tribes, including Wazirs, had behaved perfectly. So it seemed reasonable to suppose that, once they had got rid of the Mahsuds, the two corps would give good service. The events of the next fourteen years seemed to justify this assessment.

Later generations of Scouts would criticise the old Militias for being deployed in 'penny packets'. In 1910 the North Waziristan Militia, for instance, was spread out over eighteen posts, most of which had garrisons of seventy or eighty of whom fifteen or so would be on leave at any one time and at least as many required for post-defence, leaving too few for long patrols in strength. Only the main base at Miranshah could send out a proper striking force. The only outpost which could have a resident British officer was Spinwam. He lived in extreme discomfort in a mud hut, the men in tents protected by drystone walls, sleeping on heaps of straw. The fleas were awful beyond belief.

There were, however, compensations. British Officers were given generous local leave. There was a delightfully simple administration. With as yet no legal code governing the Militias, officers could make the punishment fit the crime. There was no equipment audit. There was no pay audit. A lump sum was drawn sufficient to pay the corps at its full establishment; if the corps happened to be over-strength, the extra money needed was found by the Political Agent to whom the unspent balance was handed when the corps was understrength. There was virtually no office-work. To emphasise their irregular status, officers wore irregular clothes on all but the most formal occasions. Even on operations the usual costume was a sleeveless shirt in summer, and in winter a tweed coat and cap or slouch hat.

The Militias attracted eccentric characters, British and Pathan. Lieutenant Colonel D. H. McNeile, a cavalryman commanding the North Waziristan Militia, had a passion for playing the violin, rather badly, and designing steam-engines, rather well. The Mounted Infantry of the Militia included in its ranks a Wazir with bright red hair and blue eyes, reputedly the offspring of a Gordon Highlander, whom the officers called Charlie. Tor Khan, a small, tough and wiry Afridi, Jowaki, who rose to be a Subadar Major of the same Militia, had been transferred in a hurry from the Khyber Rifles after committing sacrilege by shooting dead a Mullah who had approached his post, Koran in hand, and called upon the garrison to desert. He was the brother of Subadar Mohibullah of the South Waziristan Militia, also a killer. His nine-year-old son followed the family tradition, on a visit to his uncle Mohibullah, by cutting the throat of a seven-year-old cousin. (This son later became a Subadar of the Tochi Scouts.)

The crack-shot in the North Waziristan Militia was another Afridi, Mohi Khan, an old soldier almost totally devoid of ambition. Or, rather, his only ambition was to be orderly to Captain Bull, the Right Wing Commander. Bull, with an escort of only six sowars, went for a hack one day from Miranshah and ran into a hostile gang. The troops in Miranshah were alerted by riderless horses galloping back, and the Mounted Infantry ran to saddle up. The first sowar to be ready was promptly dispossessed of his horse by Mohi Khan, who galloped off to the rescue of his beloved Bull Sahib. Swept from the saddle by a low-hanging branch, he went on at the double – only to meet Bull's party returning to Miranshah, quite safe and sound.

Miranshah was the only place in Waziristan which offered any sort of comfort. In 1910 it even housed two nursing sisters, come to look after an officer who contracted enteritis. It was to be many a year before Miranshah saw their like again.

In 1914 Major Dodds, a former officer of the North Waziristan Militia, was Political Agent, South Waziristan. He had a personal orderly, Sarfaraz, a young Mahsud who had served with him in the

Militia. A good Pathan orderly was apt to be spoilt by his Sahib. Brave, deft, intelligent and often witty, he got his own way too often. It was a sound rule on the Frontier not to keep an orderly too long. Sarfaraz had been Dodds's orderly four years; and because Dodds ignored his wishes on the distribution of road-construction money, he shot Dodds, two other officers and three police constables with the rifle Dodds had given him.

4

Side-shows, 1914–18

In the late 1890s the British, Australian and New Zealand armies were re-armed with the Lee-Metford rifle, and by 1907 their discarded Martinis, sold to arms dealers, were flooding the market and arriving on the Frontier via the Persian Gulf in very large numbers. Although it is not a magazine-rifle and does not fire smokeless powder, the Martini is a very good weapon, accurate and long-ranged, and the tribes soon developed effective fire-and-movement tactics. When the tribes had been armed mainly with jezails and swords, a column of troops with camels and mules could march safely up a valley if the heights as far as three hundred yards on each side were piqueted: now the piquets had to be set out at least nine hundred yards, the speed of advance was reduced and the difficulties of withdrawal – all Frontier campaigns must end in withdrawal – were vastly increased. It was a much more serious business than it had been in Kipling's and Warburton's day. The Militias had Martini rifles until 1912, when they were rearmed with the long magazine Lee-Enfield.

At the start of the First World War there were about 5,000 trans-Frontier Pathans in the regular Indian Army, including ten companies of Mahsuds. Their performance was patchy. Those who reached the Western Front and East Africa fought magnificently, particularly the Mahsuds, and won numerous medals for bravery; an officer who commanded Mahsuds in East Africa waxed lyrical in their praise. But many deserted rather than fight against the Turks, for the Sultan of Turkey was the Khalif of Islam, Commander of the Faithful, Shadow of God upon Earth. The trans-Frontier Pathans' ambivalence is illustrated by two Afridi brothers, Mir Mast and Mir Dast. Mir Mast deserted in France, was awarded the Iron Cross and sent back with a Turkish mission to the Tirah where he made much mischief. Mir Dast was awarded the Victoria Cross in France and never wavered in his loyalty.

Fortunately the Amir of Afghanistan did not take advantage of our difficulties by proclaiming the Jehad (Holy War). Even without this, Waziristan from 1914 to 1918 was far from peaceful.

On 7 January 1915, Captain Eustace Jotham of the North Waziristan Militia and a dozen Mounted Infantry rode out from Miranshah to locate raiders from Khost, in Afghanistan. Jotham was a romantic; recently on leave he had won newspaper fame by rescuing passengers from a blazing railway-carriage and now he was furious at being stuck in a mud hut in Waziristan while his battalion would soon be fighting Turks or Germans. At Spina Khaisora, fifteen miles west of Miranshah, he and his small patrol were ambushed in a deep nullah and almost surrounded by some 1,500 tribesmen. Jotham and his men galloped for safety, but just as he was getting clear, the horse of one of his sowars was shot. Jotham turned back to rescue him. He was quixotically carrying a sword, with which he is said to have cut down several of the Khostwals before he fell himself, riddled with bullets and bleeding from a dozen slashes. At almost the same time his Daffadar, a Wazir named Darim Khan, dismounted to give covering fire to the remainder of the patrol, and remounted and made off only when they had got safely away. Jotham was awarded a posthumous VC. Darim received the Indian Order of Merit and, subsequently, the Croix de Guerre. He lived to become one of the Frontier's most famous characters.

Two weeks later another Khostwal lashkar, estimated at 10,000, again advanced on Miranshah. Under their Commandant, Major G. B. Scott, the North Waziristan Militia and a section of Mountain Artillery made a long night march to get across the lashkar's line of retreat, and a regular brigade from Bannu attacked frontally at dawn. The enemy were driven back on to the Militia and across the Durand Line, with heavy casualties. After this the Khostwals and local tribesmen gave no more trouble for four years.

In South Waziristan the Mahsuds were more than troublesome. The anti-Government party led by Fazal Din, son of the Mullah Powindah, was spoiling for a fight, and in 1914 committed several outrages. The Government was exasperated, for the last thing it wanted then was a frontier campaign; but in 1915 the Mahsuds committed one hundred and eighty major crimes which claimed a hundred victims dead, seventy wounded and ninety-three Hindus kidnapped. In November a piquet of the South Waziristan Militia was ambushed, ten were killed, three wounded and thirteen rifles lost. In April 1916, there were no less than seventeen Mahsud raids into Dera Ismail Khan district.

At the end of February, 1917, Mahsuds attacked the Militia post at Sarwekai, garrisoned by 250 men under Major Hughes. Plagued by long-range sniping from Garesi Sar, a hill commanding the post from about 1,400 yards, Hughes sent a hundred men to occupy it. There was no difficulty in putting them there, but great difficulty in keeping them supplied. So Hughes reluctantly decided to withdraw them and took out fifty rifles half-way to Garesi Sar to cover the withdrawal. The Mahsuds were, as always, quick to seize their opportunity: both the covering party and the withdrawing party were rushed, and attacked with bayonets and knives. Hughes and twenty of the men were killed, ten wounded, eleven captured and reserved for a more unpleasant end at the hands of the Mahsud women. The situation was saved only by the courage and skill of Subadar Mohibullah, IOM, the Mahsud-hating Afridi, who withdrew the survivors into the fort and held it until relieved.

In April and May 1917 the total Mahsud bag, nearly all regular army, was 207 killed, 140 wounded and, most disgraceful, 238 rifles captured.

On 10 May a force from Sarwekai moved out at night to intercept raiders. It consisted of 250 Gurkhas and 120 Militia under Mohibullah again. At dawn with fifty Gurkhas and fifty Militia he surprised and shot up a party of Mahsuds cooking their breakfast. The Mahsuds were caught off their guard – no ordinary occurrence – but counter-attacked with extraordinary ferocity. There were four or five hundred of them, all armed with magazine rifles, and the troops were forced back to Sarwekai, losing thirty-nine killed (including two British officers), sixty-three wounded and seventy missing.

At the end of the month a well-known hostile named Musa Khan carried out an astonishing coup. He led by night, right up into the Tochi Valley, a gang of Abdullai, real hard-liners. Their objective was the North Waziristan Militia post at Tut Narai. Because the post was well outside Mahsud country, the garrison had become careless. Briefed by ex-Militia men, Musa Khan timed the attack for a holiday, knowing that everyone but the Quarter Guard would be off duty, their rifles locked in the Armoury, the men washing their clothes or bathing in the pool below the post. No patrols would be out who might discover the gang hiding in nullahs and holly-oak jungle close by.

In mid-morning five apparently unarmed tribesmen and two 'women' stopped to talk to the Militiamen hanging about outside the wire. It is likely that the 'women' were taken for dancing boys, dressed as girls, favourite entertainers on the Frontier. Three of the men then approached the sentry and chatted him up. A gullible simpleton, he was persuaded to buy them some sweets from the post canteen. As he turned to oblige them, the three Mahsuds at his heels, a more alert sentry on the wall shouted a warning. Too late! The Mahsuds produced revolvers and one shot dead the foolish sentry; two of them then made for the gate, shooting the Guard Commander as he tried to shut it, and firing on the remainder of the Guard. The rest of the party, including the 'girls', also brought out hidden weapons and engaged the sentry on the wall as thirty more tribesmen rushed up from the scrub-covered nullah. They burst in and shut the remainder of the garrison, who could not get at their rifles, in the barrack-rooms. Only the Post Subadar, seizing a dead sentry's rifle, made any sort of fight, but he was badly wounded. Then it was all over. The telegraphist just managed to get off a signal – 'Please help raiders are plundering' – before being knifed. The Abdullai got away with fifty-nine rifles and thousands of rounds of ammunition.

Worse, if anything could be worse, happened in June 1917 at the South Waziristan Militia post of Tiarza, garrisoned by twenty-five sepoys under a Wazir Havildar. A relation of the Havildar's who 'just happened' to be passing with pack-bullocks was invited in for tea. While he was refreshing himself, the Havildar sent out the entire garrison, except for an Afridi sentry, to collect firewood. As soon as they had gone, the Havildar and his relation overpowered the sentry, loaded on to the bullocks twenty-five rifles and thirteen boxes of ammunition, and departed.

In 1919, when the British and Indian armies were war-weary and demobilising as fast as possible, a new Amir Amanullah of Afghanistan did declare a Jehad and sent regular Afghan troops across the Durand Line.

5

The Third Afghan War, 1919

The main Afghan attack was a thrust into the Khyber. The Khyber
Rifles should have borne the brunt of this, but their loyalty had been
undermined by the Mullahs summoning all Moslems to the Holy War,
by revolutionary propaganda from India, and by the rumour that the
Government intended to destroy the flower of the Afridi nation by
putting the Khyber Rifles into the forefront of the battle and decimat-
ing them with artillery. After a number of desertions, the Army took
over all the Khyber posts, and the Khyber Rifles were offered the
choice of discharge or serving on. Those who opted for discharge
numbered 1,180 (but no Pathan officers), which was at least preferable
to their deserting with rifles. Of the loyalists, 146 were transferred to a
Military Police Battalion, and 200 were formed into the Khyber Levy
Corps, un-uniformed and armed with their own rifles. That, for a
quarter-century, was the end of the Khyber Rifles.

In the far north, in the semi-independent state of Chitral, ruled by its
Mehtar (prince) Shuja-ul-Mulk, the Government and allied forces
consisted of the 1/11th Rajputs (450 rifles); 23 Mountain Battery; one
section Sappers and Miners; the Chitral Scouts (1,000 rifles); the
Mehtar's Bodyguard, about 2,000 men of whom 150 had Martini rifles
and the remainder muzzle-loading rifles and jezails; and a Russian
machine-gun brought across the Pamirs by a refugee White Russian
colonel. The Chitral Scouts were part-time soldiers, called up for one
month's training every year, commanded by the Assistant Political
Agent, Major Reilly. There were also a considerable number of Kafir
volunteers whose country, adjacent to Chitral, had been conquered by

the Afghans in 1897, its idol-worshipping people offered the choice
between conversion to Islam and instant decapitation, and its chiefs
taken off to slavery in Kabul. The wildest of the wild, and totally
undisciplined, they were hardy, war-like and longing for revenge.

Opposing these forces, at cantonments in Birkot and Arnawai in the
Kunar valley,* were six Afghan infantry battalions with five more on
the way, four machine-guns and twelve mountain guns. The odds
seemed rather heavy, but the Mehtar rejected with scorn the Amir's
invitation to join the Holy War, and his people, despising Afghans,
followed his lead.

Lieutenant-Colonel F. C. S. Sambourne-Palmer, commanding the
Rajputs, assumed command of all the local forces. Reilly's command
consisted of the Scouts, the Bodyguard under the Mehtar's son, Prince
Nasr-ul-Mulk, and the Kafirs – as strange a force as was ever led by a
British officer in the twentieth century.

On 5 May 1919, Major Reilly, on his own responsibility, mobilised
the Scouts, and in the next two weeks they drove back two Afghan
incursions. It was a satisfactory introduction to war for the Scouts, who
suffered no casualties and claimed to have killed and wounded scores of
Afghans.

Against an enemy less formidable than Mahsuds and Wazirs, it was
permissible to take risks. Leaving himself with no reserve nearer than
Chitral town, Sambourne-Palmer divided his small force into four
columns for an attack on the Afghan positions at Birkot and Arnawai.
Prince Nasr-ul-Mulk's Right Column consisted of a company of
Scouts, 1,000 of the Bodyguard and some Kafirs. The Right Bank
column consisted of two Scout companies. The main body, known as
the Mobile Column, under Sambourne-Palmer himself, consisted of
two Scout companies under Reilly, the Rajputs less one company, the
two mountain guns and the Sappers. The Left Column consisted of
three companies of Scouts.

The plan for the attack was that the Right Bank column would seize
the bridge over the Bashgul near its junction with the Kunar, and attack
Birkot. The Mobile column would move down the left bank and attack
Arnawai, which would be outflanked by the Left Column moving
through the mountains. To Nasr-ul-Mulk's Right Column was allotted
the most spectacular role: guided by Kafirs, it would cross the frontier
by the high Patuk pass west of Mirkhanni; drop down into the valley of
the Istor river; follow that river to its junction with the Bashgul; cross

* The Chitral river is known below its junction with the Bashgul as the Kunar river.
  For simplicity it will be referred to as the Kunar throughout.

the Bashgul by a rope-bridge; and outflank the enemy's position by seizing the heights west of Birkot. Three hundred Chitrali jezailchis would move along the watershed between the Istor and the Kunar rivers, acting as connecting link between Nasr-ul-Mulk and the two central columns. (See Map 1.)

With most of his army almost untrained, his columns separated by mountains and a torrent swollen by melting snow, and no communication between them except thought-reading, Sambourne-Palmer's plan seemed a trifle ambitious. Had the enemy been more enterprising, one or more of his columns, separated from the others, would surely have been cut up. But it worked. The two central columns struck opposition just north of the Bashgul junction, pushed it back and attacked the main Afghan positions, capturing four guns and fifty-five prisoners. Meanwhile the Left Column had outflanked Arnawai and the Right Column duly occupied the heights west of Birkot. For good measure a single brave Chitrali crept down at night to the bridge over the Kunar which was the only link between the enemy positions at Birkot and Arnawai and cut the ropes so that it dropped into the torrent. The enemy fled south towards Asmar in great disorder; the cantonment at Birkot was well looted by Kafirs and the bodyguard. The victory was complete.

That was virtually the end of the fighting in Chitral: the regulars, the Scouts and the Bodyguard could all congratulate themselves on their performance.

The war in Chitral smacked of the Boys' Own Paper with its small forces, jezails, savage auxiliaries and deeds of high daring, all overlooked by the stupendous peaks of Tirich Mir and the Hindu Kush. The war in the Khyber was more conventional, like a sideshow of the First World War. The Afghans were not much good at it, and were soon pushed back into Afghanistan.

It was on the central front, comprising Waziristan and the Kurram Valley, that the Afghans came nearest to success. Their commander, General Nadir Khan, had considerable tactical ability, deploying fourteen regular battalions against six, and forty-eight guns against six. He also had the initiative, since the Indian High Command decided that Waziristan could not be held and must be evacuated.

In the Kurram the situation was rather different. Geographically the valley might be almost indefensible: a salient, sixty miles long from Thal in the south to the Peiwar Kotal Pass in the north, shaped rather like an inverted bottle, only five miles wide at the neck in the south, and about twenty miles wide in the north. To the west and north it was

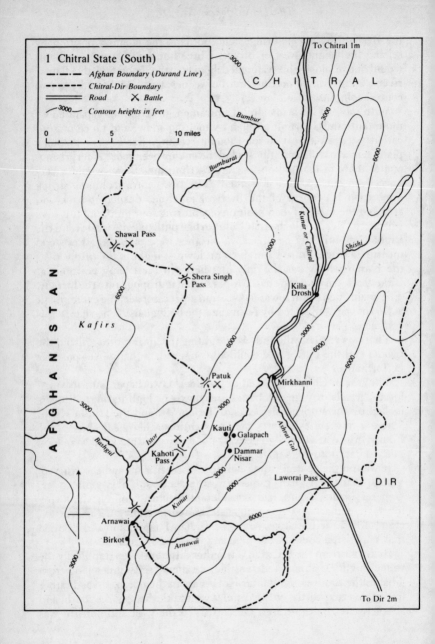

1 Chitral State (South)

— · — Afghan Boundary (Durand Line)
- - - Chitral-Dir Boundary
═══ Road   ✕ Battle
⌒3000⌒ Contour heights in feet

0   5   10 miles

To Chitral 1m

C H I T R A L

Bumbur

Bumbural

Kunar or Chitral

Shishi

Shawal Pass

Shera Singh
Pass

Killa
Drosh

Kafirs

6000

Patuk

Mirkhanni

A F G H A N I S T A N

3000

Bashgul

Istor

Kahoti
Pass

Kauti
Galapach

Dammar
Nisar

Ashrat Gul

Laworai Pass

D I R

Kunar

Arnawai

Birkot

Arnawai

6000

To Dir 2m

bounded by Afghanistan; to the east were potentially hostile Orakzai and Zaimukht tribes; and to the south, the Wazirs. The valley itself was inhabited by the Turi tribe, tough and outstandingly loyal, which made its defence possible and its evacuation highly undesirable. (See Map 2.) A regular brigade was detailed to hold the defences, constructed by Lord Roberts fifty years earlier, at Thal, in the southern bottleneck of the Lower Kurram. In the Upper Kurram a guerilla campaign would be conducted against the invaders by the Kurram Militia (1,450 infantry, eighty Mounted Infantry and two mountain guns), supported by two regular battalions and attached troops. The whole force in the Upper Kurram was commanded by Brigadier-General A. E. Fagan, the Kurram Militia by Major Dodd. Fagan's plan was to hold the regulars in reserve at Parachinar, while the Militia watched the likely invasion routes by the Peiwar Kotal Pass, fifteen miles west-north-west of Parachinar, or along the Kurram river via Kharlachi, eleven miles south-west of it; and dealt with minor incursions.

For the first three weeks of the war, nothing much happened, except that the Militia grabbed sixty head of Afghan-owned cattle. Then, on 22 May 1919, Nadir Khan marched with great speed, his artillery conveyed by elephants which have good cross-country mobility, and invested Thal. Fortunately his tactical ability was not backed by war-experience, and he contended himself with shelling the defences without putting in a serious infantry attack. The garrison had four unpleasant days before the arrival on 1 June of a relief column from Kohat. Next day Nadir Khan's army withdrew to the west. Meanwhile in the Upper Kurram the Militia were having great success. In the last week of May it drove back an incursion near the Peiwar Kotal Pass and an attack on Kharlachi Post.

The next Afghan move was to try to divide Upper from Lower Kurram by cutting through the valley via Lakka Tiga and joining forces with the Orakzais and Zaimukhts. The enemy numbered some 3,000 men with five guns. It was, therefore, bold of Lieutenant Beamish, who commanded at Lakka Tiga, to attack them with only two hundred infantry and eighty Mounted Infantry. However, this he did, on a front of no less than four miles. Although he did not decisively defeat them, he frustrated their purpose.

On 29 May an Orakzai lashkar came down from the mountains to attack the militia post of Badama. Badama was commanded by Subadar Gul Khan, who with one hundred rifles of the Militia and a lashkar of Turi villagers, waded into the Orakzais and drove them out of the valley with the loss of twenty dead.

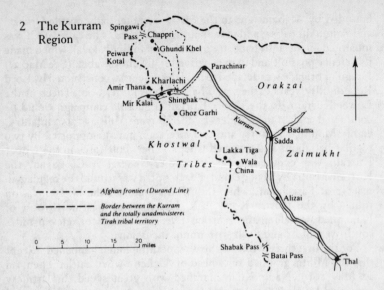

2   The Kurram Region

On 3 June the Kurram Militia invaded Afghanistan. Major Dodd took one hundred infantry and fifty Mounted Infantry of the Militia, one company of the Guides, two troops of Lancers, and two mountain guns to attack the forward Afghan post at Amir Thana. They moved out from Parachinar in the evening, and achieved complete surprise at dawn. Under cover of fire from the mountain guns, the infantry of the Militia made a valiant attempt to scale the walls. In this they were unsuccessful, but an hour later the garrison surrendered and Amir Thana fort was burnt. The cavalry and Mounted Infantry then trotted on to Mir Zaman Kalai, rushed the village and burnt it as well. They then proceeded towards Mir Kalai, headquarters of the Afghan General in those parts, who hastily decamped. Two Afghan forts and six villages were burnt, at a cost of two Militia killed and five wounded.

The Kurram Militia's last action of the war was on 30 July, nearly eight weeks after the armistice. A combined lashkar of Orakzais and Zaimukhts was again threatening Badama post. Four planes were sent to locate them, one of which flew too close to a steep, wooded mountain-side and was shot down by the tribesmen's rifle-fire, the pilot and observer being wounded. There was a dramatic race for the plane between the tribesmen and the garrison which the garrison just won, rescuing pilot and observer and returning next day to salvage the engine.

On 8 August peace was signed to end the war in which the Kurram Militia had held its own valley, harried the enemy and behaved exactly in the manner expected of it.

The Waziristan Militias had always been told that if they were attacked by regular troops and artillery which could pound their mud forts to rubble, the Army would come to their help. But now there were no troops to spare for Waziristan, so the North Waziristan Militia was ordered to pull out of all its forward posts. The decision may have been militarily correct, but politically it was disastrous, and most Militia officers thought it was wrong. The sight of the Militia burning their stores and marching out of their posts seemed clear evidence that the Sarkar was on the run, and that within a few weeks the whole country of the Pathans down to the Indus would be governed from Kabul.

On 25 May 1919, at the news that Nadir Khan was advancing down the Kaitu valley, the evacuation was ordered of the Militia posts in the Upper Tochi – Datta Khel, Tut Narai, Spina Khaisora and Boya – to Dardoni. After a fight with Wazirs during the night of 25–6 May, the retreating column reached Dardoni early in the morning of 26 May, less about one hundred and fifty Wazirs and Afridis of the Militia who had taken advantage of the darkness to desert. Also on 25 May the garrisons of Shewa and Spinwam were withdrawn in a very difficult rearguard action across open country. They had hardly left the burning fort of Spinwam when Afghans and Wazirs were in it, only three hundred yards behind them; and they were harried by Wazirs all the way back to Idak.

Thousands of exultant Wazirs milled round Dardoni, Miranshah and Idak without closely investing them. The situation was most serious in Miranshah, crammed with dejected or subversive Militia including six hundred Wazirs. At first their attitude had been satisfactory: they had welcomed the outbreak of war because they would then receive Army rations, free, instead of rations on payment; and their Pathan officers brought to the Commandant letters that had been sent to them from Khost urging them to desert with their men and join the Holy War. But they were shaken by the incidents of the last few days and the fact that most of their tribe was now at war with the Sarkar. To support the loyal elements in the garrison, two companies of the 1/41st Dogras, brave, dependable little hill Rajputs from the eastern Punjab, were sent to Miranshah on 26 May.

On 27 May after a day of indecision, nearly all the Wazirs decided to join the Jehad. Their ringleaders were the Jemadar Adjutant, Tarin, a

Tori Khel Wazir, and Subadar Pak, Madda Khel, IOM, Croix de Guerre. They did not attack the officers and an Orakzai platoon formed a cordon round the Officers' Mess to protect it. A further company of Dogras arrived with a machine-gun, and an attempt was made to persuade the Wazirs at least to hand their rifles into the armoury. They started to do so, but when some of the Dogras – disposed in commanding positions on the wall and over the gateway – began jeering, no more rifles were handed in.

Through the stifling heat of the day there was a stalemate. The Khattaks in the garrison remained loyal; the Dogras held the walls and gates, the Wazirs could not get out. But it was impossible to separate the loyal Khattaks from the disloyal Wazirs and the Afridis and Orakzais of doubtful loyalty; only eleven Wazirs, including Darim Khan, IOM, and Zeri Gul, who later became a Subadar in the Tochi Scouts, refused to join the mutiny. Lest they be shot either by their fellow-tribesmen or by the Dogras, they stayed quietly in their barrack-room. British officers were helpless spectators of their world crumbling beneath them, but neither hand nor voice was raised against them. When darkness fell the mutineers dug a hole through the mud wall and departed, with their rifles.

Of the much-decorated Subadar Pak no more was heard, but Jemadar Tarin became a well-known hostile. An ex-signaller, he used to amuse himself by tapping the telephone wires between posts and interrupting official conversations with unseemly observations and lewd laughter. He met his end in a pistol-duel with a Medical Officer – equally quick on the draw, they shot each other dead.

With the departure of the Wazirs, the situation improved and discipline was restored. In the circumstances the most surprising thing was not the desertion of Wazirs and Afridis, but the steadfastness of the other tribes. The hostile lashkars remained in the vicinity of Dardoni, Miranshah, and Idak, burnt the Miranshah civil serai, amused themselves with a lot of sniping and waited for what they thought was the inevitable evacuation. However, on 1 June two hundred and fifty of the Militia garrison in Dardoni made a successful sortie, put the enemy to flight with a loss of about ninety and blew up some fortified towers from which Miranshah was being sniped at. Morale improved; the tribesmen began to feel that the Sarkar was not on the run after all, an impression which was confirmed by the arrival at Dardoni of a relief column from Bannu on 4 June.

The South Waziristan Militia consisted of eight British officers, thirty-seven Pathan officers and 1,800 other ranks, including 230 Wazirs and 780 Afridis. The headquarters were in Wana and it also held six small posts. Its Commandant was Major G. H. Russell, 126th Baluchis, an officer very experienced with Pathans, very much in accord with them. He was thorough and meticulous over matters which he thought important, especially tactical training, the duties of sentries and musketry, but more easy-going in turn-out and discipline for what was his *irregular* corps. With the end of the First World War, officers who had been with the Militia for three or four years had departed on leave, and of Russell's five British officers now present (two being on leave) only two, Captain Traill and Lieutenant Barker, spoke Pushtu and had been with the Militia long enough to know the men. This was a great weakness.

On 21 May 1919 Russell heard that an Afghan brigade, with artillery, had crossed the Durand Line and were within twenty-five miles of Wana. Four days later news of the evacuation of the Upper Tochi posts came like a bolt from the blue. The Political Agent, after consulting higher authority, ordered that the South Waziristan Militia posts be evacuated before the Mahsuds attacked. The evening of 26 May was fixed for the start of this operation of extreme difficulty and danger. The garrisons of the two easterly posts, Nili Kach and Sarwekai, would withdraw direct to Murtaza, those of Wana and the four westerly posts, Kharab Kot, Tanai, Khajuri Kach and Toi Khula, would withdraw to the Zhob Militia post at Mogul Kot and from there to Fort Sandeman.

At six o'clock in the evening of the 26th, Captain Traill with Lieutenants Hunt and Barker left with sixty infantry and ten Mounted Infantry ostensibly on a routine patrol but really to pick up the garrisons of Kharab Kot, Tanai and Khajuri Kach. At seven, Russell assembled the Pathan officers, explained the situation and gave orders for the withdrawal. Men from the cis-Frontier tribes would be put on guard at the gate; 60,000 rupees would be loaded on to camels and donkeys, the remaining treasure distributed among the men, twenty-five rupees to every sepoy and twenty rupees to every follower. Spare arms and ammunition would be destroyed. One hour before midnight they would march out. The sick must keep up as best they could. The Pathan officers were surprised at the decision, which at the end of a victorious war seemed against the laws of Nature; but they did not question the necessity.

Major Russell's plan was never implemented. At nine o'clock Subadar Major Maqan Khan, a stout-hearted Bhitanni, rushed into Russell's office to say that seven Wazir and Afridi officers, with their platoons, instigated by Subadar Mir Zaman, Malik Din Khel Afridi, who later became a captain in the Afghan army, had seized the central keep of the fort and now held the well, rations, cash, spare arms and ammunition, and donkeys. Russell and Maqan Khan went out to try to reason with them, but they were obdurate, and fired a few shots, not to kill but close enough to make their point. The evacuation plan had to be abandoned. All that could now be done was get out of Wana the loyal elements of the Militia, the British officers and non-combatants, including Khan Bahadur Mohamad Yar Khan of the Political Department. Besides Russell, the British officers were Captain Burn-Murdoch and Lieutenant Leese of the Militia, Major Owen, the Medical Officer, and Lieutenant MacCorstie, the Garrison Engineer.

While the mosquitoes droned round and the mutineers jeered from the keep, the officers packed what they could carry in their haversacks – photographs of parents and girl-friends, a clean shirt and socks, a few items from the Mess larder. They checked that the men going with them had collected any food not in the keep. With the well in the mutineers' hands, most of their water-bottles were empty, a serious matter in the middle of the hot weather when even the night was like a furnace. Then they killed time until the temperature dropped a degree or two and it was time to leave.

At ten o'clock the gate was opened and the column filed out; there were about 290 of the Militia, including a few Mounted Infantry, but a hundred of these were recruits with very little training. The 150 followers included clerks, sweepers, water-carriers without water to carry, tailors, cobblers, washermen, shopkeepers and other followers. There were eight camels, unladen but sure to be needed to carry the wounded. A few derisive shots mocked them as they set off for Mogul Kot, thirty-four miles away across country swarming with enemies. (See Map 3.)

Sweating from the climb in the close, oppressive air, they paused to give the followers a short rest on a col of the Pir Gwazha. The British officers' thoughts were particularly gloomy: the unthinkable was happening, the Empire in humiliating retreat and they were part of it. Looking back at Wana which, if not exactly the jewel of the Orient, had been in a sense their home, they saw it illuminated by lamps and bonfires, and knew that the men they had liked and trusted, playing games with them and fighting side by side, were now ransacking their rooms, pawing over letters and photographs, smashing fishing-rods, golf-clubs and tennis-rackets. Through the gates poured excited tribesmen, milling about the parade-ground, cramming their purses

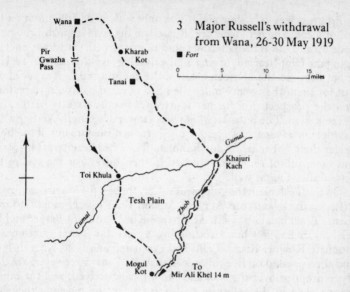

3 Major Russell's withdrawal from Wana, 26-30 May 1919

and haversacks with silver rupees, stuffing ammunition into their cartridge-belts and trying out their new rifles with *feux de joie* at the stars. There had been nothing like this since the Indian Mutiny.

A quick check among the Militia and followers showed that nearly all the Afridis had disappeared into the night. Major Russell ordered a move, and with the British and Pathan officers restraining the pace of the soldiers and goading on the civilians, they made twenty miles that night, reaching the vicinity of Toi Khula post just before dawn. Russell intended to evacuate the post, garrisoned mainly by Wazirs, and take with him any who were loyal. But the news from Wana had overtaken them during the night: as the head of the column rounded a bend of the nullah and came within sight of Toi Khula, it was fired on from the walls and from the hills to the east.

With his long tail of followers and recruits, Russell had no option but to by-pass Toi Khula. The Wazirs had wasted no time and the sniping from the hillsides was increasing. Major Owen was tending the wounded and tying them as well as he could to the camels' pack-saddles. They stopped to drink and fill their bottles from the warm trickle of the Gumal, and then breasted the steep rise to the Tesh plateau. Fourteen miles to Mogul Kot.

Progress was very slow and it was only with great difficulty that the column could be held together. Russell on his good English-bred pony rode up and down the faltering column, joking with the brave, encouraging the faint-hearted, urging on the limping laggards in the rear. Had it not been for the non-combatants, the column could have raced on; but for them the twenty miles they had covered had been purgatory, and the prospect of a further fourteen was only slightly better than Wazir knives. The Subadar Major was a tower of strength , setting a fine example in adversity. A platoon of Sheranis turned up out of the blue, under their Subadar, Abdur Rahman. They had deserted from Wana but now, full of remorse, returned to their duty. For the rest of the retreat they fought well.

On the Tesh plain the going was easier, though the Wazirs continued to harass flanks and rear. At noon Captain Traill's party caught up with them. Traill had done well. At Kharab Kot Lieutenant Barker and his ten sowars had left him, trotting on to warn the Tanai garrison and evacuate Khajuri Kach. Traill had evacuated and fired Kharab Kot, and then pressed on five miles to Tanai. In Tanai were seven Wazirs: three dropped over the wall and ran off as he arrived, and the others were locked in the cells. By half-past two in the morning they had loaded on to the post's camels the spare rifles, cash and ammunition and set off for Toi Khula twelve miles away.

They arrived there not long after Russell had left and, like his party, were fired at. Supposing that the garrison had mistaken them for hostiles, Jemadar Taza Gul, Adam Khel Afridi, went up to the post to ask what the hell they were up to. When he demanded to be let in, the post commander replied with some cock-and-bull story of the gate-key being lost. How Taza Gul gained entry is not known; once in, by sheer force of personality he put under arrest eighteen Wazirs in the garrison, opened the gate and let Traill's party in. As there was no fuel to burn the spare rifles and ammunition, the rifles were smashed, the ammunition dumped in the well and the party hurried on towards the Tesh plateau, reinforced by the Toi Khula loyalists.

So intense was the sniping during the afternoon that Russell's column had been obliged to piquet their route to keep the enemy at a distance. As the trained sepoys, less than two hundred, were too few to provide piquets, advance guard and rearguard, Traill's party was very welcome. The advance guard came down off the heights of the Zhob river valley at about six in the evening, and some sowars of the Mounted Infantry were sent on ahead to Mogul Kot to ask for help. For the last two or three miles their route was piqueted by the Zhob Militia.

Barker meanwhile, having left Traill at Kharab Kot, had trotted on via Tanai to Khajuri Kach, forty-seven miles from Wana (a long ride in the hot weather) arriving there in the afternoon. He no longer had ten sowars with him – four Adam Khel Afridis had slipped away during the night. Khajuri Kach was held by 120 rifles, Orakzai and Bangash. They obeyed Barker's orders to burn the stock of forage in the post, foul the well with oil, and load rifles, ammunition and cash on to the post camels, although they seemed sulky and reluctant. He rode out of the fort on his last lap, his six sowars leading, the post garrison following with the camels. As they emerged, they were heavily fired on and the camels, already terrified by the flames and billowing smoke of the burning forage, broke free and galloped down the Gumal river, bucking and shedding rifles, ammunition boxes and cash. Seeing that the Orakzais and Bangash had no intention of following him, and that the camels could not possibly be caught, Barker and his faithful six trotted on up the Zhob river. The tribesmen were too busy chasing the camels to molest them and, free of encumbrances and of doubtful comrades, they felt quite gay and light-hearted, despite the seventy miles they had ridden since the previous evening. They joined Major Russell's column a mile or two short of Mogul Kot.

Mogul Kot was held by twenty-seven Mounted Infantry and eighteen infantry of the Zhob Militia, under a Brahui Jemadar. It seemed as though their troubles were over. But this impression was erroneous. The food and forage in the post was quite inadequate for the influx from Wana; Russell reckoned there was enough for only two days. The water-tank within the walls was designed for fifty men, not 450; attempts to bring water from the river cost eight men wounded and the bullocks pulling the water-cart killed. There was no room for the camels and horses inside the walls, and outside they were picked off by snipers. The little fort was packed to suffocation; the heat, dust and flies were appalling, as was the sanitary problem.

Russell would have liked to push on next day, 28 May; but the followers were exhausted and could not move before the morning of the 30th. Arrangements were made by wireless for one hundred infantry and one hundred Mounted Infantry of the Zhob Militia to leave the next fort, Mir Ali Khel, fourteen miles away, at three o'clock in the morning and piquet half-way to Mogul Kot. Russell's column would move out at six-thirty. The wireless set then broke down, so there was no further communication.

By six-thirty there was no sign of the Zhob Militia who, under Captain A. F. Reilly, were having to fight their way through hardening opposition. Major Russell set fire to the magazine and stores and at eight o'clock ordered the gate to be opened; but in the face of heavy fire it had to be slammed shut again. With crow-bar, pick and shovel, a hole was hacked in the wall at the back of the fort, out of which Lieutenant Barker and his Mounted Infantry sowars led the fourteen surviving horses. Under fire they galloped up the river valley looking for a fall-back position, giving a good field of fire and cover for the led horses. They had ridden a mile before they found one. There they dismounted, three horse-holders took the horses into a nullah, and the remainder prepared to give covering fire to the infantry.

It was some time before these appeared. The first piquet went too far, ignored signals to return, and seemed to be making off. At this inauspicious sight morale, already strained to breaking-point, broke. Nor did it help that this was the first day of the Ramzan fast when religious feeling might be strong and confidence in Faranghi officers low. (Nevertheless at no time did they turn on their British officers, and Barker recalls that throughout mutineers and deserters 'treated us pretty decently'.)

It was impossible to get any piqueting organised. By twos and threes and whole sections the men straggled away, some up the wide Zhob river valley, others into the hills. British and Pathan officers tried to get them under control, but as soon as they rallied one party and went on to the next, the first party drifted away. By the time they reached the Mounted Infantry, who were giving what covering fire they could, Burn-Murdoch, Traill, Leese, McCorstie, Mohamad Yar Khan and eight Pathan officers had been killed, Hunt wounded. Then Russell was shot through both legs, and his pony in the stifle and jaw, but kept going.

They straggled past the Mounted Infantry who thereafter acted ('in theory', said Barker years later) as rearguard, dismounting to give covering-fire and then trotting on to catch up. As they distanced themselves from Mogul Kot, the Wazirs turned their attention to looting the fort. About five miles further on the disorderly mob met the first piquet of the Zhob Militia, whose commander, Captain Reilly, had been killed as he lay pinned under his wounded horse. They reached Mir Ali Khel, and in a stupor of exhaustion went on through the night to Fort Sandeman.

About 350 of the South Waziristan Militia, including a hundred recruits, had left Mogul Kot; about 140 reached Fort Sandeman. There is some doubt about how many rifles were lost. The Official History said that 'very few' retained their rifles; a contemporary, and somewhat inaccurate, account, written apparently by a clerk whose command of English was poor, says that only nine arrived with rifles. But Barker, when shown these figures, said, 'No, I cannot credit that. We would not have taken them back,' that is, no man would have been retained in the corps if he had thrown away his rifle, and most of the men who reached the end of the long march were retained. It does, therefore, seem probable that of those who got to Fort Sandeman, comparatively few disgraced themselves by arriving unarmed.

Some of the stragglers from Mogul Kot and Khajuri Kach made their way in small parties through the hills to Murtaza. The garrisons of Nili Kach and Sarwekai had been withdrawn without trouble. But of the Militia's total strength of 1,800 perhaps a hundred were killed and 1,100, nearly all Wazirs and Afridis, deserted with their rifles. The tribes won 1,200 good Lee-Enfield rifles and 700,000 rounds of ammunition.

The Official History concludes the dismal tale:

> Regarded merely as a feat of endurance at this period of the year, the withdrawal of the party was of itself a fine achievement; but taking into consideration the almost insurmountable difficulties which beset it on the road and the dangers through which it emerged, the exploits stand out as one of the finest recorded in the history of the Indian Frontier.

Well, yes. But one wonders if that is how Major Russell saw it. However for their personal conduct he was awarded the DSO, Lieutenant Barker the MC, Subadar Major Maqan Khan the IOM and Jemadar Taza Gul, the IDSM. Taza Gul's exploit at Toi Kullah was very remarkable, for Afridis did not distinguish themselves at that time.

Harrying the demoralised survivors of the South Waziristan Militia, the exultant Wazirs were joined by the Pathan tribes of the Zhob, Sheranis and Mando Khel, and by Suliman Khel nomads from Afghanistan. The Mullahs preached the Jehad, telling of Afghan armies pouring into India like the hordes of Mahmud Ghuznavi.

It was all too much for the Zhob Militia. Eight hundred of its Pathans deserted and most of its posts were abandoned and looted by tribesmen. On 3 June the post at Manikhwa, twenty-four miles east-north-east of Fort Sandeman, was tamely surrendered to Wazirs and Sheranis. The garrison was composed of nomadic Ghilzais from Afghanistan, who had elsewhere shown themselves to be thoroughly unreliable (not surprising in the circumstances); and their Pathan officers when they made their way to Fort Sandeman, explaining the mishap, said that the enemy had put a spell on their rifles which would not fire. But that was the last really bad performance put up by the Zhob Militia. There remained true to their salt two companies of North-West Frontier Pathans, mainly Orakzais, one squadron of Pishin Kakars, a fairly tractable Pathan tribe in Baluchistan, and a squadron and a company of Brahuis, a very wild, hairy and almost unknown nomad tribe, not Pathan, from the desert country south-west of Quetta. But so shaky and unreliable did these faithful remnants appear that when, on the approach of a large enemy lashkar, the garrison and civilians of Fort Sandeman were withdrawn inside the perimeter, they were left outside. When, however, Fort Sandeman was attacked, and the bazaar burnt, it was the Zhob Militia who drove the enemy off.

There followed some weeks of scrappy fighting along the Fort Sandeman-Loralai road in which several small columns were cut up by mixed Wazir-Sherani-Suliman Khel lashkars, culminating in a spectacular disaster near Kapip. An entire convoy and its escort were routed in hand-to-hand fighting, four British officers and forty-nine other ranks killed, seventy-one wounded, all the carts and two guns lost. 'After this,' says the Official Report, 'all was chaos and the troops, with the exception of the rearguard of Zhob Militia, split up into twos and threes and made their way to Fort Sandeman during the night.'

The honour of the Zhob Militia was further restored by a fine exploit of Subadar Major Gulab Khan on 11 October. After leading fifty rifles on a forced march of sixty miles, he surrounded the village of the doyen of Militia deserters, ex-Subadar Haji Mir, killed him and ten of his followers and recovered twelve Government rifles.

In Waziristan and Zhob the loss of magazine rifles was particularly serious. The tribes had acquired modern rifles by theft and capture from ill-trained, post-war army units, by purchase from Afghanistan, and from the Middle East which for four years had been flooded with arms, distributed wholesale by the British and Turkish Governments to any Arabs who might take their side. Moreover they turned out in tribal rifle-factories, with simple hand-tools, foot-operated lathes and looted rails, remarkably good imitations of the Lee Enfield service rifle, complete with regimental numbers, which were nearly as accurate as the genuine article until, after about 300 rounds, the rifling began to wear. It was not unknown for soldiers to sell their rifles for 500 to 600 rupees and buy for 150 rupees replicas so good as to pass all but the most expert annual inspection. For as little as 40 rupees a poor man could buy a single-shot Martini-action rifle firing the ordinary ·303 ammunition. The Mahsud factories at Kanigurum were not very accessible, but the Afridi factories beside the Kohat pass were only a few yards across the Border, a popular tourist attraction. They did seem to be cocking a snook at the Sarkar, and from time to time consideration was given to closing them down. But what was the point? They would merely be established a few miles back. It would be more effective to concentrate on preventing the tribesmen acquiring bullets and empty cartridge-cases from rifle-ranges, with which to replenish their ammunition with the help of cordite and caps smuggled out of Kabul Arsenal. Rifles and ammunition in Tribal Territory were expensive, but there was no real shortage.

There are differences of opinion about tribal marksmanship. The popular image of the bearded sniper able to shoot the eye out of a gnat has been challenged by those who ask, 'How could he afford the ammunition for practice enough to make him a crack shot? Was not his skill really in field-craft and concealment, in never squeezing the trigger unless he had a good chance of a hit?' But it is on record that the South Waziristan Scouts, better shots than most army battalions, invited a Mahsud team to enter for a falling-plate competition. The Mahsuds, using Government rifles and ammunition, won.

The Army, back from France, Palestine, East Africa and Mesopotamia, was ill-trained for the special conditions of the Frontier. Accustomed to fighting against conscripts who sprayed the country with lead but were not noted for straight shooting, officers and men found it disconcerting in Waziristan that every shot seemed to be aimed at each of them, personally. To safeguard the long, vulnerable columns of camels, mules, horses and lorries every height within 1,500 yards of a brigade's axis of advance had now to be piqueted, slowing to snail's pace every advance and seriously complicating every withdrawal. The new rifles fired smokeless powder; no longer could a sniper be located by a puff of smoke every time he fired. In the 1890s a Pathan lashkar with its coloured banners had shown up like a field of flowers on the mountainside; now it was seldom visible since the tribesmen, including thousands of ex-soldiers, soon adapted their tactics to their new weapons, slipping from shadow to shadow, from brown-grey rock to grey-green gurgura bushes, covering every knife-rush with accurate long-range fire, and in pursuit of a withdrawing piquet dropping from foothold to foothold like wild goats, bounding down the steep scree like falling boulders.

Having nothing else to do with their time, they would study for days or weeks the habits of a convoy-escort, a standing piquet, a watering- or range-party until they saw develop some careless habit or tactical error − a patch of dead ground or thorn-scrub left unchecked, men moving across the open without a supporting section lying prone, a round in the chamber, finger on trigger, ready to give instant covering-fire. Then they struck − a volley and a knife-rush and away into the hills with their captured rifles and ammunition, leaving half-a-dozen mutilated corpses, a hideous offence under the sky.

It is strange how little has been written about the military organisation and chain-of-command of the tribes, which must have been sophisticated enough to control lashkars numbering thousands, carrying out complicated tactical movements. It was similar to the Scottish Highlanders' system, each family, sept and clan following some proven war-leader who was not formally elected, but was nevertheless the tribe's choice. There were also marauding outlaw gangs drawn from several tribes, attracted by the fame of some Robin Hood whose raids were generally successful.

The formidable character of Mahsuds and Wazirs and the respect − awe − they inspired may be judged from extracts from an army pamphlet produced by HQ Waziristan District in 1924:

> The physique, powers of endurance and experience gained by the Mahsud and Wazir in years of incessant raiding made him a formidable enemy in his own hills, and there are quite 3,000 to 4,000 of them who have served in the Militia or Regular Army, and have an intimate knowledge of our habits and tactics . . .
>
> Owing to his activity on the hillside and general watchfulness it is almost impossible to outflank him or cut off his retreat . . .
>
> When the troops commence to retire, it is astonishing how numbers of the enemy will appear in places which had seemed to be deserted, and the rearguard will be harried in the most determined manner. Every opportunity which occurs of cutting off small parties will at once be seized . . .
>
> The Mahsud or Wazir is an expert at attacking convoys or small detachments and is assisted by the nature of his country, the ravines being narrow and winding, while the hillsides in the western tracts are often thickly covered with bushes. He attacks systematically, with special parties told off for specific duties, such as the neutralising of adjacent piquets by fire, supports to his advanced parties of swordsmen, etc. . . . Ambushes may sometimes open by a few shots

from one side of the nullah. Untrained troops rush to cover on the side from which fire comes. This is what is waited for. Heavy accurate fire from the other bank then finishes the party.

Against troops proceeding to take up position the usual plan is to ambush the leading party of the advanced guard, firing a volley and charging immediately. Knives are used to cut free rifles and equipment, and the tribesmen make off in the inevitable confusion before a counter-attack can be organised . . .

Do not let a man approach you in enemy's country scratching his stomach, he is looking for his knife. Hit him on the elbow with a stick and he'll drop it . . .

Avoid shaking hands with strange Pathans. They will seize with their left hand and stab with their right on occasions . . .

Mahsuds or Wazirs brought to bay always fight desperately. Should a party be surprised completely without hope of escape, an immediate and determined counter-attack must be expected.

The fiercest fighting of 1919–20 took place after peace with Afghanistan was signed. There was a real war against the Mahsuds and, to a lesser extent, the Wazirs. Never had the tribes been so well-armed, never had their morale been so high. And the Army was not at its best, the war-time soldiers having been discharged, and the ranks filled with young recruits, many battalions with little mountain warfare and no Frontier experience. An unusual feature of a very savage war was that from time to time it was halted, temporarily, by the arrival in the British camp of parties of enemy with flags of truce, wearing their war-medals, come to shake hands and chat with the officer who had commanded them in East Africa.

Of the South Waziristan Militia, one company, carefully selected, operated as an integral part of a regular battalion. They performed well and went some way to restoring the Militia's good name. Otherwise the remnants of the corps remained at Tank, re-training and re-forming. The North Waziristan Militia, who remained in Dardoni, Miranshah and Idak posts, were involved in minor piqueting and patrol actions.

6

The New Model Scouts

The post-1919 plan for Waziristan was that it would be dominated from within, when the necessary motor-roads were completed, by one brigade at Razmak and one at Wana. A circular motor-road would be built to link Jandola, Wana and Razmak, and descend from Jandola to Tank. This road system would be linked by the Central Waziristan road to the Bannu-Miranshah-Datta Khel road, and with the Kurram.

What part would the Frontier Corps play in this?

After the unhappy events of 1919 there were plenty of soldiers to say, 'none at all'. Lord Reading, the Viceroy, recommended that the Frontier Corps be converted into Frontier Constabulary and officered by the Indian Police, which was in fact the fate of the ephemeral Mohmand Militia raised in 1917 and disbanded three years later. The Khyber Rifles were disbanded. The Zhob Militia barely survived, but later made a good recovery. The Chitral Scouts and the Kurram Militia had come through the ordeal with credit; the Gilgit Scouts had been on the sidelines. But what was to be done with the Waziristan Militias?

They had been based on a fallacy: that good officers can make reliable soldiers of trans-Frontier Pathans serving in their own districts and often fighting against their kith-and-kin. The desertions had been confined mainly to Wazirs and Afridis; other tribes – cis-Frontier Khattaks, Yusufzais and Bangash, trans-Frontier Orakzais, Mohmands and Bhitannis – had in the main remained loyal despite strong religious and political pressures. It was decided that, reformed on different lines with the Army always at hand to support them, they could still play a useful role. So from the loyal elements of the North and South Waziristan Militias and the Mohmand Militia were raised the Tochi Scouts and the South Waziristan Scouts (SWS), based on a more realistic appreciation.

The Tochi Scouts had a Headquarters Company of specialists (signallers, armourers, etc.), two troops of Mounted Infantry, each fifty-nine strong; and two infantry 'Wings', each the equivalent of a battalion. Its total strength was twelve British officers and 2,278 Pathans. The South Waziristan Scouts (SWS) had a Headquarters Company, two troops of Mounted Infantry and three infantry wings, a total of fourteen British officers and 2,774 Pathans. Each corps was commanded by a Major, Wings by Captains, companies by Subadars, platoons and troops by Jemadars. Each rank carried far more responsibility than in the Army.

British officers in Scouts were not, as was widely believed, the insolvent and the dissolute, on the run from moneylenders and irate husbands (at least, not all of them). They joined the Tochi Scouts, SWS, Kurram and Zhob Militia (Chitral and Gilgit were rather different) for a variety of motives, the most common being a wish to see active service, during what was expected to be a lifetime of dull, peaceful soldiering. No man would join unless he had a strong liking for Pathans, whom many Indian Army officers profoundly distrusted. An active outdoor life was an attraction, far better than sitting in some citadel of military bureaucracy. Some joined to give themselves time, in the long, lonely evenings in outposts, to study for the Staff College, some to have three months' leave every year, either to go home, or to trek into the high Himalayas, three weeks' march from Srinagar, to stalk *ovis ammon*, markhor and ibex. Last but not least was the financial motive. Scouts officers drew quite generous mileage allowances, and what was in fact a sort of hard-lying allowance or danger-money, though it was not called that. There was a large lump sum for passing the Higher Standard Pushtu examination, and it was impossible to spend much money in Ladha or Datta Khel posts. This meant that officers who were in debt, or saving up to get married, were drawn to Scouts. A large proportion came from 'Piffer'* regiments, which were traditionally Frontier-minded. Not many cavalry officers joined the Scouts since it took a man away from serious polo. (Those who did generally gravitated to the Mounted Infantry, but they had to do six months in an infantry wing first. Lurid was the language of Carlo Platt

---

* Punjab Frontier Force. Originally irregular units stationed always on the Frontier. They lost their irregular status and their near-monopoly of Frontier postings during the Kitchener reforms, but they still *thought* Frontier.

of the Eighth Cavalry when he discovered after his six months' obligatory foot-slogging in the Tochi Scouts that he could no longer get into his beautiful Maxwell polo-boots.)

Officers were seconded from the Army for three years, extendable to five. At the end of his term there would be a magnificent farewell party in the Officers' Mess, a farewell feast with the Pathan officers, and next morning with bursting head the officer would drive away, the men cheering and the Mounted Infantry galloping alongside letting off firecrackers. After three or four years with their regular battalions and regiments, they could, and many did, do second and third tours with Scouts; but whereas a single tour was an asset to an ambitious soldier, more than one was liable to put him out of the running for the Staff and for high command.

When the reputation of the new model scouts had become well-established, that is by about 1924, there was much competition among British officers to join. It was rather like joining a very small, very exclusive club. Not only did a candidate have to have a first-class report from his regiment, and some command of Pushtu (which generally improved in outposts when he was speaking little else), but he had to stay a couple of weeks with a corps, at headquarters and in outposts to be 'vetted'. A man might be a very good regular soldier, but still be unsuitable for Scouts. There were very few British officers in a corps; they might have to spend weeks alone or with another officer in an outpost, and this required a certain temperament. Loneliness or an uncongenial partner could drive some men to drink, murder or suicide. If a man was idle, or too earnest, cantankerous, a bore, physically soft, could not hold his drink, or had the wrong approach to Pathans, he was out. A veto from a single officer, a hint from the Subadar Major that he would not quite do, and that was that. No officer on his first tour with Scouts could be married. Not only were officers' wives not allowed in Waziristan, but the Treasury had strong objection to paying a widow's pension for forty or fifty years.

Most British officers, knowing some Pushtu before coming to Scouts, worked up to Higher Standard during their first few months. If they had difficulty in passing, they were sent to Peshawar for a month's cramming under the famous *munshi*, Ahmed Jan. He was an inspired teacher, and a tyrant. Ralph Venning, still with his battalion, went to him to learn enough Pushtu to speak to shikaris and such. Ahmed Jan told him, 'You are only a lieutenant of Gurkhas, so my fee will be one hundred cigarettes. But you will come to me for Higher Standard, and then I shall *rook* you.' His cramming course was no rest-cure. The day started with one hour's lesson under the Master himself; then another hour with an old man who in a very broad Afridi accent told tales of *The Thousand and One Nights*, unexpurgated and very 'interesting'; in the afternoon an hour's conversation with Ahmed Jan and a group of Frontier Constabulary sepoys of various tribes and various accents; then home-work — grammar exercises and translations, always using the Persian script. Ahmed Jan was not the only Pushtu-teacher, but he was the only one who could show a testimonial signed by Captain A. P. Wavell of the Black Watch in 1906.

Major Russell continued in command of South Waziristan Militia through its disbanding in 1921 and its re-forming, with elements of the Mohmand Militia, as the South Waziristan Scouts. In the past he had believed implicitly in Pathans, believed that one could *always* trust them, and he had chosen his orderlies from the wildest trans-Frontier tribes. According to Barker, during and immediately after the mutiny in Wana, Russell had been surprisingly philosophical and tolerant, insisting that the scuttle from Waziristan had tried loyalty too far. But brooding over these events, his attitude had hardened. Never again would he wholly trust a Pathan. On two points he was adamant: there would never be less than two cis-Frontier Pathans to one trans-Frontier in the corps and he would have no Mahsuds or Wazirs at any price. He retained the tribal companies — Khattak, Afridi, Yusufzai, Orakzai, Mohmand, and others — but as administrative, not operational units. Never again would any post be garrisoned wholly, or even mainly, by men of one tribe; its garrison would be drawn from several companies. The arrangement was administratively clumsy, and not conducive to good training, but it was, Russell thought, a necessary precaution against mutiny. He never talked about 1919, and left his juniors to make up their minds about Pathans. As a result they usually did what he had done — preferred the wilder trans-Frontier tribes and chose orderlies from them, rather than from the more reliable, less colourful, Khattaks, Bangash and Yusufzais.

Denis Ambrose was a subaltern in the 1/6th Rajputana Rifles at Sararogha fort in 1923. Fourteen miles to the south, at Jandola, the new South Waziristan Scouts were still searching for a new identity, while being responsible for piqueting about twenty miles of road from Kotkai through Jandola to Khirgi. Convoys of camels, mule-carts and, as tracks were up-graded into roads, an increasing number of lorries, passed back and forth every day. There was an ambitious programme of road construction to open up the country to trade and, incidentally, to troops – Jandola to Ramzak, Jandola to Wana, and eventually to Razmak. Waziristan was officially at peace, but there were many hostiles who considered themselves still at war, and the weekly casualty list was quite heavy.

To Ambrose and his fellow-subalterns:

the Scouts were something of an enigma. We knew that they had mutinied and killed most of their British officers only three years previously. Yet here they were trusted with our protection over two of the most dangerous sectors of the road, acting in conjunction with the Khassadars.* Now the Khassadars we could see. They sat by the roadside and grinned as the convoy passed. But the Scouts, who were primarily responsible, we never saw during the day, except perhaps for a British officer, dressed in a semi-mufti uniform outfit, going up to the Column Commander (never the Adjutant or Company Commander) and assuring him in the friendliest manner that he might safely proceed. But whether the Khassadars or the Scouts were responsible, the casualties did not occur in the Scouts' sector. Sometimes the shooting would occur immediately after leaving their sector, when the Army piquets began to take up their positions; and of course it would be whispered that in all probability the Scouts and the Mahsuds were working together and that the whole episode had been fixed up between them. However, these ideas were later modified when we learned that the Scouts too were getting a weekly casualty list.

The Scouts officers whom Ambrose met spoke well of Russell, enjoyed being in Scouts and liked the men.

Their main point was, why serve on the Frontier with a regular regiment, sitting in camp behind barbed wire, and never moving out except on regular piqueting routine, when, instead, you can have the freedom of Scout life, the whole countryside to roam over, carrying a shot-gun instead of a revolver.

So Ambrose and a fellow-subaltern, H. G. Boulter, applied for secondment to Scouts, and a few weeks later they were told to report to Jandola for interview. Russell talked to them outside his tent, a

---

* Un-uniformed tribal levies, armed with their own rifles.

short, stocky man, red-faced, hatless, dressed in a grey flannel shirt, shorts and heavy chaplis.* Ambrose records:

> His main idea seemed to be to find out why we wanted to join the Scouts ... It was difficult in those days to give an adequate reason, for the Scouts were still heavily under a cloud and had not attained the prestige which came many years later. Perhaps we were obviously keen, for to our relief we were accepted on three months' probation.
>
> The camp at Jandola was not very different from the army camp at Sararogha, except that it was not so tidy. There was the same barbed wire, behind which were rows of tents. Whereas the army was provided with a certain number of huts, the Scouts had none, for the policy was eventually to build forts.
>
> At the time the Scouts were recruiting heavily. Consequently there were always several hundred recruits under training. The recruits themselves were fairly smart in their turn-out and drill, but as soon as a party of them joined the ranks of the 'old soldiers' it seemed to be a point of honour with them to forget all their drill and become as lax and slovenly as the rest. The idea was that the Army was smart, the Army went in for spit-and-polish. But look how useless they were when they got into the hills! Look at their rate of progress on the march! Look at their ponderous piqueting! Compare that with the speed, the endurance, the tactical sagacity of the Scouts! So the Scouts and, sad to say, the junior officers of the Scouts were inclined to look down on the ability and utility of the Army ... whereas the Army frankly mistrusted the Scouts.

Before 1919 discipline under Russell had been on the soft side, now it was harsh – twenty-eight days' Rigorous Imprisonment for quite a minor offence. A Summary Court Martial, consisting of Russell and one other officer, could sentence a man to a year in Bannu jail; the Political Agent could sentence him to death. Russell was equally severe on the Subadars and Jemadars, having many sacked in the early days, and they greatly feared but respected him. Subadars commanding companies had wide disciplinary powers and often awarded punishments not in the book.

Newly joined officers were kept fully occupied just as they would be in a regular battalion – on parades, range-work, platoon-training, office-work, the study of Pushtu. Occasionally, with a more experi-

---

* The Pathan sandal, now obtainable in any Brompton Road shoe-shop.

enced officer, they went out on a patrol, known in the Scouts as a 'gasht'. But these gashts were quite short, generally through the foothills to protect a convoy's flank. When Ambrose joined the South Waziristan Scouts in 1923 the Jandola-Razmak road had not got far beyond Sararogha, and work on the Jandola-Wana road had not begun. None of the Scouts forts had been built so they lived uncomfortably in oppressive heat or snow in tents surrounded by dry-stone perimeter walls. The longest outing from Jandola was to escort the weekly convoy of camels through the dangerous Shahur Tangi to provision the Scouts' posts at Chagmalai at the bottom of the Tangi, Splitoi at the top, and Sarwekai, where Bowring had been murdered. It was three days out and three days back. Such was the sinister reputation of the Shahur Tangi that Ambrose was not entrusted with this outing until he had been some months with Scouts and could speak fairly good Pushtu.

Occasionally the patrol would come across a Mahsud gang on its way to or from a raid, shots would be exchanged, a man or two might be hit, but, says Ambrose,

> I do not recall any brilliant captures in those early days. On the other hand there were no serious losses of arms or of men from the Scouts patrols, which, considering the state of training and the absence of high morale, was probably the best one could expect ...
>
> [One night] there was a shout from the Medical Officer who woke up to find a man in his tent. The rifle-thief and two of his companions got out through a gap in the wire, and a volley of shots from outside covered their escape. Every piquet blazed away into the night, but apparently no one was hurt. All the raiders got was the MO's revolver. But next morning Russell's wrath fell heavily on the camp piquets in the vicinity of the cut wire: chiga* party drill was intensified and security tightened up. There were no more such cases.

Early in 1924 Russell was appointed Inspecting Officer of Frontier Corps (IOFC) with a general supervision over (but not operational command of) the South Waziristan Scouts, Tochi Scouts, Kurram Militia, Chitral Scouts and later the Zhob Militia. He was succeeded in command of the SWS by Major S. P. Williams. Williams had missed the war; because he had defied a vindictive CO by marrying too young, he had languished in a training depot for four long years and escaped

---

* A party of about platoon strength ready in every camp for immediate pursuit.

only to go to the Zhob Militia. The young officers of the SWS, who regarded themselves as the tough boys of the Frontier, viewed his appointment with misgiving: they needed no paterfamilias from the Zhob to teach them their job.

How wrong they were. Williams – 'Stanley Pip' as they named him – turned out to be tall, sinewy, very tough, with a jaw like a battleship's prow, slightly stooping and rather deaf. His outlook differed from Russell's. Not having been with the Militia in 1919, he had suffered no disillusion, and he blamed the Government's policy rather than the men themselves for those unhappy events. He genuinely loved Pathans as a race, placed them far above any other martial race of India, had no wish to serve with any other, and had helped build up the morale and efficiency of the Zhob Militia. His wife was the niece of the famous Frontier officer, G. O. Roos-Keppel, from whom he learned a thing or two.

His Pushtu was excellent, but it was the classical Pushtu of Peshawar, comparable to 'the King's English'. One day, inspecting a squad of recruits, he stopped to ask one a question. The youth, his ear attuned only to the broad dialect of his tribe, taken aback by the formidable Faranghi addressing him incomprehensibly, turned helplessly to a neighbour and asked, 'For God's sake, what does he say?' Stanley Pip exploded – but was instantly penitent, and soon had all the recruits grinning.

He retained the 2:1 proportion of cis- to trans-Frontier tribes and he retained the tribal platoons. But in order to make the company an operational as well as an administrative unit, he grouped into one company five platoons of different tribes of which never more than two were trans-Frontier. Thus a company might have one Afridi and one Mohmand platoon from across the border, and Khattak, Bangash and Yusufzai platoons from British India. Its commander and second-in-command would be from none of those tribes; they might perhaps be Orakzai, Bhitanni or Mullagori. The result was an increase in efficiency, a rise in morale, and a strong, non-tribal, company *esprit de corps*, a competitive spirit in sports and emulation in action. The Mounted Infantry was composed of two troops of mixed tribes. Nevertheless, although a complete company could thereafter be used in operations, the basic operational unit was the platoon. Scouts spoke and thought in terms of gashts or garrisons of nine platoons, not of two companies. A Subadar commanding A Company would often find himself commanding a gasht which included platoons from B and C Companies.

The Khattaks, living mainly in the Nowshera, Bannu and Kohat districts of British India, were the most heavily recruited Pathan tribe, both in the Army and the Scouts. Afridis affected, not very seriously, to disparage them as not true Pathans. *'Bhang largai na shi,'* they would say scathingly, *'Khattak serai na shi.'* ('The cannabis plant cannot be wood, and a Khattak cannot be a man.') But they were valued highly as being more reliable than other Pathans, having taken on some of the characteristics of their neighbours the Punjabi Mussulmans, backbone of the Indian Army. The Yusufzais had in the past provided most of the Pathan recruits for some famous regiments, but by the late 1920s had become somewhat infected by politics, rather commercial-minded, and perhaps a little spoilt by the easier life consequent upon canal-irrigation. The third cis-Frontier tribe were the Bangash who lived around and west of Kohat. They were a smaller tribe than the Khattaks but similar in character and reliability. Adjacent to the Turi, they included some Shiah sections. They were better educated than most Pathans, and their young men provided the backbone of a celebrated football team, Kohat Shining.

Foremost of the trans-Frontier tribes were the Afridis, something of an enigma. In 1897 a large British force had invaded the Tirah, burnt villages, destroyed crops and felled walnut and chenar and mulberry trees; but they had then withdrawn in mid-winter in some haste and confusion, leaving the Afridis with the impression that in the end they had won – the Sarkar would never again invade the Tirah. Nor did it. Sir John Maffey, Chief Commissioner of the North-West Frontier Province, wrote in the aftermath of 1919 of

> the flash of Pathan eyes and the frenzy of the drums echoing from the rocks when over the campfires the Afridis sing their ballad of 1897: *'Ai! People of Islam, the Holy War!'* Through it all, when peace and friendship come again . . . for we do like one another . . . we remain always the enemy, the infidel power which tries to take from them their God-granted slagheap of mountain trash. But without avail! To Allah the praise!

Yet after 1919 Afridis in Scouts behaved splendidly, and provided more than their share of outstanding officers. They made excellent fighting men, using their brain as well as their brawn, though inclined to be distracted from the job in hand by private feuds and sectional differences. Between 1919 and 1941 recruitment of Afridis in the Army almost ceased, because they had proved so unreliable; so the Scouts got the pick of the tribe.

The Mullagoris are a small, cheerful and well-behaved tribe living in the north of the Khyber. The Orakzais, the second most heavily recruited tribe, live in the south of the Tirah and are steadier in character than the Afridis. They, like the Bangash, have some Shiah sections. They are great travellers, many going to sea as deck-hands and stokers. The Mohmands, from the great mountains north of Peshawar, were also regarded as being too unreliable for army recruitment, and had a reputation for cruelty and treachery, but in the Scouts they made good soldiers. The Bhitannis live in the hot, stony, arid hills east of Jandola. They are neighbours and enemies of the Mahsuds, and pride themselves on being 'the stone on which the Mahsud broke his teeth'. In fact, the Mahsud generally got the better of their raids and counter-raids.

All this and much more about the tribes had to be known by a Scouts officer. Nor was it enough to know that Naik Gul Sher Khan was an Afridi; one had to know whether he was, for instance, a Malik Din Khel from the proudly independent Tirah where no Faranghi had set foot since 1897, or an Adam Khel from Kohat pass – Tribal Territory, to be sure, but so accessible to troops and police that he could almost be regarded as a cis-Frontier man.* One had to know whether an Orakzai was Sunni or Shiah. It was symptomatic of Scouts' attitudes that a Pathan was seldom mentioned in reports or orders without his tribe, and often his section being specified. Thus one reads that Subadar Major Mehdi Khan, Saghri Khattak, was awarded the IOM; that Havildar Mastan, Orakzai, Ali Khel, was promoted Jemadar; that Naik Khial Badshah, Afridi Sipah, was killed.

Nothing was more important than the choice of the right men for promotion. Theoretically this should be decided entirely on merit, but the officer who made merit the only criterion, ignoring seniority and a rough tribal balance, would find himself commanding a resentful, even mutinous, rabble.

Claude Erskine, the first Commandant of the Tochi Scouts, with his young face and grey hair, was a man similar in ideas and style to S. P. Williams and his corps developed on similar lines. There was one notable difference: under pressure from George Cunningham, the resident, Waziristan, the Tochi enlisted about a hundred Wazirs to take advantage of their local knowledge and contacts. Half were trans-Frontier, and half men of the Jani Khel who lived near Bannu,

* In calculating the proportion of cis- and trans-Frontier men, the Adam Khel were counted as half-and-half.

just inside British India. They produced some good Pathan officers, but were always an anxiety. How should they be organised? At first they were formed in two platoons, one Jani Khel, the other trans-Frontier. But this was risky, and besides it was not making use of their local knowledge, which was the main reason for their enlistment. It was decided to split them up, a couple of Wazirs to each non-Wazir platoon. They felt affronted at the obvious slight and complained (probably not without reason) that they did not get a fair deal in promotions. So they were re-formed in two platoons. Then it became hard to fill the trans-Frontier platoon. Tori Khel, Manzar Khel and Khaddar Khel were all tried in turn, and none was satisfactory: the young men preferred the less exacting service of a Khassadar. Eventually, after the Khaddar Khel had notably misbehaved, the trans-Frontier platoon was disbanded, but the Jani Khel platoon remained and did good work. Another difference between the Tochi and the SWS was that in the former the Subadar commanding a company and his second-in-command were generally of tribes represented in that company.

Among the officers of the Tochi Scouts in the early days was 'Nat' Cosby, short, stocky, square-jawed with a shining morning face and generally a Burma cheroot sticking out of it. He had sailed round the Horn before the mast in a square-rigged ship; he had planted tea in Ceylon; he was the only officer in the 5th Royal Gurkha Rifles who was present at the landing on V-Beach in Gallipoli and at its evacuation, having collected in the meanwhile three wounds and an MC. Later he became a stickler for turn-out, but there is an agreeable picture of him in the early days of operations with the Razmak Brigade, clad in 'rat-catcher' (a loud tweed coat and cap), bounding down an adjoining precipice to the feet of the Brigade Commander, politely raising his headgear and saying, 'Your right flank is secure, Sir'.

He had in his Wing a very reliable Subadar who was a Tori Khel Wazir; he taught Cosby a lot about the tribes, and the first thing he taught was that when the garrison of a post changed, the locals would at once find out who were the new officers there, British and Pathan. On this they based their behaviour. A good post-commander had very little trouble; a not so good one, the reverse.

With British officers coming and going, continuity and *esprit de corps* depended mainly on the Centurions of the Corps, the Pathan Officers.*
All were men of immense experience and awesome authority, particu-

* It is difficult to know what to call them. They used to be called 'Indian Officers', but after partition that is inappropriate. They cannot be called Viceroy's Commissioned

larly in their own tribal platoons with whom they had almost a paternal relationship. They had gained their commissions after not less than twelve years' service in the ranks. They knew inside-out the internal economy of the corps; they knew exactly how to control a gasht, place a piquet, conduct a difficult withdrawal. They knew in dealing with tribesmen when to be tough, when to be flexible, when to be genial and when to bluff. Many were illiterate and intended to remain so. The strange anomaly was that these splendid veterans, as they nearly all were, should cheerfully take orders from Subalterns younger and less experienced than themselves, albeit far better educated and more technically instructed. But the British officer would be very unwise, both in problems of man-management and in the field, if he did not ask the advice, generally offered with tact, of Pathan officers. Socially they were treated with the utmost respect by British officers, who invariably gave them the honorific of 'Sahib', and by other ranks who saluted them. Race, language and cultural differences implied a certain separation between British officers and Pathan officers, but there was no feeling of social superiority on one hand or inferiority on the other. They ate normally in their separate Messes, but were always glad to accept one another's hospitality. Pathan society is essentially democratic, and this was reflected in the very close relations between British officers and Pathans when they were together in small posts for weeks on end. Henry 'Flathead' Cubitt-Smith was even consulted by a childless Subadar on the intimate subject of marital techniques. 'The wonderful thing about Scouts', a newly-joined officer was told by his mentor in the SWS, 'is that when they get to know you, you make *such friends*.'

The Senior Pathan Officer was the Subadar Major who had no command but was the Commandant's confidential adviser on everything pertaining to the corps. His badge was the major's crown. Subadars (badge, two pips) commanded and were second-in-command of companies. They were supposed to be, and quite often were, above and unswayed by tribal prejudices. Jemadars (one pip) commanded platoons of their own tribes. In each platoon was a Havildar (sergeant), and Naiks and Lance Naiks commanding sections. The Mounted Infantry used the cavalry rank-system: the equivalent of Subadar was Risaldar; of Havildar, Daffadar; of Naik and Lance Naik, Lance Daffadar and Acting Lance Daffadar. A private soldier in the infantry

Officers, a term which came into use in the Army to distinguish them from Indians holding the King's commission, because their commissions were from the Chief Commissioner, later Governor of the NWFP. So let them be termed 'Pathan Officers'.

was a Sepoy, in the Mounted Infantry he was a Sowar. Outside this chain-of-command were the Jemadar Adjutants, one to each Wing, and Drill Havildars, who were responsible for recruit-training and NCO cadre classes. There were also Signal Jemadars and Quartermaster Jemadars.

Being fallible humans, selected by fallible humans, the Pathan Officers occasionally failed; but failure was rare.

Many were characters, some could be described as 'cards', such as Subadar Khan Baz, Afridi, Malik Din Khel, of the SWS. He was a formidable warrior – but much more. He was an inspired clown. Henry Cubitt-Smith's loving aunt sent him a bullet-proof waistcoat. He could not wear it on gasht: he would die of heat-stroke, unless he died first of ridicule. But it was just the thing for Khan Baz, about to depart on two months' leave in the Tirah which was crawling with his blood-enemies. So Cubitt-Smith presented it to him – and a few minutes later heard a clanging like a dozen blacksmiths at work, and shrieks of laughter. Investigating, he found Khan Baz sitting in a chair, wearing the waistcoat, being charged by several happy sepoys with tent-pole lances. He wore it again that afternoon, keeping goal in a football match.

He could neither read nor write, but employed as his amanuensis a more accomplished Signals Naik. At the start of every parade each Subadar was required to report his company's parade-state – so many Pathan officers, NCOs, sepoys, signallers etc. This, of course, was done verbally, formally, at attention – except by Khan Baz, who simply held up his hand, on the palm of which the numbers were written in indelible pencil.

In the battle-backchat which sometimes accompanied skirmishes between tribesmen and Scouts, who often knew one another by sight and by name, his stentorian voice was conspicuous.

'We're leopards!' would come a cry in the Mahsud dialect from the rocks above. 'Keep your distance!' (A bullet cracked overhead.)

'And I'm Subadar Khawn Bawz, Afridi, Malik Din Khel. *Staré mashé!*'*

'May God strike you dead, Khan Baz!'

'And may your arsehole split, Sher Dil!'

To the British officers he was generally known as KB, but the

* *Staré mashé*, 'May you not be tired' is the stock Pathan greeting, to which the proper reply is *Khwar mashé*, 'may you not be poor' — sometimes the height of irony as between a ragged tribesman beside the road and a British officer at the end of a 30-mile gasht.

Pathans called him '*Tabrur*', 'Cousin', with macabre irony since he was supposed to have killed most of his cousins. Going on furlough he begged Jock Scotland, his Wing Commander, for some rounds of ball for his twelve-bore shot-gun, far more lethal at close range than a ·303 bullet. He needed them, he explained with patent insincerity, for bear and panther. On his return, Scotland asked if God had prospered his shikar. 'I got the bastard!' chortled KB, 'I got him! Even his bedclothes caught fire!'

Whatever might happen on leave, blood-feuds within the corps were absolutely forbidden. There were two Mohmand officers, Subadar Hujum, a dour veteran in the South Waziristan Scouts, a crack shot, and the flamboyantly moustachioed Jemadar Akram of the Tochi Scouts. Whenever they met in Waziristan they got on perfectly well. But by arrangement between the two Adjutants, they were never allowed on leave at the same time, nor were their leave-dates announced beforehand. One year someone slipped up: their leaves overlapped. Only Hujum returned, slightly less dour.

Recruits joined young, about seventeen, vouched for by Pathan officers and NCOs from their sections. What induced them to join? To some extent, money. Their emoluments may not seem lavish: by 1929, fifteen rupees a month basic pay, plus six rupees Ration Allowance, plus a Local Allowance of three rupees a month for the Tochi and five rupees, because of the more unhealthy climate, for the SWS. But to trans-Frontier Pathans, this was a considerable sum. Army pay was higher, but in the Army a man might have to serve far from Pathan country. Besides – an important point – if a tribesman died in the Army, he might be buried anywhere; whereas in the Scouts he was nearly always sent home for burial. Some villages were traditionally Army villages, some Scout villages, and on the whole recruiters did not poach. Recruits were certainly not drawn to Scouts by loyalty to a Faranghi Government, or to British officers whom they had never met. Some were attracted by tales told by older friends and relatives, some sought adventure, and the Pathan's sheer love of fighting was certainly a motive. But the greatest incentive was *izzat*, honour, for during the 1920s and 1930s the Scouts gained enormous prestige from one end of the Frontier to the other. A Scout on leave in his village, rose-bud over one ear, gold-embroidered waistcoat and *kullah*, telling tall tales of battle against Mahsud and Wazir, was a person to be envied and emulated. The recruits all came from the yeoman-farmer class. They enlisted initially for three years, which could be extended three years at a time to a maximum of eighteen years. They were entitled to three months' furlough after every fifteen months, and generally a whole platoon went on furlough together, so that the effective strength of a five-platoon company was four platoons.

Recruits either came in under their own steam, or were brought by brothers and cousins returning from leave. They were inspected by the Adjutant, told to take off their shirts, sent for a run, medically inspected and given a few simple co-ordination tests. If they passed, they were put on the *Umedwar* (Hopeful) list and sent back home, to be called up as vacancies occurred according to their gradings – Excellent, Very Good, Good and Very Fair. The best Recruits Squad Victor Wainright, as Adjutant of the Tochi Scouts, knew, was one recruited wholly from Maliks' sons. Heredity or environment? Recruit training, known always as 'the Drill', took about six months, and was the responsibility of the Adjutant and Jemadar Adjutant.

Many Pathans – as in other aggressively martial races – are given to buggery. It is socially more or less tolerated, as in London and New York. The famous Pushtu love-song the *Zakmi Dil* (Wounded Heart) extols the charms of

> A boy across the river with a bottom like a peach,
> But alas! I cannot swim.

Like Knights Templar in their Syrian castles, and sailors at sea, Scouts lived for months without even speaking to a woman. But the official attitude to buggery was far from permissive, for whenever it occurred, there had been trouble – NCOs competing for the favours of a 'milk-faced boy', or a virtuous recruit shooting a randy old Havildar. The Pathan officers, with their knowledge of a recruit's background, and the Medical Officer with a sharp eye for physical evidence, nearly always managed to weed out potential Ganymedes, but there were occasional scandals. There was a young Bhitanni who complained that he had been raped by every man in a piquet. The Commandant, S. P. Williams, after exhaustive enquiries, concluded that he was lying in order to get an NCO into trouble, and sentenced him to a term of detention. A couple of years later Williams said to the Subadar Major, 'I was right in that case, wasn't I?' The Subadar Major looked him long in the eyes. 'No, Sahib, you were wrong. His story was true, every word of it.' In the Tochi, at a later date, a Bangi Khel Khattak shot dead an Orakzai Naik and sepoy who, he said, had tried to bugger him. It was a fiendishly difficult case for the Commandant. Eventually the Khattak got away with twenty-eight days' Rigorous Imprisonment and dismissal for 'accidentally wounding'. But the whole Wing had to be reorganised so that Orakzais and Khattaks were not in future in the same company, lest the former regard it as a case for a blood-feud.

Unlike Major Russell, S. P. Williams and Claude Erskine believed that smartness made for good morale. They instituted a tremendous drive on drill and saluting. However irregular Scouts might be in the field, on parade and quarter-guard everyone had to be immaculately turned out — uniforms starched, leather and brass gleaming, rifles of course spotless, the hair of the northern tribes cut very short, of the southern Khattaks and Bhitannis combed, oiled, cut in a neat straight bob just below the ears. Drill, up to Guards' standard.

But on gasht their turn-out was entirely functional: khaki *pagri* wound tightly round a dome-shaped, padded *kullah*, *shamleh** hanging loose to shade the back of the neck; a shirt (in cold weather, perhaps two shirts and a brownish pullover) of khaki in the Tochi, and in the SWS of *mazri*, a stout, coarse blue-grey cotton flecked with black, khaki shorts in summer and in winter *partog*, baggy Pathan pyjamas of *mazri*. (The Mounted Infantry wore *partog* all the year round.) The footwear was a heavy leather chapli, studded with soft iron, broad-headed nails. Fifty rounds were carried in a leather bando-lier over the left shoulder, and twenty more in two belt-pouches. From the leather belt hung a short bayonet. The quart-size aluminium water-bottle was larger and of better design than the Army model. In a haversack would be some wholemeal flour or parched gram, a couple of onions, a pinch of tea, sugar, a needle, thread and nails for repairing chaplis, and perhaps a grenade or two. British officers might include in their rations a tin of sardines or bully beef, but lightness was all: nothing must be carried which reduced speed. In night operations a rolled woollen cap-comforter was worn for warmth, and 'grass' sandals (actually made from dwarf-palm fibre rope) for silence. Sometimes in very cold weather the partog were tucked into hose-tops to give a plus-four effect. The grey and khaki blended perfectly with the land-scape, especially as the shirt hung loose, flapping, Pathan-fashion, outside shorts or partog so that there was no straight, revealing line where shirt and shorts met.

Gone were the days when British officers wore 'ratcatchers' on operations; nor could they wear Sam Browne belt and topi. To avoid

* The *pagri*, turban, was wound round a *kullah*, skull-cap. The *shamleh* was the loose end of the *pagri*.

becoming targets for every sniper, they dressed exactly like the men. An officer's pagri was generally tied in the manner of his orderly's tribe, since it was his orderly who had taught him how to tie it. Not that this get-up effectively camouflaged him: tribesmen could always tell a British officer by the way he walked.

In fairly peaceful times officers usually carried revolvers on gasht, in open holsters, slung on a strap over the shoulder, with loops on the strap to hold spare cartridges. In safe areas, where partridges were plentiful, they often carried shot-guns. But in bad times it was better to carry a rifle, as Ralph Venning of the SWS was instructed by Subadar Mohabbat, Aka Khel Afridi. 'Very well,' he replied, 'but I'm damned if I'll carry seventy rounds as well.' Mohabbat nodded implacably. 'Seventy rounds is seventy rounds.' And so it was.

The Scouts' weapon was the same as the Mahsuds', the ·303 rifle, the Short Magazine Lee-Enfield (SMLE) Mark III which had served the British Army so well throughout the First World War and was to be retained, slightly modified but by no means improved, throughout the Second World War. Although it has not the high rate of fire of semi-automatic rifles like the FN and the Kaloshnikov, it is far more accurate over a much longer range. A marksman can put all his shots into a 4-inch diameter bull's-eye at 200 yards, 15 inches at 600 yards and 24 inches at 1,000 yards; he can fire more than 15 aimed rounds a minute. And Scouts were marksmen, far better on the average than regular army soldiers; perhaps because they had no light machine-guns and carried less ammunition, they concentrated (like the tribesmen) on single-shot accuracy.

The Scouts had their own motor transport, at first heavy, slow but reliable Albion lorries. In 1928–9 these were replaced by six-wheeler Morris three-tonners, lighter and faster, but more temperamental. They managed to keep the old Albions as well.

The Mounted Infantry were a *corps d'élite* open only to the best men of three years' service. Their value was that, over suitable terrain, they 'could git thar the firstest with the mostest'.* They then dismounted and fought on foot. The horses were hardy countrybreds of about 14.2 hands, smaller and usually quieter than cavalry horses. Every few months the officer in charge of the Mounted Infantry, accompanied by a Risaldar, a party of sowars and a Veterinary Assistant went to the

---

* A tactical principle attributed to the great Confederate cavalry General, Nathan Bedford Forrest.

horse fairs at Amritsar or Dera Ghazi Khan. There would be horse-races and camel-races and donkey-races, tent-pegging, wrestlers, jugglers, snake-charmers, dancing boys – all the fun of the fair in choking clouds of dust and an incessant din. There was no formal auction: the officer looked at likely horses, bargained with the owners, called on the Veterinary Assistant to make sure they were sound and the mares not in foal, and somehow contrived to get them into the specially-fitted horse-wagons on the train. 'Fitz' FitzMaurice of the SWS, a sharp-faced, humorous fox-hunter, speaking fluent Pushtu with a West Cork lilt, recorded one of these occasions: 'Saw 120 horses. Rode 30. Bought 12. A long day.' From railhead they were led up to Jandola or Miranshah, where those that were unbroken were lunged for a few days, backed and schooled in the Remount Ride. After six or eight weeks they were fit for gashts. Most of the training took place close to the rifle-ranges, to accustom them to rifle-fire. Each corps carried out its own equitation training, and potential instructors and remount-riders did a course with the nearest cavalry regiment. Every sowar carried on gasht two spare horse-shoes, fore and hind, and nails, and could in an emergency cold-shoe his pony.

The sowar carried his rifle in a short bucket, only a few inches deep, attached to the saddle, in which the butt rested, the rifle being held upright by the sling passed over the right shoulder.

Fighting only on foot, the Mounted Infantry had to have some arrangement for holding horses in cover and moving them as required. The cavalry practice was for one horse-holder to ride his own and lead three horses. To put more men into the firing-line, Scouts sometimes had one mounted horse-holder leading as many as seven horses – a very difficult feat, practised more during training than on operations.

Up to 1928 Scouts operated what was known in cavalry as the *silladar* system: each sowar owned his horse, buying it at a special low price out of stoppages from his pay. It was his property, he was responsible for looking after it, if it died or became unsound, he would have to replace it. If he did not live too far away, he would take it home on furlough. In theory, the system saved the corps money, and the sowar would take better care of his horse if it was his own. In practice horses were apt to return in poor condition, because in most villages there was not the good forage to which they were accustomed. The Scouts, therefore, like the cavalry, dropped the *silladar* system, and horses became corps property.

In the early 1920s, before increasing prestige attracted a better type of recruit, Scouts had a great deal of wastage from desertion. No one much minded a man taking himself off without his rifle; he was assumed to be a young fellow who did not know his own mind. Such unauthorised departures numbered 136 from the two Waziristan corps (out of a total strength of about 5,000) in 1922–3, but as the quality of recruits, their motivation and conditions of service improved, the number dropped steadily to twenty-seven in 1928–9. Desertion with a rifle was far more serious, a black disgrace on the deserter's platoon and company. If the deserter was later killed, none of his former comrades would think it anything but a good riddance. In the early 1920s such desertions numbered four or five a year, but by the end of the decade there had been none for three years.

A more serious cause of wastage was sickness. Waziristan is malarial in places, the Scouts were living in tents for years until new outposts were completed, there were no fresh fruit and vegetables, and sanitary conditions were not all they should be. Malaria, scurvy, dysentery and jaundice all took their toll. In 1924–5 the Tochi Scouts lost twenty-nine men by fatal illnesses, the SWS not less than seventy; half their strength had to be admitted at some time of the year to hospital. But during the next year mosquito nets were issued, and land was acquired for fruit and vegetable gardens. There was a determined effort to improve sanitation, reduce fly-breeding and eradicate the anopheles mosquito in the vicinity of posts. The results were dramatic: hospital admissions were far lower, and during the year 1925–6 the Tochi and the SWS lost only eight and nine men respectively.

Nothing shows up better the improvement during the 1920s in discipline, morale, living conditions and the standard of recruits than the steady reduction of wastage by desertion and sickness. But nothing could make Waziristan a health resort; mosquito nets could not be used on gasht and on night operations; the anti-malaria prophylactic, mepacrine, had not yet been invented. And even mosquito nets were no protection against the tiny sandfly and the debilitating fever it caused. So malaria, sandfly-fever and diarrhoea were hazards that had to be put up with, helped by doses of quinine, aspirin and chlorodyne, and applications of citronella oil.

Each corps maintained a semi-private fund, known in the South Waziristan Scouts as the 'Corps Fund' or 'Garden Fund', into which went profits from the sale of milk, vegetables and fruit, and fines levied on the men for minor disciplinary offences; out of the Fund payment was made for seeds, milch cows, garden implements and such like. Somehow the Fund escaped the attention of the Military Accounts

Officer, until one paid an unexpected visit to Jandola and Nat Cosby had to come clean. At first the visitor was horrified and asked, 'What authority have you for this?' Cosby replied, 'Thirty years of usage and custom.' Proof that everything purchased had, indeed, been for the good of the corps mollified the Accounts Officer, and he gave good advice off the record on how to run this equivocal fund in future. It was of the utmost value to commandants to have money for immediate needs without prolonged arguments with accounts babus, brown and white.

Each Wing trained its own recruits before they passed into the ranks. In 1924 there were three officers at Sarwekai – Captain E. D. Moorhead, Captain Denis Ambrose, and Lieutenant G. H. Tapp. The last was in charge of recruit training with the Jemadar Adjutant. There was a squad of forty recruits just due to complete 'the Drill' and pass into the ranks. To Tapp it seemed that a final polish could be given by taking them up the Barwand Raghza where they were sure to experience a little long-range sniping and have the opportunity to shoot back.

The Barwand Raghza is an open plain, about four miles wide, beginning close to Sarwekai and stretching north-eastward for some seven miles. It is an old talus fan of gravel shot out from the hills to the north, seamed with gullies and dry nullahs and traces of old terraced fields. Each time a gasht went beyond a certain point, a couple of hundred Mahsud villagers would swarm out and open fire on them. A lot of rounds would be fired on both sides and occasionally a man or two hit: the villagers never came very close, and their shooting was a mere protest, a 'trespassers will be prosecuted' warning. Next day the Political Agent would fine them a few country-made rifles, and a month later the same thing would occur again. Just the right experience, thought Tapp, for the recruits. In this he was abetted by Moorhead who could not abide a no-go area under his very nose, and enjoyed the excitement of a scrap, the pitting of wits and skill and courage against a worthy enemy.

The forty recruits, under the Jemadar Adjutant with the drill Havildar and a couple of Naik instructors, made an excellent 'advance to contact' over the open plain, well spread out, two sections in turn moving forward, the other two in position to give covering fire. In the distance some grey-clad figures were seen running from a village on the left, and soon the drums started thudding first in one, then in other villages. Tapp began to feel the exercise was getting out of his control as, indeed, it was; he should never have crossed the Barwand Raghza with less than four platoons of seasoned Scouts. He gave the order to withdraw.

'They'll be shooting soon,' warned the instructors; and, sure enough, they did. Scores of tribesmen were getting closer, screened by the nullahs and scrub, and working round the flanks. However, the recruits behaved with admirable steadiness, two sections giving covering-fire while the other two leap-frogged back past them. Then one in the rear section was killed, and immediately afterwards his section commander. The section, leaderless, retired in disorder, leaving the bodies of two men and their rifles, which had to be recovered. The tribesmen were now firing at close range.

Tapp halted the retirement and went back with his orderly and a Naik for the rifles, and for the men if they were still alive. They lay in the open about half-way between the rear section and the tribesmen, a hundred yards from each. Tapp and the men with him had not a chance: he was killed, they were both wounded. There were now five rifles and bodies left out in open ground.

The Jemadar Adjutant had got the remaining recruits under control, firing steadily to stop the Mahsuds approaching the bodies, but shots were coming at them from both flanks and almost from the rear. They could move neither forward nor back, and were now outnumbered four or five to one.

Fortunately the firing had been heard in Sarwekai, and just as their position was becoming desperate, the chiga platoon was seen moving fast across the plain, followed by four more platoons under Ambrose. Confronted by a hundred seasoned Scouts, the Mahsuds withdrew to a respectful distance.

Tapp was recommended for the VC but did not get it − perhaps because he had no business to be engaging in that sort of exercise.

The new tribal composition produced corps which were reliable in that it would be unlikely for a whole company to be infected at the same time with the same grievance or cause for disaffection; but because they included few Wazirs and no Mahsuds, the SWS and Tochi Scouts lacked really detailed local knowledge, topographical and personal. Pathans, serving in one district for years, acquired a far better knowledge of it than regular troops, but they could not know it as well as men who had been herding goats there as little boys, familiar not only with every nullah and path and patch of thorn-scrub, but every house and fortified tower − who owned it, how many sons he had, whether he was to be deemed a friend or enemy. For this the Scouts had to rely on tribal police known in Waziristan as Khassadars, in Baluchistan as Levies. Armed with their own rifles, un-uniformed and, by and large, unreliable, they were nevertheless useful for road-protection and escorts in more or less peaceful times, since a neighbour would be reluctant to fire on them lest this start a tiresome blood-feud. For that very reason Khassadars were reluctant to fire on a neighbour, though they would fight raiders from outside. They looked upon themselves as servants of the tribe, helping the Jirga to carry out the Sarkar's policy, not as servants of the Sarkar. If, therefore, the tribe was at war with the Sarkar, the best that could be hoped of them was neutrality. 'Spit and no polish' was said to be their motto.

Tribal misbehaviour was met by a graduated response. If the Khassadars could not or would not settle the trouble, the Scouts were called in. If it was too much for the lightly armed Scouts, then along trundled the Razmak, Wana or Bannu Brigade with its artillery and machine-guns, its cavalry and armoured cars and light tanks and attendant aircraft. *Was* was a word much in Mahsud and Wazir minds and on their lips. It means power or force. The success of a Political Agent, a Scouts Officer and a Malik depended on maintaining a balance of, and exerting the right amount of, *was*. It would be a bad Malik who, in the supposed interests of his tribe, provoked the Political Agent into bringing in the steam-roller of the Army; a bad Scouts officer who used excessive force where persuasion would have done the trick; a bad Political Agent who appealed unnecessarily for military support. Subadars of Khassadars – one of them was Darim Khan who had won the IOM with the North Waziristan Militia in 1915 – were very expert at estimating *was*.

The South Waziristan Scouts and the Tochi Scouts each regarded itself as the hardest fighting, longest gashting, deepest drinking corps, raising more hell on leave in Peshawar or Kashmir. The SWS boasted of having bigger mess-bills than any unit in the Empire; but the Tochi drank their beer out of *quart*-sized silver tankards.

Their style was subtly different. On leave in the Peshawar Club one would see Tochi officers in flannels and 'brothel-creepers', but SWS officers in mazri shirts and heavy chaplis. In efficiency there was nothing to choose between them; but the Tochi were the more relaxed, they had more social contacts with the tribesmen; the SWS, perhaps because they had Mahsuds to deal with, were the more 'regimental', the more aggressively on their toes, a tauter ship. Also, according to the Tochi, they were more addicted to bullshit: 'the sort of fellows who wear posteens in Delhi'.

7

The Militia Corps after 1920

The Kurram Militia was spared many of the problems which beset the two Waziristan corps because the local tribe was the ever-trusty Turi, the local lashkar regarded almost as a reserve for the Militia. Its role was not to police the tribe, which hardly needed policing except when there was a Sunni-Shiah conflict, but to stop raids and incursions from the Afghan tribes to the west and north, the Orakzais and Zaimukhts to the east and the Wazirs to the south-west; also to be, as in 1919, the first line of defence against a serious invasion.

The strength of the Kurram Militia in the 1920s was five British officers and 1,341 Pathans, organised into twenty-two platoons of Infantry and two troops of Mounted Infantry. They had their own artillery, two 10-pounder pack-guns, carried by mules or camels, which could be dismantled and assembled in a couple of minutes.

While most of the corps were Turis of the Shiah sect, there was as a counterweight a small Sunni element of two platoons of Khattaks and one each of Mangals and Chamkannis, handsome, cheerful people from the snowy hills along the Afghan border.

In 1927 the Khattaks were replaced by two platoons of Mahsuds, a triumph of hope over experience. True to type, several deserted with rifles. However, Harry Garland, when he commanded the corps, valued the Mahsuds. When a vacancy occurred for Subadar Major, the Inspecting Officer of Frontier Corps advised him not to give it to the senior Subadar because he was a Mahsud. 'But', wrote Garland, 'I did promote him, and he turned out absolutely first-class. Had I passed him over, the Mahsuds in Parachinar would have created merry hell, and the situation would have been incredibly unpleasant. The Mahsuds in my time did extremely well, and I liked them very much.'

The Kurram was a true Militia, in the sense that it was composed mainly of local men defending their own country against the enemies who surrounded it. During the 1920s they were deployed in ten small posts, with garrisons varying from half a platoon to a platoon-and-a half, far less than any in the Tochi or SWS. These posts were too small to send out long, strong gashts; their role was local policing and the gathering of intelligence – not difficult since the locals were their friends and relations; and to act as staging posts for proper gashts sent out from the Militia's main fort at Parachinar where there were twelve platoons, the Mounted Infantry and the guns.

The Turis are fine, big fellows – bigger than most Pathans – and tough, brave soldiers, but the fact that they were an island of Shiahs (and very devout, indeed fanatical Shiahs) surrounded by Sunnis, and that they would serve only near home, had an effect on their character. They were rather introverted, much given to intrigue over, say, promotions which were, of course, nearly all in one tribe. They were flatterers, which is not a Pathan characteristic. 'The Sahib speaks wonderful Pushtu,' a Turi would say, knowing perfectly well that the Sahib did nothing of the sort. They even used to kiss the hand of the Turi Subadar who was a direct descendant of the Prophet, a military salutation which British officers deprecated.

Terence Phillips was invited to the Turi Mohurram celebrations, when they mourn the deaths at the Battle of Karbela (680), of the martyrs Hassan and Hussein, grandsons of the Prophet, who had opposed the Umaiyids' claim to the Khalifat. It is from that date that the Sunni-Shiah feud began. Phillips was at the time in the Tochi Scouts which had two platoons of Turis. But similar Mohurram celebrations took place in the Kurram Militia. He describes the scene:

The lower barrack was all hung with printed cotton cloths and carpeted with rugs. Up at the end was the Mullah, with a solid mass of Turis nearest him. I could see nothing but bobbed heads sticking out of blankets. I thought I had better take a seat at the back, but was taken up to the front. The Mullah, a nice old man, was talking apparently in Arabic, but later changed to Pushtu, and we had the story of Hazrat Isa (Jesus Christ) from the conception by the Holy Ghost right through to the Crucifixion. Then he said something about Hassan and Hussein and the whole crowd hid their heads in their blankets and started sobbing, their shoulders shaking with grief

... All got to their feet and took off their shirts and to a chant of Hassan from one side and Hussein from the other, began beating their breasts with both hands clasped ... Two men stepped into the middle with a kind of flail formed of a bunch of chains on a wooden handle and began beating their backs with rhythmic shouts of Hassan-Hussein, and the crowd became more and more excited, jumping in the air and shouting the names louder and louder ... [So, with tears and flagellation, the ceremony continued until] many backs were raw ... Kadam Ali, my orderly, who stood about six foot four, was particularly devoted and his back was a mass of raw red marks with a brown background. Standing up in the light of the oil lamps he looked like some pagan god, Thor or Odin, with the steel chains swinging round his head, giving off flashes of light as they caught the rays of the lanterns ... Soon it was all over and they sat down, and Mohamad Taqi told me I could go.

Such an exhibition was totally alien and indeed abominable to Sunni Pathans, and it says much for the discipline and tolerance of the Tochi Scouts, in whom the Turis formed a small minority, that they put up with it.

Most of the Kurram posts were on craggy hilltops, accessible only by mule or on foot. The most common 'incident' was a fracas between Sunni and Shiah, usually corrected by billeting a Sunni platoon on an offending Shiah village or vice versa. Every year there were cases of minor robbery or lorry-shooting, but nothing on the Waziristan scale. The Militia had a few casualties, for example when men returning from a course or leave-details were shot up on the road; occasionally they went out against Orakzai, Zaimukht or Khostwal raiders. It was quite an event when the garrison of Lakka Tiga post (one and a half platoons) was attacked by a lashkar, or when the Para Chamkannis shot up the Political Agent's Jirga and had to be seen off by a Militia gasht. In 1930 the Kurram Militia actually suffered thirty-four casualties in tribal skirmishes and the Viceroy granted them a bonus of one month's pay for all ranks; but most of the fighting done by this fine corps after 1919 was when from time to time they sent detachments to help the Tochi Scouts and the SWS. However, they did the job for which they were raised. Parachinar could turn out in half an hour a formidable little army, eighty horse, five hundred foot, two guns. Ian McHarg, their Commandant, found the sight of this column operating against the background of the snowy 15,000 feet Safed Koh one to stir the blood.

There were, for British officers, compensations for the quiet life.

The climate of Parachinar is delightful; officers' wives and children could live there. It lies on a long, shaly slope overlooked by the Safed Koh and the Peiwar Kotal. The Government station is above the town, amid its fruit and vegetable gardens. Everywhere there are streams from the mountains, nourishing great chenar, walnut and mulberry trees. Every fruit and vegetable seems to grow twice as large as anywhere else. The Quarter Master's duties included keeping the tennis courts verdant, the asparagus-beds in full production, the swimming-pool clean and the Brahmini milch-cows in good condition,.

There was excellent shooting. Four or five guns could pick up fifty brace a day of chikor, sisi, black and grey partridge, teal, snipe and mallard. The mahseer fishing, with fly-spoon or light plug, was first class, with plenty of two-pounders and an occasional fish weighing over five pounds. Ian McHarg, a skiing enthusiast, when Commandant had built a ski-hut on the slopes of the Safed Koh. There was a magnificent thirteen-mile run. They were often, recalls McHarg, shot at, but travelled too fast to be in any danger; so the frustrated marksmen relieved their feelings by burning down the hut. The MI ponies supplied the traction-power for ski-joring round Parachinar itself.

The valley was a paradise for birds. Terence Phillips describes

the most exciting day for birds in my life. There was an osprey on the lower Taida jheel. My orderly instantly recognised it as a Mach Khorak, an Eater of Fish, so it must be quite common. There were at least two hundred Harriers, mostly on the lower Taida. Half of these were Marsh Harriers of both sexes, old and young birds, all mixed. There were a good many Pallid Harriers, but more Montagues, a beautiful bird. It was very dark and an overcast day, and there were thousands of Kulan [cranes] flying up the valley in their great clanging formations and, finding the pass blocked by cloud, coming back down again. In the evening the light was very bad but just enough to see a hundred wagtails, nearly all yellow-headed but a few grey-headed with their yellow throats and very dark grey, almost black in the light crowns and still darker cheeks. There were some indeterminate greeny-grey females which I have been unable to identify, though they were very tame. Stonechats were very common and there were a few Rufous Backed Shrikes and I saw one King Crow. As I crossed the river a flight of eight terns, big and gull-like and seeming all white except for one which I saw had a black cap, passed over me. These and the wagtails are the only birds seen today which I cannot identify. The boy I had left to watch the car had shot a

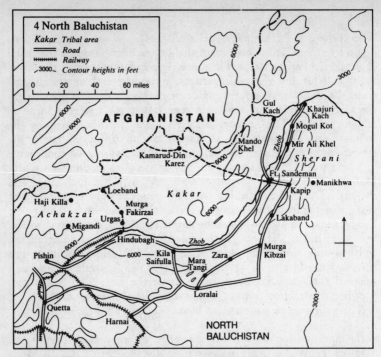

4 North Baluchistan

Kakar   Tribal area

Road

Railway

_3000_ Contour heights in feet

0   20   40   60 miles

AFGHANISTAN

Gul Kach   Khajuri Kach

Mogul Kot

Mando Khel   Mir Ali Khel

Kamarud-Din Karez   *S h e r a n i*

Ft. Sandeman   • Manikhwa

Loeband   *K a k a r*   Kapip

Haji Killa   Murga Fakirzai

A c h a k z a i   Urgas   Lakaband

Migandi

Hindubagh   *Zhob*

   Murga Kibzai

Pishin   6000 — Kila Saifulla   Mara Tangi   Zara

Quetta   Loralai

Harnai   NORTH BALUCHISTAN

green willow warbler with his catapult, which was a new bird to me. As I came back I came on a hundred white storks in the trees by the roadside and they sat still as I passed only ten yards away.

The Baluchistan Politicals were usually out of step with their colleagues across the Gumal. They did things differently and, they thought, better. Whether the comparative placidity of Baluchistan, up to 1919, was the cause or the effect of the success of Sir Robert Sandeman's policy of indirect rule right up to the Durand Line, was much debated – probably a bit of both. Certainly the tribal authorities in Baluchistan had more control over their people than the Waziristan Maliks; and the country was more open, more friendly to regular forces than to guerillas. (See Map 4.)

After the collapse of Sandeman's system in Zhob, the Baluchistan Politicals in 1920 looked at their private army and came to a conclusion exactly the opposite to that reached by the Waziristan Politicals.

The Annual Report for 1919–20 recorded:

The old corps had been altogether too highly organised and its objects misconceived. Drill, discipline, uniform, training had been introduced, which were foreign to the whole spirit of the tough

76

tribesmen who formed its rank-and-file. Standards of efficiency were set up which were neither desirable nor capable of achievement in an irregular corps, and which robbed it of what was much more important, initiative and mobility. The object now aimed at is to have a homogeneous body of men irregular in fact as well as in name, loosely disciplined but mobile, incapable of forming fours but thoroughly acquainted with the country and its people, able to move as silently and rapidly as the raiders they are out to catch. The tribes who proved failures in the 1919 débâcle have been removed, and their places taken by Brahuis and Baluchis. There are still a large number of Orakzais in the corps. But as time goes on it is hoped that this foreign element will disappear . . . There is no need for a body of foreign mercenaries in Zhob.

It did not work out that way. The new Zhob Militia* was composed of five British officers and 1,200 tribesmen, organised into two companies of Brahuis, one of Baluchis, one of Pishin Kakars, two of Orakzais, one of mixed North West Frontier Province Pathans, and two troops of Mounted Infantry. Nearly twenty years later the Orakzais were still the backbone of the corps. In uniform, discipline, organisation and training it became very like the Waziristan corps. Nothing else would suffice in the situation in Zhob in 1919–20.

Before May 1919, the Zhob Militia had held ten posts besides Fort Sandeman. All but two were evacuated or surrendered to the tribesmen while the loose administration collapsed like a house of cards – the local officials demoralised, the Jirgas ceasing to function, the tribal Sardars and Maliks sitting on the fence. A year later, after the murder of his predecessor, Major R. H. Chenevix Trench took over as Political Agent, Zhob.

He found that there was still no functioning administration: conditions were just like those in the Tribal Territory of Waziristan. Jirgas were making no attempt to re-establish their authority, the local officials were still demoralised, the Sardars and Maliks still sitting on the fence. Not a rupee of revenue had been collected for a year – financially of no significance because the revenue from Zhob was small, but a barometer of the efficiency of the administration.

The brightest feature of a gloomy scene was the Zhob Militia under Captains G. A. R. Spain and N. L. St P. Bunbury. Except for the

---

* After the débâcle in 1919 the Zhob Militia was renamed the Zhob Levy Corps, but soon reverted to the old name of Zhob Militia. So, let us call it the Zhob Militia throughout.

Baluch and Brahui companies, it was up to strength; over seven hundred recruits had been trained during a year in which it saw far more action than the SWS, Tochi Scouts and Kurram Militia combined. After its deserters had departed and its Ghilzai company had been disbanded, it had acquitted itself very well, and it was now ready to take on more responsibilities, especially the posts which had been lost a year earlier, not only in Zhob but in parts of Pishin and Loralai districts.

In the autumn of 1920 the Zhob Column, a brigade group, ventured for the first time in a year to Mir Ali Khel. From there the Brigadier, Political Agent, half-a-dozen officers and a troop of Mounted Infantry rode on to the Moghul Kot and back. Their route was piqueted to half-way and they chanced the rest, sighting no Wazirs. Mogul Kot was littered with split cartridge cases, from Major Russell's firing of the magazine. On their return they were shown the place where Burn-Murdoch, Traill, Leese and MacCorstie were said to be buried, and the place in the dry river-bed where Reilly had been killed. The bones of his horse were there, but his remains must have been washed away in a spate. Shortly after this, the Militia took over the two posts again.

It now remained to restore the loose administration and, as a pre-requisite, some semblance to law and order. There were three over-lapping obstacles: (a) The Wazirs; (b) the Suliman Khel, nearly as tough and nasty as Wazirs, migrating through the Zhob twice a year on their way between Afghanistan and India; and (c) local hostiles of the Sherani, Mando Khel and Kakar tribes, including Militia deserters.

The locals were the first to weaken. One by one, on safe conduct, the leading hostiles came into Fort Sandeman to negotiate their return to house, home and respectability. 'It goes against the grain', wrote Trench, 'to let them off scot-free, but after all the object is a return to normal.' It does not seem to have gone much against his grain. One outlaw, 'a cheerful knave, touched me for 200 rupees and a camel. As a proof of his good feeling, he told me he had me in his sights twice in ten days, but refrained from squeezing the trigger.' Another gave the Political Agent a beautifully embroidered, astrakhan-trimmed posteen. It would not be seemly, he said, to come empty-handed. People began to resort to law. An early litigant was a reformed Sherani outlaw who in the heady days of 1919 had bought from a plausible Mullah an amulet guaranteed to deflect bullets from the wearer. To try it out, he tied it round the neck of his favourite fighting cock, took careful aim and blew the unfortunate bird to pieces. He now complained to the Political Agent that the Mullah had taken his money under false pretences.

Trench advised him to seek redress from the Jirga which, with its new-found confidence, awarded him substantial damages against the man of God.

The Suliman Khel gave more trouble. In 1921 they killed an American geologist and they massacred a caravan of Nasars, another Powindah tribe and their hereditary enemies. Trench with a Militia Mounted Infantry escort found the Nasar corpses. It was not a pretty sight: 'the Suliman Khel had gone out of their way to be unpleasant.' In March 1921, a hundred Suliman Khel raided the chrome mines at Hindubagh, getting away with 250 camels. The chiga party from the Militia post followed, a pekinese pursuing a mastiff, and managed to shoot a couple before the raiders crossed the Afghan border. Worst of all, a lashkar of eight hundred to a thousand Suliman Khel, Wazirs and Kharots spent eleven days in British territory hunted by three columns of regular troops and Militia; they stole hundreds of cattle and camels, looted several villages, and got clear away. In a private letter Trench wrote, 'A little *suppressio veri* is necessary to keep on good terms with the soldiers, but the naked truth is that the raiders were never hustled out of a walk.' In a rugged, roadless country the three columns, with no wireless communication, were looking for a needle in a haystack.

Besides these misdeeds, the Suliman Khel owed thousands of rupees for their misdemeanours in 1919, and had no intention of paying. Their caravans kept well clear of Fort Sandeman and the Militia posts. Trench's Assistant Political Agent, Khan Bahadur Sherbet Khan, an Afridi, came up with the answer. The richest of the Suliman Khel were not in Zhob at all, but in Calcutta, lending money (in defiance of the Prophet's injunctions) to the mild Hindus, to whom their annual visit, to extract ruinous interest with the dagger and a heavy iron-bound cudgel, was a time of terror. It was arranged with the Calcutta police that they should arrest the most eminent and send them up to jail in Fort Sandeman, there to remain until the tribe paid its dues. 'Imagine the disgust of these rich merchants of Calcutta', wrote Trench, 'I have a dozen in jail. We are very good pals. I tell them they are my guests: meat, tobacco, good food and no work. Their protestations of innocence and promises to settle if they are allowed back to their sections would melt a heart of stone!' Sherbet's device was within the letter of the Frontier Crimes Regulations, but perhaps not quite what its framers had envisaged.

Trench reinforced the Hindubagh area and told the Militia they could have 'the rifles, money, clothes, boots etc. of any raiders they may lay out. The resultant increase in keenness is very marked. "Even if it is a magazine-rifle, Sahib?" The price of a good magazine-rifle is equal to three years' pay, or the price of a wife.'

The chief object was to get the local tribes to defend themselves and help the Militia against the raiders. They would do so willingly, said the Sherani Maliks, if the Sarkar would give them magazine-rifles, but they had only Martinis. 'The Wazirs, Sahib, allow no one to bring a Martini on a raid.' But matters were slowly improving. In June 1921, a man came running into Fort Sandeman with news of a Suliman Khel gang in a village only eight miles away. The Militia chiga troop rode off but only twenty rifles: all the rest of the Mounted Infantry were on a gasht. However the Sherani Jirga was in session, which enabled Trench to put it to them that this was their chance to show their worth. 'They responded with alacrity, law-givers and litigants alike. Within a few minutes the court had broken up and sixty Sheranis, some mounted and some on foot but all with rifles, were following hard on the Militia's heels.'

The Suliman Khel purged their past offences, realising that the time of unbridled licence was past. The Wazirs did not. The Amir of Afghanistan, in order to de-stabilise the Baluchistan border, settled seven hundred Wazir families, 'real die-hards, with a bitter hatred of us, every man and boy with a ·303 Lee Enfield magazine rifle,' at Shahjul, across the Durand Line north of Hindubagh. From this sanctuary, immune to retaliation and too far away for easy surveillance, they were ideally placed to cross the border anywhere in six hundred miles.

Trench heard that they had killed a Veterinary Officer and cut up a company of the 92nd Punjabis on its way to relieve the besieged Zhob Militia post at Haji Killa, in Pishin district. (In Waziristan no one in his senses would move a single company about like this.) As the Zhob Militia were involved, and the Political Agent, Pishin was at the far end of the district, Trench drove to Pishin, picked up some Militia and riding camels, and hastened to the scene of the fight. They met six wounded and naked Punjabis who had been released by the raiders, gave them their camels and continued on foot. Then they met eight more, sent them back on horses borrowed from a village, and resumed the hopeless chase. They learned that the company had run into three to four hundred Wazirs and put up a good fight until the two British officers were killed, when the Wazirs rushed the survivors. Forty Punjabis were killed, twenty captured and eighty rifles lost: a first-class disaster. The prisoners were stripped and made to carry the Wazir wounded to safety. Then the Sikhs were decapitated and the Moslems released, naked, to make their way home. The lashkar summoned the

Militia post at Haji Killa to surrender, but the Subadar in command told them to go to the devil, and they went on across the border into Afghanistan.

In March 1922, Trench temporarily took over Pishin district, expecting it to be a soft posting. Within a few days of his arrival there, at six-thirty in the evening, in came Lieutenant-Colonel Boswell [not his real name], commanding a Punjabi battalion, with news that five of his officers had gone off chikor-shooting that morning and only three had returned. These said they had been fired at while walking up birds in line; they had lost touch with the other two, but had made their way to their car and got away, which was probably the best they could do with only shot-guns against rifles. 'Anything more insane than to go out without a rifle or two among them, I can't imagine', commented Trench. 'Added to this, they had been warned there were raiders hanging about the area, and had actually been ordered not to go there.'

Trench, Boswell and forty Punjabis piled into lorries and drove hard for Migandi where the incident had occurred.

It was bitterly cold, freezing hard and a cruel wind. But we reached Migandi by ten o'clock in spite of a bad road, numerous breakdowns and practically no lights. I then knocked up some villagers who told us that the raiders, about a dozen in number, had passed through their village late in the evening with two officers as prisoners. They gave me a scribbled note from the latter, Smith and Jones [not their real names], to the effect that they were unhurt and that their captors were prepared to let them go if I released and sent to Haji Killa certain men whom I had in jail. They also laid down other terms on a liberal scale! The leader of the raiders was one Nadir who has come into prominence during the last year. Well, there was obviously nothing to be done at Migandi. The raiders had a three-hour start and might have been anywhere in the hills to the north. It was pitch-dark and quite impossible to follow their tracks. So we started back and reached Pishin, half-frozen in spite of posteens, at one o'clock, I spent most of the night waking up people in Quetta with 'Clear the Line' wires. It gave me a quiet satisfaction!

Meanwhile the Tahsildar at Pishin, hearing from another source a garbled version of the affair, had sent word to a troop of Militia under Risaldar Khairo Khan, Kakar, telling him if possible to cut the raiders off.

Next day the Agent to the Governor General, Sir Armine Dew,

arrived and fairly blew his top. Not merely had the five idiots disobeyed
direct orders, but they were poaching, for chikor-shooting in that area
had been closed for a year. Meanwhile Trench had gathered in various
headmen of Nadir's tribe.

There were only two courses open. We could either accept the
raiders' terms, in which case it would be next to impossible to run the
show in future, or we could put up a bluff. Dew decided — and I
think rightly — on the latter. His main and immediate object is to get
back the two British officers safe and sound, but he also has to
consider the province. So we selected half-a-dozen of the most
influential Maliks of Nadir's tribe, put the fear of death into them,
and sent them off this afternoon with orders to go to Haji Killa, get
into touch with the raiders and tell the latter that unless they returned
the prisoners unhurt, their relatives would swing, their villages be
burnt and their tribe ruined. I never saw men more frightened.

Dew left for Quetta, and half-an-hour later a special messenger arrived
from Risaldar Khairo Khan to say that he and local villagers had come
up with the raiders, killed Nadir and were continuing the pursuit. What
was he to do with Nadir's body?

Khairo Khan has done splendidly, but one does not know whether to
be glad or sorry. It all depends on whether any relative of Nadir is in
the gang. If he is, he will kill Smith and Jones. It's beyond our control
now ... I had the best reason to suppose that Nadir and his gang,
under the indirect pressure I was putting on him by incarcerating his
relatives, would have come in in three or four days, when the folly of
Boswell's officers presents him with a card beyond his wildest hopes!

When the raiders started shooting, Smith and Jones had become
separated from their companions whom they saw making off in the car.
They had no choice but to surrender.

The raiders relieved them of their guns, assured them they were not
Wazirs and that they were not going to be killed. They all then
trekked up north across the hills for the Barshore valley, going hard
until the morning. The raiders gave the prisoners the best of their
food, a blanket apiece and an ox to ride on, and were much amused
that they had come out to shoot and had themselves been pinched.

During the day Nadir and two others left the road to look up friends in a village. While he was there, up came Khairo Khan and his troop and shot Nadir dead. The rest of the gang pushed on until four in the afternoon when, reckoning they had outdistanced pursuit, they stopped at a house for refreshment.

Three very comely young women in it made tea for captors and captives alike, all sitting (girls included) chock-a-block round a fire to drink it. While they were refreshing themselves, Khairo Khan and his MI came up and started firing through the door and roof at 200–300 yards' range. One of the girls who had a small baby went and hid among the cows, but the others merely moved out of the line of fire. The raiders then turned ugly and were about to shoot S and J when a local man rushed in between them with a Koran. He was dashed to the ground, but Smith and Jones guaranteed the raiders' lives and liberty if their own lives were spared. The raiders agreed, but made them sign a bond for 2,000 rupees before they were allowed to leave the hut and get Khairo Khan's lot to cease fire. They had difficulty in inducing KK to do so because he wanted to mop up the whole gang. A short parley followed, after which Smith and Jones with their rescuers made off, leaving the gang in possession of their shotguns and the field!

It was with marked reluctance that Trench paid 2,000 rupees to the raiders' emissary a few days later.

By the end of 1922 there was a visible improvement, thanks largely to the Zhob Militia. There were still a few small raids, by Wazirs, not local tribesmen, but the locals were passing information in to the Political Agent and the Militia forts. Maliks were bringing their disputes to Fort Sandeman, and were accepting tribal responsibility for law and order. Even the light taxes were being collected by junior officials who could move safely around with a small escort.

By the mid-1920s Zhob was at peace. The Militia gashted about the district and piqueted for the Zhob column on excursions to the Gumal River and the Afghan border. They had occasional trouble from the Suliman Khel, and sometimes an outlaw took pot-shots at a lorry. Most gashts were very different from those in Waziristan — leisurely circuits of the outposts taking from four to fourteen days, with baggage camels and furtive assignations with five-rupee informers whose news was always weeks out of date. Occasionally they were sniped from afar, but they had no real fighting. Zhob became a sort of addiction for many

Political and Militia Officers, though it is difficult to see wherein lay its charm. Geoffrey Hawkins said that his three years as a Wing Officer of the Zhob Militia there were the happiest in his whole service.

> I enjoyed the change from regular soldiering . . . six officers commanding 2,400 men, instead of fifteen officers commanding 800 according to the rule-books. Then there was the land, so unattractive yet encouraging you to explore it. It was hot. It was cold. It rose up in long scrawls of hills and then settled down. You had to fight it, and when you did, you appreciated each other. It held about two humans to the square mile. Villages, far apart, hid themselves in cracks in the earth, valleys in which were small, mud-walled patches of green where grapes and apricots grew. It was a country of silence, except sometimes for the sound of the wind. And you went where you wished, except over the Border.

There was polo on the gravelly maidan below the rocky hill on which perched Sandeman's Fort. There were wonderful chikor shoots with lines of Militia beaters driving the birds fast as grouse over the guns, swinging round the spurs and over the gurgura bushes. There was good mahseer fishing in the Zhob river; the *gud*, the wild sheep of the Frontier, could be found on many mountains; and officers with abundant energy and a head for heights could stalk straight-horned markhor on the precipices of the Takht-i-Suliman, and descend gingerly to the narrow ledge where Solomon had landed his magic carpet to allow his Indian bride a last look at her home.

The tough boys of the South Waziristan Scouts and the Tochi Scouts used to say that the Kurram Militia was the life of a country gentleman, and the Zhob Militia the life of a *retired* country gentleman. To which the Kurram and the Zhob might have retorted, 'In so far as your statement has any validity, it is because we, in the early 1920s, won our wars, making the Kurram and the Zhob too hot for hostiles. You are still fighting yours – not, if we may say so, with conspicuous success.'

8

The Scouts at Home

The fort at Jandola, completed in 1923, housed the headquarters of the South Waziristan Scouts: one Wing Headquarters, thirteen Infantry platoons and one troop of Mounted Infantry. Officers from the other Wings (based on Sararogha and Sarwekai) resorted to its Officers' Mess on average about once a month for two or three days.

Jandola is on the Mahsud-Bhitanni border, in a country of arid hills. From the outside it resembled a mediaeval castle with loopholed, crenellated walls some fifteen feet high, towers at each corner from which attackers could be enfiladed and another tower over the massive gate. The walls enclosed a space of rather more than an acre: inside, backing on to the walls, were the British and Pathan Officers' Messes and quarters, and barrack rooms and the armoury, quartermaster's stores and other offices.

The Messes and living quarters looked on to a well-watered lawn. There was a red-flowered pepper-tree, a gorgeous powder-blue flowered jacaranda outside the British Officers' Mess, a miniature box-hedge and climbing roses. Outside the walls were the triangular, walled tahsil where the Pathan Tahsildar held court. It was usually crammed with litigants, five-rupee informers, and hostages held as security for someone's good behaviour. (After residing in Jandola for a few weeks, a hostage was usually replaced by some other member of the family.) Outside too were the Mounted Infantry horse-lines and the motor transport park and workshop, protected by lower walls against snipers. Nearby was the mud fort of Old Jandola, converted into a civil hospital.

'Stanley Pip', wrote Denis Ambrose, 'was a great gardener, so we all became gardeners too.' The gardens, some six acres, lay between the fort and the Tank Zam. There were grown in abundance peaches, apricots, pomegranates, and many kinds of vegetables. Supervised by any British and Pathan officers who were interested, with unlimited labour and any amount of manure from the horses and the 130-strong dairy herd, it would have been discreditable if the gardens had not been a success. Garden work was popular with the men, as was garden produce. Among the gardens was a tiny officers' swimming pool and two grass tennis courts. Jandola, only 2,300 feet above sea-level, was hot in summer, but all this greenery made it bearable. Water for the fort and the gardens was pumped up from the Tank Zam. The pump-house, wired and booby-trapped, could have been the Achilles heel of Jandola, but was never actually sabotaged. To discourage long-range sniping, there were two stone-built piquet-towers, on ridges about a mile away to east and west.

The basic building was done by the Sappers and Miners, but the corps was responsible for many improvements and extensions, especially after it was discovered that good bricks could be baked from the local clay. The Akora Khattak platoons produced many good masons, bricklayers and carpenters; when cement was difficult to obtain, they made lime from a special kind of grey rock.

Like the gardens, the Officers' Mess was the creation of Major S. P. Williams. It consisted of ante-room, dining-room, card-room and billiards-room, with the 'usual offices'. Other rooms might keep to military tradition – leather arm-chairs, shikar-trophies, captured weapons and corps photographs – but Williams made the ante-room, known more appropriately as the drawing-room, the greatest possible contrast; its chintzes and water-colours, its luscious brunette over the mantelpiece, afforded a real relief after weeks in a lonely outpost. The drawing-room, dining-room and card-room were inviolate: parties were confined to the billiards-room. Denis Ambrose describes the scene:

On a guest night (which occurred whenever we had a guest) Stanley Pip, slightly deaf, would be seated in the drawing-room reading and sipping a weak whisky-soda, quite oblivious to the pandemonium in the billiards-room, with billiard balls hurtling through the air in energetic fives and crashes of broken window-panes, accompanied by a piano and bawdy songs. Next morning as a routine procedure the glass would be swept up before breakfast and the panes replaced by the ever-helpful sapper. Although parties frequently carried on to 3 a.m., they were never allowed to interfere with the 6 o'clock gasht next morning, the most effective medicine for very thick heads.

The Jandola Mess acquired a reputation for hospitality and guests were numerous. Among the earliest, in 1924, were a party of VIPs including Sir Alfred Mond, Chairman of ICI, and Lord Inchcape, Chairman of the P & O Line, touring India during the cold weather. The Scouts decided that something special should be laid on for them, such as a 'typical' Frontier outrage. So some slightly puzzled Mahsuds, who had hitherto been forcibly dissuaded from anything of the sort, were paid five rupees each to fire a few shots over the Mess roof during dinner. All through the meal bullets cracked and ricochets whirred overhead, to the manifest delight of these eminent persons, who felt they would have something to dine out on in Belgravia. A good time was had by all, except for the sole casualty, an unfortunate donkey.

Another early visitor to Jandola was Lawrence of Arabia, in the guise of Aircraftsman Shaw, benighted there by a broken-down truck and accommodated in the Officers' Mess. He capped their tales of rifle-thieves, kept them enthralled by tales (some, perhaps, almost true) of far Arabia, and left them a volume which is still treasured by the SWS officers.

This book [he inscribed on the fly-leaf] was written by me, but its sordid type and squalid blocks are the responsibility of the publisher. It is, however, the last copy in print of *Revolt in the Desert*, and I have much pleasure in presenting it to the officers of the South Waziristan Scouts in memory of a very interesting day and night with them. T. E. Shaw.

The Anglican chaplain from Razmak used to hold services in the ante-room. Nat Cosby, who like many Irish Protestants may have regarded church-going as an occasion for showing the flag rather than religious devotion, issued orders at an 'O Group' the evening before. 'This is a parade, and all officers will attend. What's more you'll all open your mouths and sing: you can sing loud enough, God knows, on Guest Nights. Except you lot.' (indicating the Papists and Presbyterians) 'You'll fall in in the rear rank and keep quiet.' He greatly disapproved of 'smells and bells'. When a High Church padre took the service, and kept on darting into the card-room and emerging with a different hat on, Cosby's comments were very hurtful. The Catholic chaplain came less frequently, especially after one of his flock, Horace Draycott, who was painfully shy, made a dash for cover on his arrival, muttering to Sandy Sandison, 'Tell him I've had to go on a gasht.' But two Jesuits stayed for weeks compiling a Flora of Waziristan. No doubt, being Jesuits, they had no difficulty in integrating: they probably went out on gashts.

Food was as good as could be expected: poor beef, delicious mutton from the Frontier fat-tailed sheep, plenty of fresh vegetables and fruit and as many luxuries as they could afford. Most of the officers drank a good deal – beer, whisky, gin and champagne whenever a celebration was called for, which was as often as possible. In Jandola this was an antidote to the hard life outside: they all needed it, some needed it more than others.

There were other Mess entertainments besides billiard-fives. (Were proper billiards and snooker ever played?) Trick revolver-shooting kept the 'ever-helpful sapper' busy next morning – but not, more by luck than judgment, the 'ever-helpful doctor'. Ambrose records that

fire-blowing became very popular. This consisted of filling one's mouth with paraffin and spewing it out over a lighted match, producing a long flame. One night young Boulter was performing this fascinating trick when he hicupped in the middle of it, causing the flame to blow inwards instead of outwards. He was in hospital for three weeks with singed lungs.

A visitor, offered a drink by Haggis Gardyne, would observe his host taking a drink too, and then nonchalantly chewing up and swallowing the glass. M. J. O'Connor was a member of the Magic Circle, enlivening many a difficult Jirga by producing an egg from a Malik's beard, or a lighted cigarette from his ear. His most celebrated coup was getting four senior officers playing bridge, after dinner, with fourteen cards each: they never noticed. Geoffrey Keating would clear the floor and, to the music of the gramophone, dance ballet. He was a most competent performer – entrechats, fouettés, pirouettes, the lot. He was part-Russian, and during the Second World War became one of Churchill's Russian interpreters. Denis Ambrose, while himself preferring Beethoven, Mozart and Chopin, could whack merry hell out of a piano; he and three others made up a hot jazz-band, piano, drum, trumpet and guitar, but, alas, no girls to dance to it. FitzMaurice and Felix Williams had fine voices, specialising in Irish and Welsh songs respectively. Fitz's *Me Mother-in-law* and Felix Williams's *One Meat*

Ball, in the early hours of the morning after a guest night, were things to remember.

Sir Philip Chetwode, Commander-in-Chief, India, visited Jandola as a guest; he had, it must be remembered, no authority over Scouts. Late in the evening FitzMaurice gave a spirited rendering of *The Croppy Boy*, followed by more seditious Republican songs. He then turned to the C-in-C with a genial smile and said, 'Now you can court-martial me if you could, but you can't, can you?' The C-in-C acknowledged that he would if he could but he couldn't.

Officers' quarters – a bedroom and a bathroom each – had, of course, no electric light, electric fan, pull-plug or running water. Instead there were hurricane- and pressure-lamps, the bhisti with his water-skin, and the sweeper hovering in the background with bucket and broom.

Sanitation was a problem. In the early days it was by what was euphemistically known as 'tribal custom' – i.e. the men going out in the early morning to the nearby bushes and nullahs. This was not insanitary – the sun soon dried it up – but it was hardly safe: a Scout engaged in the earliest business of the day was a squatting target. And it was certainly not suitable for posts with garrisons of two or three hundred. So during the 1920s post-sanitation was modernised. There were bucket-latrines inside the walls for use at night, and deep-drop latrines, outside the walls but protected from sniping, to which the men resorted in a rush in the early morning.

There was a Commandant of the Tochi Scouts to whom all this unused compost was a challenge. The best stuff in the world, wasted! Think what those clever Chinese would have done with it! Should it not be spread on the vegetable gardens? But the Pathan is very fastidious in these matters, and the thing must be managed with care. It was obviously a matter to be delegated to the Quartermaster, who at the time was Captain Mohamad Sharif, a burly Kuki Khel Afridi, one of the first trans-Frontier Pathans to hold the King's Commission. So 'Sharifo' was told to get on with it.

After prayerful thought (for there might well be trouble) he decided that the business had better be done by the Kuki Khel platoon, his own tribe, supervised by himself. All went well. The oldest latrine-trench was first opened up; the contents were quite unobjectionable, a fine, friable compost with no smell at all. Then suddenly the man at the bottom of the trench flung down his shovel and exclaimed the Pushtu equivalent of 'I'll soldier no more!'

Sharifo drew a deep breath. This was the moment of truth. Any mishandling of the situation by himself might produce mass-disobedience, even mutiny. The Frontier in flames from one end to the other, and he responsible for it!

'Why?' he asked, with a calm he was far from feeling.

'Not with this bloody shovel. It's the one we use for stirring our pilau.'

The Quartermaster's main job was, of course, not the gardens, but the procurement and issue of all rations and equipment. Except for arms and ammunition, everything was obtained through civilian contractors. Victor Wainwright, when Quartermaster of the Tochi Scouts, was advised never to negotiate with a contractor unless his shorthand clerk was in the room next door, head in a wall-cupboard, notebook and pencil ready. It was a precaution which more than once proved its worth in dealings with local and minor entrepreneurs. But the permanent Corps Contractors (one to each corps) were Hindus of the utmost integrity. To obviate delay in the payment of Mess-bills by officers who might be beleaguered in outposts, the Corps Contractor drew all their pay and allowances, settled their bills and credited the balance (if any) to their private bank accounts.

The Scouts' posts needed a great deal of firewood, which was brought in by local contractors, piled in heaps outside the barbed wire, from time to time weighed in enormous scales, and the contractors paid. One dark night the sentry at Jandola heard the sound of heavy movement and called the Pathan Orderly Officer. After listening for a while, they realised that the contractor was busy moving wood from the pile that was weighed and paid for, on to the unweighed pile, so that it would be paid for again. The sentry, young and bloodthirsty, wished to discourage this enterprise with a grenade, but the Orderly Officer thought this might be over-reacting, and told him to do nothing to interrupt the work. Next morning a fatigue party reversed the process – transferring nearly all the 'unweighed' pile of wood to the weighed, and paid for, side. When the contractor returned for his money, he marked with expressionless face the huge pile of wood for which he had supposedly been paid, the mini-heap for which he might now expect payment, the smiles of the Scouts – and made no comment.

Hockey was the principal Indian Army game, though Gurkhas preferred Association football. But hockey was not suitable for Scouts: it was too difficult, in stone- and shale-country, to produce a smooth, mud-and-cowdung hockey pitch. So S. P. Williams made football and basketball the main SWS games. Any number of men could kick a ball about any level space, and basketball could, if necessary, be played inside the walls of a post, uninterrupted by sniping. Scouts basketball was an extremely rough game; being tackled by a bony and exuberant Pathan was as bad as being tackled by an Irish Rugby international, and cost more than one officer a broken rib or collar-bone. Scouts football was marked more by vigour than by science and was not really up to good Gurkha standards, but Scouts liked sharpening up their game against Gurkhas and British troops. Jemadar Mukhamed, Orakzai, tough as old boots, became very friendly with Jemadar Bhim Sing of the 9th Gurkhas, another all-out competitor on the football field. They would go at one another hammer-and-tongs for ninety minutes, then finish up with a warm embrace and gurgles of delight. After a particularly hard match, a beaming Mukhamed announced to his Wing Commander, 'Bhim Sing will dine with us tonight – provided none of his people know.' It was unheard of for a Gurkha, indeed for any Hindu, to eat with Scouts, so strict secrecy had to be preserved. Bhim Sing and Captain H. R. 'Hutch' Hutchins sampled together the produce of Scotland, which is, of course, forbidden to Moslems, and then had a rare old evening with the Pathan officers.

Football served a more Machiavellian purpose. The Subadar Major allowed the local boys to use the ground and casual questioning by a friendly Scout, with a handful of sweets, often paid dividends. 'How's your uncle Mahmud, Ali?' 'He hasn't been home for ages.' 'Staying with his cousin in Makin, I suppose.' 'Oh, no, they're not friends these days.'

On the lawn in front of the Jandola Mess croquet was played. The Pathan officers took delightedly to this vicious and vindictive game. Soon they were up to all the dodges, legitimate and otherwise, and argued heatedly the finer points of a pastime usually associated with vicarage garden-parties.

The most prestigious sport, of obvious military value, was the *khud*-race, five or six miles of the roughest possible going, up and down almost precipitous slopes.

For officers there was tennis twice a week, always on different days and at different times, after a patrol had searched the maize- and sugar-cane fields within rifle range.

For the men a popular entertainment was Khattak dancing. The sword-dance, to the wild music of drums and pipes, with blades flashing, full white shirts swirling and the young men's bobbed hair tossed back and forward, was one of the sights of the Frontier.

The Mulagoris were great singers, musicians and bird-fanciers. A Mulagori Scout would often be seen walking out in the evening followed by his tame chikor, or bouncing up and down in his hand, to strengthen its leg-muscles, his favourite fighting quail. A Mulagori leave-party was always unmistakeable – singing, and its lorry festooned with bird-cages.

Miranshah, the home of the Tochi Scouts, had much the same atmosphere as Jandola, but it was an older fort, its gardens were longer-established, producing delicious grapes. It lay in an open plain, separated from the villages and cultivated fields along the Tochi river. Food, amenities and entertainments were much the same as in the SWS.

The well-watered lawn was always green, and kept so by successive generations of captive Demoiselle cranes which consumed the wire-worms, leatherjackets and other enemies of green grass. However they exercised a reign of terror over the officers' dogs, even the bull-terriers backing away from their dagger-like beaks. A new-broom Commandant expelled them from the garden. Promptly the lawn became covered with unsightly brown patches; the Demoiselle cranes were brought back and the dogs had to put up with them.

The fort at Miranshah was bigger than Jandola, because it included within the perimeter wall the Political Agent's office and house, and a RAF flight with hangars, workshop, British officers' and Other Ranks' quarters and Messes. The RAF had its own compound, but there was a short cut between the Scouts' and the RAF Officers' Messes up an iron ladder, over a flat roof and down another ladder. This occasionally presented problems after Guest Nights, as in 'Operation Prender' when John Prendergast of the Tochi, weighing at least seventeen stone, had to be carried back to his quarters after dining with the RAF. It was explained to the Scouts sentry, staring fixedly to his front, that the Sahib had been suddenly taken ill – quite a reasonable cover-story until the Sahib himself blew it by bursting into a loud but tuneful rendering of *Come, Landlord fill the flowing bowl*. The suspicion then dawned on his devoted and exhausted bearers that they had been had. The Scouts sub-alterns so impressed a newly-posted Medical Officer about the danger from snipers (in fact, negligible in Miranshah) that he used to crawl across the flat roof on hands and knees.

The Politicals usually messed with the Scouts. One Assistant Political Agent wore a kilt at dinner, so a light-fingered Scouts subaltern crawled under the table during a festive occasion and unfastened the buckles which held it up. Rising to the Loyal Toast, the Assistant Political Agent was revealed to the scandalised Mess waiters as a true Scot.

The Tochi Scouts, on the whole, had a more varied social life than the

SWS. The delights of Bannu, Kohat and Peshawar were comparatively accessible, while for the SWS civilisation consisted of two Mission nurses and the Political Agent's family in Tank, reputedly the third hottest place in the world. Miranshah had a better climate than Jandola, drier and cooler. There was a squash-court as well as tennis-courts. And the Tochi played polo, while the SWS took the austere view that if the Mounted Infantry ponies played polo, they would inevitably be bought with a view to polo rather than gashting. It was mainly a British officers' game, but some of the Mounted Infantry were keen and dashing players.

When the Army re-occupied Wana in 1929, the SWS detachment there could ride with the Wana Drag Hunt, 8½ couple, which hunted twice a week in the protected area. Occasionally they got on to a jackal which took them further afield, but the local Wazirs generally had the good feeling not to shoot at them. The Mounted Infantry of both corps went in for tent-pegging, a favourite sport of eastern horsemen, though it was not good for the horses, giving them a taste for tearaway galloping in a straight line.

Both North and South Waziristan offered fairly good shooting, when and where it was safe to shoot without being shot at: chikor, sisi, duck, snipe and an occasional woodcock. The Dhana chikor shoot, on the plain west of Wana, was an annual event. In 1930 it was well and truly shot up, Wilcox of the SWS getting a bullet in the backside. Thereafter shoots were generally accompanied by a Scouts gasht, and the Jandola Mess Game Book contains in the 'Various' column an enigmatic entry: '2 Wazirs'. South Waziristan had quite good mahseer fishing in the Tank Zam, and there was no case of an angler being shot up. Pathans have great sympathy for the mentally afflicted.

The Agency Surgeons at Miranshah and Jandola were busy men, treating not only Scouts but the locals. Gunshot and knife wounds were the commonest complaint. These doctors were pioneers of plastic surgery. Many an injured husband cut off the nose of his erring wife, and then, regretting his hasty action, took her to the hospital to have it sewn on again. The graft was made by cutting a flap from the forehead and letting it fall down over the missing feature. There were problems in treating the tribal ladies, since any husband would far rather his wife died than that her body should be seen, let alone touched, by another man. In cases where modesty was at risk, the patient's husband would describe the symptoms while the doctor, on the other side of a screen, asked questions and prescribed treatment.

All Pathans, including Scouts, dreaded operations under anaesthetics, not least because they feared that an infidel surgeon might, when they were unconscious, incapacitate them from getting the full enjoyment from the Houris of Paradise. It could take hours, when every minute counted, to persuade a Scout to have his appendix removed, or a bullet-smashed limb amputated. One morning Nat Cosby was told by the Medical Officer, 'I have an appendix case on the table, but he won't let me operate. Can you come over?' Cosby wrote:

I went across, and found a young Afridi boy very scared, who said (using the English word) he did not want operation. I told him that as he had had so much pain, the Doctor Sahib would put him to sleep, and he would wake up with the pain gone. He persisted, 'I don't want operation.' I sent for the Subadar Major who reasoned with the boy, without success. Then I tried the hard line and said, 'Well, if you won't have an operation, you'll be no good for the Scouts, and you'll be thrown out.' He looked at me like a beaten dog and said again, 'Oh Sahib, I don't want operation.' Things did not look hopeful. Then I said, 'Suppose I take *Zamanat* (Security) for your life, will you agree?' He thought for a moment and replied, 'Sahib, if you will take *Zamanat* for me and stay with me while the Doctor Sahib works, I will agree.' I said, 'That's fine, we'll go ahead.'

The operation was successful, and the boy soon fit and well.

Geoffrey Hawkins of the Zhob Militia was asked by the Medical Officer, Jimmy James, 'I wonder if you'd give me a hand? I have to operate on a man's spine and need some help.' Hawkins

got into some white hospital kit, and when the patient had been put out, and certain preliminaries carried out by Jimmy, I was given a long spoon-thing and told to push it up and down the patient's spine. But with the terrible scraping noise, and lots of blood, I went out like a light.

Hawkins had to be revived by a large brandy: Nature had not fashioned him for a surgeon. The patient recovered.

A Medical Officer at Miranshah was standing outside the civil hospital near a group of tribesmen, squatting on the ground with their rifles between their knees. Suddenly one upped with his rifle and took a pot-shot at the doctor, miraculously missing. He then made a bolt for it. He probably knew enough about Scouts' habits to assume that the recruits drilling on the parade ground would not have ammunition in their bandoliers. What he did not realise was that there was also a cadre-class of Havildars, seasoned men of eight to ten years' service, who did have live ammunition. He had not a chance. Two dropped to the sitting position, took careful aim at the running figure and fired a single shot each, dropping him before he had run two hundred yards. Then began a search for the doctor. It was some time before he was found – taking refuge in the women's purdah ward.

The Wing Headquarters forts were completed, Sarwekai and Sararogha in the south, Khajuri in the north in the early 1920s. They were smaller versions of Jandola and Miranshah, with vegetable and fruit gardens, but fewer amenities. The smaller posts were at first mere camps, surrounded by barbed wire and bullet-proof drystone walls, the tents dug down to give more headroom, warmth and protection from sniping. Each Wing garrisoned two or three of these outposts, initially as follows:

South Waziristan Scouts

Jandola	Corps Headquarters and 1 troop Mounted Infantry
	Wing Headquarters and 13 infantry platoons
	3 infantry platoons at Chagmalai
Sarwekai	Wing Headquarters and 11 infantry platoons
	1 troop Mounted Infantry
	3 infantry platoons at Splitoi
Sararogha	Wing Headquarters and 9 infantry platoons
	5 infantry platoons at Kotkai
	2 infantry platoons at Ahnai Tangi

Later, in the 1930s, Chagmalai and Splitoi were handed over to Khassadars, and new Scouts posts were built at Tanai, Tiarza and Ladha. The SWS road-post system resembled a wishbone with the two arms joined at Jandola. On the right arm the posts were Kotkai, Ahnai Tangi, Sararogha and Ladha; on the left arm, Sarwekai, Tanai and Tiarza.

Tochi Scouts

Miranshah	Corps headquarters and 1 troop Mounted Infantry
	Wing Headquarters and 10 infantry platoons
	4 infantry platoons at Datta Khel
	2 infantry platoons at Boya
	2 infantry platoons and 1 troop Mounted Infantry at Mir Ali

Khajuri	Wing Headquarters and 9 infantry platoons
	7 infantry platoons at Spinwam
	3 infantry platoons at Shewa
	2 infantry platoons at Razmak

Later the Tochi Scouts left Razmak and built a new post at Dosalli, which replaced Khajuri as a Wing Headquarters. Khajuri, Mir Ali, Miranshah, Boya and Datta Khel were on or near the road running westward from Bannu; Spinwam and Shewa were on the road running north-west from Mir Ali to Thal; Dosalli and Razmak were on the Central Waziristan road which linked the North and South Waziristan road system (see Map 10, p. 240).

Life in the camps was never comfortable. The dug-in tents, lit by pressure-lamps, were hot in summer, very cold in winter, alive with mosquitoes, sandflies and fleas. As each fort was completed, the corresponding camp was demolished and the garrison moved into the fort. It might not be a home from home, but it was far more comfortable, safe and healthy than the camp. After 1927, posts were armed with Vickers machine-guns, for post-defence only, not to be taken on gasht because they would cramp mobility.

Every fort had a mosque, built by the men and (to the annoyance of the Garrison Engineer) always askew to the rest of the layout since it had to be meticulously aligned, with atlas and prismatic compass, on Mecca.

John Prendergast spent two months with no other British officer in Datta Khel fort. He writes:

It was difficult to fill in time, and boredom hung heavily on my soul. We continued to carry out a weekly gasht on foot over the steep, shaly hills, but we encountered no hostile tribesmen. We played football on the level, stony waste outside the fort: it was terribly hard falling and I bear scars to this day. From the fort I spent hours watching the changing light and colours on the hills in the distance. There was not a single growing thing in the tremendous sweep of the wide valley and it looked as smooth as if swept by a giant broom. But this was deceptive as, being a soil-eroded country, it was scored by deep ravines or nullahs, any one of which could have concealed scores of tribesmen . . . Then my gaze would drop to the inside of the fort. Its walls were of the usual clay and chopped straw, that extraordinarily durable mixture that archaeologists have found to last over a thousand years in this dry climate . . .

In the centre there was a pitch on which we played a peculiarly rough kind of basketball. There was none of your squeal and pass. You grappled with the man who had the ball to make him surrender it. The men's quarters were built round this, backing on to the walls. They had pulled their string beds out into the sun for airing; some were pouring boiling water on to the frames to destroy the bed-bugs. They were polishing away – one was twanging musically on the strings of a rabab – others were singing in high-pitched, nasal voices of bygone forays and abductions. There was a smooth walk-way above the quarters round the crenellated walls and at each corner there was a tower, loop-holed for medium machine-guns ... The nights were long and I used to hear the sentries on the wall shouting their numbers in order: number one sentry, number two, and so on. If a sentry was asleep and he didn't shout his number, the fact was immediately detectable ...

Sometimes the Pathan officers used to invite me down to wonderful feasts of mutton pilau and thick, flat, wholemeal bread served piping hot. I would return the compliment, of course, using their cooks but paying the bill. The senior Subadar, Kabul Khan, was a tough, pock-marked Afridi from high up in the Tirah. His land was lavishly covered with conifers and his family had the wood-contract for far-off Peshawar. Great beams were carried down on hefty Bactrian camels. This part of Afridi territory had never been penetrated by the British. I remarked that his country must be very beautiful and I would like to come and see it. He replied, 'If you did, I would shoot you.' I gathered that it was a matter of principle and not personal ... We finished off the feast with green tea which was brought in brick form from China by camel. This, spiced with white cardamon, makes a wonderful carminative after a full feast.

Kabul Khan and his five brothers in the Tirah owned a proper, modern 3·7 ins howitzer, with ammunition, acquired by devious means from the Afghan army. Despite his toughness and undoubted efficiency, he had a touch of a small boy, evinced one bitter January day at Datta Khel when he snowballed the senior Madda Khel Malik, a huge, sour-tempered fellow who failed to see the joke. This Malik was reputed to have buried under his house 20,000 golden guineas and 20,000 Russian gold coins. When he brought his daughters in to be treated by the Sub-Assistant Surgeon, the little girls' headscarves were sewn all over with gold pieces.

Harry Garland was commanding Datta Khel post in 1930 when his

Commandant, Frank Mardall, arrived with an unexpected visitor, well known by his pen-name, 'Ian Hay', as the writer of Great War novels. For someone so familiar with the military scene, 'Ian Hay' showed an almost childish desire to fire the Vickers gun. Garland did not think this a good idea; he had not time to clear the area, and did not want accidents to the local tribesmen or their livestock. However Mardall said, 'Let him have a go, Harry.' So 'Ian Hay' sat down behind the gun, selected as his target a harmless rock and pulverised it with a whole belt of 250 rounds. A gasht had to be sent to ensure that no one was hurt and no bogus claims for compensation would be lodged. That night they slept on the roof, owing to the heat, and were awakened by shots cracking over them; someone was expressing disapprobation of the Empire by sniping from the vegetable garden. 'What should we do?' asked 'Ian Hay'. 'Stay in bed,' Garland replied, 'go back to sleep.' Eventually the sniping stopped. Next morning the Man of Letters returned to Bannu, delighted with his exploits in the furthest outpost of Empire and full of praise for the young officer's sang-froid. But it was not sang-froid: by an exercise in simple trigonometry Garland had ascertained that any shot fired from the vegetable garden must either smack into the parapet or pass at least four feet overhead. One was perfectly safe in bed, but in some danger out of it.

Talk at the Pathan officers' tikalas ranged far and wide, for they had many interests and were well informed on world affairs. At a tikala given by Terence Philips at Datta Khel

> We covered the decline of the English birth-rate, the price of rifles, the number of beards in England, and matrimony. I said it must be very hard on the married men seeing their wives only on leave, and Zeri Gul, the Jani Khel Wazir, said, 'Ah yes, but, my goodness, we make the most of it! You can always tell a married man when he comes back from leave because he can scarcely put one foot in front of another.'

The conversation then turned to the exorbitant cost of brides:

> Aman Gul said, 'If I wanted to marry, I should have to pay three thousand rupees for a bride, and it is hard for a young man to find so much money, so most of us have to wait until we are near middle-aged.' Everyone condemned this selling of brides, and Zeri Gul said, 'Up in Swat a girl comes with a dowry.' When I asked why he did not go to Swat for a bride, Lal Mohamad replied, 'No, it would be no

good. A girl who has brought in so much money would think herself far too grand to work as our wives must.'

Datta Khel had a remarkable fruit and vegetable garden, producing quantities of vegetables, peaches, apricots and grapes literally by the hundredweight for the garrison. It had an all-ranks swimming pool. The Tochi valley was one of the main bird migration routes, and the garden was full of them in spring and autumn. Philips noted harriers; and chaffinches,

here at the extreme eastern limit of their range for though I saw several in the Datta Khel garden, they had been reported only once before in India. Rosy Pastors, too, a sort of pink starling, besides four other races of starling, the Himalayan, Central Asian, Finsch's and Hume's, all with a different distribution on their feathers of brilliant glossy green, purple, copper-purple, purple-red, violet-purple, bronze copper and blue; and the hills round about in the hot weather were full of the sweet-singing Bay Backed Shrike.

As part of their general awareness of the world, many Scouts had a good knowledge of birds, naming not only the common varieties but, for instance, the Bluethroat, and the White-capped Redstart, distinguishing between the Scarlet and the Little Minivet, the pied and yellow wagtail and knowing the names of even such exotica as Stolieza's Mountain Finch. To Philips this was a revelation.

However content he and others were with life in the posts, not every British officer could put up with it, which was why the vetting of would-be Scouts officers was so carefully done. Even so, there were unhappy times. Two officers, together for weeks, never communicated except by written notes; two more actually came to blows over the emotive question of whether an aircraft signalling panel be laid out on this piece of flat ground or on another or on another piece ten yards away. Outpost life would have been unbearable but for the remarkable affinity between British officers and Pathans.

In the South Waziristan Scouts the last of the posts to be completed, in 1936, was Ladha, 7,000 feet above sea-level, surrounded by well-wooded hills, in summer cool and healthy, in winter often under snow. It cannot be said that the Scouts were welcomed by the local Mahsuds. Said one old man, 'We'd rather have four brigades of infantry than a thousand Scouts. The Army will sit quietly within its wire and we can sell it eggs and chickens, and if they march out we will know exactly where they are going and how far they can go. But the Scouts come from anywhere, and go anywhere, and we never know from which side they are coming next.'

It was in the small posts that the British officers got to know the local tribesmen, provided they wished to be known. At Ladha Ralph Venning and 'Bush' McDonald had as their nearest neighbour a plump, moustached, pippin-faced Mahsud named Shah Pasand, which may be translated as 'Prince Charming'. His fellow-tribesmen, however, generally called him *Kurnail*, 'Colonel', because he had been commandant of the Amir's Bodyguard in Kabul until 1930 when, seeing the writing on the wall, he had anticipated his royal master's deposition by decamping with as many rifles and boxes of ammunition as could be loaded on to a hastily-improvised mule convoy. With this as his nest-egg, he had settled down near Ladha as a gentleman of leisure, building an imposing mansion complete with a fortified tower. He was never actually detected in crime or hostile action, and was on the friendliest terms with the Ladha officers; but no one trusted him a yard. In 1942 he was joined by his brother who as a young man had emigrated to Burma where, by industry and honest ways, especially in the management of a chain of lucrative brothels, he had become exceedingly rich. He had got out one jump ahead of the Japanese – no mean feat for one of generous proportions and sedentary habits. From Ladha, like a retired Indian Army Colonel in Bournemouth, he looked back with nostalgic longing to the good old days. 'People here,' he complained, 'do not know how to live, they are savages. When will the British re-conquer Burma?' The two brothers, both highly concupiscent, found as they aged that desire outran performance, and took their problem to the Scouts Medical Officer, who kept them supplied with a stock of 'Buck-you-up-o pills', air-dropped with the Ladha mail on the not infrequent occasions when their fellow-tribesmen blocked the road.

Each fort and post kept a chiga platoon ready to sally out at a moment's notice, usually by an inconspicuous, defiladed 'chiga door' (also known as 'the thieves' door') to deal with any untoward situation. Benjie Bromhead was in charge at Sararogha when:

The little fort at Ahnai Tangi reported firing across the road. Now the tribes were free to shoot each other so long as the shooting did not happen within the vicinity of government posts or property, but the road was inviolable. So the chiga platoon was summoned by the banging of the Quarter Guard gong, a short piece of suspended rail. At this tocsin, they fell in and raced across the plain towards Ahnai, whilst a support company stood to. I went ahead in my car with the senior Pathan officer and we were met at the foot of the slope below Ahnai by a group of men from the garrison. Firing had ceased, and we found a wounded Mahsud lying on the road beyond the fort, shot in the stomach, his entrails protruding. He was a tough bearded man with eyes of stone, and he made no murmur as we laid him carefully in the back of my car. We drove back slowly, the chiga party following, and the Medical Attendant soon dealt with his wound pending the Agency Surgeon's arrival. He survived, and I visited him in hospital, to be met with the same hard stare and little to say in answer to my questions. He was a silent man, with hatred in his eyes, and I felt almost sorry for those who had tried to kill him.

In July 1935, Victor Wainright of the Tochi Scouts took over the Scouts post near Razmak.

This was a tented camp for four or five platoons on the bank of the algad running from the Sui Dar to Razmak camp proper. It was there to try and prevent the constant bickering between the Abdullai Mahsuds and the Tori Khel Wazirs about the grazing around the algad.

Mir Hamza, Jowaki Afridi,* was the senior Subadar. He was a wiry little man, knee-high to a duck, very smart, very fit and very bloodthirsty – a sort of human combination of Kerry Blue, Bull Terrier and Staffordshire. Although intelligent and full of nous, his immediate reaction to any trouble was to rush at it bull-necked. He was quite alarmingly outspoken and the greatest fun. His closest friend was the senior Aka Khel Afridi Subadar, Kabul Khan, of much the same age and seniority, both young for their standing. Kabul was as brave and as capable but either more intelligent or given to thinking a little longer. Miry and Kabul were like affectionate brothers and together behaved like mischievous prep-school boys, always playing practical jokes with the object of making the victim late for parade or look stupid in some way. They would then have terrific mock quarrels and go round telling anyone who would listen what a shit the other was.

Anyway, my first Sunday, I was just lighting my after-breakfast pipe when there were shots around the camp, the chiga-gong went and Miry in gashting order appeared in the door of the British

* Son of Hony Captain Tor Khan, one-time Subadar Major of the North Waziristan Militia. See page 25.

officer's hut looking remarkably like a hunt-terrier with the leash half-off. I asked him what cooked, and he replied more or less in one breath, 'It's Mahsuds and Wazirs, and by the time you've got on a uniform shirt, pagri and pistol the chiga platoon plus the Kuki Khel platoon will be ready to move.' A few seconds later I said, 'What shall I do?' The answer was polite, 'I suggest you order me to chase the Wazirs like hell up the left bank with the chiga while you do the same to the Mahsuds up the right bank with the Kuki Khel. With any luck the buggers will fight, but they are much more likely to surrender and say it was all a mistake or hop it through the scrub.' By this time the rest of the post were standing to along the perimeter wall, so we streaked off, uphill, against the wind, on a very hot morning in thick thorny scrub at 7,000 feet plus.

The Kuki Khel – very tough, with egg-shaped heads because their mothers bind them when they are tiny -- grabbed three or four less active Mahsuds, full of injured innocence about being quietly grazing their goats when they were shot at by dastardly Wazirs. After we had gone a mile or two the shooting stopped, so we halted in a defensive position and Miry came across to say he had done the same. I decided to call it a morning and hand the prisoners in to the Tahsildar at Razmak. At this juncture my Aka Khel orderly, who was very like me in build and colouring and tied my pagri exactly like his, handed me a rather odd-looking bullet and said, 'Who's a lucky boy to be hit by a spent one? It bounced off your leg and you'd better send it home to your Mum.' Sure enough, the mark was there on the front of my thigh, rather like a deep burn.

A few days later some Abdullai Maliks came in to say that they were rather grateful to their gallant friends the Militia, because actually they had been caught on the hop and badly outnumbered. Would I like to go unarmed with my orderly next Sunday to shoot a bear on Sui Dar? They would feed us and lend me a good rifle; I accepted with alacrity. By this time Mir Hamza had gone on leave and the senior Subadar was Sar Gul, Kuki Khel, commonly known as Mian Sahib* because he was one. I told the old boy (about 40) of the Mahsud invitation and he said, 'You'll do nothing so foolish.'

'Subadar Sahib, may I remind you that I am commanding?'

'Sahib, that is no problem. My Kuki Khel platoon will restrain you. I'm going on pension in less than a year, and I'd prefer to risk disciplinary trouble than be derided for the rest of my life as the

* A Mian is a kind of holy man.

Subadar who let his young officer be had for a mug by Mahsuds.'

When I pointed out that one of the Maliks was a pensioned Subadar from my cousin's battalion of the Baluch regiment, he replied with several interesting Pushtu proverbs, variations on the theme *merde alors*.

So Wainright never did get his bear-shoot, and the Mahsuds never did get Wainright.

They nearly got Neville Williams (Stanley P's son), however, a few years later, when he was with the SWS in Ladha. On the mountain above Ladha lived Wali Zar, universally acknowledged to be an out and out rogue. He invited to dinner Williams and James Watson, a tough, hard-drinking little Scot, older than most subalterns, who came to the Indian Army and Scouts from the Digboi oil-fields. Everyone warned Williams against accepting the invitation, the Pathan Tahsildar telling him, 'Wali Zar first class rascal *dé*'. But Williams, with a family tradition to uphold, regarded it as a challenge. He did, however, as a precaution tell the Post Subadar to send out the chiga platoon if he was not safely back by six o'clock. He was regaled with a terrific spread, every kind of Pathan delicacy till he was fairly bursting, the rice oozing out of his toes. In the East it is for the host, not for the guest, to intimate that it is time to go; and Wali Zar was in no hurry to give 'the permission'. Williams became more and more apprehensive, but could not depart without grossly insulting his host; Watson afterwards recalled 'Och, you know we were sitting there and there was nothing more to be said, and I could feel the hair rising on the back of my neck, and I knew that something was *wrong*'. Suddenly there was an uproar from outside, two or three rifle-shots rang out and in burst the Ladha chiga platoon. The Post Subadar, thoroughly disapproving of the whole enterprise, had sent it off half an hour before Williams had ordered. Thirty armed Mahsuds were flushed from the vicinity, some hiding actually under the floor-boards of the house.

A different kind of emergency occurred at Khajuri in the Tochi when Nat Cosby was commanding it in the 1920s. This is his account:

A caravan of Powindahs returning to Afghanistan from India camped about five hundred yards from our post. Through my glasses I saw intensive digging going on. A local said they were burying many people. I sent my Sub-Assistant Surgeon across to find out what was the matter. He returned saying, 'Sir, many men are dying of vomiting and diarrhoea.' Suspecting cholera, I rang up the Medical

Officer at Miranshah who came down and confirmed my suspicion. The caravan was upstream of us, and we in the fort and piquets all drew water from the Tochi river. Immediate action was to draw water only from midstream, since the cholera germ likes sluggish water near the edge and does not survive in fast running water. Immediately our first case occurred. I had isolation tents pitched between the walls and the barbed wire apron. We were lucky to get away with four cases, of whom three were saved by a saline intravenous drip. The men readily queued up for cholera inoculations as this epidemic really scared them.

9

Gashts, Baramptas and such

The main purpose of an outpost was to serve as a base for gashts. The term 'gasht' is more descriptive than 'patrol' because it conveys the impression of speed. In Scouts' English it was used as a verb, 'to gasht'; or as a noun, 'a gasht of twenty-five miles' or 'a gasht of four platoons'. The gasht was the commonest Scout operation, a patrol of about four-platoon strength. It had six objects:
  (a) Training
  (b) Peace-keeping between the tribes
  (c) Discouraging raids and the assembly of hostile lashkars. It was better to deter than to punish.
  (d) Acquiring detailed topographical knowledge
  (e) Giving moral support to friendly tribes
  (f) Demonstrating that Sarkar's forces could move where and when they wished, right up to the Durand Line.
It was Major S. P. Williams who developed the long gasht in the South Waziristan Scouts, made possible by the construction of forts to replace camps. High-walled, loop-holed and wired, a fort needed fewer guards than a camp, which meant more men could be spared for gashts which could venture further afield and stay out for longer. Soon twelve miles was a mere morning stroll and gashts of twenty-five to thirty miles a day were commonplace. In order to appreciate the gasht, it must be compared to a move by regular troops in Waziristan, usually a brigade group known as a 'column'.

Whatever form a daylight operation took – advance to make contact, formal attack, destruction of a hostile village, rearguard, convoy protection — the basis of it was piqueting, known to our grandfathers by the more picturesque term of 'crowning the heights'. Any column was accompanied by an immensely long train of camels, horses and mules, carrying artillery and machine-guns, rations and ammunition, blankets, greatcoats and tents, barbed wire, picks and shovels, picketing ropes and stakes and telephone-wire, water-pumps and canvas troughs, clerks and field post-offices and cooks — all the clutter and impedimenta and non-combatants which seemed just as necessary to an Indian Army column in the 1920s as television and press correspondents, photographers and television cameras and sound-recorders, typewriters and teleprinters and Public Relations Officers are to a British Task Force sixty years later. They made a target which no sniper could miss, even at a thousand or twelve hundred yards. Therefore no column moved without first placing small bodies of troops — a couple of sections, a platoon, or a cavalry troop in more open country — on any hill within range of the axis of advance. This made movement very slow and laborious, but the Government was concerned that the job should be done with the least possible casualties, and 'sweat saves blood'.

The method of posting and withdrawing a piquet was laid down in exact detail: it had to be, since the piquet, perhaps fifteen hundred yards from its parent unit, had no communication save flag and helio, and perhaps only a junior NCO in command.

Piquets were found by a unit reserved for that purpose, and placed by the advanced guard commander. As the column moved along the road, which was nearly always along a valley, they fanned out to the commanding heights as indicated to each piquet commander with a pointer-staff. The piquet moved up a ridge and over open country so that ambushes were avoided and it was clearly visible to the supporting artillery and machine-guns. It operated according to the normal principles of fire-and-movement, generally with a Lewis gun covering the advance of the rifle-sections. The piquet-commander prominently displayed a small canvas screen, khaki on the side facing towards the enemy, orange on the side facing down into the valley, so that his position could be clearly seen by his friends. Having reached his objective, he disposed his men for all-round defence, dug or built up such cover as was practicable, 'rocked' any dead ground immediately beneath him, and stayed there, keeping a very good look-out, until recalled.

He had meanwhile left two 'road sentries' on the line of march with a chit giving the piquet's serial number, strength and position. These were handed to the rear-guard commander. He recalled the piquet by a 'wash-out' signal with a huge red flag, and the piquet's serial number indicated by some method intelligible to the thickest Lance Naik even if the piquet signaller had been killed. This signal meant, 'Pull out as soon as you like but as quickly as you can.'

Now came the most dangerous part of the operation, productive of the most casualties. From the enemy's point of view it was far more rewarding, as it was likely to result in the capture of rifles, to attack a withdrawing piquet in the afternoon, than an advancing piquet in the morning. Furthermore, as the tribesmen mutilated any prisoner who fell into their hands, it was unthinkable to leave wounded men behind. If possible even the dead, and certainly their rifles, must be brought down.

Lest it run into an ambush, the withdrawal should be by an unlikely route, which the road-sentries must know and point out to the rear-guard commander. It should not follow the route by which the piquet came up. First, men named by the piquet commander crawled back from the crest and ran down in pairs to a lay-back position; then the Lewis-gun section went down to that position; finally the piquet commander and the remainder of his men came bounding down from the hill, twice as fast as they ever thought they could move over such ground and waving the piquet-screen. They had to run like hell, first because the enemy, who might well have been lurking all day within a hundred yards of them, would be on the peak shooting the instant they left it; and secondly because the artillery and medium machine-guns would open up on the peak the instant the piquet was clear. If things went badly and the last man off the peak was wounded, the whole withdrawal had to be halted, and a section — a platoon — a whole company might have to be sent up again to rescue him.

Scouts were trained in piqueting; they were often employed, when under command of a brigade column, in piqueting the more distant and highest peaks. But on their own gashts, although they moved in tactical formation, they seldom sent out piquets because they had no transport to protect. While a regular Army column crawled through Waziristan at, with luck, ten miles a day, gashts raced along four and a half or five miles an hour, faster in the case of the Mounted Infantry, generally keeping to high ground and ridges because it wanted to be seen. A gasht which saw no tribesmen for a whole day would still have done its job if tribesmen saw the gasht, or even if they saw only its footprints.

A gasht could be self-contained for two or three days, sleeping rough, living on tea, onions, parched grain and *caak*, the travelling

Pathan's unleavened bread made from dough wrapped round a hot stone and baked in embers.

A Scout, officer or man, went on about two gashts a week, generally one-day affairs, sometimes longer. In more or less peaceful conditions, most gashts did more than twenty miles a day, a fact not unconnected with the modest travel allowance which officers drew for twenty or more miles. An unusually long gasht was made by Denis Ambrose, forty-eight miles in twenty-three hours, with a temperature of 100 Fahrenheit in the non-existent shade and several 1,000 foot climbs between Sarwekai and the Gumal.

It is lamentable to record that the Political Agent's private army, wearing strange raiment, speaking a strange language and claiming an expertise denied to others did not win unqualified approval in military circles. Such are the imperfections of human nature that there were even suggestions that the Scouts should be down-graded to police, or disbanded, their duties taken over by regulars who would be more reliable, since they included few if any Pathans, and better value for money, since they could be employed overseas, or on internal security duties in Bombay and Calcutta. With these considerations in mind, Northern Command decreed that one hundred regular soldiers be given a month's intensive training and then take part in a normal Scouts gasht, twenty-four miles of rough going, in order to prove that 'anything they can do, we can do better'. (The scheme was hatched by a senior officer who had, years earlier, been unintentionally humiliated by S. P. Williams who had taken him up and down a steep mountain in breeches and tight field-boots.) In one test a company of Gurkhas finished the course not very long after the Scouts. But over the other test a discreet veil was drawn by Northern Command: the officer was brought in on a stretcher and so many men collapsed that a squad of Scout recruits had to be sent out to bring in stragglers and rifles.

Thereafter less was said about phasing out the Scouts, but they were still regarded in some quarters with envy, hatred and all uncharitableness, and on occasions when their performance fell short of perfection, loud was the jubilation. It was not uncommon for troops new to the Frontier to mistake the Scouts in their Pathan-style uniform for tribesmen, and shoot them up. Hence the apocryphal Scouts' maxim, 'Always take cover on the side of the hill facing the enemy: they only have rifles.'

If a man, perhaps unwell, could not keep up, his friends would help him and carry his rifle. If he still could not keep up, he was left with food and water, but without rifle and ammunition, to make his way to the nearest post. If he did this once, it was a disgrace; twice, a worse disgrace; a third time, he was sacked.

With exactly the same weapons as their enemy – ·303 rifles and speed across country – Scouts were unique in twentieth-century counter-insurgency forces. But a gasht on its own, with no machine-guns, mortars or artillery, could hardly tackle a really strong lashkar. It was not meant to, there was no disgrace in retreat or going round another way. Its safety lay in secrecy and surprise, in never doing the same thing the same way three times in succession. The route for the next day's gasht was never divulged until the fort gates were closed for the night, and gashts avoided any routine of routes or halts. This was particularly important when they were accompanied by Khassadars.

Scouts signallers were trained to send messages in morse by flag, lamp and helio. But all three methods require visual contact between sender and receiver, a flag cannot be read over long distances, and a lamp is of little use in broad daylight. Helio is an efficient method of signalling up to fifty miles if the sun is shining, but to establish a helio link takes time and skill on the part of the operator who, standing necessarily in the sunlight, may be exposed to sniping. And the helio tripod, once contact is established, must not be moved by so much as a quarter inch until the message has been sent and acknowledged. None of these methods was of much use when help was needed quickly, so every gasht had four carrier-pigeons, borne in crates on the signallers' backs, which would carry a message to base. The message was written on thin paper, rolled into a cylinder fixed to the pigeon's leg, and the birds were sent off in pairs, with identical messages, to run the gauntlet of falcons.

Sometimes the pigeons would not play – or, rather, would not work. John Prendergast in the Tochi had a problem for which Sandhurst had ill-prepared him when a pair of pigeons, released to summon help when his gasht was ambushed, instead of circling round to get their bearing and then winging away to Datta Khel, perched in a tree billing and cooing at one another. They had to be stoned until they stopped philandering and got on with the job. It was equally frustrating when they would not come to hand at their destination but sat cooing on a roof, ignoring all blandishments. One unfortunate bird, believed to be withholding a message of vital importance, was shot. With urgent hands the cylinder was detached from the fluttering corpse, the precious message pulled out, unrolled and perused. It read, 'If you're as bloody thirsty as I am, God help you.'

For a newly joined officer a 'star' gasht, over twenty miles, could be an ordeal, especially in hot weather. The flies buzzing round a sweat-damp face were irritating in the sun, unendurable in the shade. Camel-flies − like horse-flies only more so − stabbed the soft skin of wrists and behind the knees. One was thirsty the whole time, but must not drink because it only made one sweat the more, and become more exhausted. The chapli took some getting used to. With its loose heel-strap, it is a wonderfully practical sandal for climbing up a dry, stony hill, but its open toe lets in grit and sand which the wearer learns to shake out without breaking step or slowing down. The occasional devil-thorn or spear-grass seed − and no one can walk a yard with it under the sole − cannot be shaken out; one must stop to remove it, then hurry to catch up. A winter gasht could be awful, with the bitter wind from Siberia cutting through shirt, pullover, and partog, mud slippery in the chaplis, snow perhaps on the ground or blowing in one's face.

But British officers, once they were fit, enjoyed gashting. It was what they had joined the Scouts for, far better than PT, drill or weapon-training behind the barbed wire of an army camp. If there was a British officer on a gasht, he was in command, and took the blame if anything went wrong. However, he would be very foolish not to consult his infinitely experienced gasht Subadar. The Pathan officers carried rolled round their walking-sticks small flags for sig-nalling, yellow for the platoon commanders, red-and-yellow for the gasht Subadar. To watch the latter handling a five-platoon gasht, moving fast and widely extended over rough country, silently with vigorous flag- and hand-signals, was an education. It required a high degree of tactical sense and knowledge of the local situation. FitzMaurice compared a gasht and its Subadar to a pack of hounds and its huntsman. A truer comparison − since a good huntsman leaves hounds to work out their own line − would be to a team of sheep-dogs watching for and obeying every signal of the shepherd. They were not super-men: platoon commanders did not always do the right thing but they were all men of experience and common sense, and if some unexpected situation developed, they coped with it.

In a country where almost every man went armed, it was one of the rules of the game that the tribesman carrying a rifle and festooned with cartridge-belts was a peaceful shepherd until he fired at you. But what about ten tribesmen who dived for cover as the gasht came within sight? A gasht commander had to make quick decisions, guided only by experience and common sense; if he was wrong, a couple of his men might die, or an innocent man be killed, starting a new tribal war.

Benjie Bromhead, large, fair and moustached, joined the South Waziristan Scouts in 1929 when S. P. Williams was still Commandant. He was posted to the 2nd Wing at Sararogha, commanded by Golly Gilbert, who, with a shock of white hair despite his youth and a large ginger moustache, was a most tolerant and efficient tutor. The 1st Wing was commanded by Bill Felix-Williams, who had the unusual distinction of playing rugger and soccer for Cardiff in the same season. He was still very active, though sometimes incommoded by pieces of shrapnel acquired on the Western Front while serving under-age in a Public Schools Battalion. Although his Pushtu was poor, he was an inspiring leader in action, less inspiring in administration.

The 3rd Wing was commanded by Jock Scotland, a burly extrovert with a tremendous zest for life and a fierce pride in his Wing. He was a noted trencherman. At feasts given by friendly Maliks, while other officers quailed at the huge piles of mutton and savoury rice, he would loosen his belt and fall to with a will, concluding with a series of reverberating belches which gave the utmost satisfaction to his smiling hosts: 'By God!' they would exclaim, 'There's a man!' His favourite hot-weather relaxation was to sit in the swimming pool at Sarwekai, listening to classical music and consuming peaches and apricots which grew there in profusion. He had a large, undisciplined and thoroughly spoilt Labrador who paid not the smallest attention to his master's stentorian summonses, 'Bongie! Come here and be beaten!' But Bongie once turned up trumps. Scotland and Henry Cubitt-Smith were taking advantage of a quiet gasht to shoot rock-pigeons. Suddenly Bongie dived into a cave and flushed therefrom an eminent Mahsud, wearing no trousers, who hared away across country in the belief that the shots he heard had been fired by the husband of the lady he was entertaining.

Every British and Pathan officer had an orderly. An orderly was not a domestic servant; he did not cook for his officer, or make up his officer's bed. He kept his officer's belt and weapons clean and was his bodyguard at all times. On gasht he had to be present even if his officer withdrew behind a rock for the purposes of nature. He accompanied his officer on leave, and on shooting and fishing trips. He had certain privileges, such as exemption from guard duties and fatigues. He might (depending on personalities) have his officer's ear and be able to 'put in a word' for someone. It was a position which was sometimes abused. But in action if an officer was hit, his orderly was expected to stay and, if necessary, die with him. Relations between officer and orderly could be very close. (But not as close as was implied by the raised eyebrows on the platform of Rawalpindi Station at the spectacle of Victor Wainright and his Aka Khel orderly embracing on the occasion of Wainright's departure on home leave.)

Bromhead was allocated Aliman, a Bhitanni, an unsophisticated, stocky youth, natural and uninhibited. Once when the brakes of Bromhead's car failed and he took a corner too fast, Aliman hacked him sharply on the ankle with a cry of 'God seize you!' followed by an apologetic smile.

Some weeks after Bromhead joined, he took a gasht through the Girni mountains south of Jandola.

We crossed over the watershed from Jandola into the Girni Algad, a short distance from its exit on to the plain, 100 rifles with a tall Akora Khattak Subadar as senior Pathan officer. He was a spare man with a tireless stride, silent but friendly. We turned up the main ravine towards the mountain, whose skirts were eroded in deep ravines. Sending a small party up on to the high ground, we moved up a deep cleft whose sides became sheer cliffs and the sky a narrow strip above. The cleft became narrower and eventually we climbed out by a side funnel to emerge with some relief on to the lap of the mountain. Its summit was a broken cliff above us and the ground rose steeply towards it. We linked with the rest of the gasht and, dispersed as far as the ground would allow, climbed to the col, a long high climb.

Before descending the west face we climbed the shoulder above the col, near which there was an extraordinary rock fashioned by time and weather into an arch. Beyond it the Derajat Plain stretched away to the Indus, invisible in the haze. Up on the hill, at about 5,000 feet, it was comparatively cool, but below us the mouth of the Gumal shimmered in the heat. We dropped again to the col, and then down steeply into the Mastang, a forbidding ravine below the west face of the Girni Sar. Here the Jalal Khel had cave-dwellings which now in the summer were empty. The lower end of the Mastang sloped down to the Shahur stream at its exit from the Shahur Tangi. On the far bank was an acre of level ground, the only cultivable soil in this part of the Jalal Khel territory. No wonder they were raiders.

As we entered the Jandola gate my Akora companion was still tireless, and the Scouts marched as if they had been but a short way. But it had been a long trek, twenty-five miles on the map across wild country, with a climb and descent of over 3,000 feet.

On another hot-weather gasht from Sararogha, they rested in the shade of ilex trees on the summit of Nishpar Ghar (7,000 feet), talking to a group of Mahsud elders whose village lay at its foot.

To have gone there without their presence would have been unwise, and with conversation they mellowed, whilst on a wooded ridge a Mahsud boy played a shepherd's tune on the flute. We descended from this Arcadia, and under the protection of the fort walls, we closed up into column, whilst the fort's musicians met us with drums and pipes to play us up the steep path with their wild and vigorous music at a pace much faster than seemed necessary, and the men marched through the gate with all the swagger a Pathan could muster.

The most surprising things could happen during a gasht, but surely none more surprising than being presented by a Scout with a small clay pot, sealed with parchment, found in a cleft between rocks. In it were thirty ancient silver coins. This happened to Victor Wainright. He kept one coin, and insisted on the finder keeping the rest to adorn his wife's head-scarf. Wainright's coin was identified by the Curator of Lahore Museum as of White Hun origin, circa 300 AD. On another gasht Wainright was offered and bought some loot from the Amir's palace in Kabul – the insignia of the KCVO, the Order of the Crown of Sweden, the Egyptian Order of the Mejidie and a very ornate Italian Order.

Wainright had an outsize bull terrier named Griffy who loved accompanying him on gasht. Towards the end of a forty-two-mile gasht with the Mounted Infantry, they were dismounted and resting beside the road watching a Ghilzai caravan pass, Wainright with his arm round Griffy for the huge, fierce Ghilzai mastiffs were snarling. When the caravan was about a hundred and fifty yards away, he thought it safe to let Griffy go. Griffy hopped off the culvert and streaked down the road after them, with Wainright, Risaldar Guli Lal and their orderlies in hot pursuit. They arrived just as Griffy had killed the biggest mastiff and was half-way through the next. Wainright was appalled, for the Ghilzai value their dogs, and felt in his pocket for money as compensation. But the senior Ghilzai Malik exclaimed, 'What a dog, Sahib, what a dog! Will you take a hundred rupees for him?'

No armed men moved faster than a Scouts' gasht in a hurry, none kept more silent and still than a Scouts' ambush, known as a chapao. The

Mahsuds claimed as their God-given prey the Derajat villages across the Administered Border. The protection of these was the job of the police and the Frontier Constabulary, but they did not pursue raiders back into Tribal Territory. S. P. Williams was concerned about this. No one could stop raiders going out: they could cross into British India anywhere in twenty-five miles. The time to catch them was on their return, encumbered with loot, hurrying home by the quickest way. If, therefore, the Frontier Constabulary could telephone Jandola immediate word of a raid, it might be possible to position ambush parties to intercept the raiders.

Williams mapped out all the likely crossing places and the routes to them from the nearest Scouts post. On word of a raid, the chiga party would immediately pile into lorries and set off to a de-bussing point, then separate into smaller ambush parties and lie in wait on the likely escape routes. It was rather like still-hunting for tiger or panther. Nothing was achieved by moving around; the only way was to lie still and silent for hours on end and let the raiders do the moving. Sometimes the raiders would not cross at once, but would lie up for a whole day or two days in the scrub-covered foothills, watching and listening for any sign of chapao, and then cross at night. Often they had a couple of unarmed men moving ahead of the main party, a stick to spring the trap. If they were stopped or shot at in the dark, they responded with loud and injured innocence, 'What, me raiding? Whoever heard of such a thing? I've just been visiting friends.' So the crafty ambush commander would let the first two men through and reserve for the main body a volley at fifteen yards.

Scouts and raiders grew extremely cunning. Sitting by a leopard kill, the hunter would know a leopard was somewhere near watching, waiting; and sometimes it could be tricked by getting up, walking noisily away and then very quietly creeping back. S. P. Williams tried this in 1924. It worked: watchers had given the all-clear; twelve raiders came jauntily through with their loot, and were all shot or captured. But for one success there were half-a-dozen failures, days and nights lying under a blazing sun or shivering in the cold, sipping from time to time at tepid water, nibbling at a chupatti – only to hear that the quarry had slipped by, half a mile away.

There were occasional unfortunate episodes, as when the volley was answered by a shout instantly identifiable as one of outrage and injured innocence. The beam of an officer's torch revealed a very angry greybeard, his groaning wife and a camel in its death-throes. Abject apologies for shooting the lady were brushed aside – 'She was too old.'

Then, realising all too late the possibilities of compensation, her husband added, 'But the camel was a *very* good one.'

However, the success-rate was enough to make raiding into British India an unprofitable investment, and by the late 1920s it had almost stopped.

In 1929 Williams was succeeded by Johnnie Johnson, a determined and remarkable man, small, dark and taciturn, not popular, who had won the MM as a trooper in a cavalry regiment at Mons. He was a hard taskmaster, and believed above all in the element of surprise. At Sarwekai after dinner one hot August night he told Benjie Bromhead to take the 2nd Wing to Jandola at once.

He asked me when I could start, and I said in half an hour's time as the men would already have turned in, the bedding had to be rolled and stacked for transport by lorry. We were told to avoid the road and make for the Mastang. We slipped out of the chiga gate and started our cross-country journey. The night was airless and after a few hours of rough going our shirts clung to our backs. Eventually we began to climb over the shoulder of the mountain between the Khuzma Pass and the Khar Gundai, a long steep climb. From the summit we dropped into the deep darkness of the Mastang, and so down to Chagmalai as dawn was breaking. From there to Jandola was easy going and we were glad to reach its walls. Johnnie was at breakfast after motoring down, with Vivian Crapp, the Adjutant. I said, 'Good morning', and sat down. Johnnie as usual said nothing except to reply to my greeting, but Vivian asked if it had been hot crossing the pass, to which I replied, 'What pass?', and he grinned hugely. But I felt I had passed Johnnie's test.

Johnson's Pushtu was not perfect, and he was not at his best when eloquence was required, for his taciturnity was a drawback, but he had great force of character; he was the sort of person who compelled obedience. He once, with only a small escort, came upon scores of Mahsuds, their war-drums thudding, the young men working themselves up into a fighting frenzy before going off to attack the Wazirs. He walked right into the middle of the pandemonium – and it stopped.

He did not remain long in command of the SWS, but in 1930 went on to be Political Agent, South Waziristan. He was succeeded in command by Nat Cosby, formerly of the Tochi, who became known to the SWS as 'PG', signifying 'pretty good', for he was a master of meiosis, the best performance being only 'pretty good', the coldest day 'pretty cool'.

His Pushtu was vigorous, ungrammatical and idiosyncratic, but no one dared misunderstand him.

A road was being built in 1932 between Ladha and Tiarza, bringing a great deal of money in khassadari and road contracts to the tribe through whose territory it passed. Mahsuds and Wazirs both claimed the land. Cosby wrote:

To settle this the Political Agent (Johnnie Johnson) decided to demarcate the boundary. For this purpose I took two troops of MI and three infantry platoons. We left Tiarza camp at about 0900 hours and soon reached the edge of a broad nullah crossing the Sparkhai plain. We halted there and could see a battle in progress between Mahsuds and Wazirs, the two sides in sangars facing one another across the plain for about 1,000 yards. In the centre on a knoll was a key-sangar about which battle raged furiously. The Wazirs had occupied it in the morning, and the Mahsuds were now trying to retake it. A Mahsud came running up and said that a leading Malik had just been killed. The PA and I sat looking at the ground for a couple of minutes, and then said simultaneously, 'This must be stopped.'

It was decided to get between them at this sangar, and to pull in a certain number of each side as hostages. A covered line of approach to the flank was spotted, and along this the force moved. Dropping the infantry on the edge of the nullah to cover us if things went wrong, the PA and I rode out of the nullah at the head of the two troops of MI and walked the whole procession slowly between the firing lines towards the sangar.

Approaching the Wazir position, I told the MI Risaldar, 'Walk on with the rear troop to the Mahsud position, surround them, dismount and cover them; while I take the leading troop on to the sangar.' The Mahsuds fired three shots close under the horses' heads, and the PA said, 'Shall we gallop?' 'Better keep a steady walking pace,' I replied.

A concealed nullah suddenly disclosed itself in which there were seventy or eighty Wazirs. The PA deliberately stopped to address them, while I got my troop round the key-sangar on the knoll and sent word for the infantry to come up as fast as possible.

I cleared the Wazirs out of the sangar, and then rode back to the PA. As soon as my back was turned, the Wazirs re-occupied the sangar, and had to be turned out again and some MI put in it. Mahsuds had the sangar taped and kept dropping bullets very close to me, but to warn, not to hit me.

The infantry seemed a longish time coming up, though actually they were moving fast, and were put in position round the edges of the nullah in which the Wazirs were still being harangued by Johnson. When they were in position, I said to him, 'OK, ready'. The PA then told the Wazirs that we proposed to take twenty-five prisoners and disarm them. After a certain amount of discussion, twenty-five representative prisoners were selected and disarmed and started back with the infantry. This all took time. Then came the job of tackling the Mahsuds which, although there were now two troops available, was a much stickier job. It was only after considerable argument that fifteen prisoners were taken and disarmed. It was a slow retirement, some of the men carrying three or four rifles and cartridge belts, others looking after prisoners. We were very relieved to reach the high ground from which we had started.

That afternoon the PA called a Jirga of Mahsuds and Wazirs and worked out terms for a settlement. After these sorts of shows we discuss the happenings rather like a football match, and one of the Mahsud Maliks said reproachfully to me, 'Sahib, you should never have tried that with less than a thousand men.'

Any officer of the South Waziristan Scouts or Zhob Militia, gashting along the Gumal valley during the seasons of Powindah migrations – north-west to the uplands of Central Asia every spring, south-east to the Indus plains every autumn, hundreds of camels swaying along with loads piled high, thousands of sheep and goats herded by long-haired mastiffs who at night would tear to pieces a stranger among the black goat-hair tents – might expect to be greeted by a cheerful hail from an old woman on the back of a tall camel, 'Wotcher, cockie!' or 'What's blowing, mate?'

This was Mary, who forty years earlier in the Australian outback had married a handsome young Afghan working camels for the goldmines. 'Nawaz Gul's my name,' he used to introduce himself, 'but Nose Gul's what the camel-buggers used to call me.' Mary was now the matriarch of the *kirri* (a nomad encampment), held in awe by Scouts, Politicals and Frontier Constabulary alike. The Powindahs had to deposit their rifles at the Frontier Constabulary post when they entered British India, but everyone knew they kept a few hidden in Mary's baggage or under her bed, where no one dared search. The Political Agents were supposed to ensure that she was content in her life-style. She was, and had no regrets. Nor was she the only Australian wife among the Powindah. One died and her bereaved husband, on his way to Bombay, told a Zhob

Militia officer, 'My mother loved her so much that she said to me, "My son, you must go back to Australia and marry another."'

A Political Agent who became more Pathan than Pathans and even turned Moslem was addressing some Powindahs in his impeccable Pushtu on where they might graze and what route they must take. 'And you're not to make trouble with the Wazirs,' he concluded. 'Do you all understand me?' He was distinctly put out when a burly Powindah answered, 'Too right, Bo. We get you.'

The Powindahs, also known by their tribal name, Ghilzai, poured in and out of India through all the frontier passes, the Kharot and Suliman Khel sections using the Gumal route. They traded in Turcoman rugs, wool, horses, dried fruit, ghi, almonds, pistachio nuts, sugar, salt, tea and the products of Russian, British and Indian factories, equally ready to buy or fight their way through the tribes along their route.

Their garments were more voluminous than those of other tribes, with long shirts and waistcoats heavy with embroidery and little discs of mica, a carelessly tied black pagri holding an untidy shock of hair, heavy shoes instead of chaplis, in winter a posteen. The women, savagely handsome, wore skirts to the ankle, black with dark red and blue patterns, striped red and black trousers, and a headcloth, some yards in length, to protect them from sun and cold – but not from the lascivious gaze of men, for they were generally unveiled. To look down from the ruins of Toi Khulla post while a couple of thousand Powindahs were camped for the night was a sight not easily forgotten. Hundreds of fires twinkled in the darkness; there was a steady hum of conversation, broken now and then by louder arguments, by shouts of friend seeking friend and of someone singing a sweet, melancholy song to the music of a lyre-like rabab. Later all was silent. At dawn all was astir again, and the caravan began ploughing through the dust towards India, with horsemen ahead, then the advanced guard of young men on foot, finally the main body and rearguard.

For the Zhob Militia they were a major problem, bullying the local tribes and up to any skulduggery. For the SWS the biennial three-weeks' camp in the Gumal valley during the migrations was an agreeable change, providing some good duck- and partridge-shooting in the autumn, and enough incident to hold boredom at bay.

It need hardly be said that the Powindahs hated Mahsuds: everyone did. There was also friction with the Wazirs, mainly over grazing. The Powindahs were not above kidnapping Wazir children to keep as slaves or sell in Kabul – but that was a game two could play. It was therefore a job for the SWS to see that both sides behaved themselves, and on the whole the Powindahs respected the forces of the Sarkar which could at any time ruin them by stopping their migration to their winter grazing. Sometimes, however, the men of the kirris, rude and truculent, fired on Scouts, mistaking or pretending to mistake them for Wazirs. There would follow violent altercations, conducted amid hordes of shrieking women, mastiffs barking and snarling, camels, goats and horses all milling round in choking clouds of dust.

When Benjie Bromhead was at Sarwekai in 1930,

Rumours spread that the Wazirs intended to hold the Gwalerai Kotal to prevent the passage of a Powindah qafila. I was sent ahead with a troop of MI while Jock Scotland followed with the main gasht bringing reserve ammunition and rations. We found a dozen Mahsud Khassadars in the ruins of the old Militia fort at Khajuri Kach, sunning themselves like lizards, while outside the fort a dead sheep, which they were too lazy to move, polluted the air. They said they knew of no rumours – and we moved clear of them and made bivouac.

Jock with the infantry gasht joined us, and we settled into a perimeter camp. An enthusiastic and experimental cook, he undertook the preparation of our evening collation. He called the result his Heart's Delight, a mixture of the contents of our two haversacks, gram, raisins, onions, dried apricots, sardines and bully beef, liberally sprinkled with pepper and with a few green chilis to give it a *je ne sais quoi*, all stewed up in a saucepan.

Afer dark, taking the MI, we started for the Gwalerai Kotal, so as to arrive there first. Riding down the steep slope to the Zhob river, Jock's horse slipping under his weight, we splashed and stumbled through the stream, and began to climb. It was dark, with the pathway a mere ghost of a track, and arriving at the summit, we spread out to dismount, hand over our horses to horseholders and occupy the high ground on either flank.

While it was still dark, we heard movement and hailed the intruders. They introduced themselves hoarsely as Suliman Khel, sent forward to secure the pass. We said we were Militia,* at which they were relieved.

At dawn came the leading parties of the kirri, composed at first of camels carrying their camping paraphernalia, and their escort, together with women to cook. There followed more women, and

---

* The tribesmen still used the old name, 'Militia'.

children, and babies with heads nodding to the rhythm of the camels' walk, and flock after flock of sheep and goats spilling down the narrow way. A laughing girl, slim as a lance, her man's rifle slung across her back, jumped nimbly from rock to rock, shepherding the flock. Some women sat and rested on the narrow ledge across the path from us. An elderly woman, staff in hand, came slowly to the top and greeted her sisters. She had the patrician features of a *grande dame*: they are a handsome race. They eyed us curiously, discussing our appearance – dressed as Pathans but walking as Faranghis. There was the sound of distant shots from the foot of the pass, and presently word came that a Powindah boy had been kidnapped by Wazirs.

We mounted and rode down the track. Fortunately the bulk of the qafila had passed, leaving our way clear. At the bottom we were told the boy had been taken up a side ravine which we followed to a place called Bunoke, 'rather a smell', because of the sulphur spring there. On a low spur above the stream was an encampment of Wazirs with their low black tents. There were women and livestock, but few men about. We told them we had come to fetch the kidnapped boy, at which they feigned ignorance. So, having taken up suitable positions, Jock told them he would drive off their livestock and take such men as were within our grasp. There was a pause for consideration, and to our relief a party of men came down the hillside with the boy, a strong youth of about fifteen.

Mounting him on the back of a horse, we set off at a trot. After a time the youth, unaccustomed to the jolting, begged to be allowed to dismount, and for the rest of the long way back to Khajuri Kach he padded happily alongside, holding a stirrup. He told us he had been tending sheep at the rear of the qafila when Wazirs fired, killing one sheep. His brother had gone on with the rest of the flock and he had stayed to skin the carcase, becoming so absorbed in his task that he had not noticed the approach of some Wazirs who fired to scare him and took him prisoner.

Everyone, including the Powindahs, was pleased with the day's work, but their head Malik exploded when a message arrived from the PA to say he would have to go back to Tank. He made a noise like a punctured tyre, an indignant 'paugh', which only Jock could imitate.

Jock had to return to Sarwekai, and I was left in case of further incident. The days were spent in exploring the empty countryside, an immensity of bare rocks and desolation. News came that another Suliman Khel qafila was on its way, and they were said to have kidnapped a Wazir boy. So we set out for the Gwalerai Kotal to intercept them, only to find that they had taken another route. This was foolish, for their guilt now seemed certain. We found them as their leading parties reached the plain, while their main body and flocks were streaming down another track over a subsidiary pass.

Climbing up against the flood, we esconsed ourselves on a spur by the track and asked for their headman. They replied that he was following so we waited. He came, a small unimpressive man for a Powindah who are often burly people, but he was as garrulous as all his tribe. We talked with him for some time before asking him about the Wazir boy. He seemed to ponder as to what sort of creature a Wazir boy might be, and denied all knowledge. He made as though to leave, but we detained him until the whole qafila had passed. We then told him we would exchange him for the Wazir, and that he must accompany us.

Protesting, he was lifted onto a horse, and we rode with him to a place outside the kirri. Leaving him with the MI and taking an escort, I rode into the encampment and explained our predicament, telling them that their headman would be exchanged for the Wazir boy. There was much indignation and a pantomime of injured innocence. Among the nomads stood the bulky figure of a Hindu merchant, dark-featured, dressed in black and armed to the teeth, a surprising and most vehement man. The argument continued and tempers became frayed, so I told them the encampment would have to be searched, and sent a galloper off to fetch the infantry gasht. After a tense wait, dots appeared spreading quickly out across the plain from the camp two miles away. It was not until the Powindahs saw that the gasht was moving towards us fast that an angry man produced the Wazir boy who was hidden in a nearby ravine. They were in no position to oppose us, but with tempers high there might have been an accident. Taking the Wazir boy, we released the disgruntled Malik at a suitable distance and retired.

A year later, in 1931, FitzMaurice was on Powindah gasht.

Thousands of Suliman Khel streaming up the Gumal. We were heavily fired on, 200 shots. The Suliman Khel said they were sorry, but they were excited and frightened. Leaving one platoon on high ground, I went down among the Suliman Khel with two platoons. I tried to find the Maliks to get an explanation for the firing. We took six or seven hostages but were surrounded by hundreds of excited

Suliman Khel who shouted at us to get out or a real battle would start. The situation looked ugly, and Khan Baz muttered, 'For God's sake, Sahib, let's get out of this quick.'

I sent off a pigeon message and dug in at Toi Kullah, leaving the Suliman Khel kirri in the Gumal. We were reinforced by Cosby and Draycott with six platoons at dusk. The Scouts took up a position astride the Gumal. There was a good deal of confusion and firing during the night and some Suliman Khel broke through. They were later stopped, for the loss of only one camel, by firing a Vicker's gun, brought out from Sarwekai, in long bursts across their bows.

The following day 'We baramptaed twenty-five Suliman Khel identified by Khan Baz and me. The PA was glad that we had not returned fire, as this would have caused a general conflagration.'

The word 'barampta', like 'gasht', is richly suggestive, almost onomatopoeic. It suggests a pounce, which indeed it is, in order to grab known hostiles, or hostages to be held until the tribe paid a fine levied on it, or livestock to be held in order to expedite a Jirga's deliberations.

Several platoons would set out at night, silent, wearing grass sandals, and surround the village before first light. When in the early morning the inhabitants came out to relieve themselves, the Scouts would stand up to show there was no escape. The next move in the game was for the village elders to emerge, their faces eloquent of bewilderment and injured innocence. Shaking hands with the Political Agent and senior Scouts officers, they would exchange the conventional greetings. 'May you not be tired . . . May you not be poor . . . Are you well? . . . Are you happy? . . . Is your disposition good?'

After these tender enquiries, 'But what have we poor villagers done? Why is the Militia surrounding our village?'

If the object was merely to round up some eminent citizens in order to give the Jirga a sense of urgency, there would be little trouble; the rules of the game were well understood: the hostages would come to no harm. The worst the Scouts could then expect was a horde of women screeching insults accompanied by unseemly gestures. 'Come on, rape us all now . . . you've taken our men, so you'd be quite safe . . . What are you waiting for? . . . Are you afraid of us? . . . Are you all eunuchs?' But if the quarry was a wanted man who had sought asylum with them, the village notables were obliged by the Pukhtunwali code at least to obstruct in every possible way, and a long argument would ensue.

Eventually it might be agreed that a British officer, a Scouts Subadar, a Khassadar and an Assistant Political Agent might conduct the search, 'of everywhere, Sahib, but the women's purdah quarters.'

'No. Of everywhere.'

There would be another long argument, and at last that would be conceded too, the women having been moved out and herded together apart from the men. It was dangerous, poking about in half-dark rooms, going through doors behind which there might well be a Ghazi dedicated to death and determined to take a Faranghi with him. But generally the bird had flown, or had never been there at all. Sometimes, however, the Scouts had a stroke of luck. There was a SWS officer, Major E. E. 'Balu' French, plump, pink-and-white, rather soft in appearance but hard as nails, a perfectionist with an eye for detail like a hospital matron's. ('One against nine hundred,' he would say of his efforts to make his Wing as methodical as himself.) On one barampta he cast an eye over the village damsels – and noticed one. 'Her feet beneath the petticoat like little mice peeped in and out': but these feet were far from little; they were suspiciously large. He insisted, against loud protests, that she unveil, which disclosed the bushy beard and well-known features of No. 3 on the Wanted List. Further investigation, on the same lines, disclosed several more wanted men. French's subalterns were impressed: they had not thought of him as a connoisseur.

Benjie Bromhead took part in a very complicated barampta in 1930 of the predatory Jalal Khel, in their winter quarters in the Mastang.

Ambrose with the main gasht would search the caves and collect any wanted individuals and livestock. A separate gasht under Gilbert would occupy the attention of the Jalal Khel in the Girni. A gasht under FitzMaurice was to cut across the high ground overlooking the junction of the Tormandu and Mastang nullahs. Lastly, I was to take a gasht up to the eastern end of the Girni Sar, separating the Jalal Khel in the Mastang from those in the Girni area. We were to be in position by dawn.

The following night we set off on our various ways in darkness and in complete silence, wearing grass chaplis. It was steep going and a climb of more than 2,000 feet, but we neared the top as dawn came into the sky. This was lucky, as a short distance from the top a length of cliff barred our way. The men made light of it, but I needed a hand crossing the narrow ledge, which would have been dangerous in the dark.

Our destination was a foot-track connecting the Mastang and the Girni. Above it and beyond was the narrow ridge which formed the crest of the cliffs of Girni Sar. Perched on this was a lonely shelter in which we found a greybeard and his ancient wife, and with them a minute cow like a Black Kerry. We left them in peace with a party to watch them and our flank, and ourselves settled across the pathway. Beneath us the Mastang was still dark, and far below to the east the plains stretched asleep like a pale sea.

Daylight spread slowly to the folds and valleys of the mountain. A track skirted the shoulder, and where this topped the crest a man stood. A spare man, bearded, his hair worn long to the nape of his neck, held loosely by a greasy black rag tied ropewise, his garments, once white, now so grey with dirt that they merged with the rock. He gazed downwards to where the hillside eased into the head of a narrow valley where water glinted. To one side lay a group of black tents, near them a circle of thorn hedge from whose protection sheep were slowly moving, shepherded by a boy whose cries rose to us. The man lifted his voice, cupping his hand, and shouted a long clear call. Soon figures appeared, gazing, their voices sharp and questioning. The man on the hill waved a cloth above his head and pointing eastwards with his rifle, arm outstretched, shouted 'Oh hee, Zarif Khan, the jackals have come. The Militia are round my village!'

The first sign that the search had started was the appearance of a Mahsud, gasping for breath, who ran up the steep path straight into our arms. We asked him why he was in such a hurry, and he answered bitterly, 'The jackals have come,' and spat, at which one of the men struck him across the face. We were cold, had spent a long night climbing, and were in no mood for insults.

In the Mastang Ambrose and the main gasht had taken the Jalal Khel by surprise. Ambrose, who was never at a loss when confronted by the opposite sex, while searching a cave had a greasy cloth hurled at him by an infuriated woman. He returned it to her, and it was thrown back with added venom. His orderly, not to be outdone in politeness, gave it back to her again, whereupon the poor woman collapsed in feminine hysterics.

There was no shooting, for the Jalal Khel had been caught off balance. The main gasht collected all the able-bodied men and livestock and started their retreat, slowed down by prisoners and animals.

The following morning Bromhead was on road-protection gasht.

We met a group of men making for the Mastang. One proved to be Khawas, the leading Malik of the Jalal Khel, who had been released by the PA to restrain the tribe from mischief. He was a strong, bearded man with the presence of a leader. After shaking hands and an exchange of greetings, he asked if I had taken part in the barampta and where I had been. On my pointing to the end of the cliff summit of the Girni Sar, he nodded, almost as if in approval, and then asked me not to patrol too close to the Mastang as feelings were high. He seemed satisfied that we were only there to protect the road, and left us, impressed by his personality.

The Ahmedzai Wazirs round Wana had taken to murdering loyal Maliks so the Political Agent instructed Nat Cosby, commanding the SWS, to barampta a village north of Wana and collect three wanted men.

At first light I put the MI in, to encircle the village, dismount and face inwards. I held the infantry in reserve. The wanted men were in a walled-in fort with large wooden doors. I approached the doors with the Naib* Tahsildar and called 'Open up!' From within someone asked, 'Who is in command?' and the Naib Tahsildar replied, 'Cosby Sahib. He wants Israr Gul, Sharif Ali and Hassan Gul.'

There was some muttering and Hassan Gul came out. I asked 'Where are the other two?' and after a little more delay, out came Sharif Ali. I asked, 'Where is Israr Gul?' They replied, 'He has gone out for the purposes of nature and not come back.' 'Right,' I said, 'then we'll break the door down.'

On this he emerged, came up to me and shook my hand which was holding a pistol and asked with much concern, *'Jor ye? Khushal ye?'†* This is all part of the game, understood by us all. Also always to stand back at the side of the door while talking to anyone inside, as they sometimes fire through the door. The men we took were unarmed, but where there are men, there are rifles, so our next job was to search the place. We looked in the roof and other usual hiding places, but drew blank. Then I stopped near a manger where some chickens were sitting, and a woman said to me, 'You wouldn't harm the poor chickens, Sahib.' I said, 'Search in that manger,' and the rifles were there all right, hidden under the hay. The three men were sentenced to imprisonment, and the murders ceased.

* A junior Political officer.
† 'Are you well? Are you happy?'

Scouts did not like baramptas, which were dangerous and always accompanied by a barrage of the foulest abuse from the women by which, oddly enough, Pathan officers were more abashed than British officers, perhaps because they understood more of it. One of the difficulties for British officers in Waziristan was the Mahsud, and to a lesser degree the Wazir, dialect. They had learned for examination purposes, the classical Pushtu – or, rather, Pakhtu – of Peshawar – or, rather, Pekhawur – which, with local variations, is spoken by the northern tribes, and perfectly understood by most Scouts. But not merely did Mahsuds and Wazirs turn *kh* into *sh*; they made many other consonants and vowel changes, and had innumerable words and expressions peculiar to themselves. With a little practice one could cope with one or two *mulaqatis* – men who came in with petitions, complaints or just to pass the time of day; but a Jirga was far more difficult, with disrespectful interruptions from citizens in the back row whose only object was to obstruct and annoy. However, even in a Jirga an officer usually had at his side an experienced, Mahsud-speaking Tahsildar or Subadar to whom he could turn if in difficulty. No such support was available in an altercation with a mob of screaming harridans: modesty forbade any translation of their remarks.

Lucky the officer who could reply in kind, but this was easier said than done. Pushtu is a language replete with unseemly proverbs and onomatapoea (*daz* is a shot, *poos* is a silent fart); but not only must he who aspires to answering back know the appropriate retort, he must know also the appropriate occasion to use it. To take an example, in purely male company one could observe cynically, '*Khuzza na takht ghwari, na bakht ghwari, kho ghain sakht ghwari*',* and be rewarded by Rabelaisian, male chauvinist chuckles. But such an observation directed at an infuriated virago in the presence of her male relatives might be one of those things which are better left unsaid. But some officers scored. Hugh Pettigrew, flagrantly improvising, silenced a screeching fury by bawling at her, 'Shut up, you pregnant old hen!' and Balu French demolished a contumacious Malik, who seemed to be getting the better of an argument, by the inspired throw-away line, 'Every man thinks his prick is as big as a carrot.'

Denis Ambrose, having served his apprenticeship in the SWS, went on to command the Tochi Scouts. He understood the strengths and limitations of Scouts; he was cool and clear-minded, but an opportunist. (He later made a fortune in the United States.) He was thought to

* 'A woman doesn't want a throne, and doesn't want good fortune, all she wants is … [something quite unmentionable in polite company]'

be rather unapproachable, but his Adjutant, Harry Garland, 'liked him very much. He was considerate, even though he really did work one extremely hard. He was perhaps the most efficient officer of that rank I ever met, and every moment of being his adjutant was tremendous fun, for he certainly kept me on my toes.'

He was determined to make the Tore Oba Ghilzais smart for shooting up a gasht, killing two and wounding three. Victor Wainright, commanding at Spinwam, reported that they were on their way back from India. 'Vewwy intewesting,' said Ambrose, 'Geoffwey [Keating] and I will do a gasht with you.'

He smoked like a chimney and took no conventional exercise other than a stroll round 'the Drill' or the gardens. But he led that gasht 'well over forty miles,' said Wainwright.

And when near the end I timed him, he was still doing 140 paces to the minute. There followed a Pathan officers' tikala. I, aged twenty-four, was fairly creased and ready for early bed. These two, nearly forty, were prepared to sit up all night with Denis Ambrose playing the piano, provided there was a bottle of champagne and a glass on it, preferably classical but anything (except bawdy) for anyone who wanted to sing.

The sequel to this gasht was a barampta on the Tore Oba which netted one hundred and fifty camels. But Ambrose was still not satisfied; he insisted on the Maliks making formal apology in the middle of a hollow square of Scouts. They were told that if they ever shot at a Tochi gasht again they would not get off so lightly. They never did.

Khassadars often accompanied gashts and assisted at baramptas. Their local knowledge was useful, but they were never made privy to plans beforehand. The most reliable, some would say the only reliable one, was Subadar of Khassadars in the Utmanzai Wazir country, Darim Khan, Manzar Khel, who had won the Indian Order of Merit with the Militia in 1915 and later the Croix de Guerre. Only once was he absent without leave, when the Afghans were toppling the unpopular usurper, Bacha Saquao. Darim then made his way to Kabul and returned with the jackpot – a Holland and Holland stalking-rifle, with telescopic sight, from the royal palace. Unfortunately it did not take ·303 ammunition, so he used to badger every officer to buy ·280 cartridges for him. He was a small man, tough and wiry, with an endearing habit of chuckling into his beard. With rifle slung, pistol low on his hip, knife-hilt to the right of his neck ready for a quick draw, he was a frequent visitor to the officer commanding Datta Khel post, bringing the latest news. He did not, like most tribesmen, prolong the visit *ad infinitum*; when he had had his say (always to the point) and drunk his tea, without waiting for 'the permission' he would get up abruptly and depart. For twenty-five years he was a tower of strength in North Waziristan, always ready with good advice, information and action, resisting with dauntless courage the complex political, religious and social pressures on a man in his position when war flared up in 1936. He hated, and was hated by, the Faqir of Ipi, the leading hostile. To his grief his son, Mohamad Khan, commonly known as 'Gingat' (Dung-beetle) was at variance with the Political Agent, and joined the lashkar which demanded the surrender of Darim's Khassadar post. In the course of an altercation, Gingat shot one of his cousins, whereupon Darim, lightning-quick on the draw, shot Gingat, but to wound, not to kill. Gingat was later reconciled to his father and to the Political Agent. One constantly reads in reports, 'Darim's opinion is that ... Darim's piqueting arrangements were very effective ... Owing to pressure brought by Darim, the outlaw Bararai came in to settle with the political authorities.' And so on.

Another good Khassadar was Ahwaz Khan, a hefty man with a permanent stubble on his chin. Of a Mahsud family who were hamsayas of the Tori Khel Wazirs, he got on well with both tribes. He spoke some English, and was popular with British troops who knew him as 'George'. One day he was escorting a three-car convoy from Bannu to Razmak when the second car was fired on, one officer, a sergeant and the driver being killed, and another officer wounded. 'George' at once stopped the leading car, which could have been driven to safety, and engaged the gang, defending the wounded officer until help arrived. On another occasion, when the Sappers had failed to defuse a 250-lb aircraft bomb placed to blow up a culvert, George tied his pagri round it and pulled it away. He was awarded the Albert Medal, later exchanged for the appropriately named George Medal. After being invested with it at Government House, he put on a sort of Jeeves act and bustled round handing out cigarettes and drinks. With all the appearance of a cheerful rogue, he was a brave and honest man.

10

A Sort of Peace, 1930–6

In the early 1930s a certain complacency about the Frontier became discernible, an almost reluctant belief that, with planes, light armour, improved mountain artillery, a higher scale of light machine-guns, the scales were so heavily weighted against him that the poor old Pathan would be reduced to a little long-range sniping. A pity, really, but that was progress. The events of the next decade were to correct these ideas. Keen young officers who were disappointed that the Frontier was not all it was cracked up to be, discovered that indeed it was.

The trouble originated in British India, in the prosperous districts of Peshawar, Nowshera and Kohat. In 1929 an organisation was formed called the Frontier Youth League which soon adopted a type of political uniform then fashionable and became known as Redshirts. Ostensibly dedicated to social and religious improvement, in fact it was highly seditious and tried to set up a parallel administration, levying its own taxes and setting up its own courts to punish, with fines and flogging, breaches of its own law. Its leaders were Abdul Ghaffar Khan and his brother, Dr Khan Sahib, formerly a Medical Officer of the Guides. In 1930 the Redshirts were responsible for savage rioting in Peshawar city, during which an armoured car and its occupants were incinerated. The movement never really caught on in Tribal Territory, because it was incongruously affiliated to the Hindu-dominated Congress, but there were Congress propagandists among the tribes, and hostile lashkars occasionally sported Congress flags. The Afridis and Mamunds, a small tough tribe from the mountains north of Peshawar, took advantage of the situation to come down to the outskirts of Peshawar, invade the Government Supply Depot and mine roads.

Although it was well outside their area, the Scouts became involved. The Inspecting Officer Frontier Corps, Colonel Scott, was one of a law-and-order quadrumvirate in Peshawar; he sent for Nat Cosby to act as his staff officer, and for detachments of the Tochi Scouts, SWS and Kurram Militia. Cosby wrote:

When I arrived in Peshawar, it was panic stations. The DC, a young ICS fellow, could not face up to opposition. The Brigade Commander didn't know how to cope. At the conference it was my boss, the IOFC, a tough old bird, and the Inspector General of Police who got things going on the right lines. One evening the IOFC greeted me with, 'Pack your pyjamas. We've got to spend the night at Government House.' On arrival we found a regular arsenal of weapons on the billiards table. However, the night passed quietly.

One lashkar settled itself in a deep ravine, the Zhindai Khwar, honeycombed with caves, just inside Tribal Territory close to a village called Palli. A composite force of two hundred rifles of the SWS, half Bhitannis, half Bangash, and one hundred of the Kurram Militia was sent to eject them and to barampta Palli village, all under command of Colonel Scott.

Benjie Bromhead accompanied the SWS detachment, as second-in-command to Felix Williams.

We moved into a separate bivouac on the bank of the Swat Canal, a pleasant shady place. With us was old Colonel Scott, a tough leathery man to whom comfort mattered little.

On the second night we set out. I was to lead the night march, assisted by two guides. We had been going some time when, from a flank, a bugle, atrociously played, brayed its warning. We stopped for a moment and Colonel Scott, who was deaf, asked loudly why we had halted. We went on, and when the guides showed a tendency to loiter, we knew we must be nearing Palli.

We came to the edge of a steep-sided ravine and were about to find a way down when below us a party of tribesmen scudded past, silent as a shoal of fish, grey shapes in the moonlight. Our orders were not to fire till we were in position. I hesitated, but as Colonel Scott appeared again demanding loudly why we had halted, we slid down the steep slope into the ravine. We were climbing the far bank when fire was opened from ahead, and the men made haste to reach the top, a natural reaction, but old man Scott laid about him with a walking-stick, disapproving such undue haste.

On arriving at the top, Felix went ahead with his party, making for the hills north of Palli, and my party swung right to make for the Zhindai Khwar. Almost at once Felix was fired on from behind a stone wall, but he and his men charged and quickly routed their opponents. About the same time the detachment of the Kurram Militia, who had remained at the ravine which we had just crossed, opened fire on another party of escaping tribesmen. We carried on to the Zhindai Khwar, which appeared a dark chasm at our feet.

Leaving the Bhitannis to cover us, with a platoon of Bangash we scrambled down a steep track into the chasm. It was almost dark and we were glad to find a track which led us out on to the far side. We climbed out and made for a small ridge ahead, the highest ground visible. Beyond lay the village of Palli, a tumble of low houses, and to the north the hill which Felix Williams and his party had occupied, dominating the area at long range.

The Bhitannis followed, and from the depths of the ravine came the sound of firing, echoing and reverberating within its cliffs. My heart sank, but their leading files emerged looking well pleased with themselves, followed by the rest with a handful of prisoners.

The prisoners were placed under the eye of a young Bhitanni sentry in a hollow just below the skyline, and we lay waiting for the daylight. The Bhitannis were in position facing Palli, while the Bangash guarded our flanks. The ground was devoid of cover, and soon from a row of caves in the cliff-side below the village fire was opened on us. It was difficult to see the offenders, so we held our fire. There was a noise from the prisoners behind and, turning, I saw the young Bhitanni sentry with rifle raised, pointing at these unfortunates. He was told to behave himself, and remarked innocently that as we couldn't see the enemy who were firing at us, he might as well frighten those he could see. A Bhitanni nearby said, 'There's a Mahsud!' and fired. It was curious that to him Mahsud and enemy were synonymous: the only Mahsuds anywhere near were two platoons of Kurram Militia.

Nyaz Gul, the Bhitanni Jemadar, then raced to an outcrop of rock facing the caves. It was a brave act, and he ran back unscathed to point out which of the caves the firing was coming from. So we fired on its dark interior and the sniping ceased. There was a pause, and a long silence.

At a point below the village the Zhindai Khwar took a bend and part of the ravine was visible. A wounded tribesman lay in this patch of ground and the Bhitannis, still equating the poor fellow with their Mahsud enemies, said callously, 'He will die.' In any case we were in no position to risk lives to save him.

A figure slid out from the dark doorway of a house on the opposite side of the ravine, bearded like an Assyrian with the appearance of a priest. A Bhitanni, a naive young barbarian, asked, 'May we shoot him?' to which the old Bangash Subadar with some asperity gave an avuncular 'No', and as if aware of the danger, the figure slipped back into the shadow of his door.

We shouted to our opponents in the caves to come out and surrender. After a time a small party emerged and stood on a ledge beneath the caves, whence a track ran up to the village. We called to them that if they surrendered, they would not be harmed. Foolishly they fled up the path into the village and appeared on the far side, making for the skyline. They were all shot down except for one man who disappeared over the ridge. For a moment there was silence, then a volley from the Kurram Militia.

After that the sun grew hotter, and as nothing appeared to be happening, I went in search of Colonel Scott's headquarters, taking a small escort and leaving the Bangash Subadar in charge. We found the HQ with old Colonel Scott sprawled in the hot sun on a slab of rock. It would have baked the hide off a lesser man, but he was unconcerned and seemed to enjoy the heat. After we had exchanged what information there was, I returned to the ridge where there was a general air of a rather hot summer outing. After what seemed an interminable wait we were given permission to withdraw, taking our prisoners and one or two wounded tribesmen.

With the lashkars dispersed, the Scouts returned to Waziristan, leaving the Police to deal with the Redshirts whose movement soon faded away.

There was a close relationship between the RAF, later the Indian Air Force, and the Scouts. Scouts officers often flew as observers, and RAF officers rather less frequently took part in gashts. At Miranshah there was an airfield with a resident Flight Officer for liaison with Scouts, and a duty pilot always on stand-by to help a gasht in trouble, Tochi Scouts, Kurram Militia or SWS. So efficient were communications – a carrier pigeon from gasht to fort, thence by telephone or radio to Miranshah –

that within half an hour of calling for help a gasht could expect a plane overhead.

The Bristol Fighter and Wapiti, later the Audax, biplanes were ideal for the job. They were slow enough for the pilot to stooge round, using little petrol, until he spotted the enemy, strafe them with his fixed machine-gun firing forward, and then swing up and away while the observer had a go over the side. Few tribesmen were killed, but the gasht was encouraged.

If a troublesome village had to be bombed, white leaflets were dropped over it some days before warning the inhabitants of wrath to come on a certain date; the day before the bombing, red leaflets were dropped, and the inhabitants then departed. When it was all over they came back and repaired the damage which, with those small bombs, was not very heavy. No lives were lost, but much inconvenience caused.

The biggest problem was in ground-air communications: a plane could drop a written message, but a gasht could not throw one up. Every section carried two white cotton strips about nine feet long and eighteen inches wide. The sections nearest the enemy, and none other, could spread these in a simple code, viz:

X   No enemy action

>   Am being fired on from direction of point of V

+   Am in dire danger from direction of cross of T, justifying pilot risking his life and aircraft. (Only used when under heavy close range attack.)

In addition, a gasht headquarters usually carried the Popham Panel, a canvas screen which would be spread on the ground with its black and white panels arranged in patterns in a simple code conveying such messages as 'Send ammunition ... water ... Very lights ... medical assistance'.

The best work done by these planes was the dropping, often with improvised equipment, of all kinds of supplies from ammunition and Very lights for a gasht surrounded on a hilltop in the evening, to oysters on ice from Peshawar Club, wrapped in a Lilo mattress, dropped on Biche Kashkai post on Christmas Day. The Tochi Scouts devised a sort of flying haybox in which hot curry and chupattis could be dropped, very welcome to a gasht benighted in winter.

They were used for many other jobs. 'Lotus' Lowis, Assistant Political Agent, Wana in the 1930s, made good use of a plane when the Zilli Khel Mahsuds defied the Political Agent's order not to graze their flocks in British India. From the air he spotted the trespassers, and then directed the SWS on to them. 'Gashts seized 948 sheep, 8 shepherds, 2 rifles.' Two days later, 'Put Skrine's gasht on to 1,200 sheep the other side of Spiro Khan hill. Gasht got them all.' Without a plane, the gasht would never have seen them. Holding these sheep, they could make the Zilli Khel pay a fine. 'Very good effect on Zilli Khel. The Brigadier, Wana, severely criticised me for cruelty to the sheep, but he still plays squash with me.'

The Political Agent was said to be the man who stood between the soldier and his medal. The Political Department (afterwards known as the Indian Political Service) was recruited two-thirds from the Indian Army and one-third from the Indian Civil Service. As District Commissioners they ran the settled districts of the North-West Frontier Province; they ran Baluchistan; they staffed the trans-Frontier Agencies. Most of them knew the ABC of soldiering, and many had distinguished military records in the First World War. But they were naturally inclined to be biased in favour of *their* Mahsuds and *their* Wazirs, against the brutal and licentious soldiery, if only because the entry of the Army on to the scene implied that the situation had gone beyond the Political Agent's control. Scouts officers to some extent adopted the Politicals' viewpoint: they, after all, had to live and gasht and mix with yesterday's enemy after the soldiers had departed.

The head of the political hierarchy on the Frontier resided in Peshawar. He wore two hats: he was Chief Commissioner (in 1932 upgraded to Governor) of the cis-Frontier districts, but in his dealings with Tribal Territory he was Agent to the Governor General (AGG), having under him the Resident, Waziristan, established in Dera Ismail Khan, and Political Agents for North Waziristan in Miranshah, South Waziristan in Tank, and the Kurram in Parachinar. Under the Political Agents were Assistant Political Agents, in Wana, Sararogha and Miranshah. Assistant Political Agents and upward were commissioned officers if they came from the Army, or covenanted members of the Indian Civil Service. Below them were Tahsildars and Assistant Political Officers. Before the 1914–18 war the Political Agents and the Assistant Political Agents had all been British; after it, an increasing number were Pathans and a few were Indians. The Tahsildars and Assistant Political Officers were all Pathans, but from a different part of the Frontier to that in which they served. There was a similar set-up in Baluchistan. The Political Agents of the Kurram, North Waziristan, South Waziristan and the Zhob each had an irregular corps under his general direction, but not under his operational command. In simple terms, he told the Scouts or Militia what he wanted done but not how to do it, though the precise relations between them depended, of course, largely on personalities. It was not uncommon for a Scouts officer to officiate as Assistant Political Agent.

One of the most celebrated Frontier politicals was 'Bunch' Parsons, who after six years in the North Waziristan Militia became Political Agent, South Waziristan. There he won a DSO and was badly wounded guiding RAF bombers to hostile villages which they could never have identified without him.

The job of a Political in Waziristan was as dangerous as that of a Scouts officer. Since he must not seem to fear or distance himself from his tribes, he seldom went about his work with Scout or military escort. Normally he was escorted only by Khassadars or tribal badraggas and he could never be certain that they would provoke a blood-feud by defending him against their fellow-tribesmen. The Pukhtunwali code to some extent protected him, since he was usually surrounded by Wazirs or Mahsuds in the role of his hosts. But Mahsuds in particular were notorious for flouting the code. In times of peace, an orderly and a couple of badraggas in the car sufficed for escort, but when tensions were high, as they were in the late 1930s, a Political travelled about with a whole lorry-load of Khassadars. With everyone armed to the teeth, a rose behind the ear, with music and song, the tour of an Assistant Political Agent could be quite a carnival progress.

'Lotus' Lowis, deciding one day that his escort needed exercise, stopped the lorry on a level piece of ground and told them to pick sides for an improvised game of football, refereed by their Jemadar. The referee had not the haziest idea of the rules; when these were briefly explained to him, he made a quick assessment, slipped the whistle into his pocket and strapped on a heavy automatic pistol. Someone must have told him about football 'fans'.

A good Political Agent or Assistant Political Agent spent a great part of his time just talking or listening to tribesmen. Twice a year he had to pay Maliks their allowances at informal, often light and jocular, 'Allowance Jirgas'. The Mahsuds alone had thirty Allowance Jirgas, each attended by up to two dozen Maliks, every one of whom felt he had a right to a private talk with the Political Sahib after the Jirga. In addition there were *mulaqatis* ('mole-cats'), tribesmen who waited on him with petitions or complaints, demands for road or firewood contracts, or just to pass the time of day and to receive a few rupees remuneration on what was, the Political Agent hoped, a generally understood and accepted scale, graded according to each man's importance. Political Agents' diaries are full of such items as 'sixteen mole-cats at office this afternoon', or 'a dozen mole-cats waiting for me at Boya'. This was tiring beyond words: only someone who has spent a long day listening to a Mahsud visitor 'will understand the exhaustion which comes from resistance to his importunings, the effort required to meet his plausibility, even the struggle to match his wit'.* This exhaustion was a factor in Frontier affairs: it meant that only a very exceptional Political Agent, such as Robert Warburton, half Afghan, could remain in one posting for more than about three years, which was hardly long enough to get to know the tribes. But this endless talk, arguing, warily fencing, was absolutely necessary, both to keep his finger on the pulse of the tribes, and to obtain intelligence about the tribes on which Scouts and Army relied.

Broadly speaking, a tribesman could (so far as the Government was concerned) do pretty well what he liked in Tribal Territory so long as he did not do it to Government servants. But there were limits. If a crime was committed in an Army cantonment (Razmak or Wana), or within five hundred yards of a road, or if a non-Pathan was involved, then the case was tried by the Political Agent or his Assistant sitting as a Magistrate, under the Indian Penal Code, the Criminal Procedure Code and the Frontier Crimes Regulations, and sentences up to fourteen years' imprisonment could be awarded. If there was not sufficient evidence for a Court, then the case could be referred to a Jirga. If a crime was committed within a Protected Area (roughly five miles round an Army cantonment or Scouts' post), then again the case was referred to a Jirga. 'Referring to a Jirga' meant framing the charge and referring it to about four Assessors of the Accused's own tribe, for trial either by the Shariat (Moslem Law) or by Rewaj (Tribal custom). Four or five specific questions would be put to the Assessors, e.g. Did A shoot B? Where? When? Why? What recommendations do you make?

The Assessors, representing the Jirga, might consider the Accused guilty and recommend a fine of, say, 5,000 rupees. If he paid up, well and good. If not, then his livestock, or the livestock of his family or section, might be baramptaed. If there was insufficient evidence against an individual, or he took a hundred oaths of innocence, or had departed to Afghanistan, then the Political Agent would fine his family or section, ordering a barampta if they failed to pay up.

The barampta might be a complex operation of a dozen platoons with cordon, covering party, reserve and search-party to round up the tribe's

* Sir Olaf Caroe, *The Pathans*, page 404.

eminent citizens who would not be released until the case was concluded, and whose relatives would use their influence with the Jirga to
expedite proceedings. Or it might not amount to more than a platoon
driving a flock of goats into the post perimeter and telling the goat-boys,
'Be off, now, and tell your dads the Militia are very hungry. They'll eat a
goat a day until the Jirga settle the case.' The holding of livestock on
rapidly diminishing grazing wonderfully concentrated the Jirga's
mind.

A blockade might be imposed, cutting off an offending tribe from its
trade with British India or preventing its annual migration to winter
grazing. Only if all these failed, would the Army mount a punitive
operation; or the RAF bomb the fortified towers of the offender.

Essentially the Scouts' job was to lend muscle to the Political Agent's
wishes. For an example of how it worked, take the case of the murder of
Captain Roy Beatty, an officer of the Tochi Scouts acting as Assistant
Political Agent in North Waziristan.

In 1936 a Madda Khel Wazir named Zawel was flogged by the
Afghan authorities for robbery, taunted with robbing only Moslems,
and challenged to try his courage on a Faranghi. Smarting under this
treatment, he collected a gang of seven Madda Khel worse than himself,
ascertained when Beatty would be taking the Khassadars' pay and laid
an ambush at a sharp bend in the road where the car must slow down.
Beatty and two of his escort were killed, one Khassadar and his clerk
wounded. By the time his escorting Khassadar lorry arrived, Zawel and
his gang had got away with 32,000 rupees, three rifles and a revolver.

The Political Agent then went into action. First he laid on a Scout
barampta which netted ninety eminent Madda Khel. Then he called
upon the Jirga to hand over the gang. Meanwhile he held in his hand a
strong card: in 1934 one hundred Madda Khel rifles had been taken
from them as surety for good conduct for one year. In 1935, 1936 and
1937 the Madda Khel's conduct had been far from good, so the hundred
rifles, held as surety, were then confiscated; but the Jirga complained of
sharp practice by the Sarkar and, after some argument, the Political
Agent conceded that the rifles would not be confiscated but would
continue to be held as surety for good behaviour. There they were, still
in the Bannu armoury, available if the Government thought it politic to
use the carrot rather than the stick.

Under pressure from the relatives of the hostages taken in the
barampta, and stimulated by air-action against the villages which were
harbouring the gang, the Jirga brought to trial the three least important
members. But prosecution witnesses failed to turn up, the three

accused took a hundred oaths of innocence and were released. Zawel and the other four, said the Jirga, were in Afghanistan. Forty of the hostages were released, but fifty more rifles were taken as surety for a final settlement. This settlement eventually comprised a fine of 25,000 rupees, as well as the return of the 32,000 rupees which had been stolen, plus fifty more rifles. Madda Khel timber contractors paid most of the money and those hundred rifles, taken in 1934, were accepted as payment of the balance. The remaining hostages were then released.

Often affairs were complicated by the action of the Afghan authorities who were seldom conspicuously helpful. In 1937 a gasht of Tochi Scouts, infantry and Mounted Infantry, under Denis Ambrose and Balu French, escorted the Resident, Waziristan, Colonel 'Bunch' Parsons, on a tour of his parish. To make a point, they went right up to the Durand Line and were there fired upon, from across the border, by Tannis, an Afghan tribe, and by Dawegar Saidgis on the Indian side. It was a time when it seemed particularly important not to annoy the Afghans, so the gasht prudently withdrew with only a couple of men wounded.

Delhi then sent a strong protest to Kabul; Kabul replied with regrets that the esteemed Colonel Parsons had been incommoded and 'proof' that the Scouts had invaded Afghanistan, massacring, wounding and raping peaceful citizens. To avoid such deplorable events in future, suggested the 'God-given Government', would it not be wise for the Afghan authorities to be given prior notice of every military force approaching the Durand Line? For obvious reasons, it would not. His Britannic Majesty's Ambassador in Kabul then weighed in with some unhelpful observations, implying that he swallowed the Afghan case hook, line and sinker; it was decided, therefore, that nothing more would be done about the Tannis. The Dawegai Saidgis, however, a small tribe not usually obstreperous, had been downright impertinent. So they were blockaded, cut off from all trade with India, their livestock prevented from moving to greener pastures, until the culprits were tried by the Jirga and duly acquitted after taking oaths of innocence. Eventually the tribe was punished by a fine of 500 rupees – hardly vindictive.

It was a curious way to run a turbulent frontier, and not one that would have been followed by Russians or Americans. But it worked – in a sort of way.

It was obvious that no Scouts post could fall to tribesmen armed only with rifles unless the garrison was treacherous or amazingly incom-

1. (*left*), Captured Zhob raiders

2. (*below*), Raw material for the Zhob Militia, Baluchi tribesmen *c.* 1900

3. A Wazir Malik

4. The South Waziristan Militia *c*. 1905

5. South Waziristan Scouts: two Pathan officers with signalling flags on gasht, overlooking the Gumal River

6. (*left*), Tochi Scouts: puddling mud for building

7. (*below left*), South Waziristan Scouts Mounted Infantry, in a hurry

8. (*right*), Gilgit Scouts: 'Meat on the Hoof,' a *shapu* bagged on gasht

9. (*below*), The Wakhan side of the Kotgaz Pass

10. (*above*), The Officers' Mess at Jandola

11. (*left*), Subadar Amir Shah, Orakzai, dancing for joy at the news of his promotion

12. (*above right*), Datta Khel Fort

13. (*right*), South Waziristan Scouts using 'Walkie-talkie' sets

14. Tochi Scouts, with two Sapper officers in attendance demolishing the headquarters of the Faqir of Ipi near Arsal Kot

petent. It was equally obvious that enemy artillery could make any garrison very uncomfortable. Mahsuds and Wazirs saw the point and showed great ingenuity in acquiring from Afghanistan or manufacturing simple artillery pieces firing solid shot and, later, high explosive shells. One of the earliest of these pieces was Sadde Khan's gun.

Sadde Khan was a Shabi Khel Mahsud, a semi-professional hostile, ambitious to extend his influence. Early in 1930 he commissioned the Kaniguram armourers to construct a gun which would demolish any Scouts post and drive the Faranghi out of Waziristan. It was a breech-loader of 2¾ ins bore, firing a 9-lbs solid iron shot about nine inches long with a copper driving-band to take the barrel's rifling. It was fired by a ·303 blank cartridge which ignited a black-powder charge. Barrel, carriage and wheels were detachable and could be loaded on to camels.

Attracted by this gun and stimulated by Congress propaganda that the Scouts were ripe for mutiny and the Army wholly committed to a war against freedom fighters in India, there assembled a sizeable lashkar under three well-known Mahsud hostiles, Gulin, Khaisor and Ramzan; and, of course, Sadde Khan himself. It included the Jalal Khel Khassadar company, but the Mahsud tribe was by no means united in its support; the Khassadars of Ladha fired on the lashkar, the Abdullai of Makin told it to move along; and when it announced its intention of blowing up an important road bridge, the women of the Shabi Khel sat on the bridge until the lashkar went away. They would not, they said, have their houses destroyed just to please Gulin. The lashkar, however, advanced on Sararogha.

Sararogha squatted on a plateau amid its wire entanglements with something of the solidity and menace of Krak des Chevaliers, the great Crusader castle in Syria. Eastward it frowned down a 500-foot cliff on to the vegetable gardens and pumping station beside the Tank Zam and to the hills beyond. Upstream, to the north-west, there was a view up the Barari Tangi between steep khud-sides and precipices, beyond which were higher, wooded mountains. Downstream, a long rifle-shot from the fort, was a higher ridge on which a stone blockhouse deterred any ill-wisher from sniping at the football ground, parade ground or landing-strip. Further to the south a succession of ridges and ravines stretched down to Jandola, fifteen miles away and 1,800 feet lower. The country around was not a no-go area, but the Mahsuds were far from friendly, and gashts had to watch what they were about.

The garrison consisted of three British officers, Captains Felix-Williams, FitzMaurice and Horace Dracott; three company commanders, Subadars Ghulam Haidar, Swati, Khan Baz, Malik Din Khel Afridi, and Umar Din, Bangi Khel Khattak; nine platoons (374 rifles) of trained Scouts, and eighty-two recruits. The civil authority was represented by the Assistant Political Agent, Captain Abdur Rahim Khan, and the Tahsildar. About a mile to the west was the Langar Khel piquet, a stone-built tower, garrisoned by Havildar Gul Dar and twelve Malik Din Khel sepoys.

Already messages wrapped round stones had been thrown into the Scouts' latrines promising rewards, in this world and the next, if they handed over their Officers. On the evening of 6 July 1930 a Shabi Khel Malik warned Williams that the lashkar was near; if he lied, he said, the Sahib could take revenge on his sons who were in Sararogha. At eight-thirty that evening the telephone wires were cut, and later the Sararogha Khassadar post was attacked. Its commander, Gulgai, brother of the local Malik Shah Bahram, was wounded, but killed a Wazir lashkarwal and wounded the enemy commander, Ramzan. (Later he was obliged to pay compensation for the death of the Wazir — such were the vagaries of war in Waziristan.) The Khassadars were withdrawn and the post was burnt.

At daybreak on 7 July about six hundred hostiles were in position on all the high ground around the fort. Two patrols slipped out of the chiga gate, searched the nearby nullahs but drew blank. They were not fired at, but were called upon to hand over their officers, in particular Khan Baz; if they did so, they would be allowed to depart in peace. A gathering was seen about 1,600 yards away being addressed by a Mullah in white, and scattered by a burst of machine-gun fire.

Williams and the Assistant Political Agent were faced with the difficult problem of what to do about the Mahsud loyalists in and around Sararogha. They were a mixed bunch, including a reformed outlaw nicknamed Parang (Leopard), Khassadar Subadar Gul Rakhman, Malik Shah Bahram, and an extinct military volcano of immense distinction, Honorary Captain and retired Subadar Major Mir Badshah Khan, MVO, IOM, one-time Aide-de-Camp to His Royal Highness the Duke of Connaught. Prudence and a knowledge of frontier history argued that every Mahsud should be cleared out from every building close to the fort, and from Malik Shah Bahram's village on the cliff-top opposite. But this would mortally offend influential loyalists and might well turn them into furious rebels. A factor to be considered was that Shah Bahram's brother, Gulgai, was lying wounded in the civil hospital and his children had been brought in for safety. Moreover it would be of great political value if eminent Mahsuds were seen to be fighting against the lashkar. The eventual decision was to trust them. Ten, including Gul Rakhman and Parang, would hold the thick-walled school, easily covered from the fort, and the remainder would hold Shah Bahram's village and the adjacent caves. The decision was amply justified. Not only did they hold their positions, but throughout the siege they supplied the Assistant Political Agent with accurate information about enemy movements and intentions.

The RAF bombed and strafed the enemy many times. The bombing was disconcerting to those unaccustomed to it, but the tribesmen learned to watch and shoot at the planes until the bombs were released, and then dive for cover.

The night of 7–8 July was spent by the enemy in taking out the Khassadar posts in the neighbourhood. As these were not supposed to stand up to serious attack, one after another was evacuated; most of the Khassadars withdrew in good order to Shah Bahram's village. Half-hearted attacks on Langar Khel piquet and on the village were beaten off without difficulty. More serious was an attempt on the pump-house, in the vegetable gardens four hundred yards from the fort. In a long siege in hot weather its loss could have been serious. Controlled fire was aimed at it when hammering on the door was heard, and the enemy retired without doing much damage.

The tribesmen still based their hopes on the 'Militia' defecting, and during the night they again called upon them to hand over their officers. 'We can't hear you,' replied Khan Baz. 'Come a little closer so that we can talk properly.' Imprudently they approached close enough for a well-aimed volley from the walls, and retired cursing Afridi perfidy.

Next morning, 8 July, a party of twelve was seen coming up the road. Luckily they were recognised as Khassadars, and sent to join the garrison at Shah Bahram's village. Another large gathering was seen being harangued by a man in a blue shirt. The Assistant Political Agent sent out Gul Rakhman, Parang and three others to find out who they were and what they were up to. Back came word that they were lashkarwals, so at the next opportunity they were machine-gunned. Blue-shirt and another were seen to fall, and Williams earned good marks from the Mahsuds by allowing them to be carried away. In the middle of the scorching afternoon, the Assistant Political Agent's orderly bravely carried Very lights and snuff to the isolated garrison of Langar Khel piquet who had signalled their need of them. Throughout the day all those not on guard carried out normal training in the morning and played basketball in the afternoon. Morale was very high.

At stand-to in the evening a Congress flag was planted about eight hundred yards from the fort and numerous tribal standards were seen on the hillsides, such as had not appeared for fifteen years. They were, perhaps, an indication that the Mahsuds regarded the siege as more of a propaganda exercise than as a serious operation of war, and were relying mainly on the 'Militia' changing sides. The enemy was estimated as anything up to 20,000; Williams thought there were about 5,000, of whom not more than half would be armed with modern rifles, and the rest hoping to acquire them.

Captain Abdur Rahim, the Assistant Political Agent, heard during the day that Sadde Khan's gun had now arrived. He also received a sketch-map of the fort, showing the sectors which would be stormed by various Mahsud sections and the Wazirs – the signal for the assault being the first shot from the great gun. At last light several camels were seen approaching and it was surmised that they carried the gun. At ten o'clock that evening Parang and a Malik who had been sent out to reconnoitre reported that the gun had actually been mounted where the Congress flag had been, and that a large crowd had collected to see the fun. They were dispersed by Very lights and controlled rifle- and machine-gun fire. There was a lot of shouting from outside the wire, and one loud-mouthed fellow kept calling, 'You've put up a good fight. Now come out!' Subadar Umar Din directed a section's fire at the loud voice of which no more was heard. 'You have your answer,' he shouted.

At eleven o'clock there was a reverberating boom and a hurroosh overhead: Sadde Khan's gun was in action. Sniping redoubled, and the garrison awaited the assault. A second shot, better aimed, smashed into the wireless room. A third, and a fourth, followed. Disclosed by its flash, the gun was engaged by machine-guns and did not fire again that night. The assault, for which the garrison had been eagerly waiting, did not take place.

Next morning, 9 July, the patrol moving out of the chiga gate was heavily sniped and had to return until the first planes appeared overhead and engrossed the tribesmen's attention. The patrol went out again, and succeeded in locating the gun in a new position, a sangared cave 1,600 yards north of the fort. The area was bombed and machine-gunned, but Sadde Khan's gun had fired its last shot; some failure in the breech-block mechanism, or an overcharge of powder, had prevented it from locking, and the block had been blown back through the master gunner's stomach.

That was really the end of the siege. The destruction of the great gun and the realisation that the 'Militia' had no intention of defecting took the heart out of the lashkar, which had shown less than the usual

Mahsud determination. During the night of 9–10 July it disappeared. As for Sadde Khan's gun, it was hauled into Jandola and set up on the lawn outside the Officers' Mess.

It had not been much of a siege. The greatest loss was of fruit and vegetables consumed by the enemy somewhat unripe, and of fruit-trees damaged. But the point was made that the South Waziristan Scouts of 1930 were a very different corps from the Militia of 1919. Their victory was celebrated in a lavish feast provided by the Resident, Waziristan.

About the same time the Tochi Scouts post at Datta Khel was also attacked. Years later Subadar Aman Gul, who had been a young Naik there, told Terence Philips about it.

Subadar Sayed, Afridi, was in command, and Faujoon, Yusufzai, was second-in-command. Sayed was in the garden talking to the gardener when a Madda Khel informer came running in and said, 'Close the gates and stand-to. A lashkar is upon you.' Sayed hurried back to the fort and the gates were closed with a bang. At the same time some five hundred armed men were seen running towards the fort from the rifle-range. There was no time to close the gaps in the wire, and the last man of the garrison had only just time to get in through the chiga gate when the lashkar surged in a wave up to the walls. It all happened so quickly that the guards hardly had time to take post and the chiga-platoon was still falling in. There was a babble of yells, 'Let us in! We're all Pathans and Mussulmans. Give up the fort!' They began beating with poles on the gate and all heaving against it so that it started to bulge inwards. Subadar Sayed was warning them that he would open fire when a plane appeared overhead. Either someone inside the fort found the strain too much and fired or else one of the lashkar fired at the plane. Instantly a hail of rifle-fire swept the packed mass outside the gate, and those who could run made off through the wire. The space between the wire and the wall was a shambles. The Wazirs left thirty dead, and carried off nobody knows how many wounded.

11

A Sort of War, 1935–7

The Redshirt movement throve in the settled areas on the frustration of being denied the limited self-government which other provinces of India enjoyed. In 1935 this was granted, and in 1937 the North-West Frontier Province attained full provincial self-government, including responsibility for law and order, the Chief Minister being Dr Khan Sahib, brother of the Redshirt leader. He had no responsibility for the trans-Frontier tribes, and did not interfere with their administration; but the spectacle of a Pathan as Chief Minister, giving orders to British District Commissioners, was an unsettling one.

In 1935 there was trouble among the Bajaur and Mohmand tribes north of Peshawar, necessitating two operations against them which eventually sucked in four brigade groups. It was noted for a sharp defeat inflicted by the Mohmands at Wucha Jawar on one of the best Frontier battalions, the Guides (5/12 Frontier Force Regt) who in two hours lost three-quarters of the company-and-a-half engaged. The Pathan evidently still had a bite in him.

The Scouts were not involved in these campaigns, which were well outside their area, and the numerous Mohmands in the Scouts remained loyal throughout. The decision was made that they should go on leave and furlough as and when it was due. Indeed the South Waziristan Scouts Subadar Major Manawar Khan, a Mohmand, on his return from the Jubilee of King George V was sent on special leave to learn the story of Wucha Jawar from the Mohmand point of view.

There were certain features common to all Frontier campaigns. The first was that in the end the Sarkar was bound to win; it was unthinkable that it should fail to defeat a few thousand tribesmen and compel them to pay for their misdeeds and to submit to their country being opened up by a road. Both sides knew this perfectly well. The tribesmen could not win, but they could make victory so expensive for the Sarkar that no attempt would be made to occupy permanently their homelands and govern them. The Mahsuds, Wazirs, Afridis, Orakzais and Mohmands did just that; their achievement was to be left more or less alone for a hundred years.

It was important that the butcher's bill should not be too high. British public opinion might accept a thirty per cent casualty rate when the stake was national survival, but not when the stake was pushing a road through the Khaisora valley. To minimise casualties, tactics were adopted of which the common feature was that they were very time-consuming. One was 'crowning the heights' or piqueting, already described; another was the perimeter camp into which every brigade column crammed itself at night.

Early in the afternoon the day's march came to an end. Protected by piquets all round, colour parties marked out their unit lines, packed together as close as possible, and a staff officer marked out the perimeter. Each unit moved into its allotted space and set to work, with all haste, digging its own sector of the perimeter ditch and building the stony soil into a bullet-proof wall some four feet high. Then each man dug himself a hole or built himself a sangar in which to sleep; only the camels, horses and mules were without some protection. Before night-fall all sentries were posted, some piquets called in, machine-guns set on fixed lines, and the brigade stood-to, each man in the place he would occupy in the event of an attack. In fact an attack against machine-guns and rifles firing at point-blank range was most unlikely. Instead there could be sniping, light or heavy, all through the night. It was a waste of time to reply to this, except perhaps with the fixed-line machine-guns, but the snipers might sometimes be stalked or ambushed. In general all the column could do was put up with it, lying in their shallow pits while bullets cracked overhead, whined away after a ricochet, or occasionally thudded into an unfortunate camel.

Against an enemy equipped with artillery and mortars, a perimeter camp would be a death-trap, but on the Frontier it made sense. Undeniably, however, it slowed down operations, taking hours off the day's march. Scouts on their own never built perimeter camps, except when they were established for long in one place. If ever they spent the night in an Army column's camp, it was not expected (least of all by themselves) that they build their sector of the wall, for they were always last in at night and first out in the morning; and had, moreover, no picks or shovels.

After any skirmish, it was absolutely necessary to recover the wounded, if possible the dead and certainly their rifles. A prisoner who fell into the tribesmen's hands was lucky to be simply decapitated. He was more likely to be disembowelled and castrated, his privy members thrust into his mouth; to be flayed alive; or to be pegged out, his mouth open into which the women of the tribe urinated until he drowned. So if a man fell wounded during the withdrawal from a piquet, the platoon – company – even a whole battalion might have to put in a counter-attack to rescue him. Scouts, although Pathans, were more at risk in this respect than Indian or British soldiers, for a gasht, with neither machine-guns nor artillery, might be quite unable to counter-attack a strong lashkar.

Captain Tony Gibb survived a Mahsud knife-rush. He was with his Army battalion, commanding his company which was moving up a narrow ridge thickly covered with ilex trees. There was a sudden volley and he was knocked spinning by the sledge-hammer blows of two soft-nosed bullets. Lying shocked, helpless and terrified, he saw twenty or thirty tribesmen, brandishing long knives, burst through his leading platoon and tear down towards his company headquarters. He just had strength enough to roll down a precipitous slope, landing in a snow-drift where the counter-attack found him unconscious an hour later. When he came to, he found that a third bullet had hit his wrist, cutting his watch-strap. He later joined the South Waziristan Scouts hoping, he said, to find the bastard wearing his watch. But though he then made light of his experience, he had nightmares about it for months.

There were occasions, very few, when Mahsuds and Wazirs did not act true to form. In 1920 the group of Mahsud hamlets and fortified kots known as Makin was being burnt as a punishment. A gasht of the North Waziristan Militia, under Lieutenant Barlow, was piqueting a hill overlooking the scene. Smoke from the burning obscured the hilltop, and a machine-gun opened up on it, hitting Barlow with several bullets and knocking him down the enemy side of the hill. He came to rest on a ledge beside a badly wounded Mahsud. Their common misfortunes struck some chord between them. Barlow handed his water-bottle to the Mahsud, who took a swig from it and said, 'Our people will be here soon, Sahib, and will kill you if they find you. Roll down under that rock and hide.' Barlow just managed to do so before he passed out; and was eventually rescued.

Despite the unpleasant habits of the tribesmen, and occasional forbidden reprisals, there was little ill-feeling between the two sides. The tribesmen knew that, if they fought well, they would not be shamed even though they were sure to be defeated. Soldiers were quite pleased if the enemy put up a good show. The enemy in no way threatened the British rule of India; it was far better to have a frontier battle than a riot in Calcutta.

The soldier's view of the Frontier was strictly professional. No doubt the higher command worried about the implication of tying up at a time of international tension two divisions of regular troops in chasing these scallywags, but to the ordinary regimental soldier the Frontier provided the excitement of not too arduous or too prolonged active service with first-class training for all ranks. And Scouts within days of a fight could be cheerfully discussing it with the ex-enemy.

As for the Politicals, simple soldiers professed themselves quite at a loss to know which side they were on. There are many versions of the tale of a Political Agent attached to a column who interrupted a conversation about Mahsud casualties, 'You're all wrong. We haven't lost nearly as many as you think.'

Politicals always seemed to be advising military thrusters not to do this or that because of the bad effect it would have on the Abdullai, or the Tori Khel, or some other gang of unmitigated blackguards whom the Brigadier had never heard of and had no intention of inviting to tea. In normal circumstances their view would prevail. Only in something like full-scale war did the army assume control, with the GOC taking over the role of Resident. Then the Political Agent could only look wise, advise and deplore.

In 1935 the Mohmands sued for peace and the four brigades withdrew. But many people felt that Waziristan would be next to blow up. A generation had grown up who had been nurtured on their fathers' tales of 1919 but were as yet unblooded themselves. And blow up it did.

The trouble started early in 1936 not with some dramatic act of colonial oppression or freedom fighters' defiance, but with what should have been no more than a police court case.

A Moslem student in Bannu abducted a Hindu girl, more or less willing, who became a convert to Islam, more or less willing, and her abductor's bride, more or less willing, taking the name of 'Islam Bibi'. But she was a minor, so her parents took the matter to Court – not to the Jirga, since they were Hindus and the abduction had taken place in British India, but to a British Indian Court.

The case immediately took on a communal aspect, with angry

Moslem mobs demonstrating in Bannu and even threatening the Deputy Commissioner's house. He was an officer of the Indian Political Service, Lieutenant-Colonel Evelyn Cobb, so famous for his loquacity that the expression 'Cobbologue' had passed into Political and Scout parlance. His first reaction when confronted with a hostile mob was to climb on to a chair and talk to it. And talk. And talk. Gradually by ones and twos, then a dozen at a time, the mob melted away, until Cobb was addressing only his orderly and a few policemen.

But the case of the abducted girl could not be so easily dismissed. Agitation spread to the Daur tribe, not as martial as Wazirs but very fanatical. They were roused by a holy man named Haji Mirza Ali Khan, better known as the Faqir of Ipi. He had not hitherto been active in politics, but had a reputation for piety and good works. He now flared up as a firebrand, preaching that Islam was endangered, every Moslem must rally to the Holy War. He raised a Daur lashkar which the Tochi Scouts dispersed without bloodshed. He then established himself in the Khaisora valley among his own tribe, the far more formidable Tori Khel section of the Utmanzai Wazirs.

Frontier experts used to point to the Tori Khel as an example of the success of peaceful economic penetration. There was no tribe less likely to cause trouble. They owned good irrigated land in the Tochi and Khaisora valleys and around Bannu itself. They owned huge flocks of sheep. They drew large sums in Maliki and Khassadari, in road- and timber- and firewood- and meat- and milk-contracts, and in rent for the land on which Razmak cantonment was built. They were almost hamsayas of the Government. They seemed perfectly content – but the truth was they bitterly resented, while profiting from, the Government's presence in their country; their rapacity was insatiable and unsatisfied; and they spent much of their wealth in the purchase of ·303 rifles.

In the mid 1930s they, like all Pathans, had been aware that changes were taking place which would not be to their advantage. Politically they were neither naive nor ill-informed. They might discount Congress propaganda while pocketing Congress money – but they saw the Government of India Act of 1935 as a concession to Hindu pressure, and a Hindu majority in the Legislative Assembly as the first step towards Hindu rule over the Frontier itself. Odious as was the erosion of their independence by the British, it would be far worse if the British handed them over to the Hindus.

For an annual sum of 7,500 rupees the Tori Khel had agreed to the construction of a road southwards from Mir Ali into the Khaisora valley. But the usual dissatisfaction over the distribution of this money and of road-construction contracts developed into hostility to the road itself. By the autumn of 1936, although the first instalments of the 'Khaisora Allowance' had been paid, work on the road had not started. The Tori Khel also felt that the Government had been unfair to them in its adjudication of a boundary dispute with the Mahsuds. They were therefore in a receptive mood to the Faqir's preaching and saw in the case of 'Islam Bibi' a test of the intentions towards Moslems of a Hindu-biased Government.

The case came up early in 1936 before the Magistrate in Bannu who awarded custody of the girl, until she came of age, to a respectable Moslem gentleman. Every Political must have sighed with relief and most Army officers with disappointment. But in August 1936, the Judicial Commissioner, reversing the Magistrate's judgment, sent the girl back to her Hindu parents. Later the Court of Appeal was to return her like a shuttlecock to the respectable Moslem gentleman, but already with the Judicial Commissioner's judgment the fat was in the fire. The Rule of Law is doubtless the most precious gift bestowed by Britain on a grateful sub-continent. Well, yes, but . . .

The Faqir now redoubled his preaching, with the special theme that never must the infidel Sarkar drive its impious road through the Khaisora. He promised the faithful immunity from bullets, shells and bombs, with the rider that anyone who was hit was obviously lacking in faith and therefore deserved it. The Government called on the Tori Khel Jirga to honour its undertaking on the road; the Maliks agreed, but the young men, spoiling for a fight, refused.

The Tori Khel must be shown who was master. A plan was drawn up that on 25 November the Razmak brigade (Razcol) would start from Damdil and move eastward down the Khaisora valley. The Bannu brigade (Tocol) would start from Mir Ali and move southward over low hills. They would meet and spend the night at Biche Kashkai in the Khaisora valley, and return next day to their bases. Razcol moving over the more difficult country, along the boulder-strewn bed of the Khaisora river overlooked by high ridges on each flank, would do about thirteen miles each day; Tocol over easier country about sixteen miles. It was too far if opposition was encountered, but opposition was not expected; it would be an exemplary demonstration of the Government's might, enlivened perhaps by a little long-range sniping. (See Map 5.)

In both columns the Tochi Scouts had vital tasks. With Razcol, eight platoons would provide distant flank protection, out beyond the close piqueting of the regular troops, and six platoons would operate in front

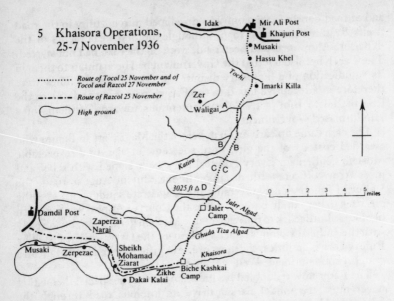

5 Khaisora Operations,
25-7 November 1936

.... *Route of Tocol 25 November and of*
Tocol and Razcol 27 November

—·—·— *Route of Razcol 25 November*

⬭ *High ground*

of the advance guard, flushing out opposition before it could delay the
column's advance. With Tocol, four infantry platoons would act as
right flank guard and two Mounted Infantry troops* as left flank guard,
also outside and beyond the close piqueting.

Hopes of a peaceful promenade were soon proved illusory. On
reaching Zaperzai, about one-third of the way to Biche Kashkai, Felix-
Williams (formerly South Waziristan Scouts and now commanding the
Tochi Scouts) with the platoons leading Razcol was warned by Khassadars that there were hostiles on the hills ahead. They soon came under
fire and, as yet unsupported by the column's advance guard, took the
first of the high features. Subsequently, with the help of a company of
the Guides, they took, one by one, the ridges on both sides of the
Khaisora and held them while the column passed through. They came
down the road in darkness, half-an-hour after the rear party had passed
through, and followed the column to camp after having been moving
and fighting for thirteen and a half hours during the Ramadan fast. It
was one of the rules of Frontier war that empty cartridge cases must not
be left to be collected and refilled by the tribesmen. It required nerve

---

* Under Tim Taylor, the only Frontier Corps officer to become a Major General in the
Australian Army.

systematically to collect empty cases while under fire. These six platoons fired 1,800 rounds and brought back 1,760 cases.

The flank piqueting was described by John Prendergast, a Wing Officer, on a hilltop far to the left flank of the column:

I could hear the deep note of the medium machine-guns and the sharper one of the light automatics, with the occasional crump of our little howitzers. Clearly there was quite a party going on. As the day wore on, the noise grew fainter. It became hotter and hotter, until you could have fried an egg on the rocks and I was beginning to feel the terrible pangs of thirst. I eked out my water prudently, though it was by then as hot as tea and came straight out as sweat ...

In the late afternoon we were to withdraw to our fort at Dosalli. The opposite force had to cross over the valley towards us to get to the road and we had to cover it with brisk fire as it was closely followed. Then we trudged up the steep road to Dosalli. It had been a blazing hot day during the month of Ramadan when the Scouts were forbidden to drink in the daylight hours. They were exhausted and scarcely able to carry our casualties, who must have suffered horribly too. Stretcher-bearers had to be changed every hundred yards, officers taking their turn.

Tocol had a rougher time, mainly because the brigade staff did not have proper control, and one of its battalions, the 3/7th Rajputs, was a new arrival. Felix-Williams, anticipating difficulties in communicating with brigade, attached a Scouts signals terminal to the main column. With it also went the Scouts Medical Officer, George Graham, and a Mess servant with a camel laden with appropriate provender. The Scouts Mounted Infantry were to act as distant left flank guard, and four infantry platoons under Victor Wainright as right flank guard, initially piqueting Zer mountain – quite unnecessarily, in his opinion, since it was at least two miles from the axis of advance. He viewed with apprehension

a slightly complicated operation with a scratch column. Zer is a pig of a feature, full of great outcrops of rock which make observation difficult. Moreover my gasht was to be a mixture of Right and Left Wings under Subadar Shawal Dad, a tall, scraggy Barak with a great beak of a nose and both eyes peering out of the same hole. Miry and Kabul reckoned that his mouth was the most efficient part of his head.

However, one of the platoon commanders was Lal Din, Mohmand, a modest, self-effacing little man known as 'Tank' because of his habit of going bald-headed at any operation and his apparent invulnerability to bullets. Although the Tori Khel Maliks warned that there would be trouble, and Roy Beatty, acting Assistant Political Agent, told the Brigadier that tribesmen were building sangars, Brigade did not really expect opposition. Wainright's

orderly, Baz Gul, put a couple of tins of Gold Flake into my haversack. When I called him an idiot because I hadn't smoked for months, he said I'd be glad of them by the evening.

We set off very early to secure Zer before the column approached it. The leading platoon as they cleared the crest saw about thirty tribesmen making off in a hurry. They were almost certainly hostiles: friendly shepherds would have stayed to chat and delay us. But we were still observing the rule of not firing until fired upon, so we had to let them go. I reported to brigade, but throughout the day getting anything out of them was very difficult. In comparison with Razcol, with whom we usually worked, Tocol seemed a very straggly affair.

Shooting started at about A—A [See Map 5], and built up with a lot of automatic and machine-gun fire, and by B—B the column's progress was slowed right down. We were not fired on, and we saw no tribesmen moving in from our side. We skirted to the right of a Rajput company which did not look too happy, officers and NCOs walking about a lot between sections instead of staying under cover or moving fast. As we came down from Zer, the leading platoon killed two tribesmen who shot at them, one a huge fellow; they looked like Mahsuds. Twice I asked brigade for orders, but the only answer I got was 'get on' – nothing sensible like 'Take over as vanguard,' or 'Continue as flank guard but a little closer in.'

I noticed three or four sangars, C—C, on the far side of a nullah and roughly at right angles to the column's axis of advance. Fire from these was holding up the Rajputs who were very brave but hadn't a clue and got shot down in clumps, losing all the British Officers of their two forward companies. As we approached the nullah I dropped Shawal Dad with two platoons on the near bank to give covering fire and with the other two, Akoras and Lal Din's Mohmands, fixed swords and went for the sangars, killing six or seven. I cannot honestly say I saw any bayonetted, they were probably shot as they tried to get away. We caught one Mahsud, took his rifle and dagger and put a rope on him. We had one killed and two wounded, and several near misses, bullet holes through our loose shirts and partog.

Soon after this the column halted and the Brigadier held what would now be called an 'O Group'. It was well past the time for settling into a perimeter for the night, and I made myself unpopular by saying so with rather more vehemence than my age and rank warranted. The Brigadier, however, chose to ignore my advice and press on to Biche Kashkai in the dark.

The Mounted Infantry were sent back to Khajuri (George Graham saw two sowars leading horses with their dead friends' bodies tied over the saddle, arms and legs dangling) and the column moved on at six-thirty, with Wainright's gasht as Advanced Guard, accompanied by Roy Beatty. (What business the Assistant Political Agent had up in front is not quite clear, but as an officer of Hodson's Horse and the Tochi Scouts as well, he thought it was the right place.)

We moved in a rather tight diamond formation, Lal Din's Mohmands leading, slowly in the dark. The popular Khassadar, 'George', came through from behind, and told us that Razcol had reached Biche Kashkai but with many casualties. I believe he was carrying a message for Razcol. Personally I always thought him a very suspect character, sucking up to the Razmak garrison and far too matey with Wazirs for a so-called Mahsud.

Between nine-thirty and ten there was a sudden burst of fire, about thirty shots, from a bit to the right of our axis of advance close to the far bank of the Ghuda Tiza Algad just as we were about to cross it. The muzzle-flashes were most unpleasant. Baz Gul and I hit the deck, and the Mahsud prisoner broke away and dashed off to the left. I was carrying an automatic pistol and was so slow in getting off the safety-catch that I missed him. I shouted to Shawal Dad to get the right hand platoon on to where the fire came from. No Shawal Dad. There was some rustling in the thick grass and, thinking it might be the prisoner, I went after it with my pistol, only to encounter Roy with his hand full of iron stalking me. By this time the main body had joined in the shooting from behind us, and I shouted in English, Urdu and Pushtu to cease fire and give me a chance to sort things out; being the meat in the sandwich wasn't my idea of fun. Shawal Dad turned up and told me he had been taking the right hand platoon forward. I didn't believe him.

Some time after ten o'clock it was decided to camp in the Ghuda Tiza area, and I was told to build and occupy two platoon-strength piquets. I built one with the left hand platoon and told Shawal Dad to

build the other with the rear platoon. It was slow work in the dark.
Lal Din had the forward platoon well sited for all-round defence, and
I told him to wait half an hour and then withdraw with the right hand
platoon to the camp. Some time after midnight I was satisfied with
the piquets and went back to the camp myself, reporting to the
Brigade Major who was comfortably tucked into pyjamas and
sleeping-bag, which I rectified. I then found the Mess servant who
gave me a large slice of plum-cake and a treble whisky-and-soda. He
said the firing had stampeded a lot of animals into the night,
including the Brigadier's own horse.

Light is thrown on the staff-work and signals of this operation by the
fact that when the commander of Razcol wished to inform the commander of Tocol that he had reached Biche Kashkai, he was obliged to send
word by a Tori Khel Malik. And when the commander of Tocol wished
to inform the commander of Razcol that he was still well short of Biche
Kashkai, he was obliged to send word by the Khassadar, 'George', who
was stopped by the enemy but talked his way through, 'Come on, let a
chap earn an honest penny.'

Next day Tocol, with loads to collect that had been lost in the night's
stampede, could not move until mid-morning and reached Biche
Kashkai in the afternoon. As the troops were rationed for only three
days, plans were changed and it was decided that both columns would
march to Mir Ali on 27 November.

For that move ten platoons of Scouts under Felix-Williams acted as
Advance Guard Mounted Troops, covering a front of 2,500 yards well
ahead of the Advanced Guard. He told Wainright, 'Stay with the
rearguard until you have extricated the camp piquets and then keep
running until you reach me in front.'

Wainright recalls:

So we tightened our straps and jogged for about four miles until I met
Felix talking to Major Fisk of 7th Bengal Mountain Battery. Fisko
handed me an enormous flask and, when I spluttered, said, 'Good
God, boy, you didn't think I'd dilute it for a job like this?' Felix sent
me back with three platoons to do laybacks for the left flank guard. I
saw one interesting incident. The first wave of a piquet of North-
amptons came off nice and steadily. When the second wave came off
there was a lot of shooting and one man rolled over and lay still. Two
stretcher-bearers went back for him like rockets, but when they got to
him, booted him to his feet and down the hill. He wasn't hit, only

frightened. A little later I was almost knocked over by a terrific kick in the seat of my partog by George Laman. 'Stop walking about like a spare f—g lamp-post,' he said. 'It's cost the taxpayer thousands to train you!'

On the right flank Wainright's friend 'Miry', the fierce little Jowaki Afridi Subadar Mir Hamza, won a remarkably good IOM by cornering in a fortified tower and capturing an entire gang of hostiles. 'At Miranshah,' said Wainright, 'after it was all over an ammunition check produced more empty cases than rounds fired. Claude Erskine asked me what I had felt like in the Ghuda Tiza Algad, and I replied, "Rather frightened and very angry." He reckoned that was about normal.'

In three days ten Scouts platoons and two troops of Mounted Infantry had twenty-six casualties, and won an MC, an IOM and two IDSMs. The two brigades of regular troops had one hundred and seven casualties. It could not really be claimed that the Tori Khel had been taught a lesson, but everyone agreed that the Scouts' performance had been brilliant.

The enemy were mainly Tori Khel, with a few Madda Khel Wazirs and a stiffening of irreconcilable Mahsuds. The Faqir's propaganda was obviously successful, and there was every chance of a major Frontier war. Therefore the General Officer Commanding Northern Command assumed control of all military operations, and also political control of Waziristan, with the Resident, Waziristan, as his Chief Political Officer. Reinforcements were brought in, the Rawalpindi Brigade, two light tank companies, and two extra batteries of mountain artillery. The Tori Khel must be punished.

Jimmy Gimson was a Captain of the Guides Cavalry, now a Wing Commander of the Tochi Scouts, all steel wire and ginger with piercing blue eyes, a bristling moustache and a dangerous temper combined with charm and consideration for others. He returned from home leave and marriage just too late for the November fighting, and wrote to his wife on 13 December that the war was 'diminuendo'. Work on the road into the Khaisora valley, from Khajuri to Biche Kashkai, was progressing under Scouts protection. On 16 December he celebrated Id-ul-Fitr, the end of the fast, in an immense feast with the Pathan officers.

To punish the Tori Khel the troops were burning some villages and Gimson, watching from the hilltops, was 'very sick to see small villages where I had been hospitably entertained going up in flames. Unfortunately the Army do not have to gasht in this country as we have. It will be a long time before we are welcome here again.' Then came Christmas sports and a chikor shoot near Dosalli post.

Victor Wainright spent a lonely but restful Christmas in Biche Kashkai camp, three weeks

> with the culverts down, telephone wires cut and the wireless on the blink. A rest-cure except for the occasional *daz-maz* [sniping]. A plane from Miranshah used to fly over every morning and drop my mail, a newspaper, and a loaf of bread on the sort of parachute small boys make with a handkerchief, string and a stone. My Christmas dinner consisted of a light snack of *pâté de foie gras*, turtle soup, whitebait, turkey and ham, and Christmas pud dropped in a parcel of tins sent by a girl friend from Fortnums.

By the end of the year the Tori Khel, disgusted at the paucity of support given by their fellow Moslems, had had enough. They were summoned for a full Jirga to discuss peace terms, including the fine they must pay, and sent back home to think about it. The rifles and hostages demanded as surety for good behaviour were handed in, and on 11 January 1937 the Jirga accepted the Government's peace terms, which included a stiff fine and the requirement that they control or expel the Faqir of Ipi.

There was still, however, a constant influx of hostiles from the Afghan province of Khost, Tannis and Zadrans and Mangals, who knew like the backs of their hands the paths across the Durand Line. They had to be stopped, lest they stir up more trouble. It was rather similar to the SWS chapaos for gangs raiding into Derajat, except that the Khostwals had to be intercepted on their way in, not like the raiders on their way out, heavy with booty. The cold on these January nights was arctic, as men had to keep still for hours. Gimson wore vest, shirt, four sweaters, greatcoat, pants, two pairs of trousers, two pairs of stockings and socks.

But he had his reward. After three failures, he set a chapao two miles west of Dosalli. 'At 1030 the lashkarwals lit fires a quarter of a mile to the east. I started off with the reserve platoon to stalk them, but meanwhile they ran into the ambush of the other two platoons. There was a ten-minute battle, and three Madda Khel were captured.' The next night he tried with five platoons four and a half miles east of Dosalli. The gang walked straight into them and they held their fire until the last possible minute. 'Two enemy dead and a third picked up dead the next day.'

'War now really over,' wrote Gimson to his wife on 20 January. He took fifty recruits out to scour the plain for bustard and played in a polo match, Scouts against Brigade HQ. There was a NCOs Promotion Course, and practice began for the annual Scouts sports. His Wing were to build and occupy a new fort at Khaisora, with fifty Sappers and Miners to help with the skilled jobs. 'The Tori Khel have brought their families back,' he wrote on 31 January, 'so there will probably be no more trouble.' He actually had a meal with a Tori Khel Malik. The Faqir of Ipi, persuaded by the Tori Khel Maliks that he was *persona non grata*, departed for pastures new. Political control of Waziristan was handed back to the Resident. Things were getting back to normal.

Six days later, on 6 February, Captain Keogh of the South Waziristan Scouts and his orderly were shot dead on the road near Ladha, and on the following day occurred the murder of Captain Roy Beatty, by a Madda Khel gang near Boya, to which reference has already been made.

The Faqir was in business again. He had promises of support from several tribes on both sides of the Durand Line. Early in March he issued a decree calling upon all Khassadars to desert, on pain of being denied Moslem funeral rites. 'Khassadar Subadar and twelve Khassadars deserted,' wrote Gimson on 3 March, 'a bad sign.'

On 29 March the newly-arrived (Abbottabad) brigade had heavy casualties, two British officers, two Gurkha officers and thirty Gurkhas being killed, forty-four more wounded. Next day Gimson 'gashted over the scene of yesterday's fighting. We brought in the bodies of five Gurkhas, ammunition, stores and four enemy bodies.' The war was not, after all, over. The GOC resumed political control of Waziristan; the Tochi Scouts and SWS were placed under Army command, and all leave was stopped.

Meanwhile the Mahsuds, never on cordial terms with the Tori Khel, had withdrawn the skirts of their garments from these unseemly disturbances. A few hard men had gone north, but the tribe as a whole remained neutral. Their Khassadars actually shot up fellow-Mahsuds whom they found cutting telephone wires, and put up a good fight against a Powindah lashkar which was up to no good. This Powindah laskhar, half-Suliman Khel and half-Kharot, led by a Kharot whose father had been killed by the Zhob Militia, gave Wana brigade a run for its money on 17 February 1937, about twenty-two miles west of Wana at Obo Sar, near the Afghan border.

At first light the Advanced Guard had moved out of camp, followed by the main body, while four infantry platoons of SWS under Douglas Robertson and one troop Mounted Infantry under Ralph Venning stayed to see the transport and followers safely on their way, and then act as rear-guard mounted troops. When hundreds of mules, camels and followers were jammed tight trying to get out of the perimeter and follow the main body to the north-east, the enemy suddenly opened a heavy fire on them from the high ground along the Afghan border. The whole lot stampeded, bolting not north-eastward along the piqueted route, but to the south-east where they would have no protection. The Scouts infantry platoon manned the perimeter wall and fired on the enemy; Risadar Gulab of the Mounted Infantry said to Venning, 'You know what they'll do next, Sahib? They'll get on to that hill to the east and cut off the transport and followers.' Venning gave the order to mount and (feeling painfully conspicuous on the only grey horse) led the Mounted Infantry at a gallop for that hill, dismounted at the bottom and raced up to the top, arriving there just before the enemy. Lotus Lowis, the Assistant Political Agent, with the SWS infantry and Khassadars helped round up the animals and sort out the confusion, but four rifles and much ammunition were lost.

'Two battalions up from India were awful,' he wrote. 'Four platoons of SWS, with MI, were superb and did most of the rearguard and flank guards, losing two killed, a horse and a sowar wounded.' They were sniped all day, and Venning on his grey horse was glad to reach camp.

A grand Jirga of the Dré Mahsud was called at Sararogha on 8 March, under the walls of the fort, covered by machine-guns, to hear the Government's decision on a fine on the whole tribe for the murder of Captain Keogh in Mahsud tribal limits. The Political Agent was 'Barnie' Barnes, than whom there was no better man at handling a difficult Jirga. He understood well that it was no good issuing orders to a Jirga: they would just walk out on you; they had to be argued into agreement. Barnes was convincing in English: 'Well, in Pushtu he's better still,' wrote Lowis. 'He puts the most difficult things across in such a way that the Jirga can do nothing but agree. I'm inclined to get angry, which gets one nowhere.' Barnes, sitting at ease (one did not address a Jirga standing), started off by warning the tribe that they must control their troublemakers. This was ill-received. There was a lot of heckling, 'That's not our job, it's yours . . . That's what you're paid for. You're the Political Agent aren't you?' A fellow with a voice like a bull bawled out, 'You're the Political Agent. Haven't you got any balls?' It was a bitterly cold day. Barnes thrust his hands into his trouser pockets, groped about and shouted back, 'Well, I thought I had. But it's so bloody cold that now I'm not so sure.' It brought the house down, the Mahsuds rocking with laughter, and the atmosphere at once improved.

In the end they agreed to pay 75,000 rupees for Keogh's murder, to expel the Faqir should he enter Mahsud territory, and to control their troublemakers, assurances which they more or less honoured.

Could it be that the Mahsud had changed his spots? No, it could not.

Perhaps the greatest advantage the Government forces now enjoyed was motor transport. (But not only Government forces: a Wazir lashkar was brought to the front in hired buses.) Motor convoys escorted by armoured cars seemed so secure that the roads were not usually piqueted for their passage, except by Khassadars.

At daybreak on 9 April 1937, a routine convoy of forty-nine lorries and two private cars left Manzai for Wana. It carried military and civilian loads, leave details rejoining their units, and some officers returning from a language examination. It was escorted by four armoured cars, distributed at equal lengths from front to rear of the convoy. There was also an infantry escort of fifty-one with two light machine-guns, and most of the leave details were armed. The convoy- and the escort-commanders were both very experienced, and the convoy seemed well-found and secure. There had been reports of a hostile named Konia Khel in the vicinity and of tribesmen 'apparently engaged in a tactical exercise' in the Shahur Tangi. Unfortunately no one put two and two together, except the Political Agent and the SWS Commandant, Major Skrine, who drove seventy miles to Waziristan District Headquarters to advise against running the convoy that day.

The Shahur Tangi, on the Manzai-Wana road, was a notorious place for ambushes in the days of animal transport. It is a defile three miles long formed by the Shahur nullah, generally dry or a mere trickle, running between steep rocky hills. The road runs, with three sharp bends, along the north side of the defile, above the nullah bed, and for about two miles the defile is very narrow with steep slopes above and below the road, which is not wide enough to turn a vehicle except with much forwarding and reversing. On either side of the nullah are innumerable boulders, caves and catchment-drains from which it is easy to enfilade, at point-blank range, stretches of road up which lorries must crawl in low gear. There were stone-built posts at Chagmalai and Splitoi, bottom and top of the Tangi, but these had been evacuated in the comfortable circumstances of the 1930s. An early morning flight by the RAF disclosed nothing suspicious; but the convoy commander, as he entered the defile from the Chagmalai end, noticed with surprise that there were no Khassadars there either. (See Map 6, p. 160.)

At a quarter to eight, when the leading armoured car was two-thirds

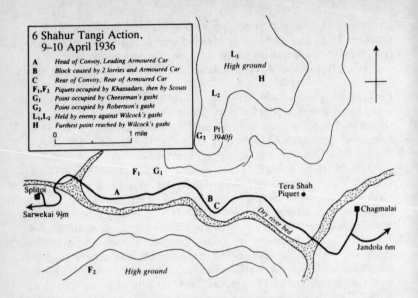

of the way through, the rear well inside the Tangi and the convoy crawling up the steepest part, intense fire was opened along its entire length and continued for about fifteen minutes. Nearly all the officers, sitting beside the drivers or in the two private cars, were killed or wounded in the first minutes. Many of the escort were shot before they could jump down from the lorries, and many drivers killed or wounded who, from the Army of 1937, could not readily be replaced; their lorries, jammed together or slewed across the road, made a total block. The Mahsuds knew their job. Their positions were just above the maximum elevation of the armoured cars' machine-guns. The survivors were pinned down in the ditches beside the road or culverts under it, cowering from the tribesmen's soft-nosed bullets. Thus in the centre there was a sort of stalemate and a Medical Officer, Captain N. M. Durrani, himself a Pathan, heroically walked towards the tribesmen calling on them in Pushtu to cease fire while he brought the wounded under cover. He was shot dead.

Lieutenant Hopkinson in the leading armoured car managed to get out of the Tangi with the three leading lorries, one driver being wounded. He sent them on, and returned to give what help he could. The other three armoured cars, spaced at intervals down the column, were all immobilised by stranded lorries, but able to use their machine-guns to cover the road, except at one point where it was defiladed and the tribesmen came in with knives, mutilating and finishing off the wounded officers and several others.

The nearest Scouts were on a road protection gasht from Sarwekai, one troop Mounted Infantry and four platoons under Captain Cheeseman. At 7.55 they heard firing and marched to the sound of the guns. But Lowis, the Assistant Political Agent, was at Splitoi before them, with a lorry-load of Maliks and Khassadars from Wana, where he had heard the news by wireless. He put the Khassadars into two permanent piquet-posts (F1 and F2, see Map 6) without opposition, climbed over the wall of the fort, opened the gate and found the telephone working, the line miraculously uncut. He was thus able to establish communication with Jandola. (Throughout, this was a soldiers' battle, everyone doing the best he could with very little central direction since the Scouts from west and east were separated by the full length of the Tangi, and detachments of Scouts, armoured cars and Khassadars arrived piecemeal at the scene of action.) Cheeseman and his Sarwekai gasht arrived about mid-day taking over Splitoi post and the piquets from the Khassadars.

On the same day the Jandola and Sararogha garrisons were changing over, and when the news arrived, only three platoons were in Jandola. Although they had just marched in from Sararogha, they piled into lorries with Major Skrine and Lieutenant Wilcock and drove at top speed to Chagmalai. They debussed and, following the first principle of mountain warfare, made straight for the high ground north of the Tangi, with orders from Skrine to try to link up with the Scouts from Sarwekai and to prevent tribesmen streaming down from the north to join in the battle. A plane arrived to support them but, with one bullet in the petrol tank and another in the pilot's ankle, it had to force-land on the road, crumpling a wing against the only tree for miles. Other planes, however, gave some support during the day and at least encouraged the survivors of the convoy.

Advancing towards the highest peak (L1), about two miles west of Chagmalai, Wilcock's three platoons came under very heavy fire from the front and right flanks and were in danger of being cut off by tribesmen hastening towards the Tangi. Regulars from Manzai arrived at Chagmalai, including an officer senior to Skrine who assumed command, and decided that Wilcock's platoon must be withdrawn. The withdrawal was closely followed up by overwhelming numbers of tribesmen, and Wilcock was shot in the shoulder.

The rear platoon was commanded by Havildar Multan, Sipah Afridi.

He was a very fine shot, a wonderful exponent of 'fifteen rounds rapid', his head and the rifle pressed into his shoulder as steady as a rock, his right hand working the bolt with the regularity of a metronome. During the withdrawal along a knife-edged ridge he was badly wounded and could go no further. Knowing that the wound was mortal, knowing too his fate should he fall alive into the tribesmen's hands, he *ordered* his platoon to leave him to cover their retreat. For some minutes they heard the well-known sound of Multan's rapid fire: then it stopped. In the late afternoon three more Scouts platoons arrived at Chagmalai and established a piquet three-quarters of a mile west of the post.

Meanwhile Cheeseman's Sarwekai gasht had seized the high point (G1) north of the Tangi, preventing tribesmen from coming down from the north. They commanded the west end of the Tangi and their covering fire helped a section of armoured cars from Sarwekai under Lieutenant Wetherell to unblock the head of the convoy. The leading lorry was slewed across the road, its civilian driver lying wounded beneath it. Under a hail of bullets Wetherell pulled out the driver, started the lorry and drove it clear. But there was still a block, for the driver of the next lorry was dead and the engine shot through. With great difficulty a tow-rope was attached and, steered by a volunteer, the lorry was towed away by an armoured car. But the third lorry was then hit in the petrol tank and burst into flames, preventing all further efforts to unravel the knot from the front. The rear armoured car, trying to force its way between two abandoned lorries, became hopelessly jammed between them, forming an impassable obstacle.

A busload of Maliks arrived and tried to remove their fellow tribesmen by sweet reason. One, Koran in hand, was shot dead, and the rest prudently withdrew, abandoning their bus just where it contributed most to the blockage and confusion.

Douglas Robertson, a slight, very fair young man, was commanding the SWS fort at Tiarza, north-east of Wana.

My HQ was at Tiarza with detachments at Wana and Tanai. I had made a visit to Wana and on the day in question had left on a gasht to visit a Wazir friend and hoping to pick up a few teal and snipe on the Wana Toi pools. I had left a helio on Gibraltar* and unfortunately just as we got to the first pool the helio began winking and we were ordered to return as *fast* as possible. We arrived to find the main road lined with lorries. I told my gasht to fill water-bottles, etc. and get

---

* Gibraltar. A high peak above Wana.

into the lorries. I asked for information but there was little except that the convoy had been ambushed. I asked for messages to be passed to Tanai and Sarwekai to order all but a few sentries to be ready in gashting order on the road. We picked up almost a platoon at Tanai and about as many at Sarwekai.

On arrival at Splitoi we found the Khassadars at their posts and the line through to Jandola. I spoke to the Commandant and was told to get down the road in a hurry and 'bail out the convoy'. Of course I said 'Yes, sir,' to him, but to myself, 'Like hell.'

I had a good look at the high hill (G2, Pt 3040) above Splitoi and decided Konia Khel would not have his rear protected. So I agreed with the Pathan officers we'd take that and work along the ridge and down the spurs. So we moved off well spread both laterally and in depth. We came under fire about half-way up and from there on individuals and pairs moved as and when they could from rock to rock. The bravest deed I saw that day was a Barak signaller walking down a spur waving his flag across his body to stop an armoured car firing at us.

We encircled the peak and pushed the Mahsuds off. I came round a huge rock face-to-face with a Mahsud coming round the other way. I winged him − we both fired together − and then like a damn fool followed him down the reverse slope. It was then that I was hit from the left. Entry just below shoulder, hit a rib and exited a quarter of an inch from my spine. Of course I was bowled over like a rabbit. In a flash my Orakzai orderly and a Khattak were down and had me back on top again, where field dressings were applied and I was strapped up like a dummy in two pagris. The dum-dum had left a large hole. They laid me in a fairly flat gully and wanted to evacuate me. I refused and spent the night there. Meanwhile the advance along the ridge and down the spurs was progressing well, and soon all quietened down.

Robertson got up, walked about and organised his gasht into an all-round defence of the peak for the night. They had a hand-to-hand fight in the darkness, bayonets, knives and grenades, and killed several Mahsuds. He walked into Splitoi in the morning, where Lowis got him to lie up.

While Robertson's and Cheeseman's gashts were shooting up the enemy from their rear, Lowis judged the time ripe to send the Maliks and Khassadars in. He sent sixty straight down the road into the Tangi. No one fired at them and they occupied the culverts and sangars from which their fellow-Mahsuds withdrew. It was then possible to get thirteen more lorries out. This was the Khassadars' finest hour, and an unexpected end to the front of the convoy's long ordeal.

As it got dark, the enemy made repeated efforts to rush the convoy, but except in two places were beaten off by fire from the armoured cars and survivors of the escort who were collected into small groups round each armoured car. At the same time Scouts from Splitoi worked to take out the wounded and extricate more lorries, an operation not helped by the fact that many were civilian vehicles of doubtful reliability, as indeed were the drivers. When at first light the Scouts advanced along the ridges and into the Tangi, they found the enemy had flitted. The last vehicles were removed during the afternoon, thirty hours after the ambush. The convoy losses were ninety-nine, including seven officers. The SWS had seven killed and two officers wounded. The enemy, initially only about eighty but increasing during the day to over three hundred, lost about sixteen killed and twenty-six wounded. It was evident that motor transport had not solved all convoy problems.

After this episode Konia Khel became Public Enemy Number One in South Waziristan, in disrepute even in his own tribe which did not want to be drawn into the Tori Khel's war. Lowis took up three Mahsud Maliks in a plane to try to identify his house.

At first they were glum and almost sick. Then there was a yell as someone spotted it, and from then on things went with a swing. Picture the cabin, not very large, with three Mahsuds, Aslam (APO) and I bounding about and two British Other Ranks trying to take photographs.

But when the Scouts went to call on him, Konia Khel was not at home.

An attempt was made to take him out by bombing. A plane, laden with two 250-lb bombs, crash-landed on the steeply sloping football ground at Ladha and ended up nose-down in the perimeter wire, the bombs fortunately unexploded. Because Ladha was cut off by blown-up bridges and mined roads, the pilot and air-gunner remained Venning's involuntary guests for many weeks, Corporal Power proving a most effective trainer of 1st Wing football team.

Konia Khel was next seen in unexpected circumstances. Hugh Pettigrew and the SWS Subadar Major were invited to a farewell tea-party, in the Political Agent's garden in Tank, for Barnie Barnes on his departure. 'Who', wrote Olaf Caroe, 'does not remember those farewell tea-parties when men who have made your life a burden for months and years all at once come round with fervent hand-clasps and, bidding you God-speed – could it be with a tear in the eye? – make you half-believe that the burden was worth carrying?' There were about fifty Maliks, senior Khassadars and Scouts present, including some well-known hostiles who, as was customary, had come in under safe-conduct. Suddenly the Subadar Major leaned close to Pettigrew and whispered, 'Look, Sahib, at the next table, the tall man with a black beard. It's Konia Khel!' The worst cut-throat in Waziristan was placidly nibbling sweet biscuits and sipping tea in the Political Agent's garden, perfectly safe until he re-crossed the border into Tribal Territory.

The Resident, Waziristan, at that time was Johnny Johnson, the ex-cavalry trooper and former Commandant of the SWS. He adopted a surprisingly 'Political' bias: the tribesmen were never in the wrong, Scouts and Army always at fault. Lowis wrote that, 'Johnson's consumption [sic] of responsibility and clearness of decision are really first-rate. He does everything off his own bat and never consults anyone. Johnson is the hell of a chap.' But he was 'not impressive in a Jirga. Pushtu fluent but not good, delivery rotten. Barnie much better in Jirga.' This did not, perhaps, make for easy relations between them. When the Resident came on tour of South Waziristan, 'on at least two occasions Barnie called Johnson "Sir"!'

Barnie Barnes's swan-song in Waziristan was a real *tour de force*. Major-General A. F. Hartley (in Lowis's opinion 'an ignorant little tyke, both of mountain warfare and of tribal affairs, and anti-Barnes') ordered that the tower of a notorious hostile in Makin be demolished. The Politicals argued that this would bring the Mahsuds into the war.

So Barnie and Aslam after a fearful argument got the Maliks to undertake to demolish the kot and bring in the bad man. Armed with this undertaking, he tackled Hartley who, after more argument, agreed. There was a full-scale Jirga near Makin, camp sniped at night, but Hartley took it well. The Jirga was an hour and a half late in producing their man and there was more argument about burning the kot, an operation which had been stopped by rain. But at last they burnt it. This was a great achievement on Barnie's part. A hostile Makin on the L of C would have been serious.

Barnes became Political Agent, Zhob, where he was murdered by a fanatic across his office table.

12

War, 1937–8

Meanwhile the Tochi Scouts had had several successful chapaos, intercepting Afghan tribesmen and Madda Khel Wazirs on their way to join the Tori Khel lashkars. One under Felix-Williams (hardly, perhaps, a Commandant's job) brought in eleven Mangals including two killed and two wounded; others accounted for fourteen Madda Khel.

On 30 April 1937 Jimmy Gimson was ordered to evacuate Khaisora post, which he had so recently built, as it was difficult to keep supplied and no longer served a useful purpose. 'We had an extremely strenuous twenty-four hours. We had to pull the whole place to pieces and I had orders to leave nothing whatever behind. However we got finished in time and sent back sixty-four lorries of stores.' Naturally the Faqir made the most of this, announcing that the Faranghis feared to stay in Khaisora and would soon be bolting from Razmak and Wana also. A number of optimists actually arrived in Wana with camels to carry away the loot.

Victor Wainright was on an operation with the Mounted Infantry.

One afternoon Guli Lal, the tough little roly-poly Seni Khattak Risaldar, told me that a patrol had brought in rather an odd chap, and it might be interesting for me to be in on the questioning. 'Dump your cigarette-case and lighter,' he said, 'and cadge Marouf's cigarettes. In your partog you'll pass as a Pathan, but if you want to talk you'd better rattle some stones in a tin can in your Afridi-brogue act.' Polite chap, our Guli.

The prisoner turned out to be a Khostwal, a rather nice little old chap with a long heel-rope wound round his tum. He said that rumour in Khost was that the British were on their way out and loot was easy, so he was looking for a horse or mule to take back. We gave him something to eat and a handful of chupattis to carry, and told him to go home and say the British were so rich that even the poor Pathan Militia could afford to feed horse-thieves.

The problem remained of bringing the enemy to battle. The Faqir's headquarters was believed to be at Arsal Kot, a complex of caves and fortified towers in the Shaktu valley, which runs parallel to the Khaisora and five to ten miles south of it. They could hardly hope to catch him there, but his prestige would take a knock if he were chased out of it. The Tori Khel might stand and fight to prevent this. For the operation a division was formed of the Bannu and Abbotabad Brigades under Major-General A. F. Hartley, and concentrated at Dosalli. His orders were to defeat the enemy lashkars and occupy Arsal Kot.

The first objective was the Sham plain, a high plateau five to six miles south of Dosalli, which formed part of the watershed between the Khaisora and the Shaktu river systems and was an important summer grazing ground of the Tori Khel. From Dosalli there were two possible approaches: the obvious one up the Sre Mela nullah and gorge, which from the Sham plain runs down steeply in a northerly direction to the Khaisora near Dosalli; and another approach, far more difficult, along the top of the three-mile long Iblanke ridge, rising from north to south one to one and a half miles east of the Sre Mela.

The Iblanke ridge has been compared to a lean and mangy lion. Its tail is the Khaisora valley. Its spine, one and three-quarter miles long, rises steeply to the high points corresponding to the lion's right and left shoulder-blades; then down the neck (half a mile) between the ears, up the scruff of the neck (quarter of a mile) to the skull, then down between the outstretched forelegs to the Sham plain. (See Map 7.) But little of this was apparent in Dosalli on 7 May, for the map bore no relation to reality, and air-photos were equally unhelpful.

Hartley had taken over only two weeks previously. Stigmatised by Lowis as 'an ignorant little tyke', he was perhaps too ignorant of mountain warfare to follow the customary procedure of a slow, slogging progress up the nearest valley, piqueting as he went. This the enemy had anticipated, constructing many sangars artfully concealed from which he could make the forcing of the Sre Mela gorge a very expensive operation.

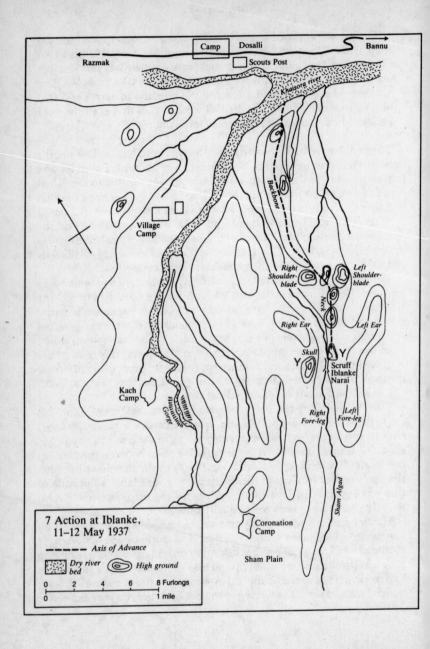

Razmak ← | Camp | Dosalli | → Bannu

Scouts Post

Khaisora river

Backbone

Village Camp

Right Shoulder-blade

Left Shoulder-blade

Neck

Right Ear

Left Ear

Skull

Scruff Iblanke Narai

Kach Camp

Gorge

Right Fore-leg

Left Fore-leg

Sham Algad

Coronation Camp

Sham Plain

7 Action at Iblanke,
11–12 May 1937

– – – – Axis of Advance

Dry river bed   High ground

0   2   4   6   8 Furlongs

0   1 mile

Hartley decided to outflank the enemy's preparations by a night advance by the Bannu Brigade (commanded by Brigadier F. H. Maynard) up the Iblanke ridge to the Sham plain. It was a very bold concept. Maps and air-photos being useless, and reconnaissance impossible without giving the game away, he could rely only on recollections by sundry Scouts, who knew the route from past gashts. These included no British officers. Fortunately this was a popular gasht, for from the Iblanke Narai at the top the Orakzais could communicate by helio with Samana fort, in their home country. The consensus of opinion was that the path along the ridge, although extremely difficult, was passable at night by laden mules. On this Jimmy Gimson staked his military career and Hartley the Bannu brigade. Had the Scouts been wrong, dawn might have found the brigade jam-packed and immobile on a knife-edge ridge, fired at from three sides and unable to bring its own weapons into action – recipe for a disaster far worse than that of the Guides at Wucha Jawar.

Since the essence of the plan was surprise, and Dosalli was crawling with Wazir Maliks, Khassadars and contractors, a convincing deception-plan was necessary. Fortunately there was one at hand. From Dosalli a road ran south-west to Razmak, eighteen miles away. But the enemy had broken it in many places and sabotaged the pumping station at Razani, six miles from Dosalli. What could be a more likely task for the Army than to re-establish road-communications with Razmak? Elaborate written orders were issued, with a wide circulation, for that operation, and Gimson was

continually being sent for to answer questions about the country, water, etc. Yesterday morning I was out with a gasht from 7 am to 1 pm to protect a recce party, and no sooner had I returned than I was asked to take a sapper officer out to look at a possible camp-site 4 miles from here. It is a bad bit of country and I was worried we might find the enemy behind us as we started for home, however all was well. I was seized as soon as I got back to discuss a plan for Scouts to occupy a camp at Razani and am just about to go off with an armoured car to look at the place ... *Later*. Made two trips to possible sites at Razani. Water supply not enough. Decided to move Abbotabad brigade up the valley towards the Sham plain.

The last sentence refers to the establishment of a camp, known as Village Camp, one and three-quarter miles up the Sre Mela. This could be taken as the first move of an orthodox bash through the gorge, and was vigorously opposed. But the real purpose of this camp was to be the base for a supply-route passable by animal transport and, later, MT, up the Sre Mala to the Sham plain after the plain had been occupied. So successful were these cover-plans that the enemy kept a lashkar of four hundred on the Razmak road, and went on building sangars on both sides of the Sre Mela, but did not suspect that the advance would be by the Iblanke ridge.

It was to be on the night of 11–12 May. Commanding officers were given verbal orders only on the morning of the 11th, and written orders not before five o'clock. It was not until after six o'clock, when the camp gates were closed, that the deception-orders, for the move to Razani, were cancelled.

Eight platoons of Scouts, commanded by Gimson with George Laman and John Prendergast, moving at their own speed, were to lead the advance, take the 'shoulder-blade' heights, and hold them until the Advanced Guard, the 2/11th Sikhs, arrived. (It was not then realised that the shoulder-blade heights were overlooked at close range by the Ears and Skull heights.) Behind the Sikhs, the 2/4th Gurkhas was charged with close-piqueting the route, not so much for protection as to prevent people going astray. Piquets of five men would be posted every hundred yards, on alternate sides of the path and not more than ten yards from it. To ensure that the next piquet was ready, each piquet-commander, on his predecessor being posted, was to seize the hand of the Commanding Officer and hold it until he was posted. (The Adjutant had some difficulty in impressing on young Lance-Naiks the importance of this familiarity with the man who controlled their destinies.)

Behind the Gurkhas would come the 2nd Argyll and Sutherland Highlanders less one company; the 7th and 19th Mountain Batteries; the 12th Field Company Madras Sappers and Miners less one section with the Advanced Guard; the 8th Field Ambulance; the Supply Issue Section and the second line pack transport of the column. The rear guard was to be the 1/17th Dogras, less two companies which, with one company of the Argylls, was to provide close protection and help with the mules.

Obviously it was necessary to cut the number of mules to a minimum, but it was no use the brigade reaching the top of the ridge unless it packed a punch heavier than the rifle-armed Scouts. This meant that the battalions' medium machine-guns and two batteries of 3·7 ins howitzers, all mule-borne, with all the ammunition they would need, must accompany the column. In addition the column would require one blanket per two men, tea and sugar for two days, water, picks and shovels for building a camp, signalling and medical stores. All this required a total of 725 mules. No riding animals were to be taken, and no mules addicted to braying. Because of the very difficult going, a leader was to be provided for each mule.

Every man was to carry two days' hard rations. It was hoped that rations would arrive via the Sre Mela by 13 May, but in case this was not possible, an air-drop was arranged.

The pace of the brigade (but not of the Scouts) was to be no more than one mile an hour, set by an officer at the head of the main body. Scouts were provided to act as guides for the Advanced Guard, brigade HQ and rear guard. Inter-communication was to be by runner, and by pack wireless sets (mule-borne) with brigade HQ, the Advanced Guard, the rear guard and the Sappers and Miners.

Gimson wrote to his wife on 11 May,

> We are making a big push tonight, starting off from here at 8.30 pm and going over the hills to the Sham plain. I've got eight platoons Scouts, Laman and Prender. We are all carrying two days' rations on the man and apart from that nothing but a gasht sheet to sleep in . . . It's really a big gamble, but I have a feeling that it will be a successful one. We are certain to have a battle tomorrow.

After it was all over, he wrote,

> I was feeling, to say the least, very anxious. The responsibility of getting the brigade there and of having said that the mules could get over the very difficult ground was on my shoulders, and if the expedition had failed, I would have been for the high jump.

By eight-thirty a moon in its first quarter gave too much light, and the Scouts did not start until nine o'clock. In pitch dark, carrying only rifles and ammunition, wearing grass sandals, they moved silently as wraiths, climbing continuously until they occupied the 'shoulder blade' heights half an hour after midnight. There they were within shouting-distance of the enemy, and in the customary exchange of taunt, challenge and innuendo learned that the Wazirs had no idea that the whole brigade was on the move and were quite confident of stopping the 'Militia' alone: 'The Iblanke Narai is closed,' they shouted.

For the brigade struggling along behind the going was appalling – a very steep climb to the ridge, sloping slabs of rock on which mules skidded helplessly, two-foot steps up which each one had to be induced to jump. On either side of the knife-edged ridge were precipitous slopes down which mules rolled until brought up by a bush or tree; they then had to be re-loaded, coaxed, pulled and shoved up to the top again. They were terrified, trembling the whole time, but only two were so damaged that they had to be destroyed. Nothing seems so snail-like as an advance in darkness, but however slowly the van is moving, the rear is always hurrying to keep touch. The worst, atavistic, fear is of being lost, alone in the dark. To John Masters of the Gurkhas it seemed that the din of their progress reverberated through the mountain.

We tried to be quiet, but our passage boomed indescribably loudly in the silence of the hills. Boots clashed on the stones; mule-harness creaked, hooves struck sparks from the rocks. There was no path on the spine of the ridge, and men and animals foundered on up, panting, among the bushes and concealed rock-outcrops. Sudden storms of louder noise burst over us as mules loaded with shovels or radio-sets lost their balance and crashed down two hundred feet of mountain among us. There were soldiers everywhere – on the ridge spine, lost along the sides, down in the dark gullies looking for fallen mules. I heard swearing in ten languages and saw soldiers cut mules' throats and manhandle the loads on up the mountain.

But all the Scouts could hear was an occasional crash and clatter as a mule went over the side; and the tribesmen, further away still, heard nothing. Gimson wrote,

By 1230 hours I had reached my first objective, just short of the pass leading to the Sham plain. My orders were to wait until they closed up on us and we expected them by 1.30 ... When they had not arrived by 4.30 my heart was in my boots and I thought they must have got stuck. In addition, for the last two hours the enemy had been shouting to one another on the heights all around us. At 5 am a message came from Brigadier Maynard to say the brigade was some way behind and telling me to push on and secure the hills on either side of the pass [Y—Y on Map 7]. Dawn was breaking, and as soon as we moved forward we came under heavy fire from the front and both flanks.

Prendergast recalled that

I looked back and saw a close-packed column of the 11th Sikhs below me in the gathering light – close-packed as they were edging along the narrow spine. At the firing the column bent like a cornfield and for that sort of vital second all training was forgotten and panic reigned. I heard a high, calm voice. It was their commander, Colonel Keyes, as he called them to order. They knew him and steadied at once ... A Scout near me was firing calmly and deliberately. His wadded skull-cap round which his turban was wound showed a puff of cotton-wool. A bullet had pierced through it and missed his skull by an inch.

As the Scouts went forward, the guns and machine-guns came into action. Shells from the howitzers burst along the enemy position, machine-gun bullets crackled overhead, knocking dust and stone chips off the sangars. Gimson wrote

By 7 am, we had taken our objectives, with the loss of 3 Pathan officers and 2 other ranks. By 8 am the brigade Advanced Guard had taken over from us and I was ordered to push on and secure the camp-site. We went straight over the wooded hills, about 2½ miles, fighting all the way, and got the enemy really on the run, secured the camp-site and sat down to wait for the brigade which arrived just after mid-day. The camp was officially named Coronation Camp, and we drank the King's health in weak whisky and water out of an Eno's bottle.*

On 18 May the Bannu Brigade moved on to a new camp-site at Ghariom, four miles south-south-east of Coronation Camp, better placed for an attack on Arsai Kot. The Scouts were protecting the right flank. They came under fire, and Gimson sent Prendergast forward to take charge. Prendergast describes it,

As I moved up with four of the leading platoons we were positively and sharply held up along a lip. The tribesmen could cover every movement across a flat piece of bare ground, some three hundred yards wide. Bullets were cracking an inch or two above our heads. Being normal, I had horrid visions of having my brains scattered by the next shot. The crack of the bullets was so unnervingly sharp and close as to turn my eardrums into singing deafness. I found myself very frightened indeed ... Was this me, trying to dissolve my whole quaking body into the very soil? Flatter and flatter I pressed myself into the ground. One thinks fast in moments like this and I thought,

* On that day King George VI and Queen Elizabeth were crowned.

'This is terrible, I'm supposed to be a leader.' Then the thought came back, 'Well, lead then.' So, still terrified, and with an awful feeling that my legs were made of rubber, I rose and waving my puny revolver tried to get a forward charge going. In a split second I was covered with dust from bullets which struck the ground at my feet and at the same instant I knew that the men were not going to follow me. The nearest rifleman looked up at me and I saw stark fear in his eyes, so I quickly went to ground. After all, I argued facilely, it was my job to make the enemy die for his country, not me for mine.

I then slid down from the lip out of fire and tried to get something started. I moved one platoon round to the left under cover of the lip to get rapid fire going from a more enfiladed position. Then swearing at the three other platoons and getting bayonets fixed, I led them over the edge with a loud Pathan shout of '*Halla, halla*' ('Attack, attack') ... and raced across the bare three hundred yards. I knew my stout stature made me a marked man, so I zig-zagged as I tore across the intervening space ... Some men fell, but the enemy did not stop to face the bright line of bayonets coming on so swiftly. There was some blood spattered on the ilex scrub to show that the tribesmen had not got off scot free, but when we got to the crest and looked down on the thick scrub on the far side, there was no trace of them.

The column pushed on to Arsal Kot, razed it to the ground and blew up the Faqir's cave-headquarters. Lowis was there with a party of Khassadars:

the 'Vicarage'* was twelve paces deep with two side-rooms six yards deep and a big room at the end, seven to eight feet high. Ipi had left some days earlier. Fleas frightful, very hungry, swarming up stockings. I could not have stuck on a postage stamp without covering a bite.

A distressing feature of these operations was the appalling incompetence of a British battalion, a very famous one with a great fighting record. It was ambushed, it was surprised, it was caught on the hop, it lost rifles, it left out its dead and wounded, of whom there were far too many. 'The —— bought it again,' wrote Gimson on 2 June. 'They really are hopeless and all their casualties have been due to their own incompetence. I personally consider that the enemy realise that they are easy meat and wait for them to come along.' Lowis wrote on the same

* The Faqir's supposed HQ.

theme, 'The —— lost many rifles, left wounded out and were sent off in disgrace for six weeks' training. Right up to the end they were quite pleased with themselves.'

A day or two later Hugh Pettigrew was out with a SWS gasht, the Subadar being Khan Baz (KB). The passed a string of camels, whence emanated an appalling stench.

'What on earth is that?' asked Pettigrew.

'Mahsuds,' replied KB rather louder than was necessary. 'Just Mahsuds, they all smell like that.'

The camel-leaders muttered crossly among themselves, touching on KB's ancestry, the indelicate habits of his aunts and the unwholesome relations between Afridis and goats. But the smell was so awful that Pettigrew asked what the camels carried wrapped up in sacking.

'Corpses.'

'What corpses?'

'British soldiers. We found them in the Shaktu and are taking them to Sararogha for burial. Doubtless the Assistant Sahib will give us a reward.'

In mid-June there was a report that the Faqir was residing in a tower known as Gul Zamir Kot, about a mile from Arsal Kot, on the Wazir-Mahsud boundary; and a purely Scout operation, with eight platoons of Tochi Scouts under Felix-Williams and eight of the SWS under Skrine, was laid on to catch him – a forlorn hope, thought Gimson, 'as he has probably moved on somewhere else by now. News from informers is always very stale and unreliable.' They left Dosalli in the evening and were lorried to Ghariom, five miles from Gul Zamir Kot. They marched at 11 pm to a point on the Shaktu river two miles from Gul Zamir Kot and then separated, the Tochi Scouts moving forward over the high ground north of the river and the SWS south of it. At one time, hearing the sound of stealthy movement, then running feet in the darkness, the Tochi Scouts thought they were being shadowed by the enemy, but discovered just in time that it was the SWS who thought they were being left behind.

By 3.45 am a cordon had been formed round three towers, and at first light the search began. The bird, of course, had flown, but the operation was rewarding. Ten Mahsuds and one Tori Khel were captured, the last being Arsal Khan, the owner of Arsal Kot and for many months host to the Faqir. Two Hindus were found, in a pitch-dark room, their feet locked in stocks. They had spent nearly four months in that position, were in a shockingly emaciated condition and were overjoyed at being rescued.

Some Mahsuds were getting obstreperous, though not the whole tribe. It was decided that Razcol would establish a camp at Torwam, between Razmak and Wana. To facilitate this, the SWS would build a temporary camp at Sharawangi Narai, in wooded country about six miles north-east of Torwam. Ralph Venning, summoned to Divisional Headquarters to be issued with these orders, immediately objected on the grounds that there was no water within half-a-mile of the camp site. David Williams, his Wing Commander, backed him up, and there was an acrimonious argument. Eventually the Army agreed to provide water-tanks and mules to keep them filled, and the SWS agreed to build and occupy the camp. But it did the SWS no good in military eyes; a young know-all may be forgiven if he is wrong, but not if he is right.

The Politicals warned that at the sound of firing Mahsuds would swarm in from the populous Baddar valley to the north-west, and the Scouts had information of a big lashkar in the neighbouring hills. However, Divisional Intelligence knew better and anticipated no serious trouble.

The operation started on 23 June. To cover Razcol for the first part of its move from Chalweshti Camp to Torwam, and the building of the Scouts camp at Sharawangi, Tocol would piquet three miles of road, returning to Chalweshti in the evening. The maps were unhelpful, the country broken and thickly wooded, with ilex trees growing right down to the road-verge.

There was no opposition until Tocol HQ reached Sharawangi Narai. The infantry of Tocol consisted of the 2/11th Sikhs, the 1/17th Dogras and the 2/4th Gurkhas. From the Narai the Sikhs took over advanced guard and piqueting, while the Scouts started unloading lorries, carrying up supplies and collecting rocks for the perimeter of their new camp.

The Sikhs omitted to piquet a ridge running parallel to the road and to the right of it. At eight o'clock, their forward platoons at S-S-S (see Map 8) came under heavy fire and could advance no further. A company and a machine-gun platoon of Dogras was then sent up to the ridge at D; and an Adam Khel Afridi platoon of Scouts, under Jemadar Shah Zamir, was ordered to fill in the mile-wide gap between the Dogras and the Sikhs by piqueting a knoll at Sc. It moved, well spread out, along an undulating spur which sloped down from the camp-site and then sharply up to an intermediate knoll seven hundred yards from the camp. As they approached this they were fired at from a few yards range and then rushed by scores of Mahsuds who had lain concealed in the undergrowth. In fierce hand-to-hand fighting two of the Adam

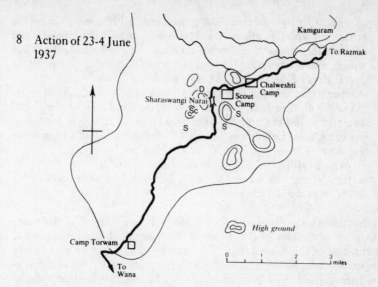

8 Action of 23-4 June
   1937

Khel were killed and eight wounded, including the platoon commander, and the remainder were forced down off the knoll. The exultant
enemy, following up closely, were checked by machine-gun and artillery fire which wounded at least one more Scout. David Williams,
commanding the SWS detachment, ordered Subadar Mohabbat Khan,
Aka Khel Afridi, to counter-attack with three platoons, which he did
brilliantly, establishing a piquet on the knoll Sc and recovering all but
one of the casualties' rifles.

The Gurkhas then came up, relieving the Scouts' piquet at Sc and
providing a company to help build the camp. Here is Ralph Venning's
account:

At about 2.30, a driving hailstorm from the north (wooded) side of
the camp blew up. Guessing the tribesmen would use this at their
backs to stage an attack on the half-built perimeter, I got permission
to take a patrol round the edge of the wood. We took the attackers by
surprise and scored a nice 'one-up'. About 4.30 the Tocol retired to
Chalweshti and we were on our own in the midst of a well stirred
hornets' nest. That evening at stand-to a party of about a dozen
tribesmen strolled up the road right in the sights of Havildar Barak
Khan, a big Akora Khattak with splendid moustaches, who was in

charge of the medium machine-gun. I ordered him *not* to press the button on which his thumb was itching because I thought by their careless demeanour that they *must* be some of the PA's Maliks. I was wrong, and missed a golden opportunity. They saw us and dived for cover. Barak Khan never let me forget it.

After dark there was some fairly vicious sniping. I was about to get out of the shallow hole that David Williams and I were sharing, and do a trip round the guards, when there was the most extraordinary wheezing noise beside me. 'Oh God!' I thought, 'David's been hit in the chest.'

'Are you all right?' I asked rather fatuously.

'Just letting the air out of my Lilo, getting another six inches down', was the laconic reply.

Next morning Tocol marched on to Torwam, helped by the three platoons of Scouts under Venning who piqueted the high ground south-east of their new camp. They surprised and shot up about sixty tribesmen whom they met on the way, but came under fire simultaneously from the enemy and from their friends, medium machine-guns of Tocol.

The effect on the Scouts was a tendency to jumpiness and shooting at shadows. Mindful of having only seventy rounds a man, I told Subadar Khan Baz to pass word around to use only aimed fire at seen targets. KB never did things in quite the orthodox way. In a stentorian voice and the thickest Afridi brogue he bawled, 'God preserve you, my children, don't shoot them. Grab them by the balls!' As we reached our objective, we received four very unwelcome 3·7 howitzer shells, one of which almost hit our orange piqueting screen. I later protested to the gunner who replied, 'Sorry, old boy, I didn't think you'd get as far as that.'

Unfortunately the successful little operation was the occasion of an unseemly row between Army and Scouts. David Williams, then second-in-command of the South Waziristan Scouts, was a man of strong character and decided views, not a glad sufferer of fools, rather prickly and by no means averse to digging in his toes if his men were given a task which might cost them unnecessary casualties. His objections to the waterless camp-site had not been well received, and it was not the only time he objected. Nor was the Army blameless. Some weeks earlier Claude Erskine, the Inspecting Officer, Frontier Corps, had drawn up in conjunction with the Army Commander a memorandum on the characteristics of Scouts and their proper use in co-operation with regulars. This the Waziristan District Commander, who was not over-burdened with Frontier lore, had not bothered to read. A week after the Sharawangi Narai camp was established Lotus Lowis, rather given to pungent criticism, wrote in his diary:

The Scouts have got themselves into thoroughly bad odour, by petty obstructiveness, mostly on the part of David Williams. Their name is complete mud with the District Staff and the really good shows they have put up in the past will now be discredited. Parsons* is now in Simla and is exercising some control over that madman Cassells.† Also Barnie has told Skrine what he is up against with the local military, and Skrine is going to tackle them and will probably get this right, or at least stop the rot.

But some of the resentment lingered on and in some military eyes the Scouts could do nothing right. However, two of the senior members of the District Staff, 'Jumbo' Mays and Pete Rees knew the form and were good friends of the Scouts.

The same could not, alas, be said of the Resident, Waziristan, Johnnie Johnson. He knew the form, all right, but was far from friendly with the Scouts Commandant. He and Williams each irritated and exasperated the other. Perhaps this was inevitable. It was like a hunt in which the retiring Master is elected Chairman, and cannot help criticising everything his successor does. Claude Erskine, on his retirement, warned Williams

I was glad I was strong enough to defeat the people (and Johnnie was, I think now, the chief) who wanted to remove you. Just be very careful until peace comes and try to suffer the Army gladly. It is quaint for me to give you this advice, as I have never been able to follow it myself ... So be careful of Johnnie and the Army. I know you will command the corps splendidly.

He did.

The grumbling about Scouts continued, inspired mainly by jealousy and a lack of understanding of their role. But the last word was with General Hartley, senior to the Waziristan District Commander:

* Sir Arthur Parsons DSO, formerly Resident, Waziristan and an old Militia officer.
† Sir Robert Cassells, Commander-in-Chief in India.

Dear Williams, an official communication has been sent to you today to the effect that I consider the allegations made against the Scouts ... to be totally unfounded. I should like you to know that it was extremely distasteful to me to be compelled to take notice of the various stories and tittle-tattle which were in circulation, and nobody is better pleased than I am to find there is no truth in them.

The retirement of Claude Erskine, who had been the first Commandant of the Tochi Scouts, was much regretted. He had been a superb IOFC. No one could have been better. He was experienced, perceptive and had a wicked dry sense of humour. On visiting a Post he would ask the most searching questions in the most disarming way, and generally he knew the answers. A visit from Erskine, said Victor Wainright, 'was like a month's pay, ten days' leave and a big tikala, especially if there was trouble about. He was a great man, and the Scouts loved him.'

The Tochi Scouts and the SWS spent most of the second half of 1937 protecting the road-construction designed to open up central Waziristan and to link the road systems of North and South (see Map 10, p. 240). The strain on the Tochi Scouts was great because, owing to the increased responsibilities, they had to expand by no less than twelve platoons (from forty-one platoons). The Kurram Militia helped by sending two platoons into North Waziristan, and the SWS by lending drill instructors. But such a sudden influx of recruits diluted the well-trained pre-war platoons.

There was the usual trouble over the allocation of road contracts, and demands for payment in advance; the Faqir denounced the roads and tried to organise resistance and non-cooperation. But by the end of September five thousand Wazirs and two thousand Mahsuds of fighting age, who might otherwise have been less beneficially employed, were drawing regular wages for pick-and-shovel work. A pioneer battalion of Mahsuds – unarmed – was raised, and did at least keep one thousand young Mahsuds out of mischief. They worked better under some sort of military discipline than as contractors' labour, and best of all to the vigorous music of their drums and pipes.

At the end of 1937 the Tochi Scouts camps at Biche Kashkai and Ghariom were up-graded to Scouts posts, the building being done by Sappers and Miners, Scouts, the Army and the Mahsud Battalion, all in three or four weeks. Each post was surrounded by a six-foot wall, later raised by the inmates, and two belts of double-apron wire fence. At two corners of the wall were towers armed with medium or light machine-guns. There was a water-tank holding 48,000 gallons, a magazine, and stores containing three days' rations for an infantry brigade. The light machine-guns were Vickers-Berthiers, commonly known as 'VBs', similar to the later Bren, lighter and less liable to stoppages than the Lewis-gun. 'Have you any VBs?' asked the Viceroy visiting the Tochi Scouts. 'They sometimes catch it in Bannu, Sir, on their way back from leave,' was John Auret's reply.

Hugh Pettigrew with 'Beetle' Lowis (cousin of 'Lotus') was commanding the escort for a sapper extending the road from Sararogha northwards to meet a road being pushed south from the Tochi valley. It was dull work, with no real gashting, until the road-head was so far from Sararogha that it was decided to set up a new camp at Janata, eight miles north of Barari Tangi.

A strong gasht from Sararogha protected the building of the camp, and the Political Agent harangued the local Maliks, promising lucrative contracts if they kept their young men under control. As soon as the Commandant had chosen the site and marked out the perimeter, a couple of hundred Scouts worked hard on the wall and barbed wire. Pettigrew wrote:

By late afternoon, when the main gasht withdrew, Beetle and five platoons were safely settled in, with two sangar piquets on the ridge above the camp. Beetle and I took a real pride in Janata ... We were determined to make the camp so secure that we would not mind if half the Mahsud nation decided to have a go at us. The perimeter walls rose to seven feet with a fire-step all round, and head-sized rocks at irregular intervals to stop the sentries from being spotted. To prevent a rush-attack, and to keep any visitors from throwing bombs at us, we put up two barbed wire aprons, one close under the sentries' eyes and the other beyond grenade-throwing range. A gate was made for the camp entrance and a stone screening-wall built to cover it from snipers' bullets. All the tents were dug down and low stone walls built round each.

The Mess had started off as a mere 180-pounder tent, but quite soon stone walls replaced its canvas sides and the uprights were placed on stone pillars to lift the ridge pole two feet higher. The result was more space, better headroom and some protection from bullets. Light came in through a large gap in the wall by day, and from a petromax pressure lamp at night ... One night I was in the Mess writing a letter. Crack! A slight pause. Then again Crack! Crack! Three bullets had gone unpleasantly close to my head. I was on the floor before the third, and in another moment or two had stretched up an arm and turned off the lamp.

Next day the window-sill was raised a foot higher.

David Williams took over command of the SWS in December 1937. He was hardly a comfortable character, nor what Dr Johnson called 'clubable', but he was a most efficient Commandant with original ideas, a ready pen and imagination. He was a keen amateur flier. (Too amateur, sometimes, as when he dropped a crate of Guinness through the roof of Jandola hospital.) He had a disconcerting familiarity with bombs, booby-traps and explosives of all kinds, planting round the Sararogha pump-house a veritable bulb garden of '36-grenades', and crawling about them with complete unconcern. On their way to Ladha, he and Hugh Pettigrew were warned by a Khassadar that an ill-wisher had planted a bomb in the road. Pettigrew recalled,

> David Williams jumped out of the car and began to search. In a matter of moments he had found the loose spot on the metalled surface, and soon had the bomb prised out, a cylindrical cigarette tin, filled with gelignite and fitted with a crude plunger and cap. He held it up in his fingers for inspection, inches from the cigar that he was smoking, and then slowly wandered to the edge of the road and tossed it down the khud. Whump! From my running position half way towards the shelter of the car I heard it go off ... with his quick sideways smile he got in and we went on our way.

Williams was an innovator. He did not change the principles of Scout work, but set out to correct the weaknesses of a gasht. First, communications. Pigeon, helio and flags were all useful, but surely in 1937 something better could be devised? While on leave he bought (out of the Garden Fund) and, with his teenage daughter, tested on Dartmoor some Marconi Type H9A lightweight radio-telephone sets. Soon the SWS were using 'walkie-talkie' sets long before the Army. The set was light, eighteen pounds complete, it was robust, and any part damaged could be easily replaced. Unlike flag and helio, it was invisible in operation, and did not disclose the user's position; it could function in all weathers, including cloud and mist which put helio out of commission; it could be operated on the move. Since it was for speech only, not morse, the user did not have to be a trained signaller, and messages could be sent and received far quicker than by morse. It did not, like the carrier pigeon, philander while on duty. And it cost only £18.

If there was a direct line of sight between sender and receiver, it could function easily up to twenty miles, but a hill between reduced the effective range, and might prevent communication altogether. On a dead-level plain, the curve of the earth's surface limited its range to two to three miles. But it was generally better than the previous combination of flag, helio and pigeon. Pigeons, however, were still carried by gashts – just in case.

Williams next turned his attention to increasing the gasht's firepower without reducing its cross-country mobility. The Vickers-Berthier light machine-gun was too heavy. But what about a machine-carbine? The British and Indian armies had no use for it, but the Germans had, and they knew a thing or two. So he bought (Garden Fund again) some 9 mm Steyr-Solothurn machine-carbines, made in Austria and Switzerland. They weighed, with magazine, less than a rifle. They had a magazine-capacity of 30 rounds and fired at a rate of 700 rounds a minute. They were essentially short-range weapons, useful at night to check a knife-rush, or poking about in dark houses and narrow lanes during a barampta. They were invaluable in chapaos.

Lieutenant Mohamad Yusuf Khan was the first of the so-called 'Indian Commissioned Officers' in Scouts. In fact he was an Afghan, a Durrani, of a family settled in Abbotabad, his mother-tongues being Persian and Pushtu. He came to the SWS with an MC won in his regular batallion, and was a 'natural' for Scouts. He had two absorbing hobbies – horses and classical music. On leave he was a hard rider to the Peshawar Vale Hounds, in Waziristan to the Wana Drag; and he spent much of his spare time schooling and jumping the Mounted Infantry ponies. In whatever post he was stationed, there was an expensive gramophone, and his Wing became accustomed, if not reconciled, to the works of Beethoven, Mozart and Chopin.

The Ahmedzai Wazirs carried out a big raid in Dera Ghazi Khan district, and sixteen platoons of SWS were deployed for six nights in chapaos to intercept them on their return with the loot. Yusuf's gasht of six platoons lay up every day in the ruins of the old Militia post of Nili Kach, in the empty wilderness south of Chagmalai. Every evening after dark the platoons moved out to different chapao positions, and returned before first light to Nili Kach where they remained concealed during the day. They were not detected there, but had to hold three Wazirs who came upon them fortuitously. The heat during the day was blistering, anything up to 105 in the shade for those lucky enough to find shade, which made it very difficult to sleep. At night it was cold, with nothing but thin mazri gashting sheets to keep them warm. They ran out of food, and almost out of water, but could send for no more without giving away their position. On the third night one of Yusuf's chapaos heard men approaching from the south. They waited until they were close and then opened rapid fire in the glare of Very lights. Next morning they found two bodies, and various items of loot dropped by the raiders in their flight. They afterwards learned that they had wounded nine more – a very good bag.

In the morning camels brought them tea and chupattis, but the chupattis were too rotten even for famished Pathans. A plane, reading their Popham-panel appeal for food, dropped some tins of sardines, but as there were too few for all to have a bite, nobody ate any; and the men trudged back to Chagmalai with light hearts but empty bellies.

In April 1938, there was a hostile gathering in the area of the Dargai Sar, a 5,740 foot mountain four miles north-west of Splitoi Scouts post and the same distance south-west of Kotkai Khassadar post. It was well placed for more mischief in the Shahur Tangi, so two converging gashts of SWS were ordered onto the Dargai Sar to frustrate any such intent. One of the six platoons under Captain Ian Dewar, accompanied by a newly joined Lieutenant Alderman, were told to move up from Splitoi; the other of five platoons under Major Woods, Captain Babington and Lieutenant Pettigrew would approach it from Kotkai. Before the arrival of the Marconi 'walkie-talkie' sets, there was no direct communication between the two gashts; but that was a commonplace of widely dispersed Scouts operations.

Dewar's gasht reached the peak without firing a shot. Woods's gasht advanced across the plain and up the Spin Ghara ridge which sloped up to the Dargai Sar by a series of knife-edges. Pettigrew recounted the affair:

The leading platoon had reached the first tangled pile of rocks and their leading Scouts were moving across the narrow concave stretch of the ridge, sweeping up in two hundred yards to another jumble of rocks. Suddenly there was the crack of bullets, not a fusilade but just five or six shots, and the platoon in front went to ground. I had been moving a little way behind them with my Subadar, Said Badshah, Orakzai, and it took only a few moments to double forward to where the platoon commander was lying ... The shots had come from the next group of rocks, one of the two point Scouts had been hit, and both were now lying half-way between us and the enemy. When I raised my head to get a brief glimpse of the enemy several bullets came unpleasantly close. One ricochetted from a rock and hit my orderly lying beside me in the leg, while another splattered off another rock in small fragments, to cause scalp wounds in two Scouts on the other side of me. Lakri Woods was up with us then and his efforts to see forward brought the same savage crack and whine of ricochets . . . The next half-hour was bad. There were probably only a few tribesmen among the rocks ahead but they completely dominated the open ridge between us and them, and the ridge was too narrow for us to fan out.

Eventually we got back the wounded Scouts and extricated the forward sections mainly by keeping the enemy's head down by sustained rifle fire, but in doing so we had several more men hit. By then there did not seem to be much point in trying to advance any further. Our own gasht had opened up touch with Ian Dewar's lot who had reached the top of the Dargai Sar, the flash of their helio from the summit going a long way to offset our frustration. So with more hostiles visible from the ridge to our right and no let-up from the rocks in front, and casualties to be got away, the decision was made to withdraw.

Meanwhile Dewar on the peak had been ordered by helio to move northwards and join up with Woods's gasht. Leaving Alderman on top with three platoons, he took the other three down the ridge. Almost immediately he encountered large numbers of tribesmen and was killed. Subadar Rasul Khan withdrew the platoon to the peak, bringing Dewar's body with him. The enemy were closing round Alderman, but with six platoons he was able to move the gasht to a strong position on top of the hill, where they were surrounded. Air-support was summoned by carrier-pigeon and during the afternoon planes were often overhead, bombing and machine-gunning, which encouraged the Scouts even though the enemy were not greatly incommoded.

It was Alderman's first gasht, and his first experience of being shot at. Scouts were very expert at looking after themselves in noisy situations, and he had Subadar Rasul Khan, the big, bearded Akora Khattak, calm and capable. His platoons were a good mixture of Khattaks, Orakzais and Mohmands. They organised an all-round defence of the boulders on the peak, saw to the wounded and checked up on ammunition. Late in the afternoon, under continuous sniping and despite strict fire-control, ammunition was running rather low. As they would obviously have to stay there until relieved, they sent off the second pair of pigeons with an urgent request for more ammunition, grenades and Very lights. These were duly delivered, but the dropping equipment was at Miranshah and for his last drop, late in the evening, the pilot reckoned he would not have time to fly there, load up and return before dark. So he landed on the emergency strip of Sararogha, only ten miles away, and while men brought out what the gasht needed, he improvised a parachute from strong cord and a Mess tablecloth. Just as it was getting dark, with the Scouts down to ten rounds a man and the Mahsuds closing round and calling on them to surrender, he was back over them, flying low and slow. The spread tablecloth with the boxes swinging below landed within a few feet of the peak.

There was no serious night-attack. Faced by one hundred and fifty Scouts, concentrated in a strong position and well-found, the Mahsuds sensibly refused battle. When Woods's gasht climbed up the ridge in the morning, not a shot was fired at them.

An MC and three IDSMs were awarded for the Dargai Sar operation – and a tiny pension to Pettigrew's eighteen-year-old orderly whose shattered leg had to be amputated. The Indian Government was always more generous with medals than with money.

In 1938 the Madda Khel Wazirs became very aggressive – sniping convoys, booby-trapping roads, blowing up culverts and even poisoning the Razani water-tanks. Datta Khel post was in the heart of the Madda Khel country, less than ten miles from the Afghan frontier, and attracted hostiles like wasps to strawberry jam. At the beginning of May Lieutenant 'Loppy' Lerwill took command of the post with its five platoons of Scouts under Subadar Baz Mohamad, Akora Khattak.

The road linking them with Boya and Miranshah was cut, but for the first few days of May, life in Datta Khel was quite normal. However on the evening of 10 May, a tribal cannon opened up from about a thousand yards away and fired six solid shot through Lerwill's quarters and the signals office. At the same time there was a lot of sniping, the snipers getting closer as it grew darker. In the post was a 4·5 howitzer, manned by gunners of the Indian artillery who were training Scouts to take it over. This was brought into action against the enemy gun, the position of which was obvious from the flash and clouds of black smoke every time it fired. The blast of the howitzer, fired from inside the fort, did little good to the glass windows, but after ten rounds the unequal artillery duel ceased. The sniping, however, continued, by day and by night, for five weeks.

Datta Khel could be relieved only by a strong column pushing along the fifteen miles of road, mined and with culverts blown, which separated it from Boya. Brigadier Maynard had his priorities, among which Lerwill's relief did not come very high. His plight was uncomfortable but hardly perilous. He was in touch with Miranshah by wireless; every day planes flew over to drop his requirements. His post was strong, well-wired, well-found in food, water and ammunition. He had his howitzer in case the enemy produced another artillery-piece; he had two Vickers medium machine-guns and one hundred and fifty trained Scouts. Provided there was no treachery in the garrison of Khattaks, Mohmands and Yusufzais, it was inconceivable that the post could be taken by storm. His own chief enemy was a sense of isolation: he had no other British officer with whom he could talk and confide. Being human, on hot sleepless nights when the sentries called their numbers in turn and snipers' bullets cracked overhead, his thoughts occasionally turned to 1919, but his was not a perturbable nature, and the possibility of treachery did not weigh on him. The only mishaps which might have precipitated a crisis were a bad wound or, say, a case of acute appendicitis; but the treatment of the few wounds and sicknesses which the garrison suffered was well within the scope of the Sub-Assistant Surgeon. The worst deprivation was of fresh meat, milk and vegetables, but this did not last long enough to affect the garrison's health.

By day the enemy sniped at anything which moved, making it impossible to collect fruit and vegetables. The garrison slept, carried on normal training, watched out for targets worthy of the machine-guns, and played basketball. By night the tribesmen came closer, calling upon all good Moslems to hand over their Faranghi officer and join the Faqir. But after Subadar Bagh Khan, Mohmand, talked them within grenade-throwing range, they kept their distance. By night, too, the garrison patrolled and set up its ambushes. The most successful of these was a pre-dawn sortie, a platoon with Lerwill slipping out of the chiga gate and establishing itself on a nearby ridge. Daybreak gave them their reward – the spectacle of about fifty tribesmen in the valley below, cooking, squatting down to their morning business, or still sleeping. Ten rounds rapid caused great consternation, and the Scouts were legging it back before the enemy could pull himself together.

After six weeks the post was relieved and Lerwill returned to Miranshah where he was surprised to find himself (since there were Press correspondents there) the hero of the Conservative newspapers. Simply for (as he put it) being in the right place at the right time, he received an immediate MC and a heavy fan-mail, including an offer of marriage from a complete stranger.

It was about this time that Subadar Faujoon, Yusufzai, IOM, IDSM, of the Tochi Scouts, suffered a singular and serious misfortune. He offended a powerful Faqir who put a curse on him, the effect of which was to dry up the saliva in his mouth so that his speech became almost unintelligible, he could hardly eat and was heading for a nervous breakdown. On sick-leave, he made a tour of Moslem shrines — to no avail. Willing to try everything, he then visited Hindu shrines in Hardwar and Benares. No good. Finally he humiliated himself before the Faqir, begging forgiveness, and immediately recovered.

13

War, 1938–9

In South Waziristan in 1938 there was a very unfriendly Mahsud named Sher Ali. He possessed the necessary status-symbol for a lashkar leader, a cannon. At two o'clock in the morning of 11 July 1938 this piece opened fire at six hundred yards on Tarekai permanent piquet, defended by a dozen Akora Khattaks, which was 1,300 yards north-west of Splitoi post. Fourteen explosive shells were fired, with fair accuracy, but only one penetrated the wall, doing little damage. At the same time the piquet came under heavy rifle-fire and tribesmen crept up to the wall calling upon the garrison to come over, and were driven off with grenades.

Subadar Ghulam Hussein, commanding Splitoi post, had a 4·5 howitzer and a Scout crew recently trained in its use. The range and direction of any spot suitable for an enemy forming-up place were known to a yard. When he heard the sound of drums beating and shouts from the west, he guessed that the Mahsuds were forming up on a flat piece of ground beyond Piquet Ridge, and ordered the gunner to give them something to shout about. Two shells were fired, which by guess and by God hit the bull's eye, bringing the drumming to an abrupt stop.

Next day Splitoi was relieved. But Sher Ali had already dismantled his gun, loaded it on to camels and taken it fifteen miles across country to Katskai, two and a half miles west of Sararogha fort, within striking distance of Langar Khel permanent piquet. It was his bad luck that there had fortuitously arrived at Jandola that day, for an operation which had nothing to do with him, the Kurram Militia's two 2·75 mountain guns.

A gasht of five platoons under Captain Cheeseman was sent out from Sararogha to Wune Sar ridge about a mile and a half away, overlooking Katskai, but drew blank. He then piqueted the ridge with two platoons at the north end and three at the south. The Jandola gasht, with the Kurram guns, under Beetle Lowis and Alderman left Jandola in fifteen lorries for Sararogha. The convoy was shot up; the Kurram guns, to the delight of their crew, came into action; a supporting plane retired hurt with a bullet through the radiator, and the gasht eventually fought its way through to Sararogha.

Meanwhile hundreds of Mahsuds had closed up on Cheeseman's five platoons. He had already been ordered back to the fort, and had sent back his layback platoons, when a rush of tribesmen got to within a hundred yards. He decided that it would be better to stay where he was, so he recalled his layback; he then had three platoons on one knoll of Wune Sar ridge and two on another. As the enemy still continued to crowd him, at nine o'clock he signalled Sararogha by lamp that he would stay there for the night but needed more ammunition, which was dropped to him just before dark. The Mahsuds made frequent rushes, but were driven off by rifle-fire.

Cheeseman's situation was hazardous, and at eleven o'clock Lieutenant Warden, with four platoons and extra ammunition, was sent out from Sararogha to reinforce him. It was a most difficult and dangerous move of one and a half miles in the dark through Mahsud-infested country, up a spur towards Wune Sar ridge in the moonlight. He was several times stopped by heavy fire from the right, and had four men wounded, but at half-an-hour after midnight he reached the two platoons just as they were being attacked from two sides and were down to twenty rounds of ammunition per man. He remained with them until four o'clock, and then took half his force across to help Cheeseman. The Wune Sar positions were repeatedly attacked; the enemy were never more than two hundred yards away, and often rushed in with great determination, hurling hand-grenades and shooting at point-blank range. From Sararogha they could hear the bursts of rapid fire and the flat explosions of grenades. Guided by lamp signals, they could give some help with machine-guns on fixed lines, but the enemy were too close to the Scouts for this to be both safe and effective. Luckily there was a bright moon, which helped the defenders. At first light two armoured cars came out from Sararogha and the enemy withdrew, and at six o'clock the weary Scouts were back in the fort. They were extremely lucky to get away with six wounded, but night actions are often more noisy than lethal, and Scouts regarded a big butcher's bill as usually a mark of incompetence, nothing to be proud of.

Showing a commendable offensive spirit, Sher Ali took his lashkar across the hills to Ladha, surprising on 18 July a road-patrol gasht under Captain Babington. The first the Scouts knew of them was a burst of fire from a high ridge which wounded Jemadar Baghi Shah, Aka Khel Afridi, and two of the advanced guard. Baghi Shah, who despite a touch of Ancient Pistol was a good soldier, was more angry than hurt and wanted to get back at them, but wiser counsels prevailed. The enemy had the advantages of numbers, the high ground, and heavy wooded country; Babington therefore decided to withdraw to Ladha. At this juncture he was joined, somewhat unexpectedly, by four Mahsud Khassadars under their Subadar, Nandar, who asked for a flag and permission to parley with the lashkar. Scouts knew that in some situations 'jaw-jaw' was better than 'war-war'; but in Babington's opinion this was not one of them. If Nandar approached Sher Ali's outlaws, they would kill him, though he carried a suitcaseful of Korans.

The withdrawal was deliberate, platoons passing back in turn to successive layback positions. It was closely pressed but − an unusual circumstance in Mahsud country − was helped by local Khassadars and villagers, who wanted nothing to do with Sher Ali in Ladha. A Sipah Afridi Naik was killed, another mortally wounded, but the Gasht Subadar, Abdul Rauf, Swati, led an immediate counter-attack to recover bodies and rifles. As the gasht reached Langar Khel village the firing ceased.

Scouts were not supermen. In this case they were taken by surprise and, although they fought with skill, they got distinctly the worst of it. No doubt Sher Ali looked back on the day with quiet satisfaction.

The Faqir of Ipi still had to be dealt with. He had his headquarters and organised supply dumps in the rugged, little-known Kharre mountains, close to the Durand line north of Datta Khel. It was decided to bring his force to battle there, destroy his supplies and roust him out of it. To this end the Razmak Brigade, 3rd Infantry Brigade and seventeen platoons of Tochi Scouts, designated Waziristan Striking Force ('Wastrike'), were concentrated under Brigadier F. H. Maynard. It was quite impossible to take motor transport into the mountains, and there were only enough mules available to carry two days' supplies beyond roadhead at Wushgai. This set a strict time-limit to the operation with no margin for unexpected delays.

On the night of 11 July 1938 the sledgehammer was at Degan, poised to strike the nut hidden in the dark towering mountains. On the 13th the brigades made a ponderous move north-west to Wushgai. The Scouts did a right hook against slight opposition to destroy a supply dump in the village of Kharsim and rejoined the column for the night. So far, so good.

For 14 July the Scouts were divided into two eight-platoon gashts under Felix Williams and Major 'Boob' Youngman, attached respectively to Razmak Brigade on the left and 3rd Infantry Brigade on the right. The idea was that when the brigades had seized the commanding heights of Buzoma Narai and its westward extension, Mazdak Punga, over 7,000 feet and very close to the Durand Line, the Scouts would swoop down on the supply dumps, destroy them and withdraw before dark.

The country over which 3rd Infantry Brigade had to advance proved to be far steeper than air-photos indicated, and the few paths were barely passable for mules even in daytime. The Scouts, behind the Brigade, moved at snail's pace with interminable delays. They were treated to the unforgettable spectacle of a mountain battery hurrying into action up the steepest possible slope, so steep that a gun-mule toppled over backwards and cart-wheeled down to the bottom. It picked itself up, had a good shake and tackled the slope again, clambering right to the top.

Razmak Brigade on the left, against stiffer opposition but over slightly easier ground, made better progress. By noon two battalions were on Buzoma ridge, and an hour later Felix-Williams's gasht had a toe-hold on the start-line for their raid, Mazdak Punga. Maynard had no news from 3rd Infantry Brigade, and assumed that Felix-Williams could launch off on his raid at any minute. This was not the case: his position on the start-line was precarious, the enemy were in force on his left flank, and until that flank was cleared by the 2/1st Gurkhas, he could go no further.

Acting on the principle of reinforcing success, Maynard dropped the plan for a raid on the right and ordered Youngman's gasht over to join Felix-Williams. The difficulties of moving across the grain of the country were such that they did not reach the Mazdak Punga until half-past three, and Maynard ordered that the raid must begin by five o'clock or not at all.

Boob Youngman and Bill Boulter scrambled down the steep, thickly wooded forward slope to see what was in store for them. There was much fire from the left, and a man between them was shot through the knee. Peering down into the forbidding, forested gorge which was believed to harbour the Faqir and his supplies, they reckoned that even without opposition it would take three hours to scramble down, find the dumps, destroy them and climb to the top again. But the opposition was fierce; the further down they went, the more likely it was that the enemy would get behind them, and they were sure to have casualties to carry back to the ridge. Youngman, as brave as any man alive, reckoned it was not on, and Felix-Williams agreed. The raid, the object of the whole operation, was cancelled. They pulled back to the ridge, closely followed but helped by excellent close air-support, and with two companies of Gurkhas made a perimeter camp for the night, freezing cold at nearly 9,000 feet. Next day everyone went back to Wushgai, the Scouts acting as rearguard.

'Wastrike' had indeed brought the enemy to battle, no doubt killing and wounding many hostiles. During their withdrawal they destroyed two ration-dumps and a large cave containing well-arranged store-rooms of food and ammunition. But they had been turned back, as much by the difficulties of the ground as by enemy action. The Faqir had not even been disturbed.

Some experienced Scouts officers were worried that too much was being asked of the Tochi Scouts. They had been on operations for nearly two years, and performed brilliantly. But the training and absorbing of nearly seven hundred recruits had stretched to the utmost the resources of instructors and NCOs. It is significant that for the years 1937–40 they did badly in the Deane Cup, the inter-Scout annual musketry competition, even when it was held at Miranshah. (The home-corps always had an advantage: it provided the butt-markers.) It is not, as a Scouts officer remarked, the best form of musketry training to hand a man a rifle and tell him to go and shoot a Wazir. But Felix-Williams was never one to dig in his toes (as David Williams would have done) when asked to take on too much.

However the next job was perfectly suitable for Scouts. There was a prominent outlaw named Mehr Dil, an army deserter and one of the few Khattak hostiles. He assembled a sizeable lashkar in the Ahmedzai Salient, an equilateral triangle of tribal territory, with sides fifteen miles long, which was like a broad wedge hammered into British India just north of Bannu. It was a patternless jumble of arid mountains, tortured ravines and cliffs, knife-edge ridges, with the high Junighar ridge running east and west across its centre. From this he was well placed to raid into Bannu and Kohat districts and did so frequently, up to the outskirts of Bannu. Except around Gumati in the south-west of the Salient, no one but outlaws lived and precious little grew in this

God-forsaken slag-heap. Neither the Tochi Scouts nor the Frontier Constabulary ever entered it. But it was now decided that Scouts and Frontier Constabulary must clean up the Salient.

The general idea was for the beaters to enter the covert along its southern side and drive the game over the guns which would be lined up along the northern side and round the north-west corner. Such sweeps – in this case likely to be more of a creep – are often tried in counter-insurgency operations and seldom succeed. Every shooting man knows that you cannot, however many and well-aligned your beaters, drive game in a direction it does not want to go: it nearly always breaks back or out to the side. In this case the beaters could not advance in line at all, but must enter the cover by the only two possible routes, valleys narrowing to ravines, running north and south some eight miles apart, separated and flanked on each side by almost impassable country.

The whole force, SALICOM, was commanded by Felix-Williams. The Frontier Constabulary would play the part of the guns over which the game would be driven. The Scouts were divided into three columns:

1. YOCOL, sixteen platoons of Tochi Scouts under Boob Youngman, based on Shewa and Spinwam, would be prepared either to support the Frontier Constabulary, or to operate in the north-west corner of the Salient.

2. WILCOL, twelve platoons of SWS, with two pack-borne Vickers guns and the Kurram Militia 2·75 mountain guns, under David Williams, would start from Bannu and move northwards through Gumati and up a narrowing valley to Daryobe, nine miles from Bannu; and thence on northwards as the terrain allowed.

3. FITZCOL, twelve platoons of Tochi Scouts under FitzMaurice, who had recently joined the corps as Wing Commander, would start from Domel, nine miles east of Bannu, and move up the Barganatu nullah, parallel to WILCOL's axis of advance.

Communication between columns and with SALICOM HQ was supposed to be by pack-borne wireless. In the event these sets, when working from the bottom of deep gorges, could communicate with nobody. The columns depended on aircraft to keep them in touch and to drop SALICOM's orders. Only once, when each happened to have a signaller on high ground, were WILCOL and FITZCOL briefly in helio-contact. The SWS carried for the first time their 'walkie-talkie' R/T sets, for intercommunication between platoons.

Movement was bound to be very slow, and the operation liable to take several days. Therefore a considerable number of camels (forty-seven for WILCOL alone) were taken to carry rations, water, medical stores, mountain-guns and machine-guns. Mules might have coped better with the terrain, but camels needed less water, and no one knew how much water they would find, or where. In this, and every other, respect the maps were useless.

The District Commissioner, Bannu accompanied the column with forty Ahmedzai Maliks and Khassadars – also useless.

The operation started on 20 September, and no opposition was encountered the first day. In fact the Tochi Scouts columns met with no opposition throughout, except sniping at night. WILCOL spent the night of 20–21 September in a perimeter camp at Daryobe. In the morning eight platoons pushed up the valley, piqueting as they went, until it became a sheer-sided ravine, the only possible line of advance. It opened out into an amphitheatre surrounded by cliffs, from which rapid fire was opened on the leading platoon, wounding two Scouts. Among the precipices and caves no enemy could be seen, and repeated echoes of every shot, back and forth between the walls of the ravine, made it impossible to estimate the strength and position of the enemy. The Khassadars decamped and a plane could spot nothing.

'Sod this for a lark' was the general feeling, and Williams saw that no progress could be made as long as the north end of the gorge and the cliffs of the amphitheatre were held by the enemy. The gasht was withdrawn to Daryobe, except for four platoons which piqueted the sides of the gorge all night.

Next morning the enemy had disappeared. Without difficulty, except from the terrain, they reached the Ziarat peak at the western end of the Junighar feature. Traces of a gang of thirty to forty were found, but the only hostiles seen were two briefly glimpsed in the early morning.

YOCOL meanwhile had been directed towards Ziarat from the north-west, though it was not known how far it had progressed; and some of FITZCOL had been seen moving westward along a ridge in that direction. Hopes were high that Mehr Dil's outlaws might be surrounded and four chapaos were put out for the night. The remainder withdrew to Daryobe. The chapaos had no success.

On 23 September WILCOL was ordered to move west, across the grain of the country, to Zarwam on the Kurram river. Lateral progress, east to west across the southern slopes of Ziarat, proved impossible. Movement was possible only along the line of some nullahs and by occasional goat-tracks up some ridges. Many ridges shown on the map were in fact inaccessible precipices, and those which were accessible were invariably knife-edged on top. Water was very hard to find, mainly in crevices in the rocks, but a plane was able to direct them to one or two pools. Their day's march was eight miles on the map, and took them six hours. When they reached the Kurram they found it in spate. FITZCOL was on the move, through this appalling country, for thirty-one hours non-stop. (FitzMaurice himself had for years suffered from phlebitis in one leg, for which he found the most efficacious treatment to be a gasht of about twenty-four miles which improved the circulation.) In the evening of that day about one hundred and fifty hostiles were seen from the Frontier Constabulary post at Dargai, half-way along the northern side of the Salient, and intermittent firing was heard all night. But in the morning they had disappeared.

On the fifth and sixth days the column were pulled out of the Salient, WILCOL having to ford the Kurram, which the Khassadars said was unfordable, several times at some hazard. And that was the end of that.

To David Williams the most satisfactory feature of the operation was probably the success of the 'walkie-talkie' R/T sets. The Tochi Scouts also soon acquired them but, curiously enough, made very little use of them, claiming that they did not work among hills, in hot weather and in many other circumstances. The SWS used them right down to platoon level in all ground- and weather-conditions, and they worked very well (which only goes to show that if a forceful CO takes a personal interest in anything, that department tends to be well run).

Williams next turned his vigorous mind, and those of his apprehensive officers, to motor transport. The SWS had twenty-two lorries and a few pick-up 'Vanettes'. Would it not increase their real mobility, and reduce casualties, if half-a-dozen of the lorries were armoured? Armoured troop-carriers were something the Army did not have; but then the Army did not have a Garden Fund.

Proper armour-plate was expensive, but early in 1939 some was ordered from England, five mm thick. The balance was made up of two 1/8th inch mild steel plates with a space of two inches between them. Trials showed that this would stop a ·303 bullet at point-blank range and a ninety degree impact. The engine, the driver's cab and the sides of the lorry were armoured, but not the rear, to save weight. The man who most needed protection was the driver, and behind him were his load and his passengers. Lest the cabin be unbearably hot, the armour was covered with a thin layer of wood. It was then painted green, and the vehicles were known inevitably as 'Green Line Buses', or 'Greenliners'. An armoured gun-ring for an automatic weapon could be fitted on top of the driver's cab.

'The Mahsud', wrote David Williams, 'spent an amusing year testing out these lorries as a sideline to other activities. He has scored some sixty hits on vehicles and four men have been very slightly wounded.'

Williams also needed something to transport the SWS artillery. The 4·5 howitzers, perfect for their purpose, were replaced by 13-pounders phased out when the Royal Horse Artillery was mechanised. 'The spectacle', wrote Williams, 'of a gun being dragged on its iron tyres behind a lorry (maximum towing speed 5 mph) for distances of 20 to 60 miles was not one which could be endured ... Some sort of gun-carrying vehicle had to be produced.' So to some of the armoured lorries ramps were fitted, up which the gun could be winched, and secured in the back of the lorry by its drag-ropes. A trained crew could 'unbox' a 13-pounder and get off the first round in less than ninety seconds. Eventually the 13-pounder was replaced by seven 25-pounder gun-howitzers which, having pneumatic tyres, could be towed at speed.

The toughest test for the 'Greenliners' was when three of them, carrying in all forty Scouts, were ambushed by about eighty Mahsuds on the Jandola-Sararogha road. Williams wrote

No road block was made. The reason for this was, of course, that the ambush was intended specifically for Scout lorries. Stones across the road would have stopped local lorry traffic and would have given the show away. The gang concealed itself carefully on either side of the road, while privileged spectators occupied a convenient natural grandstand some five hundred yards away. The lorries passed under very heavy fire. Three men were slightly wounded. A good proportion of the hits were made at ranges of less than fifty yards ... One bullet, fired from below road-level and slightly from in front, passed below the protecting armour and holed the casing of the timing gear pinion immediately in front of the cylinder block, but had no effect on the running of the engine.

All the hits were on the front of the lorries, aimed at the driver or the engine. If a lorry had been stopped, it would have been as bloody a business as the ambush of an Army platoon on the Kohat-Bannu road – six killed and fourteen wounded in a couple of minutes.

Occasionally the Scouts sent out their artillery pieces, particularly the 13-pounders, with a maximum range of 6,100 yards, to support a gasht in trouble. Their real use was for post-defence and to support gashts which were within range of the post. For this, elaborate range-cards were drawn up, with the bearings and distances to likely targets, so that a gasht could call for fire on such-and-such hilltop or wooded re-entrant. Scouts gunners were kept up to the mark by occasional visits from Royal Artillery officers, and became remarkably proficient. Similarly the Vickers guns were really meant for post-defence, but were occasionally taken out in support of a road-gasht and fired from mountings in the 'Vanettes'.

Early in 1939 the Empire narrowly escaped a grievous setback in Miranshah itself. The officer directly and lamentably responsible was a former Political Agent, Major Packman, who returned on a visit to his successor, Roger Bacon. Let the tale be told by Edward Lydall, the Assistant Political Agent.

Packie, having put himself on good terms with the world by the absorption of some mid-morning gin, was taking a stroll round his old haunts in company with Roger and myself. Great was his pleasure, on passing the civil lock-up, to find that it contained many of his old tribal friends who had been forced by the weight of tedium to shoot at the Army or at us, or by the laws of the blood-feud to murder their next-door neighbours.

'These poor fellows!' exclaimed Packie with rich benignity. 'There is no justice in the world.' He turned to the sentry on the lock-up, another old acquaintance. 'My friend, give me the key.'

The sentry hastened to comply and Packie, flinging open the door, addressed the inmates with radiant benevolence. 'My friends, I give you all your freedom!' Out poured quite a theatrically villainous collection of criminal types, fanning out all over the fort and going to ground in the most improbable crannies. After lunch Packie, feeling that he had righted a great and festering wrong, retired to bed to sleep it off, but Roger and I spent an anxious and exhausting afternoon winkling out his friends from their bolt-holes and replacing them one by one in the lock-up.

The next day Packie blotted his copybook again. The occasion was a high-level operations conference which, incidentally, as a mere visitor, he had no business to attend. Exasperated by a wealth of unsolicited advice from a very eminent RAF officer on how to run the Frontier, Packie turned on him, 'Listen chum, your job's to drive the f—g aeroplane!'

Two days later, and in Roger Bacon's opinion not before time, Packie's leave expired. He persuaded an RAF pilot to fly him to

Peshawar and they set off after lunch, Packie amply refreshed. As they landed at Peshawar, they saw the Governor (Sir Ralph Griffith), the GOC and most of the Frontier top brass lined up in their best uniforms to meet some VIPs. Packie descended from the plane with dignity, advanced on the Governor, tried to raise his topi, got entangled in the chin-strap, almost throttled himself and settled instead for a deep salaam. At that moment the Viceroy's plane touched down. It was the Governor who saved what promised to be a delicate situation. 'Packie!' he roared, 'F—k off!' Vaguely conscious of having been wronged, Packie wandered away into the middle distance.

When next he applied to visit Miranshah on leave, his application was returned by the Governor endorsed, 'NO NO NO NO'.

Roger Bacon had hardly recovered from Packman's visit when he had to hold a full-scale Jirga of the Tori Khel. Again let Lydall tell the tale:

They sat cross-legged on the grass in a large semi-circle, twenty or more deep. Along the base of the semi-circle, perched aloft on chairs, sat a General from Razmak, Roger, Felix, the Pathan Assistant and myself. The tribesmen all looked tremendously fierce. Nevertheless they replied politely when Roger expressed the traditional Pushtu hope that they would never be tired.

Seeing in the front row an old friend who had recently been sniping at the fort three times a week, I wagged a reproving finger in his direction. This had the unexpected result of giving him a fit of the giggles and causing him to disappear hurriedly behind his handkerchief.

Roger now opened proceedings with a short speech setting forth the sins of the tribe. They were harbouring the Faqir of Ipi, they had kidnapped twenty-six Hindus and were holding them to ransom, they had wrecked bridges by planting beneath them unexploded RAF bombs perched on the top of bonfires, and they were perpetually sniping at the troops ... The position was altogether unsatisfactory. What did they propose to do about it?

For the rest of the morning lengthy speeches were delivered by the leaders in the front row, each point being emphasised with the help of Pushtu proverbs and anecdotes. Why should they not harbour the Faqir of Ipi? He was a very holy man and a member of the Tori Khel tribe. And anyhow they were not harbouring him. The retention of Hindus was a purely commercial transaction and had nothing to do with us. As for the sniping, they had not invited us to build camps all over the country, and so could hardly be expected to feel bound by the laws of hospitality.

Steam having been duly blown off, we adjourned for lunch, leaving a clear field for the wiles of the Pathan Assistant. He was soon at work, having persuaded my giggling friend to come and talk matters over quietly. The result was that my friend agreed for a consideration to refuse hospitality to the Faqir of Ipi, to return two or three Hindus who were with him, and to cease from bombing bridges and sniping forts ... The rot now set in, and for the rest of the afternoon the house of the Assistant was besieged by keen negotiators anxious to be in on the ground floor. As a result the plenary session next day was an altogether more genial affair ... and with much handshaking the Tori Khel dispersed, pledged to be of good behaviour at any rate for a week or two.

The way was now clear for a resumption of the policy of peaceful penetration ... Money was sanctioned for the digging of wells, and a perspiring Major delighted the locals by wandering about with a hazel-wand which would on occasion rise up without warning and hit him on the nose. It was even greater fun watching a deep hole being dug at Government expense in quite the wrong place, the marks set up by the water-divining major having been moved during the night.

Throughout 1937, 1938 and 1939 the two Waziristan corps were continually in action and suffered about the same number of casualties. But they were in different kinds of action. Because the Mahsuds as a tribe were not hostile, the SWS were generally operating on their own in a true Scouts' role, while Tochi Scouts' gashts were operating as integral parts of brigades under military command.

At the end of 1938 Felix-Williams was invalided home with malaria. Under his leadership the Tochi Scouts had won great renown. He was succeeded by FitzMaurice, a dedicated Scout and a very good Commandant, if perhaps too hard on himself and not quite hard enough on others. At the beginning of 1939 political control of Waziristan, and of the Scouts, was again handed back from the Army to the Politicals, a sign that the war was again considered to be at an end.

So it was, in the sense that there were no more big lashkars in the field, except in the Datta Khel area, close to the Afghan frontier; the enemy had followed the classic tactics of guerillas, breaking up into smaller and much more elusive gangs. They became skilful with bombs and booby-traps, mining roads, blowing up bridges and culverts. Lieutenant G. P. V. Sanders lost a hand trying to defuse a bomb found near the parade-ground at Miranshah. The sniping and hold-up of civilian lorries became a popular sport, and profitable too when affluent Hindus could be kidnapped and held for ransom. (Hindus who were not worth a ransom were knifed on the spot.) In one ambush of a civilian lorry escorted only by Khassadars, the Tori Khel grabbed the corps butcher, the Sub-Assistant Surgeon and a Scout returning from leave. However, the Commandant interviewed the Tori Khel Maliks to such effect that the captives were released none the worse for their adventures.

The biggest catch was by the Shabi Khel Mahsuds: a Hindu Major in the Indian Medical Service. They used to amuse themselves from time to time by stropping a razor in front of his eyes and discussing which part of his anatomy they would amputate in order to expedite his ransom. Then one would say, 'Well, Tuesday isn't a good day for slicing off noses. We'll think about it tomorrow.' Eventually he was released unhurt, but very shaken. The Government's policy, as a rule, was to pay the ransom for its own servants, and recover it from the captor's family or clan. One gang, having stopped a lorry, was disconcerted when from its roof Darim Khan (the renowned Subadar of Khassadars) hailed them, promising to shoot the first man who laid hands on it. This made them pause, for he was a man of his word, and no one particularly wanted to shoot him and start a feud with his Manzar Khel clan. After prolonged negotiations they conceded that the lorry might return intact, with all passengers, to Miranshah. 'No deal,' replied Darim. 'This lorry goes on to Datta Khel.' And so it did.

The first SWS operation of 1939 was a barampta of all villages in the Spin Plain, fourteen miles south-east of Wana and of Utman Khel village just north of it. It was suggested, singularly enough, by the local Wazir Maliks because the villages were full of bad characters whom they and the Khassadars would identify. As the villages were scattered over an area of about twenty square miles, the operation would need a large force of Scouts, to conceal and account for whose concentration the acting Commandant, Major Woods (David Williams being on leave), evolved an elaborate cover-plan.

The regular relief of the Tiarza garrison, due a few days earlier, was postponed until the day before the barampta. Baggage lorries interspersed with troop-carrying lorries, moving back and forth between Sarwekai and Tiarza, unobtrusively dropped off three platoons at Tanai post, four miles north of Utman Khel. The change-over of Mounted Infantry between Tanai and Sarwekai was also advertised for that day; the troops from those two places, ostensibly relieving one another, met en route and returned together to Tanai. Two more platoons from Sarwekai arrived late in the evening. There were thus in Tanai on the evening before the barampta its usual garrison of four platoons, three from Tiarza, two from Sarwekai, and two troops of Mounted Infantry.

During the night of 24–25 February five platoons, taking a circuitous route which avoided all villages and kirris, positioned themselves by four-thirty on the high ground north and west of the saucer-like Spin plain. The Mounted Infantry cordoned off the east and south. And the Tanai garrison surrounded Utman Khel village. One platoon was in position on a high ridge much earlier in the night to hold anyone there who might hear the sound of lorries bringing the search-party from Jandola. Two Wazirs were captured.

At first light Captain Cheeseman with the search-party of five platoons arrived, and at the same time, with unprecedented punctuality, there arrived the Maliks and Khassadars from Wana with the Assistant Political Agent, Captain S. I. Hassan. The search started, the covering parties closed in and two armoured cars prowled menacingly around.

The Mounted Infantry spotted three tribesmen haring away westward, and two sections galloped after them. When they were within half a mile two of the tribesmen, who seemed to be unarmed, stopped and stood still; the third ran on, from time to time turning to shoot at his pursuers. The leading section rode hard after him, and while they did so, were fired on from behind by the two 'unarmed' men. It is, fortunately, difficult to hit a galloping horse at five hundred yards. Up came the second Mounted Infantry section, rounded up those two, and found a third man hiding in the crops, with a recently-fired rifle.

The leading section eventually caught up with and surrounded the Wazir who had run away. They called on him to surrender, but he was a hard man, out for death and glory, and went on shooting, his aim impaired by the fact that he had just run a mile and a half at top speed. It says a good deal for their discipline and restraint that the Scouts did not shoot him forthwith. Sowar Ghulam Sarwar broke the impasse by charging him from sixty yards in a spirited attempt to snatch his rifle. The Wazir upped with the rifle, fired – and missed. But the horse shied at the shot, which caused Ghulam Sarwar to miss his snatch and he galloped on. Nothing now remained but to shoot the Wazir, which they did – but not to kill. He was taken prisoner with the other three, treated in the hospital in Jandola and made a complete recovery, praising the All Merciful, one likes to think, for the Militia's mercy. An hour later another armed Wazir was found by the Mounted Infantry hiding in the crops. He, too, was shot down just as he was about to fire at them, and slightly wounded. The villages had been taken by surprise and the barampta was a complete success, forty-three hostiles being identified and taken to jail.

In North Waziristan a new camp was built at Khar Kamar, to fill the gap between Datta Khel and Boya. It was an unlovely place. The British officer's quarter was one room built of puddled mud and stone, with no window, which meant that the occupant had to choose between light and warmth; if the door was shut, no light came in; if it was open, in roared the savage cold wind and dust. Terence Phillips much disliked Khar Kamar because one lived on top of the men:

> every hoik and spit one hears with distressing clarity, and as they occur every two minutes, they are wearing to the nerve. Everyone going up and down to the Quarter Guard chats loudly to his friends only five yards away and that makes me feel like tearing something to pieces ... I saw two Wall-Creepers* today.

The sniping of troops on the Razmak plateau became such a nuisance that in the summer of 1939 Crocus Camp was established, for a company of Scouts, between Razmak and the Razmak Narai. This was much more pleasant: cool at 7,000 feet, surrounded by short grazed grass, and out of effective sniping distance from the hills. In August the Brigadier asked Phillips, commanding Crocus Camp, to barampta Bandiza village: 'Just nip down and back, we'll have you covered by guns and by the machine-guns of the 5/11th Sikhs.'

All this on a one-inch map which I did not examine as closely as I should or I would have seen that we would have a seven-hundred foot drop exposed all the way down and, more important, all the way back, to fire from the wooded slopes opposite and from the flanks, which completely dominated the village at the bottom of the valley. If it had been an operation laid on by Scouts, it would have been done just before dawn, with at least fifteen platoons, not five which was what I had; and the village would have been sealed off by the occupation of any heights which overlooked it.

I had a hundred and twenty-five rifles for gasht, fortunately from F Company, one of the best tactical companies in the corps, comman-

---

* A kind of bird.

ded by Subadar Jan Bahadur, a short, black-bearded Orakzai with such a reputation for integrity that he was known as 'Sharif', 'the Trustworthy'. It included a Mohmand platoon commanded by Jemadar Lal Din, IDSM, a self-effacing little man and a very good soldier.

On a beautifully clear and cool morning we reached the top of the ridge at 8,000 ft and I went forward to see what we had to do. I was not encouraged. The village occupied the place of the stage in a Greek theatre, with the Sikhs in the flies, so to speak, behind; and the enemy, if there were any, in the seats, rocky slopes thickly overgrown with holly bushes. We might be hard put to it to escape from the trap when we 'nipped down' to search the village. I protested to Brigade that I could not do it without help in holding the heights opposite, but they replied, after a long time, 'Complete your task quickly and return. You are covered by guns.'

When we had a good look into the bottom of the valley, we discovered a large kirri of Tori Khel, about which we had not known, who were apparently hamsayas of the Bandiza people, and would join them in any fight. This was an unexpected complication . . .

Jan Bahadur and I agreed that it might be very dangerous. I decided I could not go into the village without putting up a platoon on the opposite ridge, which overlooked it, and a platoon to my right, on a little isolated hill four hundred yards from the village. We were all by this time on a spur above the village. Jan Bahadur started Lal Din and his Mohmands across the valley: Makhed Gul with the Akora Khattak platoon got safely on to his isolated hill on the right, and Ridwanullah, with the Yusufzais, onto a spur on our left. That left us with only two Orakzai platoons in hand. As Lal Din moved, the people in the kirri started shouting at us to go back, and Makhed Gul saw a woman signalling from Bandiza. Shooting started almost immediately, mostly at the Akora Khattaks and some at us. Although it sent leaves fluttering down, we were well dispersed and I thought it improbable that we would be hit, but I was anxious about Lal Din and Makhed Gul who were so much closer to the enemy. The Sikh machine-guns were silent, not knowing how far we had reached, and although the guns were firing, they saw nothing to fire at and were quite ineffective over so large an area. I saw that any further advance would invite a major disaster, and signalled Brigade that I could not go on without more support. Happily I had a reply, 'Withdraw immediately.'

Jan Bahadur recalled the forward platoons by flag and they were soon on the move, covered by ten rounds rapid from us, handled splendidly by Lal Din and Makhed Gul. Miraculously they crossed the valley bottom without casualties. We then had three platoons on our ridge and two on Ridwanullah's to our left and I knew we were safe for our platoons on the parallel ridges could support each other by cross-fire. There was still not a squeak out of the Sikh machine-guns . . .

We passed through the Sikhs whose Colonel said, 'You are being followed up by two or three hundred hostiles who may attack my piquets when we withdraw. Please hold your people in reserve to counter-attack if we need you.' I knew there could not be as many as that, but passed the word to Jan Bahadur. I had not seen an enemy all day.

When we sat on the short grass to eat our mid-day meal, there was a feeling of complete confidence in the gasht, in ourselves and in each other. In the end the Sikhs got out without any trouble and we were back at Crocus by two o'clock . . . The fighting rolled away south-wards . . . The Leicesters, trying to withdraw a piquet in dense ilex scrub, had it overrun in hand-to-hand fighting, losing six killed and six wounded and having to abandon the bodies of two men with their rifles and equipment.

Lal Din was recommended for a bar to his IDSM, but it was refused, for the singular reason that his platoon had suffered no casualties thanks entirely to his virtuoso performance.

Scouts were always on speaking terms with the locals and usually, a few days after an action, someone who had been on the opposite side would drift in and talk with the Pathan officers. Sure enough a couple of days after Bandiza a Wazir came in to see Jan Bahadur. He said that two well-known gang-leaders had been on the feature overlooking the village with three hundred men. They had seen us coming and swore to let us become well involved in the valley bottom, from which we would never escape. But someone had fired too soon and sprung the trap.

A few months earlier there had occurred the curious episode of the Shami Pir. 'Shami' means 'of Damascus', and 'Pir' means 'saint'. That is what he was – sort of – a sly Syrian ecclesiastic with a venerable beard and a sanctimonious air, preaching with all the authority of a Sayid, a descendant of the Prophet, and a number of the Gilani clan. The

Gilanis, much respected for their religious associations, are found in many Moslem countries. They tended to be pro-Axis, adherents of the ex-Mufti of Jerusalem who was Hitler's instrument in the Arab world. One of them, Rashid Ali Gilani, staged a pro-Axis coup in Iraq at a critical stage in the Second World War. The Shami Pir was almost certainly financed by the Germans or Italians, but his preaching seemed harmless and not particularly anti-British.

In the South Waziristan Scouts was an Akora Khattak Subadar, Hamidullah, who was also a Sayid and, as such, had access to the Shami Pir's inner circle. He gave the Political Agent the first inkling of what the holy man was really up to — inciting Mahsuds and Wazirs to put back on the Kabul throne the Anglophobe Amir Amanullah who had been ousted ten years earlier — largely by Mahsuds and Wazirs. The last thing the Indian Government wanted was to be embroiled with Kabul, so the Shami Pir was bought off, and went on his way rejoicing. At Karachi he shaved, discarded his robes and was photographed, 'suited-booted' as Pathans say, a youngish, natty, plump Levantine such as one would expect to proffer a selection of dubious postcards.

But his activities gave notice that it was not only the British and Pathans who were interested in Waziristan.

14

Scouts on the Roof of the World

The Gilgit region is one of huge and mainly sterile mountains, intersected by deep, narrow valleys in which the heat of summer and the cold of winter are extreme. (See back endpaper.) If one visualises the Gilgit Agency as an irregular rectangular watch-face, about 100 miles north to south and 140 miles east to west, its neighbours were:

From 1 to 2 o'clock: Chinese Turkestan, entered by the Mintaka (15,450 ft) and Killick (15,600 ft) passes.

From 2 to 4 o'clock: The Karakorum Range, including K.2 (28,250 ft), the second highest mountain in the world.

From 4 to 6 o'clock: Baltistan and Astor, tributary states of Kashmir.

From 6 to 7 o'clock: The Hazara Division of the North-West Frontier Province.

From 7 to 9 o'clock: The independent territory of Kohistan, Tangir and Darel, thinly inhabited by a mixture of semi-Pathan tribes.

From 9 to 11 o'clock: The state of Chitral.

From 11 to 1 o'clock: The Afghan Wakhan.

In the Pamirs to the north-east, three empires met – the British, the Russian and the Chinese, though the two former were barely separated by the narrow strip of the Afghan Wakhan. Victorians spoke of it as 'the cock-pit of Asia'.

Within a radius of sixty-five miles from Gilgit are eight peaks over 24,000 ft, including Rakaposhi (26,050 ft) and the beautiful killer-mountain of Nanga Parbat (26,650 ft). Nowhere else in the world are there so many lofty peaks, deep valleys and long glaciers.

Only the river valleys are inhabitable or inhabited; the mountains are given over to shepherds and yak-herds. The main rivers are the Indus to the south and south-east, with 2,000 more miles to flow to the Arabian Sea; its tributary, the Gilgit river; and the Gilgit's tributary rivers of Hunza, Kuh Ghizr, Yasin and Ishkoman. All the rivers are roaring monsters, quite unfordable except in a few places in winter, and un-navigable except by a few ferry-rafts made of inflated buffalo-skins. The Indus was bridged by the Partap Pul suspension bridge, a vital link with Srinagar, five miles below its junction with the Gilgit river. There were a few other suspension bridges passable by horses; but generally animals had to swim the rivers while people with strong nerves trod carefully along the foot-rope of swaying, sagging rope-bridges. The whole area contained no wheeled vehicles, not even a cycle, but the bones of a caterpillar tractor, driven and carried with prodigious exertions from Srinagar, rested in peace where it had finally expired, in Gilgit town.

The people are divided into three main groups: the Burish or Yashkuns of Hunza and Nagar, the Dards of the Gilgit and right bank tributary valleys (also of Chitral), and the Chilasis. The people of Hunza are of an open, cheerful disposition, strong and stockily built, many with red hair and blue eyes which they (like many other frontier people) like to attribute to their descent from Alexander's army. The people of Nagar, somewhat inter-married with Dards, are darker in complexion and, living on the shady side of the Hunza river valley, darker too in character. Or so early travellers, briefed by the Hunza-kuts, used to say, and later travellers repeat. The language of both is Burushaski, which is spoken nowhere else in the world, and seems to have no affinity to any other language. Perhaps some difference in character between the people of Hunza and Nagar is attributable to the former being Maulais (followers of the Aga Khan), and noted tipplers, while the latter are puritanical Shiahs. It would be quite possible to come across a Hunzakut driving a truck in New York; but the Nagaris and Dards are stay-at-homes. As for the Chilasis, given to religious fanaticism, intrigue, robbery and blood-feuds, they are described as 'sitting in gloomy abstraction' while their women do all the work.

There is very little rain, so throughout the area crops are irrigated by water-channels known as kuhls, which bring water from the local river far upstream across mountainsides and cliff-faces, to the terraced fields where the village headmen divide it among the villagers. The kuhls need constant and skilful maintenance. They are bordered by poplars and willow-trees, growing from wands stuck in the ground in the spring, which seldom fail to strike. The poplars are used for roofing rafters, the willows for basket weaving, and their roots strengthen the banks of the kuhls.

Politically the area was part of Kashmir State, and the Government a sort of British-Kashmir condominium. That was the theory. In practice it was governed by the Political Agent, Gilgit, by indirect rule through the hereditary Mirs or Rajas of seven pocket-handkerchief sized states – Hunza, Nagar, Gilgit, Kuh-Ghizr, Punial, Yasin and Ishkoman. The system, or lack of system, worked pretty well, freeing the people from feudal subjection with intolerable taxes and forced labour, and maintaining – even improving – their very simple but healthy way of life. Chilas was governed directly by the Assistant Political Agent.

To assist him in his task, the Political Agent had the Gilgit Scouts, nearly six hundred strong, divided into ten platoons, three each from Hunza and Nagar, one each from Gilgit, Kuh-Ghizr, Yasin and Punial. The Subadars and Jemadars were mainly of the aristocratic *Gushpur* class, blood-relatives of the Mirs and Rajas. The Scouts were armed with ·303 SMLE rifles and a few Vickers guns for post-defence. The summer uniform was the same as that of the South Waziristan Scouts – grey mazri shirt, khaki shorts and hose-tops, bandoliers and chaplis. But instead of the safa, they wore the koi, resembling a rather baggy, rolled cap-comforter, made of brown goat-wool, worn throughout the Pamirs and Hindu Kush, used also as a receptacle for cigarettes and money. On ceremonial parades the koi was of white wool, real dandies wearing kois made of the soft belly wool of the ibex. In winter they wore warm woollen plus-fours, grey woollen shirt and khaki sweater. The ibex-head badge of the Gilgit Scouts was worn on the koi, backed by a coloured cloth strip one and a half inches wide, green for the Hunza platoons, red for Nagar, yellow for Punial and so on. They used flag and helio signals. Recruiting was in early spring, and was eagerly contested.

As in Waziristan, the Scouts came under the general direction of the Political Agent; but operations, training, discipline and general administration were the responsibility of the Commandant, a Major, known always as the 'Commanding Sahib'. (His wife, irrespective of personalities, was the 'Commanding Memsahib'.) His job was what he cared to make of it, but what potential, what a place and what men to serve! It was one of the most sought-after appointments in the Indian Army, considered to be a great privilege.

The corps headquarters was in Gilgit. The role of the Gilgit Scouts was to act as the trip-wire and first defence against invasion by Russia,

China or Afghanistan; and to discourage raids from Chinese Turkestan, Afghanistan and the tribal territory of the south. Thanks to the Scouts, such raids seldom took place. In the absence of any police force, they also had the general responsibility for law and order and for the arrest of blood-feud murderers, sheep-stealers and drug smugglers. They garrisoned posts at Chilas, at Gupis in the west, and Kalamdarchi, at 11,500 feet the highest post in the British Empire, at the junction of the routes from Chinese Turkestan over the Killick and Mintaka Passes.

They did not gasht like the SWS or the Tochi Scouts, widely dispersed and alert for an attack. This was unnecessary, for there were no local hostiles. It was also impracticable, for in these narrow valleys, with towering mountains on either hand, any movement off the main bridle-paths would reduce a gasht to a snail's pace, and it would take all day to piquet a single height. Any tactical move by the Gilgit Scouts would be in the nature of a forced march to reinforce Chilas, Gupis or Kalamdarchi against possible raids, or unrest among the volatile Chilasis. Where the Gilgit Scouts excelled was in the speed of their forced marches. Hunzakuts, in the course of their normal private affairs, considered sixty miles in twenty-four hours to be a brisk walk. These Scouts moved even faster than the Waziristan corps: Chilas, sixty miles from Gilgit, could be reinforced in a single day. Otherwise they had ordinary infantry training, with an emphasis on mountain warfare.

Despite the Hunzakuts' fearsome reputation as raiders into Chinese Turkestan in the nineteenth century, they were less aggressive and more straightforward than Pathans, tough and capable mountaineers, potentially excellent soldiers and unwaveringly loyal to the British element of the condominium, though with neither liking nor respect for the Hindu Government of Kashmir. They were all Moslems, Sunnis, Shiahs and Maulais, and on the whole got on well together though the Shiahs were, perhaps, less tolerant than the others. The Maulais drank wine made from local grapes, strong and quite good, and an extremely intoxicating, malodorous spirit distilled from mulberries. Some were notable wine-bibbers, including Subadar Jamshed Khan, brother of the Mir of Hunza and known to British officers as Champagne Charlie.

There was a general enthusiasm for field sports, especially falconry. 'Lend your rifle before your horse, your horse before your wife, and your wife before your hawk,' was a local saying which established priorities. Passage-hawks were preferred to hawks taken as chicks, and goshawks were considered more easily trained than peregrines. To catch a passage-hawk, the hawker marked down his roosting-tree and sat under it with a smoking fire, drumming hard. When the bird awoke and took his head from under his wing, a horse-hair noose on the end of a long rod was slipped over his head, and he was caught. Or the hawker lay in a pit under a lattice-work cover on which was a piece of meat; when the hawk came for the meat, his legs were seized. Training with the lure proceeded in the traditional manner.

Some British officers − including Evelyn Cobb when Political Agent − became falconers, but most preferred shooting. Those who were fascinated by mountain stalking − a five hundred mile walk, perhaps, for one spectacular head − could find in the Gilgit Agency the markhor, a wild goat with corkscrew-shaped horns four feet long, the ibex, another goat with horns like a knobbly scimitar, and the wild sheep known here as the sharpu. There was even a faint chance of snow-leopard, and of the gigantic *ovis poli*, Marco Polo's sheep, which at certain times of year occasionally moved from the Pamirs into the top of one Hunza valley. But already in the 1930s the ethics of shooting animals for sport was being questioned. Shooting to most officers meant bird-shooting, chikor in the lower hills, ram-chikor, the size of a capercailzie, on the snow-line, and an occasional woodcock.

The game to which all the tribesmen, including of course the Scouts, were passionately addicted was polo. Not the polo of Delhi, Smith's Lawn or Cowdray, but the game which was played in Central Asia for many hundreds of years. In the 1940s a spate washed away a gravel bank in the Kuh-Ghizr river to reveal a Dedication Plaque announcing that the King had opened a polo ground, with all the proper rites, nearly two thousand years ago.

It was played in every village, and every town; the ground was long and narrow, perhaps two hundred yards by fifty, but in villages it might be the village street. Every man between fifteen and fifty who owned or could borrow a pony played. It is not everywhere that polo is seen as a social leveller; but in Kuh-Ghizr or Ishkoman there might be seen Raja, shepherd, British officer, Scouts sepoy, and all the ragtail and bobtail of the valley playing together in perfect good fellowship and indifference to person, galloping about in a cloud of dust and enjoying themselves enormously. The best ponies, of about fourteen hands, were imported from Badakshan or the Russian Pamirs and in the 1930s cost about 200 rupees. All were stallions, which added a new dimension to the game. To keep them sound, they were 'yorrocked' before and after a match. This consisted of taking a horse for a short exercise canter, and then standing him in a water-channel, saddle on, girth loosened, head exaggeratedly over-bent, until he had staled twice. It was very effective − and needed to be, for in the traditional village polo a chukkar continued until nine goals had been scored, though in Gilgit, where alien influence had crept in, chukkars were limited to half an hour. In village games there was no limit to the number of players, but in more formal matches they were restricted to six a side.

There were no rules against crossing or foul-hooking. After a goal had been scored, the scorer enjoyed a free hit, known as a 'tambuk'. Galloping down to the half-way line, he leant forward holding the ball beside the horse's right ear and then, with a terrific underhand sweep, hit it towards the enemy goal. It was not unusual for an expert to hit three goals in successive tambuks. Another very skilful ploy was to hit the ball against the stone wall which bordered the ground, catch it as it bounced back and gallop with it through the goal while the opposition did all it could to get the ball off the striker or the striker off his horse. The famous frontier doctor, Lloyd Ledger, performed the now legendary feat of vaulting on to the ball-carrier's horse at full gallop and, riding pillion behind him, steering the horse willy-nilly through his own goal.

The game was seen at its best at the annual *jhalsa* in Gilgit when the Mirs and Rajas assembled for homage to the King Emperor (and, perfunctorily, to the Maharajah of Kashmir), to pay a small tribute in gold-dust washed from local rivers, and to receive gifts such as a sporting rifle or a telescope, with Scouts Guard of Honour and all the populace looking on. Polo matches between the kingdoms – Hunza v. Nagar, Punial v. Yasin – were the great features of the occasion. In the morning the Scouts' drums and pipes would play in the 'Commanding Sahib's' garden announcing to the world that there would be polo that afternoon. By half-past two all the Mirs and Rajas, if not actually playing, would be seated in a shamiana on the west wall of the ground, opposite them were positioned the bands of the respective teams. (Some ponies were such sticklers for custom that they would not perform without music.) The Political Agent opened the game by throwing in the ball, and then it started, fast and very furious, all the best players competing fiercely for the honour of their states while the bands played louder and louder, rising to crescendo as a goal was scored or saved. Feelings ran high, and on more than one occasion the Political Agent had to stop a match lest blood be shed and a blood-feud result. When a match was over, the losers had to dance before the winners, a ceremony which was tactfully omitted when British officers were in the vanquished team.

The Scouts were very fond of dancing, not as energetically as Khattaks but rhythmically and gracefully. The older men, particularly in Hunza, performed a spectacular war-dance with curved sword and shield. The characteristically morbid dance of the Chilasis represented vultures gathering round a dying beast.

Only an officer with a wish for adventure would volunteer for the Gilgit Scouts, and for Joe Trotter adventure began in the autumn of 1933. He had applied on impulse for a vacancy of which he heard by chance, and arrived at Srinagar with just time to purchase supplies for a year, hire a house-boat to Bandipur, and pack-ponies to take his supplies over the passes.

It was 231 miles to Gilgit, over two passes of 12,000 and 14,000 feet, and rest-houses every sixteen miles or so. Grown-ups and older children rode and walked; small children were carried by porters in doolies. Trotter had to hurry to get through; for six months in the year the passes were closed by snow, except to the dak-runner, who somehow managed to carry the mail, spending the night in huts lifted on stilts above the snow.

Gilgit town was quite a metropolis in the 1930s with the Political Agent George Kirkbride, his wife and three children in residence. There were the Scouts commandant and two subalterns; and the Medical Officer whose patients were brought even from Russian territory and from Chinese Turkestan on charpoys over the high passes. Occasionally a plane ventured the hazardous flight to Gilgit; and the pilot who carried Nat Cosby was persuaded by his intrepid passenger to fly *under* the suspension bridge, to the manifest alarm of the people and animals walking over it.

In the summer, when Gilgit could be oppressively hot, the Political Agent and Commanding Sahib moved their headquarters to small wooden bungalows at Naltar, 5,000 feet higher, a day and a half's march away. It was an idyllic site, in grassy meadows among pine-forests, with a view down the valley to the magnificent peak of Rakaposhi. The gentians, irises and ground orchids delighted all who beheld them; and for the more adventurous there were exotic fungi, far more delicious than field mushrooms, eaten with some trepidation but never any ill results. In winter there was skiing.

Joe Trotter, as second-in-command of the Scouts, was posted to Chilas. He also acted as Assistant Political Agent, in which capacity he would write the Scouts instructions from one office, and then gallop down to the other to explain why they were impracticable. He lived in an attractive wooden bungalow, roses festooning the verandah, and in summer when the Indus valley sweltered, he moved up to his 'hill station' on the Babusar pass, over which went the bridle path leading to Swat and Abbottabad.

He gashted along the low, hot valleys, among the stupendous mountains and across the glaciers, forded roaring torrents, edged across rope-bridges. If ever his gasht fired a shot, it would be for rations on the hoof, at chikor, sharpu or ibex. In his magisterial capacity he held court in village rest-houses, or in the deep shade of walnut and mulberry trees, trying cases of murder, sheep-stealing or of taking more than a proper share of water out of a kuhl. He gave logistic support to a German team attempting Nanga Parbat where, for the honour of the Third Reich and the swastika which fluttered over their base-camp, four Germans and three Sherpas died. The most important part of his job was just showing the people that the Sarkar was in business, not unduly interfering but keeping a fatherly eye on them. His most satisfactory coup was the ambush on the Babusar pass and capture of twenty *khat* smugglers,* taking the drug from where it was grown, on the slopes of Nanga Parbat, to where it would be sold, in India.

While Trotter was in Gilgit, the Scouts were converted from part-time to full-time duty; and, by agreement with the Kashmir Darbar, the State troops were moved out of Gilgit, to Bunji, south of the Indus. This did little more than give formal recognition to the obvious fact that the Agency was British-ruled, as the people all wished. With full-time duty came instructors from the Indian Army, and the Scouts became more professional.

The most beautiful time of year was the spring. The fertile, irri-gated valleys shaped like fans would begin to throb first with the sap in the willows which turned a lovely shade of red, followed by green leaves and catkins. Then came the apricot, peach and almond blossom, and soon all the cultivated valleys looked like Paradise. The wheat, barley and rice began to sprout, and one could almost feel the earth and the people of the valleys shaking themselves free of the long, cold winter. Sometimes one would find some old crone luxuriously sunning herself, but this was rare for the people had to water, manure and plough their fields. Later on the valleys would be carpeted with wild flowers – gentians, anemones, irises, ranun-culus and stonecrop.

'In the spring a young man's fancy . . .' Trotter even found time to marry the Political Agent's young sister, the ceremony being per-formed by the bride's brother in his garden. They galloped off for

* *Khat.* A mild drug, fairly harmless in small quantities, but addictive and conducive to impotence and lethargy if taken to excess.

their honeymoon to Naltar, with chaplis tied to their horses' tails, and lived happily ever after.

Ten years later 'Rosy' Milanes, wounded in Burma, was offered command of the Gilgit Scouts and accepted with alacrity. He was advised, because of his wounds, to eschew long marches, advice which he treated with contempt. He found the Scouts to be little more than policemen, and stepped up their military training without reducing their extraordinary marching speed. When there was some trouble on the Chinese border, reinforcements from Gilgit, sent up to Kalamdarchi, took three days to cover one hundred and eighty miles of appallingly difficult track, climbing by ups and downs from 5,000 to 15,430 feet, fording rivers and crossing the mile-and-a-half-wide snout of the great Batura Glacier. The Kuh-Ghizr platoon did twenty-seven miles (admittedly downhill from Babusar pass) in three hours, and were fit to fight at the end of it. Could any troops in the world match this?

Milanes's senior Subadar was Babar Khan. 'He was', wrote Milanes, 'one of the brightest and most charming of the local officers. He was about five feet ten inches tall, broad, with fair hair and bright blue eyes and a gentle, aristocratic manner.' He was a Nagari, but his sister was married to the Mir of Hunza, which made him *persona grata* in both states. Pre-eminently a man whose power depended on prestige, not his prestige on power, he was very influential, and more would be heard of him.

The state of Chitral is the size of Wales, with a population of about 100,000. The people, whose origin is obscure, are mainly Sunni Moslems in the south, Maulais or followers of the Aga Khan in the north, and a few pagan Kaffirs. They have their own language, Khowar, but, since this is not a written language, official business is conducted in Persian. The geography of the country resembles a Y; with the Lutkoh and Mastuj rivers joining five miles north of Chitral town to form the Chitral or Kunar river. Where this flows out of the state into Afghanistan, the height above sea-level is about 4,000 feet. The state includes forty-two mountains over 20,000 feet, the noblest of which is Tirich Mir, 25,263, an extremely difficult mountain first climbed in 1950. The valley is blessed with great beauty and remarkable fertility. Maize, barley, wheat and rice grow well, irrigated as in Gilgit. Grapes, apricots, peaches, plums, cherries, apples, pears and pomegranates abound; strawberries have been introduced with success. Many of the lower mountain slopes are (or were) well forested with deodars;

The Frontier Scouts

in the valley are magnificent chenar, walnut, poplar and mulberry trees.
It is an exaggeration to say there were no cars or lorries: the Mehtar had
one or two driven up through Swat and Dir to the foot of the Lowarai
pass (10,000 feet), carried by porters over the top and down to Ziarat,
whence they were driven, not without difficulty, to Chitral town.

In 1930 the state enjoyed – more or less – the benevolent despotism
of the Mehtar Shuja-ul-Mulk, a henna-bearded patriarch who had been
placed on the throne as a young lad after the Chitral Relief Expedition
in 1895. Five of his innumerable sons governed the provinces of which
his state was composed – Mastuj, Turikho, Mulkho, Lutkho and
Drosh. There was an Assistant Political Agent in Chitral, who came
under the Political Agent, Dir, Swat and Malakand. The Indian Army
detachments in the state consisted of an infantry battalion and a section
of Mountain Artillery, with ancillary services. The normal approach to
Chitral, and the force's lines of communication, were through Swat and
Dir (independent Pathan states) and over the Lowarai Pass.

Other armed forces were the Mehtar's Bodyguard, some three
thousand strong and still armed mainly with muzzle-loading rifles and
jezails; the Levies, corresponding to Khassadars in Waziristan; and the
Chitral Scouts.

The Scouts, who had done so well in 1919, had rested on their
laurels, and by 1929 were little more than a system of outdoor relief.
Most of the men were too old for military exertion, and most of the local
officers were sons, nephews and grandsons, on both sides of the blanket,
of the Mehtar, who thereby felt entitled to interfere constantly in promotions and appointments. Sandy Sandison, an energetic young Highlander, taking over in 1929, weeded out the old and infirm, started gashting and instituted a drive on training which pulled the corps into shape.

Its strength was eight hundred, divided into four companies
recruited respectively from Turikho in the far north, Murikho in the
centre, Mastuj and Laspur in the north-east, and Shishi in the
south. Each company was called up in turn for one month's training a
year (NCOs arriving ten days earlier). There was a small permanent
establishment of two British officers, the Subadar Major, the Subadar
Adjutant, and the Jemadar Quartermaster. The two last, not being
blood-relatives of the Mehtar, were viewed askance by the Chitral establishment, and tolerated only because of their skill at polo, played as in
Gilgit. The Scouts were armed and equipped like the South Waziristan
Scouts, except that they wore, instead of a safa, the pukhol, a round,
rolled woollen cap, known in Gilgit as the koi. They might not have the
dash and devil of the Mahsud and the Afridi, or the steadiness of the

Khattak, but they were good military material, very active on mountains and very keen, especially on shooting. They were full of confidence on their ability to hold their own country against all comers, be they Pathans from the south, Afghans from the west or Russians from the north.

In peace time the Scouts had no operational role, and their month was wholly occupied with training, mainly gashts and musketry; internal security was the responsibility of the Mehtar, his Bodyguard and Levies. But in war they would be embodied, as in 1919, to repel Afghan incursions and at least delay, until the arrival of regular forces, any more serious Russian invasion. It is probable that the Mehtar regarded the Scouts, British-officered, as an insurance against the sort of dynastic rebellion, by one of his relatives, which had been so common in the past, and which indeed is inevitable when the ruler has scores of sons and brothers alive whom in the old days he would have had killed. One such rebellion occurred in 1939 when Bill White was commanding the Scouts – a rising by the Governor of Drosh. White and he met by appointment – they were old friends – and discussed the matter at length while the Pretender held an umbrella over White's head to shelter him from the sun. After these civilised negotiations, the rebels dispersed and the Pretender departed into comfortable exile in Quetta.

In 1940 the venerable Mehtar died and his eldest son came to the throne (an unusual event in Chitral). This was the Nasr-ul-Mulk who had commanded a column with distinction in 1919.

The Chitral Scouts were great sportsmen, enthusiastic polo-players and most expert falconers. A Chitral-trained goshawk would fetch 200 rupees, a very large sum in the 1930s, in Peshawar.

In the summer of 1939 there was an unsuccessful attempt to climb Tirich Mir. On the expedition's departure, two of the Sherpa porters, Everest 'tigers' named Anten Sing and Tensing, remained in Chitral as White's orderlies on the strength of the Scouts. He needed them because duty and inclination moved him to carry out reconnaissances of all possible invasion routes from Russian Turkestan, through the Wakhan – a strip of Afghan territory eight to twelve miles wide – and over the Hindu Kush range into Chitral and India. The Sherpas, of whom Tensing was to attain fame as one of the first two men to reach the summit of Everest in 1953, were in the Scouts for five years. White taught them to ski. Oddly enough Tensing never really took to it; Anten Sing was much better and in the Scouts team for the All-India ski championships. Both, of course, were very fine mountaineers, and Tensing shone as a cook. His soufflés concocted at 12,000 feet on a bleak mountainside were out of this world, and his coffee- and chocolate-gateaux scrumptious.

Bill White with the Sherpas and some selected Scouts reconnoitred fourteen passes over the Hindu Kush, of which only two had been visited by Europeans in the past forty years. They varied in height from Bang Gol (15,600 feet) to Kot Gaz (17,939 feet). For this he was awarded the medal of the Royal Geographical Society. Extracts from his reports paint a picture of Scouts life far removed from Waziristan.

Andshah pass. 17,350 feet. Should only be attempted with rope and ice-axe ... First, the crossing of the Waraghi Kuh stream, fordable early in the morning before the ice begins to melt ... The second difficulty is the ice-fall at the snout of the Andshah glacier. I find the only place to attempt it was by the west bank. I had intended to get above the snout and camp, but when I saw the volume of stones and rocks coming down, I had to stop and climb up the cliff to a small hidden well of water that one of the Sherpas spotted. The place was so precipitous that we roped to prevent our falling off at night. At midnight a terrific ice-avalanche came off the centre of the spout and ploughed its way down for 1,500 feet. The third difficulty is the ice-fall on the Andshah glacier. It looks as if the glacier is closed here and one thinks the map is wrong and it is the pass. This is not so, as having passed it, one emerges on to the upper crevassed glacier which leads to the pass.

Kot Gaz pass. 17,939 feet. Difficult on the Chitral side and should only be attempted by a party equipped with ropes and ice-axes, but utterly impossible on the Wakhan side. Make the first camp at Druh, the most beautiful camp-site I have found in the whole of Chitral. A little stream bubbling straight out of the rocks through a grove of very big willows with mossy grass underneath ... masses of primulas ... The final climb from the glacier to the pass is more than a difficult toilsome scramble. The rock is exceedingly rotten and in August all the gullies are filled with slippery ice. The top of the pass is a knife-edge of rotten rock which crumbles if one touches it. The slope on the Wakhan side is stupendous: a full 3,000 feet at 60° of dry ice ... Five peaks over 23,000 feet in a circle all round.

From a lower pass, Zani An (12,789 feet), White had 'the finest ski-run in my life. Hard spring crust with two inches of newly fallen powder snow for 5,000 feet.'

He did not think he had the technical skill to reach the summit of Tirich Mir; nor could it, even by the most ingenious terminological inexactitude, be invested with military significance. But he reconnoitred five approaches, writing off three as utterly impossible, one as 'Looks unlikely to "go" because of huge crevasses and bad ice-cliffs,' and one as 'Looks feasible'. The Sherpas said the wind on Tirich Mir was worse than on Everest.

There were several lower passes from Kafiristan into Chitral, but these could not be easily reached from Russian territory. As a result of White's reports it was concluded that only two passes were feasible for a military force with mule transport: the Dorah, west-north-west of Chitral town, and the Baroghil in the far north. The Dorah was passable only in summer, when traders used to bring in Badakshani horses, highly valued for polo. This the Scouts strengthened with a system of mutually supporting sangars. The Baroghil was passable at any time of the year, and was not difficult since it was in Pamir (i.e. rolling downland) country. But from it an invader could move only down the narrow valley of the Mastuj river, and half way to Mastuj village this contracted into a gorge with very high precipitous sides. On these the Scouts constructed defences of sangars, and great piles of rocks so delicately balanced that the removal of a single key-stone would send an avalanche hurtling down onto the heads of Cossacks or Waffen SS below. It was a form of warfare well understood by Chitralis, who had used it against many an invader.

In 1943 the regular troops were withdrawn from Chitral, and its defence was left entirely to the Scouts, who were put on a full-time basis, increased by one company, and provided with a section of 2·75 ins mountain-guns and Vickers machine-guns. To help in the expansion and organisation, instructors were lent by the Tochi and South Waziristan Scouts; and to give the Chitralis the chance of being shot at, selected Chitrali officers and NCOs were sent on three-month attachments to the SWS — an arrangement facilitated by the fact that one of the Mehtar's younger brothers, Khushwaqt-ul-Mulk, was a captain in the SWS.

The whole of Chitral was infested with fairies, some of them quite good, most of them mischievous or malevolent. From Tirich Mir, they descended into the valleys when up to no good, delighting in such pranks as making a markhor vanish just as the hunter was pressing his trigger. They foretold deaths in the ruling family — so numerous that they could hardly go wrong — by moaning and wailing in the villages; and their periodic migrations caused earthquakes, known in the Khowar language as 'an army underground'.

More to be feared was the Boghazoo. John Ottley, later of the SWS, on shooting leave in Chitral, stopped to sketch an attractive tarn while his shikari and orderly went on up to the top of a col. He finished his sketch and hurried after them. It was then that he had such a fit of dizziness that he almost fainted, and the feeling of an icy hand clutching his heart. His men, full of belated concern, came bounding down the hill to help. When he felt better, he told them what was amiss. The shikari asked, 'Did you look in that pool, Sahib?'

'Yes.'

'By God, you are lucky to be alive. It is the home of a very evil creature, a gigantic frog called the Boghazoo, the very sight of whom is death!'

Back in Chitral, he told the Medical Officer that he had had a bad heart-attack. The doctor examined him, and said he had seldom seen anyone with a sounder heart or fitter in general. If he had been unfit for mountains, or had been a fey type and had heard previously of the Boghazoo, there would have been a rational explanation. But he was supremely 'mountain fit', neither fey nor imaginative, and had not previously heard of the fell creature.

There the story rests.

15

Side-shows, 1939–41

The declaration of war against Germany, in September 1939, brought no peace to Waziristan. In Jirga after Jirga the Maliks pledged support for the war effort. If, they said, the Russians dared cross the Afghan border – which in the days of the Hitler-Stalin pact seemed not unlikely – the Mahsuds and Wazirs would give them a bloody nose. But the Tori Khel, the Madda Khel, some sections of Mahsuds and even the Daurs, hearkened more to the Faqir of Ipi who churned out the Axis propaganda channelled to him through the German and Italian embassies in Kabul. He probably received more than propaganda. Two intrepid Germans set out for Waziristan with 20,000 rupees for him. The Ismail Khel decapitated the Germans and kept the 20,000 rupees, much to the holy man's annoyance. Another German was betrayed by his Afghan servant whom he had omitted to pay.

It seemed to be business as usual. The official view of His Majesty's Government was that the naval blockade and the trusty French army would soon bring Hitler to his knees; offers of military help from India were politely shelved, and only one Indian brigade went overseas, to guard dumps in the Canal Zone. To the Indian Army the war was still Waziristan, and for the first eight months there was much more action there than in France, and a steady trickle of casualties, culminating in a day when the Razmak column, with no Scouts in attendance, had over one hundred casualties and lost fifty-six rifles and three VBs.

The prospect of an invasion of India by Russia or Germany stimulated the construction of anti-tank defences on all likely invasion routes. Naturally these gave rise to feuds and bloodshed, not on the principle of

whether or not such defences were desirable, but on the far more
emotive issue of who should have the contracts for constructing them.
In the Kurram the contract was awarded to a Sikh, who thickly
carpeted with 'dragons' teeth' and other concrete obstructions all the
valleys down which the Panzers could roar. General Wavell, then
C-in-C India, came to inspect these. A man not noted for garrulity, he
drove round them for some hours in complete silence. At the end,
shaking hands with the Commandant, he said, 'Most interesting.
Thank you very much . . . Maginot-minded.' But worse was to happen.
Terence Phillips was fishing in the Kurram river when he stumbled and
the point of his light spinning-rod struck one of the 'concrete' dragons'
teeth. The concrete cracked, and sand trickled out. Investigation
showed that most of the defence works were hollow, a thin shell of
concrete filled with sand. But by that time the Sikh contractor had
departed, rejoicing in benign Government's munificence.

The 13th March 1940 was a black day for the Tochi Scouts. A
permanent piquet near the post at Ghariom was garrisoned half by
Khattaks and half by trans-Frontier Wazirs, of the Khaddar Khel
section. The Khattaks must have been appallingly gullible, for they
were inveigled out of the post to collect firewood and the seven Khaddar
Khel then decamped with fourteen rifles. It seemed a reversion to the
bad old days, and it ended the Tochi Scouts' attempts to enlist
trans-Frontier Wazirs; but the Jani Khel platoon continued to do well
under an exceptional officer, Wreshmin Gul, who was educated, spoke
a little English and was bald as an egg.

This incident fuelled a good deal of ignorant and malicious gossip
about the Tochi Scouts. After their fine work in 1936 and 1937, they
had been presented with a magnificent gong bearing the crests of all the
units who had served with them, 'In affectionate memory of close
association and co-operation.' A silver inkstand had been presented by
Divisional HQ with a similar inscription. But now most of those units
and staff officers had been replaced by newcomers who saw Scouts
either as uniformed Khassadars and hardly more reliable, or as regular
infantry in fancy-dress who should be used as regular infantry although
they had nothing like its fire-power. There was even a revival of the old
canard that they were in league with their fellow-Pathans: otherwise
how was it that they had, in comparison with regulars, so few casualties? On this Terence Phillips had some pertinent comments:

If a corps takes its recruits from a tribe where a boy is given a rifle
when he is eleven or twelve and is then required to take part in

whatever warfare his tribe, village or family may be involved, with its ambushes, stalks, sieges and defensive actions, he is good at using ground by the time he becomes a recruit. He is active and fast on the hills, hardy and probably a good shot. If at seventeen or eighteen he is enlisted and trained for six months, and is then out in tactical conditions three days a week for hours at a time with experienced officers and NCOs, he becomes an expert at fighting in country which is very like his own ground. He has a better rifle and ammunition than the local, is as fast on the hills, and is a good deal better organised. All this adds up to a quick and effective reaction to enemy attack. So the hostile tribesman does not as a rule attack Scouts gashts at close range unless he is in greatly superior strength, because he knows that it is almost impossible to surprise them . . . He is compelled to fire on them at long range, and because his rifle is inaccurate after about a hundred rounds, and his ammunition is hand-loaded and not very accurate, he does not hit many.

Nevertheless the whispers continued. FitzMaurice was told to his face that the Tochi Scouts had connived at the blowing-up of a bridge. In a cold Irish rage he took the matter up with the Inspecting Officer Frontier Corps who promised to speak to the GOC – but never did. Moreover the bad feeling between the GOC, Major General Quinan, and the Resident, Colonel Walter Campbell, rubbed off on the Scouts. 'It is a pity', wrote FitzMaurice in his diary, 'that they do not get on, and it is not Walter's fault.' Finally, it was the universal belief among Scouts officers that they did not receive proper backing from the IOFC of the day, Claude Erskine's successor.

A year later, lying wounded in hospital and quite improperly by-passing the IOFC, FitzMaurice wrote to the Governor, Sir George Cunningham, who knew all about Scouts:

I do not know how much of local gossip has reached your ears, but there has undoubtedly been criticism of the Tochi Scouts since 1938. Most of this criticism was ill-informed and untrue, but I fear that some unfair statements were almost acquiesced in by some from whom we were entitled to expect support . . . In 1939 after months of (possibly) extravagant praise, we felt in the Tochi Scouts that the pendulum had swung unduly . . . I was sometimes asked the most astounding questions by soldiers, sometimes in fairly high places . . . 'Do Scouts gasht much nowadays?' 'Oh, of course, tribesmen do not fire on Scouts' . . . The training of Scouts by 1939 was not, of course, up to the standard of 1936. How could it be? Owing to continuous actions with tribesmen, and increases in strength, and continuous movements and occupations of camps where no ranges existed, musketry and general mountain training had to be learned in action.

Cunningham replied that he had examined the gashting log of the Tochi Scouts, was completely satisfied and had told Quinan so. 'General Quinan has never spoken to me about the Tochi Scouts except with praise, though I think he must have said different things in other quarters.'

Gashting in North Waziristan in 1940 was inevitably not what it had been five years earlier. Twenty-five or thirty-mile gashts, at high speed with little or no piqueting, which had been the forte of Scouts in times of semi-peace, were far too dangerous when North Waziristan was swarming with hostiles. Gashts had to move more circumspectly, often piqueting as they went, nearly always with one platoon in firing positions ready to support the advance of another. This slowed them down and gave rise to ill-informed criticisms that they were *qillaband* ('fort-bound', afraid or unable to move out of their forts). The Adjutant wrote in a *News Letter* to former officers of the corps, 'We have heard from various sources that foot-gashting in the Tochi has stopped. From October 1st to December 31st, 1940, 216 foot-gashts were carried out ... and a total of 850 during the year.'

The Tochi Scouts were up to their best form in April 1940, on what was expected to be a routine relief of the garrison of Datta Khel. The relief column, from Miranshah, was to spend the first night, 6–7 April, in Boya post, now held by Khassadars; the night of 7–8 April in Datta Khel, and return to Miranshah on 8 April.

The Advanced Guard, a foot gasht of ten platoons, left Miranshah at dawn. It was commanded by two fire-eaters, Captain 'Bliz' Reford and 'Miry', Subadar Mir Hamza, Jowaki Afridi, neither men to let grass grow under their feet. The road ran parallel to and north of the Tochi river. They saw in the distance about one hundred and fifty tribesmen crossing the river from north to south, and when they were about two miles short of Boya they came under fire from the crops and scrub along the south bank. Leaving five platoons and a medium machine-gun mounted on a Vanette to give covering fire, Reford deployed the others to face south, and with great dash led an attack across the river in spate and into the crops on the far bank. Mir Hamza was busy as a terrier in a rat-infested barn, dashing to any place where the attack seemed to be losing momentum. They had first-class support from an Audax, bombing and strafing. The enemy withdrew, leaving one dead body and twenty-seven prisoners.

Meanwhile FitzMaurice had taken the convoy on to Boya where, after the action, Reford joined him. While they were watching the last stages of the operation, FitzMaurice was hit by a bullet which smashed his ankle. The Datta Khel relief was completed next day.

Reford got an immediate MC and Mir Hamza an IOM 1st Class, to supplement the 2nd Class he had won in 1936. But for Fitz FitzMaurice it was the end of his active career in Scouts to which he had devoted so many years and such whole-hearted enthusiasm. The wound aggravated his phlebitis and brought on tuberculosis; he was to spend most of the next year in hospital, inveighing against the IOFC and worrying about how Boob Youngman was running the Tochi Scouts in his absence.

There can have been no prouder man than Honorary Captain Tor Khan, Jowaki Afridi, formerly Subadar Major in the North Waziristan Militia, as he watched his son invested with his second IOM. He was a fierce, wiry little man with a bristling henna-dyed beard and the green pagri of a Haji, for he had recently made the pilgrimage to Mecca. Perhaps he thought it was needed, after shooting that Mullah, holding a Koran, so many years ago. No one was held in higher esteem along the Kohat Pass: even the artisans in the tribal rifle factories used to stand to attention when he strolled round examining their wares.

Boob Youngman, a South African, was a most amusing character and a great asset at Mess parties with his rousing Nationalist songs in Afrikaans, accompanying himself on the piano. He probably spoke better Pushtu than any other British officer, and could sing in Pushtu with an accent so authentic that even Afridis thought it was an Afridi singing. He had adopted the six-year-old daughter of the Chitral Scouts armourer, was paying for her education and later married her. He was a magnificent fighting soldier, singularly fearless under fire, but he was not a good administrator; and the Tochi Scouts, expanding yet again, four hundred more men on top of the seven hundred recently absorbed, needed an administrator. The usual practice in gashts was for the movements of individual platoons, *especially in withdrawal*, to be controlled by the gasht commander with flag signals. But Youngman believed that, even in withdrawal, platoon commanders should be responsible for the movement of their own platoons without interference by the gasht commander. This, and his mastery of Pushtu, suggests that he may have suffered from an acute form of 'pukhtunitis',

9   Action at Tappi, 7 August 1940

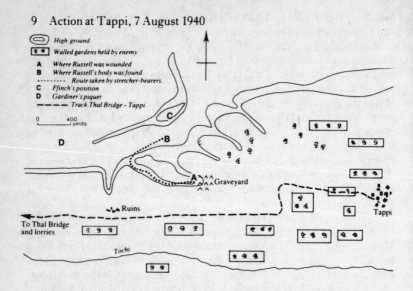

a complaint which in a milder form afflicted most Scouts officers, believing in his liking and admiration for them that Pathans, especially Pathan officers, could do no wrong. But of course they were subject, like any other race, to human error; and to base one's tactics on a doctrine of Pathan infallibility was asking for trouble. But that was the procedure in Youngman's Wing which in 1940 was to carry out the Tappi barampta. (See Map 9.)

Tappi was the largest of a group of villages on the Tochi river about ten miles south-east of Miranshah. Its inhabitants had been behaving in a very obnoxious manner – sniping convoys, looting lorries, kidnapping; so the Political authorities asked for it to be baramptaed in order that they might pull in the worst offenders. It was an operation governed from first to last by Murphy's Law: 'If anything can go wrong, it will.'

The first thing that went wrong was that the Political Agent, Evelyn Cobb, who had an encyclopaedic knowledge of the tribes and great authority with the Maliks and villagers, was away on leave, and was represented on the operation by an Indian Assistant Political Agent, a newcomer to the Frontier. The second thing that went wrong was that the opposition was underestimated. Tappi was a Daur village, and the Daurs were not highly regarded as fighting men; but they were fanatical, much under the influence of the Faqir of Ipi, and being prosperous from their rich irrigated land, very well-armed. Moreover there was no lack of Wazir hostiles in the neighbourhood; and in Tappi itself there had just arrived a party of Ghazis, holy warriors who positively sought death and Paradise.

On the evening of 6 August 1940 Youngman gave out his orders for the operation, but no other British officer seems to have been present. With hindsight, one can see that the difficulties of controlling thirteen widely-scattered platoons were not properly appreciated, and insufficient attention was paid to inter-communication. The Tochi Scouts had acquired 'walkie-talkie' R/T radio sets, but thought little of them, and they do not seem to have been taken on this operation. Nor were carrier-pigeons taken, though they might be needed if the force ran into trouble and required reinforcements. In the event most of the inter-communication seems to have been by runner and by officers to-ing and fro-ing. Lieutenant G. P. V. Sanders, the Adjutant, told the subsequent Court of Enquiry that throughout the operation inter-communication was very bad; failure to tie this up at the evening conference was the third thing to go wrong. To make up numbers, it was decided to take the Recruits Platoon. Its commander, the Drill Havildar Amir Shah, Barak Khattak, pointed out that it had no NCOs to command sections. Youngman ordered that these be provided from 'Right Wing'. One can here see the possibility of a misunderstanding, for Right Wing was his own Wing, which he was still commanding while officiating as Commandant. Anyway, it was not done, and he did not check up to see that it was done, probably because he was feeling very ill. This was the fourth thing to go wrong. The fifth thing was that two hours before the start, Youngman succumbed to a virulent attack of fever, with a very high temperature and a raging headache. Command then devolved on 'Bliz' Reford. He was a stranger to Youngman's Wing and its unusual tactical methods, and he took over at very short notice, without having been present at the evening conference. That one of the platoons, and the Recruits Platoon at that, should be going into action with no section commanders was a contingency so unlikely that it never for one moment occurred to him.

Other officers on the operation were Lieutenant Sanders, the Adjutant; Lieutenant Mike Gardiner, then at the beginning of several years in Scouts; Lieutenant Desmond Cable, another newcomer; Lieutenant Ffinch, a Gurkha officer visiting the corps on probation who knew neither the men nor their language; and Captain H. L. V. Russell, who was at the time recuperating in Miranshah and was not one of the Wing officers, but volunteered to help – the sixth thing to go wrong, for Russell weighed over sixteen stone.

Among the Pathan officers was Subadar Ali Mast, Barak Khattak, who had been a good Jemadar Adjutant in charge of recruits' training, but had recently been reported on as tactically weak and inexperienced. Fortunately there was also on the operation Subadar Wilayat Shah, Sunni Bangash from near Kohat. He was much better educated than most, spoke good Urdu and probably more English than he let on. His nickname among British officers, 'Willie Smith', implies a bursting, boyish, indeed Boy-Scoutish, enthusiasm, a readiness always to 'have a go', which was indeed his most conspicuous characteristic. On parade he would make a Guards RSM look awkward.

At one o'clock in the morning of 7 August the force debussed at Thal bridge over the Tochi river on the Isha-Thal* road and started on its four-mile approach march, through difficult wooded country, with walled orchards and crops on its right. Four platoons under Sanders and four under Russell branched off to form the right and left cordons respectively and Reford closed up on the village with the remainder, including the recruits. He established gasht HQ at the south-west corner of the village; with it was the Assistant Political Agent's party of Maliks and Khassadars.

At 5.30 am he was in touch by signalling lamp with Sanders and Russell, who each sent down one platoon with prisoners they had picked up en route. At 5.45 Khassadars went in to warn the villagers that they were surrounded; and at 6.15 it was light enough to send in the search platoons under Gardiner. Sanders and Russell themselves came in to gasht HQ for their withdrawal orders, and were told that the signal for Sanders would be a green Very light, and Russell would receive the order by flag.

There was a regular flow of prisoners, some real hostiles, others indignant villagers, for the Assistant Political Agent's party to screen. They said that a large gang was approaching from the north-east; so from Jemadar Nadir Shah's platoon (Adam Khel Afridis), which had come in from Sanders with prisoners, Reford sent two sections back to a good layback, 1,000 yards back and north of the track, on a knoll besides a cemetery, known hereafter as the 'graveyard ghundai'.

Meanwhile in the village there was much milling around while Gardiner's men separated the men from the women and children. He went down the steep main street, preceded by two sepoys. Suddenly his

---

* 'Thal in Tochi'; not to be confused with 'Thal in Kurram'.

orderly pulled him back: shots rang out, one of the two sepoys was wounded, but both got back to cover. The shots seemed to come from a house of which the flat roof, owing to the slope of the ground, was almost on Gardiner's level. He took a running jump on to it, intending to shoot the snipers as they made their escape; but as he saw no one running away, he concluded that they were still inside, and proceeded to bash a hole through which to drop a grenade. At this a harridan from the top window of a nearby house screamed unintelligibly at him, and his Subadar said she was telling them it was a mosque, and that they should not so defile a holy place. Gardiner then sent a runner to Reford, seeking guidance. Reford's first thought was to reply, 'Go ahead'; but the Subadar Major and the Assistant Political Agent both advised against it. (Looking back, Reford thinks they were right. A grenade thrown into a mosque by a Christian would have had repercussions all along the Frontier.) So he vetoed the grenade.

Meanwhile the Recruits' Platoon – boys of seventeen with no section commanders to steady them – were being regaled by a local Malik with horrific warnings of the fate which awaited them from hundreds of Wazirs even now swarming into the village. They were on the verge of panic, and Havildar Amir Shah alone could not reassure them.

As about one hundred and forty prisoners had been collected, and hostiles from all round would be swarming in to join the fight, Reford decided to call it a day. He sent the remainder of Nadir Shah's platoon back to the graveyard ghundai and called in the cordons and search-party, Sanders by runner for it transpired that no one had any green Very lights. Gardiner was furious, almost in tears at being seen off in his first Scouts operation. Russell's platoons, and the recruits, all under Russell and Subadar Ali Mast, were sent back to the graveyard ghundai. From there one platoon was sent in to gasht HQ for prisoners' escort; and the other, under Jemadar Sayid Badshah, was sent to another layback about five hundred yards back in the foothills. So there remained at the graveyard ghundai Russell, Ali Mast, one of the left cordon platoons, Nadir Shah's platoon and the platoon of nervous boy recruits.

Reford now ordered the prisoners and escort under Desmond Cable, and the Assistant Political Agent's party, all back to the lorries at Thal bridge, protected on their left by Sanders's platoons moving through the enclosures and crops, and on their right by Gardiner's platoons piqueting the high ridge which ran parallel to the track and about six hundred yards from it. He followed them with his gasht HQ.

As the withdrawal proceeded, the graveyard ghundai was fired on from the higher ground to the north-east. One of the recruits was hit in the chest and Russell, running out to help him, was hit just below the knee, the bullet smashing the bone and completely incapacitating him. Fire became heavier, and the recruits were very shaky. Leadership was now needed, and should have been provided by Subadar Ali Mast and Jemadar Nadir Shah. But Ali Mast, having told everyone to stand firm, withdrew under cover and busied himself with dressing Russell's wound — not his job at all, and hardly encouraging for his men.

At the first burst of fire, Reford had gone to the graveyard ghundai with Ffinch and his gasht HQ. He saw what had happened and hurried back to Gardiner, whom he ordered to piquet the highest point on the ridge north of the road, and stay there whatever happened. At about the same time Sanders came upon Sayid Badshah's platoon, which was under fire from the ridge, and ordered him at all costs to get on top of the ridge, clear the enemy away and hold it. This, with some difficulty, Sayid Badshah did. Thereafter he and Gardiner played an undramatic but essential role, piqueting this commanding feature, about a thousand yards apart. Had the enemy in strength got on to it, withdrawal with wounded would have been almost impossible.

While Reford was away, Ali Mast, in charge at the ghundai, detailed men to carry back the two wounded and himself accompanied them. This was all too much for the recruits. Havildar Amir Shah was able to hold only one section; the rest bolted, carrying with them some of Nadir Shah's men, Nadir Shah himself making no effort to stop the rot. They all straggled up a re-entrant leading north-west from the ghundai towards the ridge.

Reford arrived back at the ghundai and, thinking that enough time had elapsed for the wounded to be carried clear, ordered Nadir Shah and the remaining recruits to withdraw. He blamed himself later for giving the order too soon, not realising how Russell's weight would slow down the stretcher-bearers in this rough ground: they had to stop and rest every twenty yards.

Nadir Shah's men left them standing and clambered up the steep slope towards the ridge. Reford and Ffinch collected about a dozen men and withdrew slowly, covering the stretcher-party, also making for the high ground. Reford could no longer see Nadir Shah's people, but assumed that they had taken up a covering position on top. He anticipated no great difficulty in getting Russell away, and fortunately the wounded recruit had recovered sufficiently to make his own way to the rear with the other walking wounded.

The slope became too steep to carry Russell up, so the stretcher-party edged along it, hoping to find an easier way. At least they were sheltered from enemy fire, but they gradually realised that Nadir Shah was not covering them, and their own party had dwindled to a handful of completely exhausted men, largely unarmed stretcher-bearers. They could take Russell no further, so Reford collected eight riflemen, put them in covering positions and ordered them on no account to leave him. As commander, Reford had to take control of the withdrawal, the unseemly haste of which was very evident. He explained this to Russell and, with Ffinch, scrambled up to the top.

There they found Subadar Ali Mast, Jemadar Nadir Shah and about twenty men, including a signaller who had neither lamp nor helio. More men straggled in, several of them wounded. They were under fire from higher ground four or five hundred yards to the north-east. Reford's gasht headquarters had disappeared, without which he could communicate neither with the air nor with Sanders and Gardiner. At 10.30 he left Ffinch in charge of this very shaky party and went off in search of reinforcements. Fortunately the first he found were a platoon and a half under the excellent Urdu-speaking Subadar Wilayat Shah, whom he sent straight up to help Ffinch.

Meanwhile Gardiner was in a quandary. He had hardly drawn breath on reaching the top of the ridge when he received a flag-signal (it is not clear from whom) telling him to come down again. His first reaction was of disbelief; he had been told of a gang approaching, he saw figures on the hills to the north-east and it seemed madness to leave his position. Then the signal was repeated, with the addition of the words 'Russell hit'. There was a great deal of firing and he began to feel he should be doing something more active than sit on the ridge, in agonies from thirst, with an occasional bullet passing overhead. He set up a helio, and got in touch with a distant army road-protection party, but they refused to leave their road-protection duties. Should he send a platoon down? Or go down himself to find out what was happening? His Subadar made difficulties to every suggestion, but the Jemadar Adjutant turned up and Gardiner sent him down to ascertain what they were supposed to do. Shortly afterwards Sanders arrived with positive orders that they were to stay put, on no account to move. Sanders then went along the ridge to give similar orders to Sayid Badshah.

Reford arrived and was directed by Gardiner to Sanders, who told him that the Assistant Political Agent's party and prisoners had got away, and that he had sent Cable in a Vanette to Dosalli to bring up the strongest possible gasht under Bill Moberley. Things were getting under control again and Reford told Sanders, as soon as Moberley arrived, to bring him up to where Ffinch was, for a counter-attack to rescue Russell. He himself then returned to Ffinch.

Ffinch's party, when Reford left it, had been in a bad way. They were parched with thirst, running short of ammunition and under fire from tribesmen who were increasing every minute. The hilltop was made of slabs of flat rock which afforded neither cover nor material from which cover could be constructed. Although unable to speak to them, Ffinch by his mere presence encouraged the men – and they got no encouragement from Ali Mast and Nadir Shah. But there was a capable Adam Khel Havildar, Yar Shah, who worked like a Trojan, organising the men into all-round defence, directing their fire, putting courage into the faint-hearts. Then there arrived the platoon-and-a-half under Subadar Wilayat Shah, 'Willie Smith', unflappable and full of energy, 'like a breath of fresh air', said Ffinch. Wilayat Shah later told the Court of Enquiry:

> I found Lieutenant Ffinch in charge. He does not speak Pushtu so I helped him by taking charge of the whole situation under his guidance. I made a few changes in the dispositions and then awaited Captain Reford's arrival with reinforcements as it was impossible to carry out the counter-attack planned by Lieutenant Ffinch with the troops in hand at the time.

Someone arrived with a Popham-panel which Ffinch spread in the pattern indicating that he needed ammunition. Flight-Lieutenant Mukerjee,* piloting a plane overhead, flew off to Miranshah where he was handed several belts of ·303. Rather than wait for proper dropping equipment, he stuffed them into his flying boots and returned to Tappi. Flying over the beleaguered party as slowly as only an Audax could, he dropped them accurately and proceeded to machine-gun the enemy to good effect.

All this time it was assumed that Russell was safe, under cover, with eight men to protect him. But he was not. The eight had departed, leaving only his Turi orderly Lal Jan, and three unarmed stretcher-bearers. Above them was a slope almost sheer, up which they could not possibly carry a heavily-laden stretcher, but at the top of this Lal Jan saw Ali Mast with two men to whom he called for help. Ali Mast, he alleged, merely replied, 'Are you the son of a man or the son of a donkey?' and disappeared.

According to Lal Jan,

* Later C-in-C of the Indian Air Force.

Captain Russell told me to go and find Captain Reford. I said, 'I shall not desert you.' Captain Russell insisted on my going. I asked for his pistol, as I was afraid that if the Ghazis arrived they would take it. He said, 'Go off, don't worry about the pistol. I have two men to protect me.'

The Court of Enquiry did not believe Lal Jan, holding that as Russell's personal orderly he should have stayed and died with his officer. However, he went and, according to his story, found Reford who sent him with a message to the army road-protection party. This may be true. Reford did send someone with such a message, but the man never said he was Russell's orderly, or that he had been with Russell and had left him. Lal Jan next turned up, two hours after leaving Russell, at Ffinch's position, and was recognised; this was the first intimation to anyone there that all might not be well with Russell.

One of the stretcher-bearers was Khan Badshah, Barak Khattak. He told the Court of Enquiry,

> I was one of the four men who carried Captain Russell. The other three were Adam Khels from Nadir Shah's platoon. They, and Captain Russell's orderly, deserted us. I was then left alone and unarmed with Captain Russell. I heard Subadar Ali Mast telling these people to take up a position covering us, but nobody paid him any attention, they all went on, including Ali Mast. I sat beside the stretcher and saw three Ghazis coming up the nullah. One came quite close to us, he had a short clipped beard. Captain Russell said they were Khassadars, but I said 'No'. I think he said that to keep my spirits up. He then told me to go and find Subadar Ali Mast or Captain Reford and ask for men to save him, so I set off . . . The last time I saw Captain Russell he was sitting on the stretcher smoking a cigarette, his hand on his pistol.

Khan Badshah's story was confirmed by tribesmen who later said that, as they approached Russell, an unarmed sepoy was sitting beside him helping him light a cigarette. The Court of Enquiry found that Khan Badshah had been a good and faithful servant.

In mid-afternoon Captain S. I. Hassan, formerly Assistant Political Agent, Wana, now in the Tochi Scouts, driving back to Miranshah from Razmak, met two lorries on their way to Dosalli from whom he heard that things were going badly. He accompanied them, returned to Thal bridge with the first two platoons of the Dosalli gasht, and marched to the sound of the guns. He hurried along the ridge, through Gardiner's position, and eventually reached Ffinch's, where he found Reford. Soon afterwards Moberley arrived with the rest of the Dosalli gasht.

With seven fresh platoons, water and ample ammunition, Reford was at last in a position to launch a counter-attack down the steep slope to recover Russell, dead or alive. He organised it with Hassan on the left, himself in the centre and Sanders on the right; Moberley on the far right would give covering fire. It semed a very hazardous operation, for they were now under fire from hundreds of tribesmen at three to five hundred yards. Before going over the top, Reford handed Moberley his signet-ring and fiancée's photograph.

Just before they were due to start, there was a tremendous dust-storm which reduced visibility to less than forty yards, followed by torrential rain blowing straight into the enemy's faces. Although this made control difficult, it seemed the moment to attack. The signal to start was to have been by flag, and the signal to break off and withdraw by Very light. But as no flag-signal could be seen, Reford sent up a Very light and hoped that his intention would be understood. Hassan never saw it, and Sanders took it as the withdrawal signal. But Hassan had also come independently to the conclusion that this was their chance, so his and Reford's parties advanced almost simultaneously, slipping and slithering down the steep forward slope, searching corners and side-nullahs for Russell.

It was Hassan who found him, headless and stripped to a torn vest. As the rain abated, they made their way back to the top, carrying the body, and withdrew through Gardiner's position to Thal bridge and the lorries.

'How's Leslie?' asked Gardiner as they went past. 'Dead as a doornail,' Sanders replied.

The Court of Enquiry was held the next day. Its findings concluded, 'It will be fully realised what an appalling situation Captain Reford had to face. I consider that all his actions were correct, and that he acquitted himself extremely well.'

He was recommended for a Bar to his MC, Ffinch got an MC; Wilayat Shah the IOM and Havildar Yar Shah the IDSM. Jemadar Nadir Shah was permitted to depart on leave, without scandal, and not come back. Subadar Ali Mast was given the chance, which he took, of retrieving his honour at a second Tappi barampta, nine days later, and then go on pension. Russell's orderly was sacked and sentenced to imprisonment; so were the stretcher-bearers, not only for running away when (as Reford said) to stay would have been tantamount to suicide,

234

but for lying to the Court and denying that they had ever been near Russell. Reford thought this was rough justice.

In the context of 1940 it was a very small disaster. Proud British battalions had done worse and fared worse in Norway and the retreat to Dunkirk. But the Tochi Scouts felt it keenly.

The mark of a good unit is not that they should never do badly, but that they should recover and do better. The Tochi Scouts were given another chance at the second Tappi barampta, when they acted as Advanced Guard mounted troops to Tocol, fighting their way past the walled orchards and graveyard ghundai of evil memory and taking a full revenge on Tappi. Now they could hold up their heads again.

Boob Youngman was not confirmed in his acting command of the Tochi Scouts, and was replaced by Rupert Taylor from the Gilgit Scouts, a solid, rather withdrawn Yorkshireman, large, round-faced, very nimble on his feet and a fine footballer. He had been in the Tochi in the early 1930s when conditions were very different. Briefed by the Inspecting Officer Frontier Corps, he arrived with the pre-conceived notion that the Scouts were qillaband (fort-bound), and by trigger-happiness they were arousing the hostility they were supposed to discourage. He meant to restore peace-time practices, long, fast gashts and the convention never to shoot first. He soon realised that he had been badly briefed; he was astonished by the gasht logbook which showed how much foot-gashting was being done, and he admitted that he could not reconcile his duties as Commandant with the instructions he had received on opening fire. But meanwhile his attitude was resented by those who felt they had borne the heat and burden of the day. However, because he was a very decent man, he was forgiven. Not so the IOFC on whom was bestowed an injurious nickname.

Taylor, a thoroughly sensible man and a sound administrator, saw at once that the Wings were too big and top-heavy, and pushed through a much-needed reform which had been under consideration for some time – reorganising the Corps in three Wings with headquarters at Miranshah, Mir Ali (later Khajuri) and Dosalli.

But the 'softly-softly' approach which he had been instructed to introduce landed the Scouts in another traumatic experience.

In June 1941 Captain John Lowe, a newcomer to the Tochi Scouts, in command at Datta Khel, took a gasht of only two platoons up the Qalandra Sar hill, about a mile from the fort, overlooking some Khaddar Khel villages which were reported to be harbouring a lashkar. Looking down into the village of Tang, he saw it crowded with armed men, obviously hostile, and fired a single shot to test their reactions. This was an extremely rash thing to do. He should have either withdrawn, or remained hidden while he summoned reinforcements, or 'tested their reactions' with ten rounds rapid. He then moved along a ridge towards a tooth-shaped feature from which to obtain a better view.

His shot acted like a stick thrust into a hornets' nest. Up the hill swarmed the tribesmen, and as his leading platoon approached the tooth-like feature, it came under heavy fire and several men were hit. The platoon commander, Jemadar Khattak, Kuki Khel Afridi, tried to recover two rifles and was shot; one rifle he saved, before collapsing, by throwing it up the hill. But his platoon retreated in some disorder, except for his orderly Hussein Shah who stayed to protect him and the other wounded, holding the enemy off with accurate rapid fire.

The Kuki Khel are credited by other Afridis with a yokel's slowness of speech and long deliberation before speaking – not because they are stupid, far from it, but because they want to get the answer right. As Hussein Shah fired off the last of his ammunition, getting the answer right was of some importance. His officer was dead, but there were wounded Scouts still alive. He had two grenades but the enemy, closing in, were still too far and too dispersed for these to be of much use. Crouching between two rocks, he thought a while, and then hurled his rifle towards them. At the sight of this precious possession up for grabs, the tribesmen forgot Hussein Shah and made a rush for it. When they were nicely clustered, he lobbed a grenade among them to such effect that they troubled him no more until the counter-attack came down the hill a few minutes later.

In that broken ground the enemy had found two wounded Scouts and carried them down to Tang. One was still conscious. Recognising some Khaddar Khel ex-Scouts, probably the deserters of 1940, he appealed to them for a quick end. In vain. The torture was supervised by a Malik whose son had been killed that day.

Meanwhile the battle raged up the slopes of the Qalandra Sar. The gasht, greatly outnumbered, running out of ammunition and short of water on a scorching day, were in trouble. They were saved largely by a local Khaddar Khel of humble status named Maizal, who had the contract for taking water every morning to the piquet post of Akhtar, with the help of his ten-year-old son and four donkeys. Maizal now took it upon himself to organise the fort followers – shoemakers, tailors, cooks, sweepers, gardeners – and, of course, his son and his donkeys, into carrying water and ammunition up to the firing line and casualties back to the fort. When the gasht was safely inside the walls, he went down to Tang and persuaded the lashkarwals to let him take the mangled bodies of the two Scouts into Datta Khel for a proper burial, which means so much to Pathans. They were terribly mutilated, scorched and flayed with boiling water.

There was a sequel, and the officer concerned was Desmond Cable, large, extrovert, ebullient, part-Beau Geste, part-Bertie Wooster. A gang highjacked a lorry belonging to the Scouts Hindu contractor, and drove it away across country. Cable followed hotfoot, and he came up with it just before dark, finding inside one of the headquarters clerks, a nice old man, knifed and dying. But two wheels had been removed, so he could not drive the lorry back, and his gasht was not strong enough to spend the night out in very hostile country. He therefore returned to Idak Khassadar post, telephoned Miranshah for two wheels and sent out an informer to keep in touch with the gang during the night. In the early morning, the informer brought news that the gang had replaced the wheels and taken the lorry four more miles further up the nullah.

Cable, a mere subaltern, went to Mir Ali to commandeer a battalion to assist him. The senior officer there, new to the Frontier, hardly knew what to make of this strangely garbed young man demanding all sorts of things: was he mountebank or to be taken seriously? 'He seemed', said Cable afterwards in the Miranshah Mess, 'to be very worried about where he should post his piquets' – a remark greeted with hilarity as the Mir Ali plain is like a billiard table, without cover to conceal a hare. However, he took out not merely his battalion in support of Cable's five platoons, but lorries to transport them.

They left the transport on the road and pushed on at full gashting pace. A plane dropped a message giving the lorry's position, and soon the Scouts came under fire. Cable assaulted the hill from which most of the firing was coming and took it, with the loss of three wounded. From the top he saw the lorry and the gang. The colonel turned down his suggestion for a combined attack as it would be 'foolish'. Cable therefore, not being under Army command, launched an attack himself, telling his men, 'Remember Datta Khel!' 'It seemed,' he said later, 'to have quite an effect. I hadn't seen such *josh* ['dash', 'aggressiveness'] before. When they resorted to volley-fire, an awful lot of bullets seemed to go in at one side of a bush and a body rolled swiftly out of the other.' They killed six of the gang, wounded others and captured the gang-leader, son of one of Ipi's top officers. Then a rainstorm blew up and the rest of the gang got away, leaving the highjacked lorry. And that was the end of a classic small Scouts' operation.

That summer Lieutenant Mohamad Sharif Khan, the first Kuki Khel Afridi to hold the King's Commission, was in command at Biche Kashkai when John Lowe and the Garrison Engineer came to spend the night. They sat up late over whisky — lime-juice for Sharif, a devout Moslem — and went to bed in the open in front of the Mess, their beds draped in mosquito-nets, a few feet apart. Sharif was awakened by a rifle-shot, very close, and sat up with heart pounding.

There was another shot, and I saw the flash, then a third, and John Lowe disengaged himself from his mosquito-net, yelled 'Stand to!' and ran to his quarter for his revolver. As the fourth and fifth shots rang out, I ran for mine. We came out together. There was a great *hallagullah*, people shouting 'Stand to!', Very lights going up and a few shots. I thought a Ghazi knife-party had got into the officers' quarters and we would soon be split open. I ordered Subadar Lal Din to take a roll-call . . .

The Garrison Engineer said, 'I say, you chaps, I've been hit by two bullets and I'm bleeding to death.' A bullet had gone through his right thigh into his left, and he was bleeding profusely. John and I cleaned and bandaged him, and John said, 'You're in luck. Two inches higher and you'd have lost your stones.' 'Give me the whisky,' said the GE, 'I must celebrate.' One bullet had skimmed the table-top, smashing a tumbler but missing the precious whisky. Another had gone through my pillow six inches from my head, and six more had gone through the mosquito-nets. [What saved them was their big white nets. The man shooting at them could not see their exact positions.]

Subadar Lal Din came up with a long face, 'Nazar Gul, Tarakzai Mohmand, is missing.' The Tarakzai was Lal Din's own section. Nazar Gul had been on sentry-duty: obviously it was he who had tried to kill the three officers. Sharif ordered out the chiga platoon and ran off with them in a forlorn attempt at intercepting the fugitive who was probably going to join the Faqir of Ipi. After five fruitless hours they came back. Later they heard from tribesmen that they had passed quite close to the rock under which he lay hiding. When the tribesmen went down and told him to drop his rifle, he said, 'I am a Ghazi, I have just killed three officers, and my legs are all torn through forcing my way through the barbed wire. Take me to the Faqir Sahib.' He became one of Ipi's most dangerous gang-leaders, until he was killed two years later.

Rupert Taylor, the Commandant, and the Political Agent held an

Enquiry. Although there was no evidence of collusion, they decided to recommend that all Tarakzais in the corps should be discharged. At this Lowe and Sharif put their careers on the line, protesting vigorously against the whole section being penalised for the crime of a single religious fanatic. If this were done, they said, they would resign their commissions. It is not often that such protests by junior officers prevail, but these did, and the Tarakzais continued to give splendid service.

Also during that long, hot summer of 1941, Boya fort was attacked. Terence Phillips was awakened by a bugle outside the fort sounding the Cease-fire, and by rushing lights and shadow cast by a Very light.

As I reached for my chaplis, the fort was lit by a flash and shaken by a heavy explosion. The Vickers gun on the roof fired a long burst, the reiterating explosions echoing through the fort. There were running feet on the cat-walks and opened doors showed the yellow gleam of oil-lamps and the moving shadows of men struggling into their equipment.

In the well of the fort, everyone was milling round in dense dust from the bursting of a shell *inside* the walls. It had passed through the wireless room and burst against a verandah support, severely wounding in the head Jemadar Jamdad, Yusufzai, and blowing off his hand. He thought he was dying, and impressed upon me that Havildar Jalal-ud-Din, Yusufzai, should have the vacancy. Seven others had been wounded, but the Sub-Assistant Surgeon worked quickly and well.

There was no post-gun in Boya. As the walls offered no protection against proper high explosive shells – this was a 3·7 howitzer shell, manufactured in Kirkee Arsenal – Phillips and Subadar Lal Mohamad got most of the men out, dispersed behind the walls round the parade-ground and basket-ball pitch. There was little hostile rifle-fire, only a few bursts from a light machine-gun which did no damage. Another gun opened up from an orchard, its shells passing overhead, but the first gun did not fire again, its recoil mechanism having failed with damage to the breech. A plane came over and bombed in the direction indicated by oil-lamps on the fort-roof. Soon after the affair petered out, to the disappointment of the villagers who had been waiting to loot the fort when it fell. Next day they came in with gifts of fruit and congratulations. Said Subadar Lal Mohamad, 'When I saw them, I was almost speechless with rage and' – making a gesture of firing a pistol – 'I could have shot them all with pleasure.'

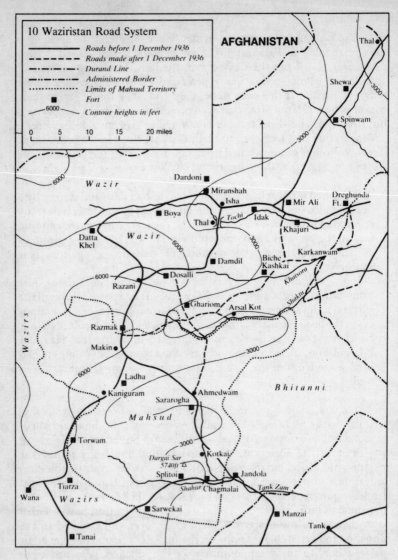

AFGHANISTAN

Thal

Shewa

Spinwam

W a z i r   Dardoni

Miranshah   Isha   Mir Ali   Dreghunda Ft.

Boya   Thal   *Tochi*   Idak   Khajuri

Datta Khel   *W a z i r*   Karkanwam

Damdil   Biche Kashkai

Dosalli   *Khaisora*

Razani   6000   Shaktu

Ghariom   Arsal Kot

W a z i r s   Razmak

Makin   3000

Ladha   *B h i t a n n i*

Kaniguram   Ahmedwam

Sararogha   *M a h s u d*

Torwam

Dargai Sar   Kotkai
5740ft

Splitoi   Jandola
Shahur Chagmalai   *Tank Zam*

Wana   Tiarza   *W a z i r s*   Manzai
Sarwekai

Tanai   Tank

had been ambushed and wounded as he drove to Bannu. It was bad luck on him, for his posting was cancelled, but good luck for the Scouts, for after he came out of hospital, he was appointed Inspecting Officer Frontier Corps on 1 June 1941.

16

Side-shows, 1941–5

The years 1941–2 were very difficult ones in Waziristan. Trained regular troops were desperately needed for the war against Germany and Japan. Razmak, Wana and Bannu were garrisoned with half-trained units which suffered serious reverses, losing men, rifles and light machine-guns. The Faqir of Ipi was at the height of his prestige and power. Every Pathan knew that the British had been thrown out of Greece and Crete, that the Germans were on the point of breaking through to the Suez Canal and the Caucasus while the Japanese over-ran South-East Asia, Malaya and Burma. With the Sarkar on the run, and with ample funds provided by Germany and Italy, probably also by the Indian National Congress, the Faqir had two enormous advantages enjoyed by no previous hostile leader. First, because he could ration and even pay them, he could keep a hard core of lashkar-wals permanently embodied, whose keep was not a burden on the local villagers. Secondly, his 'Gorwekht Militia' – as it was called from his new base in the Gorwekht mountains west of Datta Khel – included Pathans of every tribe, even cis-Frontier Khattaks and Yusufzais, with Army and Scouts deserters. They were far better armed than before, having not merely rifles but a considerable number of light machine-guns and at least four guns firing proper 3·7 howitzer ammunition, most of which was probably obtained from Kabul.

A sign of the times was the deep depression shown by Darim Khan, the Subadar of Khassadars. He was sure he had not long to live. Anyone in his position, steadfastly loyal to the British, must be marked down for death. 'Well,' said Sharif jokingly, 'there's only one thing for you to do

– join the Faqir.' Darim chuckled into his beard, 'Sahib, you know I won't do that. But whether the British go down or not, I'm a dead man.'

A greater burden than ever before was laid on the Scouts, especially the Tochi who bore the brunt of the Faqir's hostility. Nat Cosby, with his long experience of the Frontier, was worried. It was largely a matter of officers' morale. Since the fall of France and the entry of Italy into the war, it was obvious that there would be a great role for the Indian Army, and they wanted to be in on it. From 1939 to 1941 the Scouts had been carried by pre-war volunteers, carefully vetted, who had served through the heady years of Khaisora, Iblanke and the Shahur Tangi operations when Waziristan offered the only war available. But now their time with Scouts was nearly finished, and none of them would willingly extend it when they had the chance of commanding their own battalions in a proper war, or of qualifying at the Staff College for operational staff jobs. There were some very good junior officers in Scouts, who had applied before September 1939, or opted for Scouts because their own battalions seemed to be left out of the main war. Having joined for three years, some were kept on, bitterly resentful, for four, five or even six. Some war-time officers were almost shanghaied into Scouts; they knew no Pushtu and had no intention of learning it. Nevertheless there were throughout the war a nucleus of dedicated Scouts officers who more or less cheerfully did the job to hand and, whatever their heartburnings on hearing from their battalions in the Western Desert, Italy and Burma, thanked God that they were not even as those poor buggers in PAIFORCE, a dismal mausoleum of military hopes, or garrisoning the Middle East after the war had moved on, or shackled to desks or training depots or internal security jobs in India. But few of these were ready in 1941 to command Wings before taking over a corps, and the greatest need was of experienced Wing Commanders.

Disgruntled officers had a bad effect on the men. From the Tochi half-a-dozen deserted, with rifles, in addition to the desertion of half the Khaddar Khel platoon in 1940, which could be written off as a calculated risk which went wrong. Half-a-dozen out of a corps of over three thousand is not much – many regular battalions had more – but it was half-a-dozen too many. Then there was the shocking attempt of the Mohmand sentry to murder three officers while they slept. In the south Waziristan Scouts – nothing to do with the Faqir or the general war situation, but disquieting – there was a semi-mutinous, sit-down strike over promotions by the Swati platoon. Worst of all, in Cosby's opinion, was the fact that some Scouts had got into the habit of referring to the

Faqir of Ipi as the Haji Sahib, admiring him rather as the Eighth Army admired Rommel.

To Cosby it all stank of 1919. Some British officers were sent 'down the hill'. Two Pathan officers argued the toss, protesting that they could not know all that their men thought and did. 'That's what you're paid for,' said Cosby. 'You're out. You can go this afternoon.' But that was not enough: what he needed was two really good, experienced Wing Commanders for the Tochi.

Never one to waste time with minor military bureaucracy, he went straight to the Adjutant General.

'Well, Nat, what can I do for you?'

'You can give me Janson and Venning.'

'Sorry, no can do. Janson is coming up for command of his battalion, and Venning is just passing out of the Staff College.'

'I see . . .', Cosby explained his forebodings, and asked, 'If the Frontier blows up as it did in 1919, what will you need to put it right?'

'About three divisions.'

'Have you got three divisions?'

'. . . OK, Nat, you win.'

So Jan Janson and Ralph Venning came as Wing Commanders to the Tochi. With plenty of active service experience in the SWS, fluent in Pushtu and having a way with Pathans, they complemented Rupert Taylor's qualities of quiet competence and sound administration. Cosby also shanghaied Terence Philips, who minded very much, and sent him to the Kurram.

It was some compensation for Venning that he could instal his wife in Bannu, in a bungalow in the Civil Lines. One morning on the Maidan she was addressed cheerfully by a young student-type, 'Good morning, Memsahib. Your Sahib was killed today.' He drew the edge of his hand across his throat to emphasise his point. Her feelings, as she cycled back to her bungalow, may well be imagined; but she discovered eventually that it was the previous tenant, an officer of the Frontier Constabulary, who had been shot and decapitated in a fight with raiders that morning.

In the summer of 1942, with the Germans at the gates of Stalingrad and Alexandria, the Japanese poised to surge into Bengal, the Faqir of Ipi made a supreme effort to capture the most exposed of the Scouts forts, Datta Khel. It was commanded by Lieutenant Sharif Khan and its post Subadar was that superb Mohmand, Lal Din. The enemy lashkar closed round it on 1 May, beginning a siege which was to last just over three months. The harsh reality was that neither in Razmak nor in Bannu were there enough trained troops for a relief column.

Among the lashkarwals an Afridi deserter, Zamir, was in constant touch with his fellow-Afridi, Sharif, whom he called his *aziz*, his dear friend, and begged him to find some excuse to get out of the doomed fort. Sharif, hoping to persuade him that Datta Khel, so far from being doomed, was impregnable, suggested that they meet and talk things over, five hundred yards from the walls, Sharif having neither arms nor escort. Zamir replied that although he trusted his *aziz*, he would not feel happy within five hundred yards of Lal Din and two Vickers guns. Besides, what would the Faqir think? So nothing came of Sharif's suggestion.

At first Sharif was not much worried. Dhatta Khel had been besieged before for five or six weeks, and he had three months' supplies; also he had two Vickers guns, a 2·75 ins mountain-gun and plenty of ammunition. Let Ipi do his worst. But one night, his bearer having forgotten to put lime-juice beside his bed, he went down to the Mess for some. At that moment three shells tore through the walls and exploded inside; when he ran back to his room, he found his bed in splinters. The enemy had guns which fired proper HE shells far heavier and from a longer range than those fired by his little pop-gun. 'I saw fear in the faces of some of the men, and I suppose they saw fear in mine.'

A few nights later he was awakened by a bugle-call outside the walls and several shells from the Gorwekht artillery, one through the Pathan officers' Mess and another shattering the pigeon loft. This might be the preliminary to an assault, so he judged it the time to use his secret weapon, a three-inch mortar recently acquired. A rain of bombs, dropping out of the sky all round the gunflash, with no warning flash from the fort itself, so disconcerted the lashkar that the assault planned for that night was called off. A dawn gasht found tarpaulins and quilts prepared to lay over the wire as bridges for the storm-troops.

Miranshah urged Sharif to sally forth and engage the lashkar, but as the man on the spot he saw little point in this. With an average of twenty-five men down with malaria and having to leave enough to defend the fort — reinforced by the followers whom he taught to pull out the pin and throw a grenade — he could not field a gasht of more than seventy-five rifles, and the enemy numbered at least a thousand.

However, 'to hear is to obey'. At three o'clock in the morning, Sharif sallied out with three platoons and at first light was within sight of the enemy who were getting up, stretching, saying their prayers. Hearing two planes fly over, he sent up a Very light to show them where he was, and they swung round and headed for the enemy. Suddenly one began to lose height and bear away to the south, obviously in trouble. It skimmed over a low ridge about two miles away, and a moment later there was a thundering crash, an explosion and clouds of smoke. The second plane at once headed back for Miranshah for which, said Sharif, the pilot should have been court-martialled.

His first thought was that if they went to the plane they might be cut off from the fort. His second, that they must try to rescue the crew, if still alive. His third, that the plane contained thousands of rounds of ·303 ammunition. It was his first battle, and the responsibility of command weighed heavily upon him. However, Subadar Lal Din was a man of great experience, the bravest man Sharif ever knew. It would do no harm to consult him, though the decision must be Sharif's.

'What do you think we should do, Subadar Sahib?'

'Whatever you order, Sahib.'

'I think we should go for the plane.'

'Of course we must. Leave one platoon here as a layback, and run like hell with the other two.'

They doubled off with one platoon leading, gasht HQ consisting of Sharif, Lal Din, their orderlies, a signaller and a stretcher-bearer, and then the rear platoon. 'We were very fit,' said Sharif,

We ran and we ran, and we could see the enemy running too. We won the race, and shooting started – not very accurate, for everyone was out of breath. The pilot and the observer were brought to me, terribly burnt. The pilot kept saying, 'Give me water, doctor, I'm dying of thirst.' I didn't know if I should give water to a man in his condition, but I thought he would die anyway, so I held my bottle to his lips and said, 'Drink, my friend, to your heart's content.' Then I organised a stretcher-party and escort to take them by a covered way to Datta Khel before we were surrounded.

We were in a desperate plight. Lal Din had got the two platoons into defensive positions, but the enemy were coming up in overwhelming numbers and would soon be all around us. I told Lal Din that we must withdraw while we could – no need to worry about the plane's ammunition with it still ablaze. While the rest of gasht HQ took cover, Lal Din stood up in the open to signal the platoons with his flag to withdraw. A lot of lead was flying round, and I thought, 'This is all wrong, me in cover while he stands in the open.' So I stood beside him. He actually smiled at me and said, 'No. Sahib, you're the gasht commander, this is no place for you.' I thought that if I did take cover, he would never talk of it, but others would. So I stayed beside him while he flagged out his orders – platoon number, withdraw signal, then pointing with his flag to the layback position, each signal duly acknowledged. I was very frightened, thinking I was certain to be hit, and wondering where the bullet would strike. Above all I feared being taken alive, for mutilation was certain. The enemy was so close that we could hear their threats to castrate us and so on, and I saw one man chewing his beard as Mahsuds and Wazirs do to frighten you.

What saved us was the arrival of two planes, flying very low dropping 20-lb bombs and machine-gunning. We broke through the first encirclement. Then we were encircled again, but within range of the third platoon which I had left as a layback when we started the race for the plane. With their supporting-fire we broke through again. Then we heard the blessed sound of the fort's Vickers guns firing long bursts over our heads and along our flanks, and the shells from the 2·75 gun, and knew we were within a mile of safety, that we would make it.

The fort was in chaos, six or seven dead, many wounded and the Hindu Sub-Assistant Surgeon overwhelmed by a situation he had never envisaged, but doing his duty as well as he could. I sent off my report, and for hours was deluged with requests for information, including a signal from Air Headquarters in Delhi asking for a full report on the loss of the plane. I went to its crew in our hospital, both were Indian Christians. The pilot, Moses, could only ask me to send a message to his wife, which I noted down before he died. The observer, Larive, was not so badly burnt, but had two holes in his thighs. I said, 'Look, old boy, I don't want to bother you, but your people want a report on what happened.' He told me that the plane came down from some engine failure: he was thrown clear when it crashed, but got burnt pulling Moses out of the cockpit.

Two days later Rupert Taylor came over the hills with a 'star' gasht of sixteen platoons from Miranshah, to teach the lashkar a lesson. With him was Andrew Downes, a large, fair Scottish boy. Here is Sharif's story:

We set out next morning and encountered the lashkar about five miles south of the fort. It was an indecisive sort of action, both sides shooting at one another from parallel ridges, neither able to gain an advantage. I saw one Scout wounded far down the forward slope.

One of his tribe ran down to rescue him. It was a terribly hot day, and the hillside was very steep. He slung the wounded man across his shoulder and staggered up the hill, but soon had to put him down, rest and have a drink. Then he picked up his friend and struggled up a few more yards before again putting him down. He eventually reached the top with two bullets in him, and I thought, 'If this doesn't deserve the VC, what does?'

There was a big ilex tree on our ridge, and some crack shot on the other side knew the range to a yard. Every man who went near it was shot. Andrew came up and I said, 'You keep clear of that tree.' He laughed and replied – you remember he had a slight stammer? – 'I'm all r-r-right. I'm too b-b-big to be hit.' At that moment a bullet got him in the chest and in a few minutes he was dead.

In the early afternoon Rupert broke off the action. We were closely followed up, and I saw a fine example of Pathan panache. There was a platoon commanded by Havildar Karar, Aka Khel Afridi, who saw one of his men without a rifle. The boy – he was no more – said he had dropped it when he was shot, and showed his shattered wrist. 'You son-of-a- [this, that and the other],' said Karar, 'I'm not going to have these Khattaks laughing at us Afridis because we drop our rifles. Go back and get it!' Covered by fire from the platoon, the boy went down the hill and, as he picked up his rifle, he had his pagri shot off his head. He came back to his platoon.

'And where is your pagri?'

'It was shot off my head.'

'You son-of-[unmentionable shame]! What will these long-haired Khattaks say about us short-haired Afridis losing our pagris in battle? Go back and get it.'

As he picked up his pagri, one bullet grazed his stomach and another hit him in the ankle. But somehow he hobbled back to Datta Khel, a stick in his sound hand, rifle slung over his shoulder, pagri jauntily cocked.

Back in the fort it was Sharif's duty, as Post Commander, to bury the dead, of whom there were seven. It must be done outside the walls, and before dark while the machine-gunners could see to give covering fire if the burial party was shot up.

While they dug graves, I pulled some planks out of the Mess verandah and got the carpenter to knock up a coffin for Andrew. I had the bodies carried out and waited for Rupert to come. But I suppose he was very busy inside the fort, seeing to the wounded, re-organising his gasht, deciding what to do next. With only fifteen minutes of daylight left, I decided I must carry on without him. Andrew was lowered into the ground and I threw some earth on him, which is our custom too. I didn't know what to say, so I repeated the Lord's Prayer, 'Our Father which art in Heaven', which I remembered from my schooldays at Bishop Cotton's school in Simla. Rupert then arrived, and I said, 'I'm sorry, sir, it's all over.' He said, 'All right, carry on,' so I buried the others. There was a fusilade from Qalandra Sar, and everyone except Mir Hamza and I dived for cover, but we finished the job.

Rupert was very gloomy, his star gasht achieving nothing and Andrew dead. He wasn't the sort of man who can relax and unburden himself before a junior officer. We sat silent for a long time, drinking tea, before he said, 'I don't think there's any point in our staying here. We're only eating your rations, and if we don't go tonight, we may never get away.' I could only agree. So as soon as it was dark they set off across the hills to Khar Kamar, carrying the wounded on stretchers.

We were besieged for six more weeks. Sometimes we saw mirrors flashing on the hilltops and wondered if it was the relieving force, but it was only tribesmen amusing themselves. Then, three months and one day after the siege began, we got a proper helio message from Ralph Venning: 'We're all on our way. Expect us this afternoon,' and punctually they arrived, Ralph's gasht leading the Razmak Brigade. That was a good day.

His failure to take Datta Khel marked the beginning of a decline in the Faqir's power. Soon the battles of El Alamein and Stalingrad, and the Japanese blocked in Burma, indicated that those who wished to be on the winning side had better hedge their bets on the Faqir. At the end of 1942 Rupert Taylor handed over command to Jan Janson, perhaps the best Commandant the Tochi ever had. Sharif, who had not appreciated Taylor's sterling quality, was lyrical about Janson.

Jan – ah, Jan! He treated you like a friend, or a younger brother. Of course he made the decisions, but he would ask the man on the spot, 'Well, Sharifo, what would you do?' And if your ideas were sensible, he would take them up.

But Janson always said it was Rupert Taylor who nursed the Tochi Scouts out of a bad patch.

The Mahsuds felt no great sympathy for the Tori Khel and their allies, and the most influential Mahsud religious leader, Mullah Fazal Din, had a professional antipathy for the Faqir of Ipi. Of course there were hostile Mahsud gangs, and Mahsuds in the 'Gorwekht Militia', including a sort of pioneer corps expert at demolitions; but the Mahsuds as a tribe sat on the fence and refrained from provocation until they laid on a big effort which was invariably well-planned, well-led and ferocious. The Ahmedzai Wazirs followed their example.

In 1940 the South Waziristan Scouts were seriously engaged about a dozen times, some hazardous and bloody but none of particular interest except to the participants. The first significant action of 1941 was on 6 May when Neville Williams took out a four-platoon gasht from Ladha to the Tikrai Sar hill, four miles east of the fort, from which he saw in the valley below a very large tribal gathering which Khassadars told him was a big Jirga summoned by Fazal Din. As the Mullah was not then overtly hostile, Williams sent a Khassadar with polite greetings, which were courteously returned. But, scenting trouble, he thought it prudent to return to Ladha. Soon it became clear that the tribesmen, though still not firing on the gasht, were moving very fast as though to cut it off from Ladha. As a precaution, Williams wirelessed the fort orders to take out the 13-pounder and a machine-gun to a position from which they could support him if necessary. There was no *casus belli* whatsoever, and no reason why a shot should be fired, but the situation stank of menace.

Shooting started, scattered shots at first, then more and more. Williams took Jemadar Jalat's Sunni Bangash platoon to occupy a hill which flanked the withdrawal of the other three platoons. As tribesmen came hurrying up from nearby villages, the enemy strength built up to several hundred; they attacked the hill from three sides, closing to twenty yards. Williams threw a grenade at a nasty-looking hairy old man who picked it up and threw it back, fortunately without its exploding. Eventually the enemy were repulsed by grenades, rifle fire and the providential arrival of an Audax. Carrying their dead and wounded, the platoons moving back in turn, they reached Ladha after a five-hour fight which cost them three killed and eight wounded. One of the wounded Bangash just reached Ladha carrying three rifles, and died in the gateway.

It was a messy, bloody, unpredictable little affair, with a difficult withdrawal skilfully organised. But for the R/T sets calling for support from the 13-pounder and the machine-gun, the gasht might well have been overwhelmed. Among the well-earned awards was a roll of finest cloth, presented by the Ladha garrison to a Mahsud woman who carried water to their wounded.

Around this time there was a Wazir outlaw named Pirmullah, dangerous, crafty and elusive, who operated from any of a dozen villages right under the nose of Wana Brigade Headquarters. In August the Politicals thought they had him located, and called for a barampta on a group of villages north of Wana. The SWS operated in two columns, doing a right and a left hook. The right hook, ten platoons of infantry under 'Lakri' Woods, left Tanai half-an-hour before midnight and marched over very rough country in a hot, pitch-dark night to reach its place in the cordon at five o'clock in the morning. The left hook, two troops of Mounted Infantry under Lieutenant Mohamad Yusuf, crossed the Pir Ghwaza pass, a hair-raising ride in the dark with a precipice on one side, trotted briskly over the Wana plain and round the sleeping cantonment to complete the cordon by 5.20 am. The cordon was very stretched, but as it contracted, platoons could be brought into reserve. The area, thickly populated with many fields of high maize, took a long time to search. Thirteen suspects were arrested, but not Pirmullah.

At half-past nine Subadar Gul Andaz, Malik Din Khel, with one Orakzai sepoy and two Khassadars, approached the last house. They were covered from fifty yards away by Naik Shera Baz, also Malik Din Khel, one of the best shots in the corps. But after hours of searching with poor results, black with sweat, tired and bored, they were not as careful as they should have been, and did not stand to the side as Gul Andaz pushed open the door. From the darkness within a blast of fire sent all four reeling back, dead or mortally wounded, and two men made a bolt for it, to be brought down by two snap-shots from Shera Baz. They were Pirmullah and his brother. It could be said that the barampta was a sort of success.

It was Yusuf's last operation with the South Waziristan Scouts. Soon afterwards he was invalided out of the Army with pleurisy. But to the great joy of the SWS, he returned to South Waziristan as a most effective Assistant Political Agent.

Major E. E. 'Balu' French neatly outsmarted the Mahsuds, his gasht trailing its coat to lead them into a well-planned ambush. Captain John Ottley's Wing had two smart actions in 1942. In the first he was helped out of trouble by the Ladha post 13-pounder dropping its first shell with remarkable accuracy, and no little luck, on a pinpoint target he had given them by R/T. In the second, from Sararogha, he used for the first time his post-defence 3-ins mortar, taken out in a lorry. It dropped a devastating rain of bombs just over the ridge where the opposition was concentrated. Each of these actions was watched by crowds of interested but uncommitted Mahsud spectators who, when it was all over, hastened to congratulate the Militia on its success. Had the battle gone the other way, they would have been equally quick to take advantage of the Militia's failure.

In the evening of 12 April 1943, John Ottley was on the wall at Sarwekai, watching the evening roll-call.

In drove the mail lorry, and excited Khassadars reported that a lashkar including every leading hostile was sitting astride the Jandola road, about seven miles from us. The mail had got through because the local Shaman Khel were trying to persuade the gang to take their militancy elsewhere. Thanks to them, the telephone line was uncut, and I was able to talk to the Commandant in Jandola . . .

There was no point in contacting the gang at dusk: they would just melt away. I felt we should trail our coats next morning, especially as the convoy from Wana was due, which indeed they might be planning to ambush. Lakri Woods agreed, and arranged for eight platoons from Jandola to occupy Mira Khwand, a commanding hill about three miles north of the road. Having concentrated in such force, and no doubt boasted of what they would do, the hostiles must fight or lose face. It promised to be an interesting day. For the first time a dozen well-known gang-leaders were all together, men who had been responsible for most of the murders, kidnappings and miscellaneous outrages for the last decade. [See Map 11.]

The Jandola gasht was commanded by Major Khushwaqt-ul-Mulk and accompanied by the Adjutant, Captain H. R. Hutchins. 'Hutch' remembers

the enthusiasm as we piled into the Greenliners. This was not just a routine gasht, and with any luck we would all have something to talk about when it was over. We de-bussed at Splitoi and moved westward by bounds about five and a half miles to Pt 4270, a mile south-west of Mira Khwand. From there I set off up the spur towards Mira Khwand with a platoon of Orakzais commanded by Havildar Mohamad Said and a troop of MI, which had come out on foot, under Jemadar Akbar, Barak Khattak. About half-way to Mira Khwand we sighted two Mahsuds sauntering, or pretending to saunter, westward down the hill. We called on them to stop. They answered conver-

11 Action at Mira Khwand,
    13 April 1943

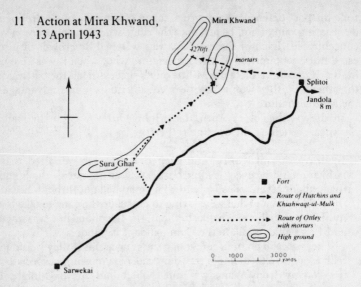

Fort

- - - - - - - → Route of Hutchins and
                 Khushwaqt-ul-Mulk

· · · · · · · · ·▸ Route of Ottley
                    with mortars

(⬭) High ground

sationally, 'We'll be back,' and disappeared into dead ground. When
next we saw them it was obvious that they had moved very fast, for
they were much further away. We again shouted 'Halt' and, as they
didn't, loosed off a couple of rounds after them before they again
disappeared. The shots stirred up a considerable gathering of
Mahsuds. The sense of urgency this produced was total: we had to
get on with it.

As we climbed up towards the crest a voice from our left reques-
ted us to 'Leave the hill to us!' The Orakzais shouted back, 'We want
it ourselves!' There was a sharp exchange of fire·as Havildar
Mohamad Said's platoon swung left to secure the vital flank, and one
Orakzai was killed.

The MI troop joined the Orakzais on top, and a young Adam
Khel sowar, with a rashness quite uncharacteristic of Afridis, ran
down the forward slope to plump himself down behind a gurgura
bush. He was shot at once, and two sowars carried him back to us. I
went across to him, and was saddened to see a little hole right
under his thorax, to which his pals were trying to apply a field
dressing. He looked at me with a bright smile and said, 'Don't
worry, Sahib, I'll just get the bandage fixed, then I'll go back and get
the bastard who did this.' 'Great idea,' I replied, 'but shouldn't you

252

have a little rest first?' 'Perhaps I will, I am a bit tired,' said the boy, and died.

Khushi now arrived with three more platoons. It was to have been the last performance of Havildar Mohamad Said, due to go on pension four days later. He moved round his men checking their firing positions, stooping low but not low enough. A bullet struck him under the armpit, passed diagonally through his body and came out at the groin, a horrid mess. As they were trying to staunch the flow of blood, some ass said something about purdah meaning that they should not expose his private parts. This was so bloody stupid that I snapped, 'This is no time for purdah,' and Jemadar Bahadur Shah, Orakzai, a grand fellow, said, 'The Sahib is right,' and opened the wounded man's shorts. But it was no good: he died in a few minutes.

We decided it might be appropriate to drop a couple of rifle-grenades behind the rocks from which the young Adam Khel had been shot. There was not a lot of shooting, but it was strictly personal. How personal I discovered when I wriggled up to have a better look at the enemy. The vicious crack beside my right ear seemed to coincide with the thump on the top of my kullah by the hand of Naik Mohamad Raza. 'Keep your head down,' he said sternly, 'We're in a very exposed position.' He took a quick snap-shot at something which flickered across his vision. '*Manam*,' said I, 'I accept that.' It was a SWS catchword, a sort of family joke used to deflate some dramatic remark or situation, and he gave me a big grin before turning to re-position in a safer place two very young Scouts just joined his section from 'the Drill'.

The Sarwekai gasht of six platoons under Ottley, starting at three o'clock, by dawn were spread along four miles of the Sura Ghar, a ridge parallel with and north of the road, from which they could cover the passage of the Wana convoy. They were in touch by R/T with Khushwaqt-ul-Mulk. The Assistant Political Agent, longing to join in the fray, trundled up the road in his lorry with his escort and, more important, two 3-inch mortars, from Splitoi and Sarwekai. At that moment the firing started on Mira Khwand. Ottley wrote,

By 11 o'clock Khushi was well and truly beset and radioed for reinforcements. But I could not send any until the convoy passed, especially as there was firing in the Sarwekai direction. But as soon as the convoy was through, I sent two platoons up to Mira Khwand, some three miles away. I took the mortars and one platoon up a parallel ridge to Khushi's.

All this took time. My party passed three casualties lying at peace under blankets in a little grove of trees. The men paused for a prayer. Then we pushed on.

(The mortars were intended only for post-defence and had no carrying equipment. For a single platoon to hump them, and their ammunition, over some three miles of rough ground and a climb of 1,500 feet was a remarkable effort.)

The Scouts' objectives were well on their way to being achieved. The Wana convoy had passed safely, under the noses of the biggest lashkar South Waziristan had seen for some time. That lashkar was now brought to battle, a nicely concentrated target for an air-strike of eight planes which had been laid on that morning from Rawalpindi. This, however, was cancelled because of a bad weather-forecast, which somewhat altered the situation.

The Mahsuds were not shooting much at Hutchins's position, but he took this as a bad sign: they were husbanding their ammunition for the gasht's withdrawal. And without air-support withdrawal would be a very tricky operation, almost impossible if they had a few wounded.

There was an excellent layback one hundred and fifty yards below our crest, but then nothing before Pt 4270 where Khushi had put a platoon of Saghri Khattaks. To stay put for the night would be even more disagreeable, in our poor position, overlooked and surrounded by the opposition. But unless we had air-support for the withdrawal, a night out seemed all too probable.

What Hutch did not realise was that the Herculean efforts of the mortar-crews and their escort platoon had brought the mortars to a position where they could support a withdrawal, behind a parallel ridge some 1,200 yards away. Moreover strong words from Jandola to Miranshah had elicited a promise from the RAF that, come wind, come weather, a plane would be over Mira Khwand at 1600 hours. R/T messages passed back and forth, and eventually Hutch was given the welcome news.

So 1600 hours became H-hour for us to pull out. It was decided that I should hold the first lay-back with Jemadar Bahadur Shah's Orakzai platoon, and we went down shortly before 4 o'clock.

The plane, an elderly Audax, arrived, and then it was all go. As it bombed and machine-gunned, the platoons peeled one by one off the crest, and as each came down, we plastered the crest behind them. I remember admiring the way they came down, beautifully extended and going like the wind. Ottley's mortars joined in with bombs dropped on to the reverse slope. In no time at all they had passed through us and it was our turn to thin out. As the men went back, I kept the Steyr-Solothurn firing irregular single shots, hoping that the enemy might think we were more than our true numbers. Eventually it was time for the last to go. 'Off you go!' I said to Bahadur Shah. 'After you, Sahib,' he replied. This was no time for courtesies. 'Be off with you!' said I, giving him a clout over the shoulders. He went off with a delightful chuckle, but only a pace ahead of me until I told him to keep to the left as we were too good a target.

Then the most tremendous storm burst.

The hills stood out livid in the late sun against a huge expanse of inky-black cloud. With the dry crackle of musketry, the rattle of the aircraft's machine-guns, the crash of bombs and the roar of thunder the effect was most exhilarating. A violent hailstorm swept the battlefield. The stones rattled down so fiercely that the mortar crews had to run for shelter . . .

[Hutch felt] a tremendous feeling of elation, they couldn't possibly aim straight in this, and then — a terrific blow on the left shoulder. No pain, and I remembered that came later. As I ran on, thanking God it wasn't the knee, I dabbed my hand on the back of my shoulder. No blood. I had been wounded by an outsize hailstone . . . It was the end of the day for us. Every feature that mattered was securely held and the withdrawal was completed in text-book fashion.

Despite the cancellation of the airstrike, the Mahsuds' First Eleven had taken a pasting. It was a long time before they gave battle again.

This was about the last Audax in action. Soon after, an astonished Tochi gasht heard a noise like tearing calico and two Hurricanes roared overhead, each firing its eight machine-guns in the general direction of an enemy which they had no time to locate. The Hurricane was not nearly as good on the Frontier as the Audax because it was too fast, it could not stooge round like a slow-moving hawk until it located a hidden enemy. 'Please sent Stratosphere Stephen home,' signalled

Desmond Cable, exasperated by a Hurricane dashing about too fast and far too high for any useful purpose. But the tribesmen loved it; until catcher-bags were fitted it scattered, like manna from heaven, thousands of good ·303 empties over the countryside, which they collected and took into the Kaniguram rifle-factories for re-filling. Provided, however, its target was easily identifiable, the Hurricane's rockets were more accurate than bombs, and could 'take out' a hostile's fortified tower without damaging nearby houses.

A couple of months after Mira Khwand the South Waziristan Scouts heard with mingled outrage and amusement that their Head Clerk, Mr Haq, had been kidnapped off a civilian lorry by a gang of Bhitannis. The Commandant acted promptly, without reference to the Political Agent who might have disapproved. Every Scout of the guilty section was sent on leave and told that if he did not return with Mr Haq, he need not bother to return at all. They returned twenty-five days later, Mr Haq, just managing a smile, in their midst. It had been a mild incarceration, with his favourite tea sent out from Jandola to the cave where he was held captive. But the kidnappers were in disrepute with the tribe, for jeopardising the jobs of sixty Bhitannis in the Scouts.

In North Waziristan, in September 1943, the Faqir made something of a comeback, returning to his old haunts in the Shaktu valley accompanied by a lashkar hired with money from Axis agents in Kabul and a gun firing 3·7 ins howitzer shells to a range of 5,000 yards. With this his 'Militia' used to shell Ghariom Scouts post, trundling his artillery back into a cave whenever a plane was heard approaching or shells from the post's howitzer started falling in the vicinity. The Assistant Political Agent, Bryan Becker, and John Auret, commanding No. 1 Wing, decided on good information that the bulk of the tribesmen were in no mood for another Holy War, though they would certainly come to the aid of the lashkar if it was attacked. But the gun was a nuisance; it killed several Scouts and severely alarmed a Subadar under whose bed an unexploded shell came to rest. The Faqir's reputation would rise if he were allowed to get away with it. Clearly the gun must be captured, or at least the cave blown up so that the gun had no cover from bombing. The Ghariom garrison could not itself turn out a gasht strong enough for the job, so a 'star' gasht was laid on, No. 1 Wing, and some Sappers and Miners for the demolition, all under the Commandant, Jan Janson.

They made the approach at night and deployed at dawn to occupy the 'gun hill'. Soon they were under fire from a fairly long range; then someone opened up from much closer. Auret recalls,

As I doubled smartly for cover I noticed Bryan Becker sort of waddling. I thought he was putting on an act and was about to tell him not to play the fool when he swayed and called out, 'They've got the APA.'

Becker's recollection is of being hit in the thigh and,

> Not wanting to be a nuisance, I got myself carried back to Dosalli by my orderly and two or three of the bodyguard who happened to be around. The bullet, having gone through my thigh, creased the forehead of my Political Assistant, a big, fair Turi, Ghulam Yahyah (of blessed memory). He died of it a few days later.

A useful 'double' for the Faqir.

On the hill the Scouts found no gun, but a magnificent cave just over the crest, on the reverse slope. Approaching it under fairly heavy fire, on a hill-top as bare as a skull, presented problems, especially for those detailed to carry explosives; so as they crawled forward, they built up low stone walls on either side. Behind these, the sandbags and explosives were passed forward from one man lying on his belly to another, and eventually reached the cave where Janson and the sappers proceeded to lay the charges. This seemed to the Scouts, with bullets cracking overhead or smacking into the stones piled beside them, to take a very long time, and they passed up a message requesting the 'Foreman' to get a move on – 'rather cheeky,' comments Auret, 'as they well knew that the "Foreman" was their Commandant, but I enjoyed passing it on.' Eventually the fuses were lit and everyone made a bolt for it before the very satisfactory explosion.

Thereafter for three years North Waziristan was troubled only by the mining of roads and sniping of lorries. Benjie Bromhead, who became Political Agent in 1944, recalled

> that it became a routine that, when a Scouts convoy went up the Tochi past Boya, some Daur in a village on the far bank would snipe at us in an ineffectual manner. We imagined him rolling out of bed and resting his rifle on his wife's anatomy, and his morning greeting would be received by an amused murmur from the men, who were quite disappointed if he failed to make it.

The Tochi Scouts reverted to the peace-time practice of officers going on duty to Bannu, and Scouts going on leave, unarmed with only

a Khassadar escort. John Auret set off on a recruiting tour, with a
leave-party, in a Scouts lorry guarded by Khassadars. A mirror started
flashing from a hilltop, a common occurrence as most tribesmen
carried little hand-mirrors for admiring their coiffures and counte-
nances, and often amused themselves by pretending it was a helio. But
to Auret it seemed that there was a curious persistence, a sort of
purpose in the flashing. Could a well-wisher be warning them of an
ambush ahead? He halted the lorry, deployed the escort and advanced
cautiously on foot. Sure enough they came under fire, and about five
hundred yards ahead a line of men started running towards them.
Looking back, they saw another party of tribesmen running to cut off
their retreat. They too ran, back to the lorry, the driver of which, with
admirable sang-froid, carefully turned it — forward reverse, forward
reverse, forward reverse — on the narrow road with a ditch on each
side, while bullets smacked into his cab. At last he had it facing the
right direction and Scouts and escort all piled in. By now the tribesmen
were quite close, but they had been running hard and their shooting
was pretty inaccurate. Bumping and swaying, the lorry trundled safely
away under their very noses.

The Army's principal concern in Waziristan was to have no trouble
at a time when every man was needed in Burma. To this end the
District Commander actually forbade the Tochi Scouts to gasht except
in the immediate vicinity of the Bannu-Razmak road. (A strange
contrast to earlier complaints that they were not gashting enough.)
Ralph Venning was so incensed by this that he took a night-gasht to the
top of the Vezda Sar, an isolated peak in the middle of nowhere, and
when there was light enough, lined up all his helios on to Gardai, where
he knew the great man would be breakfasting, to signal 'Good morning
from the Tochi Scouts on Vezda Sar'. 'Mischievous, maybe, and
tiresome certainly, but I wasn't going to have a General telling Scouts
where they could go and not go.' Soon after this, Venning left to take
command of the South Waziristan Scouts.

Dick Corfield joined the Tochi Scouts early in 1945 and within a few
days of his joining, a Gurkha battalion on road-protection duty got into
trouble and asked for help. The Miranshah gasht was already out in the
opposite direction, so a composite gasht was improvised of Drill
instructors, cadre classes, MT drivers and such, in which Jemadar
Said Gul, Kuki Khel Afridi, took over a scratch platoon of men he
hardly knew even by name, a recipe for a Tappi-type disaster. Corfield
volunteered to go too. They de-bussed at Thal-in-Tochi and moved up
the long ridge leading, singularly enough, to Tappi. Said Gul's platoon

was held up by quite heavy fire from a rocky crest, and Corfield went up to join them.

I took cover two feet away from a young Khattak, my arrival being greeted by a burst of fire and a bullet kicking up the dust between us. We both looked at the spot where it had landed, and I shall always remember the look of pure joy and amusement in his face before he fired back. He was actually enjoying it.

The scratch platoon needed a good deal of nursing, and this Jemadar Said Gul provided, moving from one section to another, positioning each and pushing it on up in turn, eventually rushing the hill-crest. For this he was awarded the first MC given to a Scouts Jemadar; previously only King's Commissioned Officers had been eligible for it. This was Corfield's encouraging introduction to the corps to which he gave his heart.

The end of the war with Germany and Japan hardly affected the Frontier. There were about one hundred and sixty cases of sniping in North Waziristan in the twelve months following VJ day, plus the shelling of posts and the mining of bridges and culverts – not headline news, but enough to keep the Scouts on their toes. One small mine was buried on Miranshah parade-ground, and blew the foot off a recruit on the Drill. Benjie Bromhead arranged for a party of Maliks from the suspect section, supervised by a Havildar of the recruit's tribe, to pull a heavy roller up and down the whole parade-ground until it was declared safe. A field-firing exercise was 'dazzed', but the only tribesmen in sight seemed to be innocent shepherds – until Subadar Khalifa, Kuki Khel, a terribly energetic old man who went up to the top of every hill on gasht, noticed that two of them were pulling-through their rifles, and took appropriate action.

The end of 1945 saw an event which seemed to mark the end of an era. Darim Khan and his son, 'Gingat', stopped at a shop in their village of Mamirogha. While Gingat went in, Darim squatted beside the door. Two strangers walked up and shot him dead. When Gingat ran out, they shot him too. Chased by villagers, they took refuge in a fortified tower.

Sharif, by now a Major commanding a Wing, was again in Datta Khel when he heard the news, and orderd a gasht at first light. On the way to Mamirogha they passed Brigade HQ at Gardai, where the Brigadier was a former Tochi Scout. It occurred to Sharif, 'Why not ask him for a gun?' He went straight in to the Brigadier who said, 'Well, Sharifo, what can I do for you?'

'You can lend me a 25-pounder, Sir. It will deal with Darim's murderers in no time.'

'Why do you say such bloody silly things? You know I can't lend an army gun to Scouts. I'd have to ask Northern Command first, and they'd think I'm mad. What's more, if you lost the bloody thing, I'd be court-martialled, and so would you.'

'Sir,' said Sharif, 'I have two hundred rifles, sturdy stock from the mountains. Every one of them will be dead before your gun is lost. Whoever heard of a Tochi Scouts gasht being overwhelmed? It would be deeply appreciated, not only by Darim's family, but by every loyalist in Waziristan. It will make an enormous impact.'

After a brief silence, the Brigadier told his Brigade Major, 'Give Major Sharif Khan a 25-pounder.' Then shaking hands with Sharif, he said, 'What a mad lot you Scouts are! And how I wish I was younger and back in Miranshah. Good luck to you.'

Sharif recalls what happened next:

We arrived at Mamirogha to find the village Jirga surrounding the tower. There was a lot of shooting going on, but when we positioned the 25-pounder, it all stopped. A greybeard shouted up, 'Come down, or the gun will fire.' One man came down, and said the other had been killed by a bullet through a loophole. He said that he and his friend had each been promised by the Faqir a rifle, a wife and 1,000 rupees for killing Darim.

The old man said, 'We must finish this feud here and now, or many will die before a settlement is made. It is simple. Darim and his son have been killed by two men, one of whom is dead. If the other now dies, that will be fair and just, and no more killing need take place. Therefore let Darim's other sons kill this man now, and that will be the end of it.'

Not a muscle moved in the murderer's face: he betrayed no emotion whatsoever. Darim's sons withdrew a little distance and talked together. They came back and one said, 'We accept.'

The old man told the murderer he must now die. He said nothing, standing with a contemptuous expression on his face. Deliberately Darim's eldest surviving son drew his pistol and shot him through the head.

17

The Scouts at Independence

In 1946 it dawned on the tribes that the British really did mean to go. Their reaction was of incredulity. 'Do you mean that, after beating the Germans and the Japs, you are being chased out of India by Hindu lawyers?' Obviously they did not particularly regret this: they were just astounded. At the same time the idea of Pakistan was seen as practical politics. The Redshirts led by Dr Khan Sahib and his brother, Abdul Ghaffar Khan, who had won an overwhelming majority in the last election before the war, with their close links with Congress, were strongly against Pakistan; but every day it became clearer that on this issue they were out of step with the vast majority of Pathans. The political ferment had its effect on Waziristan – more sniping, more mines, more highjacked lorries.

In 1945 a section of Tochi Scouts had deserted, led by a Barak Khattak named Sher Ali. He became quite a successful outlaw, operating from a group of Wazir villages near Idak and greatly helped by his knowledge of how Scouts worked. His gang was not a major menace, but one day it went too far, shooting up some recruits on Khajuri parade ground. Clearly Sher Ali would have to be brought to book – not easy, since at the first sign of activity in Miranshah, his gang used to go to ground on Zer mountain, covered with huge boulders, caves and inaccessible gullies.

However the new Commandant was Sandy Sandison, once of the South Waziristan Scouts, expert on driving game. He decided that he himself and Wilayat Shah would lead a strong gasht from Khajuri up Zer mountain in the dark, ensconcing themselves before midnight along the ridge ringing a deep re-entrant facing towards Idak. The game would be flushed by the Miranshah gasht moving out, with much lorry-din, just before dawn, and the Mounted Infantry galloping about and making themselves conspicuous around the villages. With luck the game would be moved gently up the re-entrant into the trap.

It worked. Several outlaws were bagged by Sandison's chapao, and the survivors went to ground under a huge rock. Alec Moore, the Second-in-Command, called upon them to surrender before he tossed a grenade into their cave. A voice replied that they wished to speak to Wilayat Shah, to him only would they surrender. Characteristically Wilayat Shah took the risk of going into the cave. They talked for hours, and eventually they all emerged and laid down their rifles.

On the way back, passing through a Daur village, Subadar Ramzan, a very fine Orakzai, was shot in the back. As he could move his legs, Sharif reckoned that his spine was undamaged and he would recover; but he died that night — after which his Wing was forbidden to gasht near those villages lest they exact a terrible revenge. Dick Corfield and Benjie Bromhead were with the covering force at Thal-in-Tochi. While the operation was in progress, they spotted a solitary Wazir, at least three thousand yards away, shinning up a mountain. 'Shoot him,' said Bromhead.

'What the hell with?'

Bromhead pointed to the post 25-pounder so Corfield, feeling somewhat ridiculous, proceeded to snipe a single man with a gun-howitzer. He scored no hits, but scared the daylight out of his target, and no more tribesmen broke out that way.

Sher Ali was incarcerated, while awaiting trial, in the Miranshah lock-up, from which he used to call out when he saw Sharif passing, 'Here, Sahib! Come and talk to me. You should be helping me, not hanging me, I've had you and Moore Sahib in my sights and didn't pull the trigger.'

Sharif said he would get fourteen years, but when Sher Ali was sentenced to ten, it was Sharif who persuaded him to appeal. The Governor reduced the sentence to eighteen months, of which six were remitted for good behaviour. On his release, Sandy Sandison employed him at Miranshah as a sort of private guard and general factotum, looking after Mrs Sandison who was residing there against all the rules because in 1947 Miranshah was much safer than India. Whenever the Governor arrived, she had to be put in purdah, but of course he knew all about her: Sir George Cunningham knew everything about the Frontier. 'Sher Ali and I,' recalls Sandison, 'had some very interesting talks, walking round the garden, when he recounted his exploits and the mistakes I had made.'

Another outlaw to receive special treatment was Mazrak. He was the reverse of the Scouts' usual customer, operating in Afghanistan and retiring for rest and recuperation to the Indian side of the border. His object was to topple the Amir Zahir Shah, and of this the Indian Government did not at all approve, since, on the whole, Zahir Shah had been helpful during the war and any change would probably be for the worse. The last thing Delhi wanted was trouble with Afghanistan and a possible repeat of 1919. Besides, Mazrak and his merry men were a disturbing influence in their favourite hide-out, the Ahmedzai Salient. He evaded all attempts to catch him as he moved in and out of Afghanistan, until finally the Politicals persuaded him to exchange an outlaw's precarious existence for the comfortable retirement of an Indian Government pensioner. In 1947 he surrendered to Dick Corfield at Datta Khel, a tall, imposing man, very well turned out, definitely a cut above the usual outlaw and looking every inch the Afghan noble, which he was. At Miranshah the Assistant Political Officer laid on a tikala for him, attended by all British and Pathan officers who discussed the hide-and-seek they had played with him. (He was astonished that the British officers talked Pushtu: no Persian-speaking Afghan officer would so demean himself.) Next day he went on to a commodious house in Abbotabad and a generous pension paid as long as he did not return to the Frontier.

Even before Partition the momentous decision had been made to pull the Army out of Waziristan and the Khyber and entrust the Frontier wholly to the Scouts. 'I wonder,' mused FitzMaurice, appointed Deputy Inspecting Officer Frontier Corps in Quetta, 'how the Hindu Government of India will like its Frontier being guarded entirely by 20,000 Pathans.' A new corps was raised, the Pishin Scouts; and the oldest of Frontier irregular corps, disbanded in 1919, was re-formed. In 1942 the Army had raised for overseas service an Afridi battalion. Its formation was a blow to the Scouts: it competed with them for recruits, and drew off some of their best officers and NCOs, including Khan Baz ('Tabrur') who became its first Subadar Major. On its return from overseas, volunteers from the Afridi Battalion were the nucleus of the reformed Khyber Rifles, commanded by Sharif. It was more active, less *qillaband*, than the old Khyber Rifles. Although not allowed into the Tirah, it gashted vigorously north of the Pass right up the Kabul river, and manned the frontier post of Landi Khana where it became a much photographed tourist attraction.

In March 1946, Ralph Venning, Commandant of the SWS, and Robin Hodson, Political Agent, South Waziristan, were summoned to Razmak to help entertain Pandit Jawarhalal Nehru, Dr Khan Sahib and Abdul Ghaffar Khan, who were touring the Frontier to persuade Pathans to join India, thus strangling at birth the as yet unborn state of Pakistan. The Redshirt leaders were excellent company, but Nehru was at his worst, sulky and arrogant. However, he showed courage in visiting the Frontier for a forlorn hope. From start to finish his tour was a disaster, nowhere worse than at Razmak where he addressed a Jirga of the Dré Mahsud as though it were a Congress rally at Allahabad. He struck entirely the wrong note by striding about, gesticulating and discoursing in strident tones and impeccable Urdu, which few of his audience understood, on how he had 'come to free you from the slavery of the British'. This was too much for Malik Mehr Dil, who had fought the British in 1919 and been a thorn in the flesh of many a Political Agent. 'You have the effrontery', he shouted, 'to call us slaves of the British. We've never been anyone's slaves, and we're certainly not going to be yours. And if you dare show your face here again [Mehr Dil dropped his hands to his groin] we'll circumcise you!' As the Wazir Maliks refused to meet him, Nehru must have gone away reluctantly convinced that assurances of Pathan attachment to India were worthless.

Such was the state of bloody tumult in the run-up to Independence that in April 1947 the Bhitannis, with the enthusiastic co-operation of Mahsuds, looted and burnt Tank and cut its water-supply. The Police could not cope and the Army could spare only a company. So on 16 April the Political Agent, Major 'Johnny' Raw, asked Ralph Venning for help. Tank, being in British India, was in no way a Scout responsibility, but Venning at once sent off five platoons and followed next day with a troop of Mounted Infantry and two more platoons.

Sniping, arson, the knifing of Hindus and pillaging were incessant. The South Waziristan Scouts patrolled the outskirts of the town to stop more tribesmen coming in, patrolled the streets, rounded up Hindus and moved them to a protected area, emptied the grain-stores in the city and moved their contents to the Civil Lines. They encountered several of their old customers in the unexpected role of guardians of private property, hired by Hindu merchants to protect their premises. These guards, with ample ammunition and some sort of legitimacy, sniped zealously from the rooftops, under the pretext of deterring looters, at anyone in sight, including Ralph Venning, who was not amused. It was work entirely novel to Scouts, infinitely removed from their gashts and baramptas, and they carried it out with good humour and complete communal impartiality.

There was a Mission Hospital in Tank, which for years had done wonderful work for local people and Powindahs. It was isolated, indefensible and staffed by three English nurses who were offered places, with Mrs Raw and her new-born baby, in a plane to Peshawar. Maisie, head of the Mission, asked for an hour to think it over and discuss it with the other two, and then replied that they preferred to stay.

Venning sent Major James Majury, one of his Wing Commanders, with a gasht down the Hinnis Tangi to stop more Mahsud incursions. They met two or three lashkars, quite friendly and good-humoured, who said they had heard it was free-for-all in Tank, and they were part of the all. Majury replied that they could not be more mistaken: Tank was strongly held by Scouts and Frontier Constabulary and if they showed their noses there, they would certainly be shot. At which the tribesmen quite amiably returned whence they came. After a few days Army reinforcements arrived in Tank, and the SWS returned to their proper job.

The Wazirs hoped to treat Bannu as the Mahsuds and Bhitannis had treated Tank. Large numbers set off optimistically with ropes and ladders to facilitate the good work, and camels to carry away the proceeds. But they were intercepted by spoil-sport Tochi Scouts, who turned them back and arrested a hundred and sixty.

At midnight on 14 August 1947 British rule ended and the States of India and Pakistan were born. Most British officers departed as soon as they could. However friendly towards Pakistan – and Scouts officers were very friendly – they could not escape the feeling of depression because their world was at an end. Nevertheless Scout morale was very high; however friendly they were to their British officers – and Scouts were very friendly – to Pathans it was not the end, but the beginning. This did not in the least affect the extraordinary rapport between British and Pathans. One of the last British officers to join the Tochi Scouts, who served in it for only a few months, said that he immediately felt one of a family, a band of brothers, to a degree he had never experienced in the various battalions in which he had previously served.

Some British officers stayed in Scouts, on contract to Pakistan, to help their successors into the saddle or just because they could not bear to go. Dick Corfield remained until 1950, first in the Tochi, then in the SWS. He thought that at first he might have trouble, men saying or hinting 'You are only a Faranghi. You can't throw your weight about now.' Indeed, his new Commandant, Lieut-Colonel 'George' Sadi-qullah told him, 'If you have any trouble, Dick, just let me know, and I'll sort it out.' But he never did. Or, rather, only once: Sadiqullah would not have his Moslem officers drinking, and begged Corfield to remove temptation by finishing all the booze in the Mess. Corfield manfully tackled the Herculean task, his last service to Scouts, until there was only crème de menthe left; it was never his favourite beverage, and now the mere sight of it turns his stomach.

The Scouts under Pakistani command inherited their predecessors' problems, including the Faqir of Ipi who was as hostile to Pakistan as he had been to the British. But the fact that they were Moslems, and their Government was Moslem, and there were no Faranghi, Hindu or Sikh troops on the Frontier removed one source of resentment.

The Tochi Scouts piqueted the road for the withdrawal of the Army from Razmak. Throughout the day the column was sniped by, apparently, a single sportsman armed with a Bren-gun. No one could spot him; tons of lead were poured into the mountainside in the general direction of his tock-tock-tock – tock-tock-tock. And as night fell the Scouts, who by this time had become almost emotionally involved with this indomitable hostile, actually cheered his valedictory tock-tock-tock.

Independence and Partition were accompanied by appalling commu-nal massacres, with Moslems, Sikhs and Hindus vying with one another in the slaughter of hundreds of thousands of men, women and children. But Sikhs and Hindus living among the Pathan tribes, hamsayas protected by the Pukhtunwali code, were not harassed. At Parachinar the Kurram Militia formed a refugee-camp and protected it against Khostwals and Powindahs. Three hundred Sikhs, with their families, beleaguered and in mortal danger in the heart of Peshawar City, were rescued by two platoons of Kurram Militia taken in by Denis Ambrose, the Inspecting Officer Frontier Corps, and his Staff Officer, Douglas Robertson, formerly of the SWS.

In October 1947, the Hindu Maharajah of Kashmir, although the vast majority of his subjects were Moslems, joined his State to India. Pakistan was outraged, and from all over the Frontier tribal lashkars hastened in lorries – undoubtedly with official logistic support – into Kashmir. Scouts were instructed to see nothing, hear nothing, say nothing and do nothing in this matter, although at least one British

Officer, Harvey-Kelly of the SWS, took part in the campaign. It seemed that nothing could stop these hordes of tribesmen taking Srinagar with its vital airfield. Indeed nothing did, but their own greed. The Mahsuds in particular stopped to loot, rape and murder; Indian troops were flown in and the lashkars pushed out of the Vale of Kashmir into the mountains. The Mahsuds returned home in a savage mood, having muffed an easy chance, lost the loot of Srinagar and made fools of themselves. They were burning to take it out of Hindus and Sikhs, and there was still in Wana a Gurkha battalion and a Sikh mountain battery, waiting to be escorted down to India. The task of seeing them safely out of Waziristan was given mainly to the SWS.

Ralph Venning had been succeeded in command briefly by Alec Moore, and Moore was succeeded by Lieutenant Colonel K. M. Chambers, a competent regular soldier but not one who immediately sprang to mind as a suitable Commandant of the SWS. However, he was merely stopping a gap until a Pakistani Commandant was available, and in 1947 it was hopeless to expect continuity in these matters or that a square peg would be found for every square hole. His Wing Commander in Sarwekai was James Majury, who had been in the corps four years and well knew the local form. In retrospect it seems that neither the Brigade Commander in Wana nor the Scouts Commandant in Jandola paid enough attention to the possibility, indeed probability, that the convoy of Gurkhas and Sikhs would be attacked in the Shahur Tangi. Either Political intelligence was faulty, or it was ignored. Chambers had, after providing for other commitments, twelve platoons to cover some fifty-seven miles of vulnerable road, so no extra piquets were posted in the Tangi which had, as usual, piquets at each end and one in the middle. But these were not in visual touch, and it was possible for hostiles to lie up close to the road, out of their sight. Instead it was decided that the convoy should be escorted from Sarwekai onwards by one platoon under Chambers at the head and another under Majury at the rear. Majury queried the wisdom of halting the convoy near Sarwekai, in full view of any hostiles, to enable these arrangements to be made. It was never right on the Frontier to hang about. However, this was done.

The escorting platoons joined the convoy and Majury recalls,

Then we were on our way, past Sarwekai and heading for Jandola. My party consisted of a platoon of Malik Din Khel Afridis under the command of Jemadar Shera Baz, who four years earlier had bagged the famous outlaw Pirmullah. He was captain both of the corps shooting team and of the football team, a superb soldier and potentially a future Subadar Major.

Two miles east of Sarwekai the road crossed a dry algad, on the other side of which was a low ridge surmounted by an old Khassadar post. The ground on the left sloped gently up towards the hills in the distance, but on the right it rose sharply to a ridge some five hundred yards from the road. On the Sarwekai bank of the algad was a low wall surrounding a disused garden.

Approaching this, I suddenly realised that there was trouble ahead and that the convoy was stuck in the algad. With Shera Baz and his platoon I ran down the road as fast as we could to find out what the trouble was. We found out only too soon for, as we ran down the side of the convoy, still on the road, Shera Baz dropped at my side, shot through the neck. Heavy fire was coming from the low ridge by the old Khassadar post on the far bank of the algad. The initial burst had caused considerable casualties in the Army vehicles, some of which were knocked out and slewed across the road, blocking it. The Army troops did not seem to be taking much action, sitting ducks in their vehicles, so I called to an officer to de-buss them and take up position while I with the Malik Din Khel platoon cleared the low garden wall on the right of the road and, under cover of that wall, made our way forward to the edge of the algad. The Platoon Havildar took half of them on to the high ground on the right to engage the Mahsuds from the flank while I edged forward with the remainder. As we started to deploy and assault the ridge on the far side, the tribesmen melted away into the hills and scrub beyond ... There was nothing to be gained by pursuing them: my job was to sort out the chaos and evacuate the dead and wounded. The Mahsuds had allowed the front half of the convoy through and then ambushed the rear half. The front half had gone out of sight.

Having a large number of casualties, both Scouts and Army, and hearing by radio that the rest of the convoy was ambushed in the Shahur Tangi itself, Majury took the rear half back to Sarwekai and then set off for the Tangi with the Malik Din Khel platoon. At the top of the ridge above Splitoi he found Subadar Major Umar Khan with a gasht from Jandola. They had been piqueting that end. The tribesmen had ambushed the convoy between him and the next piquet, a mile and a half on, out of sight of both. While Majury was there, Umar's gasht brought in one captured Mahsud: that was all. Driving down towards Chagmalai Majury 'saw from the damaged Army vehicles and obvious chaos that the ambush had been of extreme ferocity. It had been brief, and mostly hand-to-hand fighting.' At Chagmalai there were forty or fifty dead and wounded. By the end of the day half the convoy with its casualties was at Sarwekai and half at Chagmalai, with many damaged vehicles left on the road. From the Mahsud point of view the attack had been a brilliant success — in, kill, and out. Two days later, after negotiations with the Mahsud Maliks, the whole of the convoy was driven safely through to Jandola escorted by Khassadars. For several days odd Army stragglers turned up at Scouts posts, mostly stripped naked and very lucky to be alive.

It was very sad to lose such a wonderful man as Shera Baz. His platoon mourned him greatly as did we all. It spoke volumes for the Scouts that at a time of tumult and communal massacres down country, they remained completely unbiased and obeyed orders.

Pathans have no great love for Gurkhas, and a great hereditary dislike for Sikhs, aggravated by the Punjab massacres. But it was a matter of honour to get the Gurkhas and Sikhs safely out of Waziristan, and for that Shera Baz and other Scouts died. That their sacrifice was partly in vain was not their fault.

'The fate of Gilgit appears to rest with Major William Brown. Who is Major William Brown?' Thus minuted a Commonwealth Relations mandarin in the autumn of 1947 when Indian Army records were shuttling between New Delhi, Karachi and London, and no one could answer his question: all that could be ascertained was that Brown was aged twenty-four.

The sequence of events which led to this remarkable situation began in the early summer of 1947 when the military authorities and the Kashmir Government were looking for a British officer to see the Gilgit Scouts through the difficult period of Independence and Partition. They might have preferred someone older, but it was not easy to find anyone at that time, so the job was offered to Major W. A. Brown who had served briefly in the Chitral and Tochi Scouts, and three years in the Gilgit Scouts. A very tall, lean, dark Scot, with a horseman's stoop, Willie Brown accepted with alacrity because he liked the life in Gilgit, liked the people and 'felt that the influence of an experienced British officer would have a steadying effect during the transition'. Asked to recommend a Second-in-Command, he suggested Captain A. S. Mathieson, a year younger, whom he had known as a Khassadar Officer* in Miranshah.

Brown arrived in Gilgit in July 1947, and on 1 August the last British Political Agent, Lieutenant-Colonel Roger Bacon, handed over his functions, including control of the Scouts, to the Governor of Gilgit, Brigadier Ghansara Singh, a Dogra of the Kashmir State Forces. The Union Jack was lowered for the last time (except in Kalamdarchi where Subadar Jamshed Khan, 'Champagne Charlie', an ardent Imperialist, continued to fly it for the next four months); and the Kashmir flag was raised, at which the populace turned their backs and walked away.

Clearly the next few months would be full of interest, depending on what the Maharajah of Kashmir decided to do with his State after Partition. The most sensible, if unconstitutional, course would be to take the Hindu and Buddhist areas into India and allow the Moslem areas to go their own way, presumably to Pakistan. Other courses open to him, though not all constitutionally, were accession to Pakistan, complete independence, and accession to India. It was inconceivable that he would choose to unite his state with Pakistan. Independence would hardly be practicable nine hundred miles from the sea, even if India and Pakistan agreed to it which was unlikely. But if he did achieve it, the people of Gilgit would probably accept the situation provided they had the same degree of home rule as under the British. Accession to India would be regarded as outrageous by every Moslem, especially in the Gilgit Agency where the native population was one hundred per cent Moslem. The consequences would include the Mullahs preaching the Jehad, rebellion, fighting between Scouts and Kashmir State Forces, 'liberation' by Pathan and Chitrali lashkars, and a massacre of Hindus and Sikhs of whom there were about one hundred and fifty in Gilgit town and Chilas. There was no possibility that the Scouts would fire on their fellow-Moslems to enforce Hindu rule.

On 14 August all constitutional links between Kashmir and Britain were severed. Brown and Mathieson then became mercenaries serving an independent state, as no Europeans had done in India since the early nineteenth century. Their contract with the Maharajah obliged them to obey any of his orders, passed to them through the Governor – to do otherwise would expose them to the direst penalties. But to implement the policy of accession to India would be completely impossible, not to say suicidal, and would certainly result in a Scouts' mutiny. Resig-

---

* District Officer in charge of Khassadars, a new appointment in 1946.

nation would amount to sitting back and watching the 'worst possible case' take its course. Brown's duty, as he saw it, was to remain in command of the Scouts, and hence of the whole situation, and engineer a peaceful, orderly transfer of the Agency to Pakistan. He was emotionally committed to Pakistan but, irrespective of his sympathies, breaking his contract with Kashmir – in plain words mutiny – was the only way of preserving law and order and saving the lives of non-Moslems, including probably his own.

Brown and Mathieson agreed that, if the Maharajah did cede Gilgit to India, they, with the Scouts, would stage a coup d'état and take it over to Pakistan. Details of the operation were planned, and its code-signal would be 'Datta Khel'.

There were two complications. The first was the presence at Bunji, south of the Indus, of the 6th Kashmir Infantry battalion, about equal in numbers to the Scouts but far superior in fire-power, having a regular battalion's complement of light and medium machine-guns, 2- and 3-ins mortars. The Scouts had nothing but rifles and a couple of Vickers guns for post-defence. However, the battalion's efficacy was reduced by the fact that one of its companies was Moslem (the other two being Sikh and Dogra), as was its elderly Commanding Officer. The second complication was the existence (disclosed to Brown by his servants not, as it should have been, by the Scout Subadars) of an underground Liberation Front, ostensibly for Pakistan but to some extent aiming at complete independence with lucrative opportunities for the chief conspirators. They proposed to depose the Mirs and Rajahs – the only forces, apart from the Scouts, for continuity and experienced administration – whom one of the plotters swore to hang from Gilgit bridge. Among their leading lights was an able, influential but devious ex-Subadar of Scouts, Shah Rais Khan, a relative of the Raja of Gilgit. They had sympathisers among the more naive Scouts and in the Moslem company of the battalion at Bunji, but it was impossible to know how many.

If Brown's position was difficult, Ghansara Singh's predicament was dire. The only card he held was the 6th Kashmir Infantry, on the wrong side of the Indus. As a Dogra, he was utterly loyal to the Dogra Maharajah, but as a sensible man he must have seen that the province which he governed would never accept accession to India. If, however, he connived at a handover to Pakistan, he would lose his pension and be exiled forever from Kashmir and India. An honest, but lazy and ineffective man, he watched with dismay the unrolling of events which he could not influence. He and Brown got on quite well over whiskies and soda, but on this vital issue were poles apart.

Through August and September there were pro-Pakistan demonstrations, flag-flying and slogan-shouting. Islamic feeling was particularly militant in Gilgit town and in Chilas; there was a real danger that the tribesmen of Chilas, Darel and Tangir would declare a Jehad, probably with Scout support. But while there was any chance of the Maharajah acting sensibly, Brown could only bide his time, preserve law and order and warn Mathieson to do likewise.

The Subadar Major, Babar Khan, a Gushpur of Nagar whose sister was married to the Mir of Hunza, was a man of influence, prestige and sagacity. He was not himself a conspirator, but was probably privy to the plans of the Liberation Front. In so far as he was on the fence, Brown regarded it of great importance to get him off it on the side of union with Pakistan. They discussed the situation. He was not markedly helpful, but said he had spoken of it with the Mirs of Hunza and Nagar who recommended calm, patience and no violence. Everyone was waiting for the Maharajah to declare himself. On several occasions Brown placed all the facts before the Governor, impressing upon him that something must be done; at least he should ascertain His Highness's intentions, and advise him of their probable results. But poor Ghansara Singh seemed sunk in resignation and despair.

On 29 October the Maharajah announced his fatal decision to accede with his whole State to India, and the Governor declined to discuss the matter with Brown any further. Nevertheless on 30 October Brown insisted that he should listen to a lengthy resumé of the situation. Concluding, he urged the Governor at least to ascertain the wishes of the people in this matter. Clearly a referendum (a much-used word in those days) was impossible, but he could consult the Mirs and Rajas who would tell him their subjects' thoughts. The Governor seemed to agree generally with Brown's arguments, and said he would contact the rulers by telephone.

That evening Brown asked what they had said. Ghansara Singh replied that the Mir of Hunza had signified his complete satisfaction with the Maharajah's decision; the Mir of Nagar was out shooting and could not be reached; nor had he contacted the Rajas. Brown did not believe him, and got the Subadar Major to telephone his brother-in-law, speaking in Burushaski since the line would probably be tapped. The Mir replied that the Governor had not spoken to him and those were certainly not his views.

The next day, 31 October, Brown informed the Governor that, as his advice had been disregarded, he could accept no responsibility for the consequences and might have to take steps on his own responsibility to maintain law and order and prevent bloodshed. With these words to his superior Willie Brown crossed the Rubicon.

On the same day the wireless operator showed him an ominous message from the Mehtar of Chitral breaking off relations with Kashmir and saying he could not accept Gilgit's accession to India. Mathieson wirelessed from Chilas that the Scouts and local people were about to declare a Jehad unless there was an immediate accession to Pakistan. At evening prayers the Mullahs in Gilgit town actually preached the Jehad. The Moslem company of the 6th Kashmir Infantry crossed the Partap Pul and set out for Gilgit with undisclosed but obvious intentions. Lastly, there may have been an abortive attempt by local Sikhs to murder Brown and the Subadar Major and blow up the Scouts' magazine. It is difficult to credit this, unless one assumes a compulsive Sikh death-wish. But they are a very brave, not to say reckless, people, and subsequent searches disclosed in their possession large quantities of explosives for which they could have had no legitimate use.

Finally in the evening of 31 October Brown sent Mathieson the code-signal 'Datta Khel', and the following action was taken:

1. One platoon of Scouts under the Subadar Major proceeded to the Governor's (formerly the Political Agent's) house to take him into protective custody.

2. Detachments of Scouts cut the telephone line to Bunji and Srinagar and took over the wireless and Post and Telegraph offices.

3. One platoon gashted to Bhup Singh Pari, where the track from Bunji to Gilgit zig-zags up a near precipice, to stop any move to Gilgit by the Kashmir infantry.

4. Two platoons gashted from Chilas to hold the Partap Pul and the right bank ferry-head village of Jaglote, three miles below the Partap Pul.

5. A detachment held the Gilgit bridge.

6. Gilgit town was patrolled to prevent disorder, and the Sikhs and Hindus were removed to a protected refugee camp.

The Gilgit Scouts, elated after thirty years' peace at the prospect of a fight in the best of causes, went to it with zest and their full gashting speed.

Everything worked according to plan, except at the Governor's house. Ghansara Singh may have been supine and ineffective in a political crisis, but Dogra Rajputs are fighting men. He made no response to the Subadar Major's summons, and when the Scouts broke open his door, fired on them, killing one and wounding another. They withdrew to positions round the house. Alone, surrounded by thousands of Moslems out for his blood, with no possibility of relief, he kept up a hopeless but brave resistance, and firing continued most of the night.

Brown's main concern was that Ghansara Singh should not be lynched by the mob which clamoured to storm the house and hack the Hindu to pieces. The Subadar Major persuaded them to go down to the polo ground, where ex-Subadar Shah Rais Khan managed to calm them. The Subadar Major again summoned the Governor to surrender, but to no avail even when a machine-gun was fired high over the roof. So Brown ordered the Scouts to cease fire until daylight. At dawn Ghansara Singh gave up. If in this moment of humiliation his demeanour suggested a nervous breakdown, it is impossible not to admire his courage in hideous adversity. He was escorted to the Scouts lines where he was treated with the respect due to his rank and position.

Meanwhile in Chilas Mathieson had suppressed looting, brought Sikhs and Hindus into the fort for their safety, sent messengers up the valleys of Chilas, Tangir and Darel urging everyone to keep calm and despatched two platoons to the Partap Pul.

Next morning two to three thousand tribesmen, armed with anything from sporting rifles to daggers, were demonstrating on the polo ground for immediate accession to Pakistan, and more were roaming the streets in search of infidels. Brown reinforced the Scouts at Bhup Singh Pari and, in consultation with the Subadar Major who now disclosed that he knew a thing or two, invited to a conference the leading lights of the Liberation Front. These, it seemed, comprised ex-Subadar Shah Rais Khan; Captain Mohamad Said, attached to the Scouts; Captain Hassan, one of the few natives of Gilgit who served in the Kashmir State Forces (he had until recently been commanding the Moslem company of the battalion at Bunji, and it was not quite clear whether he was on ordinary or French leave from his post); and Lieutenant Ghulam Haidar, Brown's Adjutant, motivated purely by Pakistani patriotism and the only one of the Front's luminaries who was not entirely self-seeking.

Also present at the conference were the Subadar Major and Brown himself. The atmosphere was amicable and Brown's presence was accepted. The weakness of his position was that he was the only non-Moslem; the strength, that he commanded the Scouts, though he was under no illusion that he could lead them where they did not want to go; and that he knew his own mind on the issue of Pakistan, which none of the others did except Ghulam Haidar. They were overtly for

Pakistan, but disclosed their secret plans to set up an independent republic of Gilgit-Astor with all power in their own hands. They claimed the backing of seventy-five per cent of the Scouts, which Brown took with a large pinch of salt, and said that any who did not support them would be discharged and replaced by men from the Gilgit sub-division, Shah Rais Khan's sphere of influence. Brown argued that independence was impractical, but did not press his point, the time being inopportune for dissensions of which the Bunji battalion might take advantage. For the time being he would go along with them as they set up a provisional Government, trusting to events to show up the fatuity of their ideas.

It was essential that he should make contact with Peshawar. The message he wanted to send was such that, if it were in clear, a Moslem operator would leak it and a Hindu operator would refuse to send it. Roger Bacon had taken away the code and cypher books. Fortunately the operator was a Parsee, Mr Limbuwallah, prepared to send anything Brown wanted sent and to keep his mouth shut. Brown's messages read:

To: Khan Abdul Qayum Khan Prime Minister NWFP
From: Major Brown
Date: 1st November.
Revolution night 31st to 1st in Gilgit province. Entire pro-Pakistan populace have overthrown Dogra regime. Owing imminent chaos and bloodshed Scouts and Moslem elements State Forces have taken over law and order. Scouts Officers and Moslem Officers State Forces running administration provisionally. Request higher authority be appointed for orders immediately and reply through wireless. Commandant Scouts.

And

To: Lieut. Col. Bacon
From: Brown
Date: 1st November
Coup d'état in favour Pakistan in Gilgit. Can carry on meantime but can you help. Brown.

To Roger Bacon, then Political Agent, Khyber, it is improbable that this message came as a bolt from the blue. During the time they had been together in Gilgit, he and Brown had often discussed the shape of things to come. The reply from Peshawar said that Brown's message had been passed on to higher authority (i.e. the Government of Pakistan) and he should maintain law and order.

Brown's messages were not entirely accurate. Whatever the sentiments of the populace, the only person in authority who had unequivocally declared in favour of union with Pakistan was Willie Brown himself. Union with India had been repudiated but, except for shouting slogans, none of the Provisional Government had done anything to promote union with Pakistan. Nor did they show any haste to do so, being far too busy awarding themselves the top jobs in the Republic – Shah Rais Khan as President, Captain Hassan as Commander-in-Chief, Captain Mohamad Said as Chief of Staff, Lieutenant Ghulam Haidar as Commissioner. The Pakistan flag was raised with great rejoicing in the Scout lines, but it was a mere public relations exercise.

The military situation was unresolved and there was the possibility that the Pakistan Government, reluctant to take on more commitments beyond the northern passes and engaged in delicate negotiations with India and Britain about Kashmir, might reject their advances. The fragility of Brown's position was displayed when a fanatical Mullah called on Moslems to kill him, but Shah Rais Khan and the Subadar Major told the holy man to belt up.

The Sikhs and Dogras of the 6th Kashmir Infantry remained at Bunji, possibly unaware of what was happening in Gilgit. The Moslem company, on its way to Gilgit, encountered the Scouts at Bhup Singh Pari on 1 November and explained that their genial purpose was to slaughter any Sikh and Hindu they could lay hands on, starting with the Governor. An attempt was made to lure the Sikhs and Dogras into an ambush by a bogus message from the Governor ordering them to proceed to Gilgit and suppress a rebellion; but they did not rise to the fly. There also arrived at Bhup Singh Pari the Commanding Officer of the battalion, with the key of the Bunji magazine in his pocket.

The most encouraging feature of the situation was that the fairly simple civil administration, after stalling for two days, started up again on 3 November and functioned normally under the general supervision of Brown and Ghulam Haidar. The Treasury was left inviolate, wages were paid normally, proper accounts were kept, and the luminaries of the provisional government did not, surprisingly, draw on public funds for the generous emoluments they had voted themselves. Over the telephone the Mirs and Rajas expressed approval of Brown's actions and made quite clear their wish for accession to Pakistan.

The two-platoon gasht from Chilas under Jemadar Sher Ali, Yasin, had set out at five in the morning on 1 November, crossed the Indus by the Raikot suspension bridge and continued up the right bank. Slowed down by the post-defence Vickers gun they had with them, and not wishing to be seen from across the river in daylight, they took two days to cover forty-five miles and did not reach the vicinity of Jaglote until after dark on 2 November. There they learned from ex-Scouts that the enemy had only one platoon on the right bank, distributed between the watch-house in Jaglote village and the bridge itself, three miles to the north. In the dark they untied the Jaglote ferry and moved it down-stream, took up positions and in the morning summoned the enemy to surrender. The enemy, being Sikhs, fought it out and after an hour or so all except two, who escaped across the bridge, were dead. In 1947 not many prisoners were taken in battles between Sikhs and Moslems. One Scout was killed and one wounded.

Later in the morning Sher Ali saw a large enemy force approaching from the direction of Bunji. Since they would have mortars and medium machine-guns, it was far from certain that he could hold the bridge; and the arrival on the right bank of three hundred well-armed Sikhs and Dogras would be a disaster. Sher Ali therefore set fire to the Partap Pul, making it impassable without lengthy repairs.

Mathieson had left Chilas twenty-four hours after Sher Ali with one platoon and a Vickers gun. He too crossed over to the right bank and arrived at Thalichi on the morning of 3 November. He was almost opposite the Ramghat bridge over the Astor river, an important point because by it the battalion in Bunji could either retreat to, or be reinforced from Astor and Kashmir itself; or they could move down the left bank on Chilas. Captain Hassan (Commander-in-Chief of the Republic's forces) had assured Brown that it was strongly held by men of his own Moslem company of the 6th Kashmir Infantry. He was wrong. Mathieson, learning that it was unguarded, sent two sections to hold it. They found it damaged by villagers, but not beyond repair. Mathieson then established himself in Thalichi, covering with his Vickers gun, albeit at rather long range across the Indus, the track from Bunji to Ramghat; and he sent a runner to Brown asking for news and further orders. The enemy seemed to be rendered innocuous, bottled up in Bunji unable to move north-west on Gilgit, south-west on Chilas, or south-east back to Kashmir.

On receiving Mathieson's note in the evening of the 4th, Brown with the Subadar Major and a mounted escort set off for Thalichi, arriving there soon after midnight. In the morning they saw about one hundred and fifty enemy moving up the Ramghat ridge towards the bridge and opened fire on them, but without much effect at such a long range. For

Brown it was not enough to neutralise the Kashmir battalion; he wanted to capture the lot, with all their weapons which the Scouts would find very useful. He sent a message to the C-in-C asking for reinforcements and another Vickers gun, to enable him to cross the river and effectively encircle the battalion. This was refused, as the C-in-C had set his heart on a hazardous and totally unnecessary frontal attack on Bunji, crossing the swift and icy Indus by raft and boat. However, before the apprehensive troops embarked, news came that the enemy had evacuated Bunji and gone up into the mountains. The Scouts made an unopposed crossing, and plans were made to round up the enemy next day. This proved unnecessary, for during the night the 6th Kashmir Infantry disintegrated. Most of them probably made their way back home across the passes, some died of starvation and exposure in the mountains or were killed by villagers.

Brown, Mathieson, the Subadar Major and the Commander-in-Chief returned to a triumphal reception in Gilgit. But if the military situation was resolved, the political situation was not. Such was the intrigue and in-fighting between members of the Provisional Government that Ghulam Haidar had sent another appeal to the Prime Minister of the North-West Frontier Province and Roger Bacon to fly to Gilgit immediately, but no reply had been received. Although daily meetings of the Government were held, it was impossible to reach agreement on anything. Nevertheless the administrative machine, such as it was, functioned well under the unpractised but sensible supervision of Ghulam Haidar; so Brown and Mathieson applied themselves to redeploying the Scouts and planning their expansion and re-equipment to meet an invasion from Kashmir in the spring.

A minor social embarrassment was Brigadier Ghansara Singh. He was not in custody and could wander where he wished; but he was depressed, poor fellow, and refused to be comforted, even by a seat to watch polo matches.

As the days passed Brown's position became ever more difficult, maintaining law and order in a political vacuum. He feared that, if Pakistan did not accept the accession very soon, anarchy would result; and on 13 November he sent a third message to Peshawar saying he could not carry on unless a representative of the Pakistan Government flew up immediately. At last, on 16 November, there arrived on Gilgit airstrip Khan Sahib Mohamad Alam, a competent Pathan of the Provincial Civil Service, to take over as Political Agent. Expecting to find the Treasury looted, he brought a lakh (100,000) of rupees wrapped up in newspapers, and was agreeably surprised when these proved to be not needed. To him Brown handed over with immense relief, and the Provisional Government of the Republic of Gilgit-Astor sank without trace.

It was an extraordinary reversion, ten weeks after the end of British rule, to the practices and pragmatic loyalties of the European military adventurers in India a century and a half earlier. But the British High Commissioner in Karachi, while observing that Brown's and Mathieson's position was 'delicate', thought that they deserved credit for saving the lives of most of the non-Moslems in Gilgit, including the Governor, and that by their sense, sound judgment and steadiness they saved a very dangerous situation.

As to the end results of their coup, who can say? They include the development of Gilgit as a tourist resort; and the Karakoram Highway between China and Pakistan which was constructed by the Chinese but may one day be found very convenient for the Russians.

Postscript

The Scouts since Independence

The requirements of security make it impossible to give a detailed account of the Frontier Corps since the birth of Pakistan in 1947. Only general notes can be given.

The Government of Pakistan adopted the policy recently devised, but never implemented, by the British, of withdrawing the Army from the Frontier and entrusting it wholly to Scouts. Wana and Razmak, and most of the forward Scouts posts in Waziristan were evacuated or handed over to Khassadars.

From north to south, eight corps were inherited from the British: Gilgit Scouts, Chitral Scouts, Khyber Rifles, Kurram Militia, Tochi Scouts, South Waziristan Scouts, Zhob Militia and the Pishin Scouts raised in 1946 for the Pishin-Chaman sector of the Frontier.

In 1949 and in 1964 were raised the Northern Scouts (in which was incorporated the Gilgit Scouts) and the Karakoram Scouts for the defence against India of the 'cease-fire line' which passes through some of the highest mountains in the world. They were recruited from the tribes of the Gilgit Agency, Astor and Baltistan and have frequently been in action. The Thal Scouts, based on Thal-in-Kurram, was raised in 1949 as a general reserve for the Frontier. In 1948 the Mekran and Chagai Levy Corps, roughly the equivalent of Khassadars, were up-graded to the Chagai Militia with responsibility for the desert country in the extreme west of Baluchistan, along the Iran and Afghan frontiers. The Kalat Scouts were raised in 1965 for duties in the wild desert and mountain country, inhabited by the Brahui tribe, between Quetta and Karachi.

In 1960 the two Mahsud Labour Battalions, raised by the British in the late 1930s and employed mainly in road-making up and down the Frontier, to keep the young men of the tribe out of mischief, were re-constituted as combatant battalions, the 1st and 2nd Mahsud Scouts (*Mizh*). The Bajaur Scouts were raised in 1961 for the Bajaur, Swat and Dir tribal areas. The last corps to be formed, in 1973, was the Shawal Scouts, based on Razmak.

As under the British, most Scout units are composed of mixed Pathan tribes, a majority always being from other parts of the Frontier. Exceptions are the Northern, Karakoram and Chitral Scouts, composed entirely of local tribesmen; the Kurram Militia, composed almost entirely of Turis and their neighbours; the two Mahsud (*Mizh*) battalions; and the Chagai Militia, composed of local Pathans, Baluchis and Brahuis. Pakistan makes far more use than the British ever did of Mahsud fire and fighting quality; recruiting the young men of that tribe not only into their own corps, but into the Bajaur Scouts, Khyber Rifles, SWS and Kalat Scouts. Wazirs are recruited into the Khyber Rifles and Tochi Scouts.

The pattern of Frontier trouble has changed since 1947. In the early years of Pakistan, with the Faqir of Ipi bitterly hostile and the movement for a breakaway state of 'Pukhtunistan' encouraged by the Indian and Afghan Governments, there was quite a lot of trouble in Waziristan and the Kurram, skirmishes, sniping, ambushes, though nothing on the scale of 1936–42. Then Waziristan more or less quietened down, but there had to be operations in 1960–2 against some rebellious Bajaur tribes, tough and very well armed, who continue to give sporadic trouble and take pot-shots at the Bajaur Scouts. Baluchistan, so quiet and peaceful since 1922, is now no longer so. In 1951 there was a tribal inruption from Afghanistan, necessitating the call-up of the local tribal lashkar in support of the Pishin Scouts. The Baluchis and Brahuis are encouraged from Kabul and Moscow to complain of being second-class citizens in a country dominated by Punjabis and Pathans, and even to agitate for an independent Baluchistan, totally impracticable but keenly encouraged in certain quarters. There were operations in Zhob and Kalat.

On the whole, however, Pakistan has had less Frontier trouble than the British ever had except perhaps during the late 1920s. Undoubtedly this is due to the tribes having no innate hostility to a Moslem Government which, moreover, has poured development funds into the tribal areas and improved the tribesmen's lives by education, more recruitment and economic growth. Nevertheless the Russian invasion of Afghanistan obviously adds a new dimension to the Frontier problem, and lays more responsibilities on the Frontier Corps.

The Pakistan Government makes more flexible use of the Scouts than the British did. Thus we hear of detachments of Khyber Rifles, Tochi Scouts and SWS operating in Pishin; of the Khyber Rifles and Tochi Scouts in Bajaur. All the corps sent contingents of eager volunteers to fight in Kashmir in 1948, and in the two subsequent Indo-Pak wars, in which they won many decorations and suffered not a few casualties.

Former Scouts Officers revisiting the Frontier since Independence receive a wonderfully warm welcome from their old corps and from white-bearded veterans of Shahur Tangi and Iblanke. They find many changes, some good and some, in their opinion, not so good. The first that strikes the eye is that the pagri is no longer worn by Scouts, other than the tourist-conscious guard of Khyber Rifles at Landi Khana. The fine cotton cloth of which it is made is manufactured only in India, and is very expensive in Pakistan. So it has been replaced in Scouts and Army by the less picturesque but more practicable beret, except in the Karakoram, Northern, Gilgit and Chitral Scouts who wear the pukhol or koi cap of the Hindu Kush. The ·303 rifle has been replaced by the FN automatic rifle; there is an increased scale of machine-guns, mortars, artillery and motor transport. Except in the SWS, Mounted Infantry has been phased out, replaced to some extent, though not to everyone's satisfaction, by four-wheel drive cross-country Jeeps and Land Rovers.

Retired officers regret that less foot-gashting is done than in days of yore, a phenomenon not unknown in other armies. By no means all the officers speak Pushtu: on the other hand, the tribes are better educated than in British days, so far more of the other ranks speak and write Urdu.

But the essentials remain. The Frontier Corps are still supremely active, efficient, hard-hitting, mobile, irregular mountain troops. They have terrific pride. They still knock spots off the army at rifle-shooting. They are very much a corps d'élite.

Glossary

of Vernacular Words and Phrases

These are mainly Pushtu, although many are common to Urdu, Persian and Arabic.

Algad River-bed, generally dry.

Aziz Dear friend.

Badal Vengeance.

Badragga Armed escort, usually of Khassadars.

Bahadur Brave man, hero.

Barampta Round-up of suspected persons, of people to be held as hostages for good behaviour, or of their livestock.

Chapao Ambush.

Chapli Pathan sandal, with open toes and a heel-strap.

Chiga Pursuit. A chiga-party would be ready to sally out of a fort or a village in pursuit of raiders.

Chikor A type of partridge, closely related to the Red-Legged or French partridge.

Chupatti Disc of unleavened bread.

Daz Shot. *Daz-maz* or *dazé-mazé* means sniping. Anglicised into a verb in Scouts' parlance; 'to be dazzed' meant to be shot up.

Doolie Carrying chair, similar to Sedan chair.

Faqir A holy man.

Faranghi Frank, the term applied by Moslems to Europeans since the Crusades.

Gasht A Scouts' patrol, generally of about 4-platoon strength. Anglicised in Scouts' parlance into a verb, 'gashting' or 'to gasht'.

283

Glossary of Vernacular Words and Phrases

Ghar   Hill.

Ghazi   Fanatical warrior pledged to death and to killing infidels.

Ghundai   Knoll.

Gud   Wild sheep. *Urial* in the Punjab, *Shapu* in Kashmir, *Mouflon* in Europe.

Gurgura   A grey-green shrub similar to the sage-bush.

Gushpur   Aristocratic class of Gilgit or Chitral.

Haji   One who has made the Haj, the pilgrimage to Mecca.

Hallagullah   Uproar, confused dashing about.

Hamsaya   One living under a tribe's or an individual's protection.

Izzat   Honour.

Jehad   Holy War.

Jezail   Old-fashioned, long-barrelled matchlock.

Jhalsa   Annual ceremony of doing homage in Gilgit.

Jirga   Tribal assembly or parliament.

Jor ye?   Are you well? One of the conventional greetings.

Josh   Dash (noun), aggressiveness.

Kach   Alluvial flat on the bank of a stream.

Khassadar   Un-uniformed tribal levy, armed with his own rifle.

Khat   A mild drug.

Khostwal   Tribesman of one of the tribes inhabiting the Afghan province of Khost.

Khud   Steep, stony and rocky hillside.

Khushal ye?   Are you happy? A conventional greeting.

Khwar mashé   May you not be poor. A conventional greeting.

Kirri   Encampment, village or caravan of nomads.

Koi   The Gilgit term for the woollen cap of the Karakoram area.

Kot   Fortified tower or strongly built house, e.g. the arms-kot was the armoury.

Kotal   Pass.

Kuhl   Water channel.

Kullah   Dome-shaped, padded skull-cap round which was wound the pagri.

Lashkar   A tribal armed force. *Lashkarwal*, member of a lashkar.

Malik   Tribal headman, but without real executive authority other than that conferred by wealth and personality.

Markhor   Wild goat, with horns like corkscrews or barley-sugar.

Mazri   Coarse, blue-grey cotton cloth used for Scout uniforms.

Melmastia   Hospitality.

Mulaqati   Man who comes to visit the Political Agent or other officer with petitions, complaints or just to pass the time of day.

Glossary of Vernacular Words and Phrases

Mullah Man learned in the Koran, a preacher and lay reader, but not a 'priest'. Islam has no priesthood.

Munshi Language teacher.

Nanawati Shelter or protection.

Narai Col.

Pagri Turban.

Partog Baggy trousers.

Pir Saint.

Posteen Embroidered sheepskin coat, worn with the hair inside.

Powindah Collective term applied to many nomad tribes.

Pukhol The Chitral name for the woollen cap of the region.

Pukhtun The northern form of Pathan. *Pukhtu*, the *Pukhtun*'s language, generally known as Pushtu.

Pukhtunwali The Pathan's code of honour.

Qafila Camel-caravan.

Qillaband Fort-bound, afraid or unable to move out of a fort.

Rabab Stringed musical instrument.

Raghza Stony plain.

Safa Turban.

Sangar Protective stone wall, or breastwork.

Sar Hilltop.

Sardar Chief. Also applied to Indian Officers.

Sarishta The customary tribal pecking-order of importance of maliks and sections.

Sarkar The Indian Government. The term 'Raj' is largely a post-1947 invention.

Shamleh The loose end of the pagri.

Shariat Islamic law.

Shikari Hunter, stalker.

Silladar Irregular cavalry in which the men owned their horses.

Sisi Partridge, smaller than the chikor.

Staré mashé May you not be tired. A conventional greeting.

Tamasha Party or show of any kind.

Tangi Gorge, ravine.

Tikala Feast.

Toi Stream, pool, water.

285

Appendix 1

Indian Army and Scout Ranks

Infantry	Cavalry and Mounted Infantry	Badge
Subadar Major	Risaldar Major	Crown
Subadar	Risaldar	Two stars
Jemadar	Jemadar	One star
Havildar	Daffadar	Three chevrons
Naik	Lance Daffadar	Two chevrons
Lance Naik	Acting Lance Daffadar	One chevron
Sepoy (corruption of *Sipahi*)	Sowar (literally, rider)	

Also, Havildar Major, Daffadar Major, etc.

Appendix 2

King's Commissioned Officers in or closely associated with the Frontier Corps who are mentioned in the text

Abbreviations

Cav: Cavalry   CS: Chitral Scouts   FF Rif: Frontier Force Rifles
FFR: Frontier Force Regt   GR: Gurkha Rifles   GS: Gilgit Scouts
Inf: Infantry   IOFC: Inspecting Officer, Frontier Corps
K: Killed in action or assassinated   KM: Kurram Militia
KR: Khyber Rifles   NWM: North Waziristan Militia
Pol: Indian Political Service   Raj Rif: Rajputana Rifles
SWM: South Waziristan Militia
SWS: South Waziristan Scouts   TS: Tochi Scouts
W: Wounded   ZM: Zhob Militia

	Name	Final Army Rank	Decorations	Army Unit	Service in Frontier Corps		
K	Alderman, R. H. R.	Capt	MC	4/6 Raj Rif	Lt	SWS	1938–41
	Ambrose, R. D.	Brig	CIE, OBE, MC	1/6 Raj Rif	Lt	SWS	1923–8
					Major	TS	1931–6
					Col	IOFC	1945–8
	Aslam Khan, Sardar Mohamad	Major	CIE		Major	KR	1878–96
	Auret, J. H.	Major		3/10 Baluch	Capt/ Major	TS	1940–5
	Babington, A. M. S.	Lt Col		4/12 FFR	Lt/Capt	TS	1932–5
					Capt	SWS	1935–8
	Bacon, R. N.	Lt Col	CBE			Pol	
	Barker, A. R.	Brig	DSO, OBE, MC	2 GR	Lt	SWM	1918–19
					Capt	TS	1920–1
W	Barlow, L. M.	Lt Col	OBE, MC	Guides Inf	Lt	NWM	1920
K	Barnes, H. A.	Lt Col				Pol	
	Barton, L. E.	Lt Col		Guides Inf	Capt	KR	1898–1903

	Name	Final Army Rank	Decorations	Army Unit	Service in Frontier Corps		
	Beamish, R. P.	Lt Col		3/14 Punjab	Lt	KM	1919
K	Beatty, R. N.	Capt		Hodson's Horse	Lt	TS Pol	1935–7
W	Becker, H. B.					Pol	
	Boulter, H. E.	Brig	CBE, DSO	1/12 FFR	Lt	TS	1935–8
	Boulter, H. G.	Lt Col		1/6 Raj Rif	Lt Capt	SWS SWS	1923–6 1928–32
K	Bowring, J. B.	Capt				Pol	
W	Bromhead, Sir B. D. G. Bt	Lt Col	OBE	Sikh Pioneers 2/12 FFR	Lt/Capt Major Lt Col	SWS TS Pol ZM	1929–32 1937–8 1947–8
	Brown, W. A.	Major	MBE	12 FFR	Lt Lt/Capt Capt Capt Major	SWS GS TS CS GS	1943 1943–6 1946–7 1947 1947–8
	Bull, G.	Major		58 FF Rif	Capt	NWM	1910–13
	Bunbury, N. I. St P.	Brig	DSO	1/13 FF Rif	Capt	ZM	1921–4
K	Burn-Murdoch, C. T.	Capt		20 Punjab	Capt	SWM	1917–19
	Cable, D. J.	Lt Col	MC	6 GR	Lt/Capt	TS	1940–4
W	Campbell, Sir W. F.	Lt Col	KCIE			Pol	
	Caroe, Sir Olaf		KCSI, KCIE			Pol	
	Chambers, K. M.	Lt Col		3/8 Punjab	Major Lt Col	TS SWS	1946–7 1947–8
	Cheeseman, W. A.	Lt Col	MC	4/6 Raj Rif	Lt	SWS	1936–9
	Cobb, E. H.	Lt Col	OBE			Pol	
	Corfield, R. C.	Major		17/13 FF Rif	Capt Major	TS SWS	1945–9 1949–50
W	Cosby, N. R. C.	Brig	CIE, MC	5 RGR 5/1 Punjab	Capt Major Col	TS SWS IOFC	1923–8 1930–5 1942–5
	Crapp, W. V.	Lt Col		3/17 Dogra	Capt Capt	SWS CS	1927–30 1930–2
	Cubitt-Smith, H. E.	Brig	CBE, DSO	1/12 FFR	Capt	SWS	1930–3
	Cunningham, Sir G.		KCSI, KCIE, OBE		Pol		
K	Dewar, I. B. D.	Capt		2/17 Dogra	Lt Capt	TS SWS	1927–30 1935–8
	Dodd, P. C. R.	Major	DSO	31 Lancers	Capt/ Major	KM	1910–20
K	Dodds, G.	Major		27 Punjab	Capt Major	NWM Pol	1900–4 1909–12

288

	Name	Final Army Rank	Decorations	Army Unit	Service in Frontier Corps		
K	Downes, A. A. H.	Lt		1/13 FF Rif	Lt	TS	1941-2
	Dracott, H.	Capt		3/14 Punjab	Capt	SWS	1926-31
W	Dyer, C. J.	Capt		3/10 Baluch	Capt	SWS	1931-4
	Erskine, C. E. T.	Col	CIE, DSO, MC	Guides Inf	Major Col	TS IOFC	1922-7 1934-7
	Felix-Williams, A.	Brig	DSO, MC	1/13 FF Rif	Capt Major	SWS TS	1928-33 1936-8
	Ferguson-Davie, A. F.	Lt Col	DSO	53 Sikhs	Capt	NWM	1900-5
	Ffinch, H. D. N.	Lt	MC	3 GR			
W	FitzMaurice, W. H.	Col		6/13 FF Rif 4/15 Punjab	Capt Major Col	SWS TS Dy IOFC	1930-5 1938-40 1946-7
	French, E. E.	Lt Col	MC	5/10 Baluch	Capt Major	TS SWS	1933-7 1940-2
	Gardiner, M. M.	Major		5/13 FF Rif	Lt/Capt Major	TS ZM	1939-45 1946-7
	Gardyne, C. G.	Lt Col		3/11 Sikh	Capt	SWS	1926-9
	Garland, The Revd H. E.	Lt Col		3 GR	Capt Lt Col	TS KM	1930-3 1946-7
W	Gibb, J. A.	Lt Col		14/1 Punjab	Capt	SWS	1944-7
	Gilbert, C.	Lt Col		2/13 FF Rif	Capt	SWS	1928-31
	Gimson, W. A.	Brig	MC	Guides Cav	Capt	TS	1935-7
	Graham, G. K.	Lt Col				Indian Medical Service	
	Griffith, R. R.	Capt		Guides Inf	Lt/Capt	TS	1938-41
K	Harman, R.	Lt Col	DSO	54 Sikhs	Lt Col	SWM	1900-5
	Harvey-Kelly, J.	Major		4/10 Baluch	Major	SWS	1948-50
	Hassan, S. I.	Capt		5/10 Baluch	Capt	TS Pol	1940-1
	Hawkins, G. F.	Capt		Somerset LI, seconded to 6 GR	Lt/Capt	TS	1943-5
	Hawkins, G. J.	Col		2/12 FFR	Lt	ZM	1937-40
	Hodson, R. V. E.	Major	MBE			Pol	
	Howell, Sir E. B.		KCIE, CSI			Pol	
K	Hughes, F. L.	Major		20 Punjab	Major	SWM	1913-17
W	Hunt, R. E.	Capt		IASC	Capt	SWM	1919
	Hutchins, H. R.	Major		5/1 Punjab	Capt/Major	SWS	1941-7
	Janson, P. B.	Lt Col	OBE	1/12 FFR	Capt Major/Lt Col	SWS TS	1933-6 1942-6

	Name	Final Army Rank	Decorations	Army Unit	Service in Frontier Corps		
	Johnson, H. H.	Col	CIE, MM	2/12 FFR	Major	SWS Pol	1924–9
K	Jotham, E.	Capt	VC	51 Sikhs	Capt	NWM	1912–15
	Keating, G. F. S.	Lt Col	OBE	5/14 Punjab	Lt Capt	SWS TS	1928–33 1934–7
K	Keogh, J. A.	Capt		1/12 FFR	Capt	SWS	1936–7
	Khushwaqt-ul-Mulk	Col		4 Kumaon Rif	Lt/Major Lt Col	SWS SWS	1941–6 1948–9
K	Laman, F. E. K.	Capt	MC	5/1 Punjab	Capt	TS	1935–8
K	Leese, F. W.	Lt		29 Punjab	Lt	SWM	1919
	Lerwill, G.	Brig	OBE, MC	2/11 Sikh	Lt	TS	1937–40
K	Lowe, J. G. D.	Capt		2/17 Dogra	Lt/Capt	TS	1941–2
	Lowis, J. W. A.	Lt Col		4 GR	Lt	SWS	1937–40
	Lowis, R. H. D.		OBE			Pol	
	Lydall, E. F.					Pol	
K	MacCorstie, E. J.	Lt		1/25 London	Lt	Garrison Engineer Wana	1919
	McDonald, H. W. D.	Brig	DSO, OBE	2/12 FFR	Lt/Capt	SWS	1934–7
	McHarg, I. H.	Col	DSO, MC	4/16 Punjab	Major	KM	1938–42
	McNeile, D. H.	Lt Col		19 Lancers	Major	NWM	1909–11
	Majury, J. H. S.	Major-General	CB, MBE	R Ulster Rif, seconded to 5/15 Punjab	Major	SWS	1943–7
	Mardall, F. H.	Lt Col		3/17 Dogra	Major	TS	1929–32
	Mathieson, A. S.	Capt		Seaforth Highlanders	Khassadar Officer, N. Waz. Capt	GS	1946–7 1947–8
	Milanes, R. J. F.	Lt Col		2/12 FFR	Major	GS	1944–7
	Moberley, W. I.	Col	CBE	3/12 FFR	Capt	TS	1938–41
	Moore, A. C. S.	Lt Col		Guides Inf	Lt Major Lt Col	TS TS SWS	1935–8 1945–7 1947
	Moorhead, E. D.	Lt Col		2/16 Punjab	Capt	SWS	1923–7
	O'Connor, M. J.	Major		3/9 Jat	Lt	SWS	1924–7
	Ottley, J. F. S.	Lt Col		1/1 Punjab	Capt/Major	SWS	1940–5
	Packman, K. C.	Lt Col	CIE			Pol	
	Parsons, Sir A. E. B.	Major-General	KCIE, CBE, DSO	52 Sikh	Lt/Capt	NWM Pol	1913–19
	Paul, R. S.	Lt Col		126 Baluch	Lt Col	ZM	1917–20
	Pettigrew, H. R. C.	Col		2/14 Punjab	Lt	SWS	1937–40

Appendix 2

	Name	Final Army Rank	Decorations	Army Unit	Service in Frontier Corps		
	Phillips, T. J.	Major		9 GR	Lt/Capt Capt	TS KM	1938–41 1943–4
	Platt, J. W. C.	Lt Col		8 Cav	Capt	TS	1932–5
	Plant, W. C. T. G. G.	Lt Col		23 Cav	Capt	SWM	1902–6
	Prendergast, J. H.	Brig	DSO, MC	4/15 Punjab	Lt	TS	1936–9
	Rahim Khan, A.	Major				Pol	
	Raw, W. G.	Major				Pol	
	Reford, L. B. H.	Lt Col	MC	3/12 FFR	Lt Capt	TS KM	1938–41 1941–2
K	Reilly, A. F.	Capt		I.A. Reserve of Officers	Capt	ZM	1916–19
	Reilly, N. E.	Capt	DSO		Capt	Pol/CS	1917–19
W	Robertson, F. D.	Major	MC	1/Kumaon Rif	Lt	SWS	1935–8
	Roos-Keppel, Sir G. O.	Lt Col	KCSI, KCIE			Pol	
W	Russell, G. H.	Col	CIE, DSO	126 Baluch 4/12 FFR	Major Major Col	SWM SWS IOFC	1919–21 1920–4 1931–5
K	Russell, H. V. L.	Capt		1/16 Punjab	Capt	TS	1938–40
	Sadiqullah Khan	Brig	MC	6/13 FF Rif	Major Lt Col	SWS TS	1945–6 1948–50
W	Sanders, G. P. V.	Lt Col		5 RGR	Capt	TS	1937–40
	Sandison, W.	Lt Col	DSO, OBE	5/8 Punjab	Lt Lt Lt Col	CS SWS TS	1931–3 1933–4 1946–8
	Scotland, A. G.	Col	MC	1/12 FFR	Capt Major	SWS ZM	1928–33 1936–9
	Scott, G. B.	Col	CB, DSO	27 Punjab	Capt/Major Col	NWM IOFC	1911–19 1926–31
	Sharif Khan, Mohamad	Lt Col	MBE	5/10 Baluch	Lt/Major	TS KR	1940–5 1946
K	Skrine, P. R. H.	Lt Col	DSO	1/6 Raj Rif	Major	SWS	1934–7
	Spain, G. A. R.	Capt		103 Inf	Capt	ZM	1918–21
K	Tapp, G. H.	Lt		4/10 Baluch	Lt	SWS	1923–4
K	Taylor, R. P.	Lt Col		3/17 Dogra	Capt Major Lt Col	TS GS TS	1932–5 1940–1 1941–2
	Taylor, T. S.	Major-General	MC	5/14 Punjab	Lt	SWS	1936–9
K	Traill, H. R.	Capt		87 Punjab	Capt	SWM	1919
	Trench, Sir R. H. Chenevix	Lt Col	CIE, OBE			Pol	
	Trotter, J. G.	Lt Col		2/19 Hyderabad	Capt	GS	1933–6

Name	Final Army Rank	Decorations	Army Unit	Service in Frontier Corps		
Venning, D. R.	Lt Col	OBE, MC	5 RGR	Lt	SWS	1934–7
				Major	TS	1941–4
				Lt Col	SWS	1944–7
Wainright, V. L. M.	Brig	OBE, MC	2/13 FF Rif	Lt	TS	1935–8
Warburton, Sir R.	Col	CIE			Pol	
Warden, J. W. S.	Lt Col	MC	3/2 Punjab	Lt	SWS	1935–8
				Capt/Major	TS	1938–43
Watson, J. M.	Capt		7 GR	Lt/Capt	SWS	1941–5
White, M. W. H.	Lt Col	MBE	7 GR	Major/Lt Col	CS	1939–
W Wilcock, S. D.	Capt	MC	1/16 Punjab	Capt	SWS	1936–8
Williams, D. H. J.	Brig	OBE	6/13 FF Rif	Capt	SWS	1928–31
				Major	SWS	1937–41
K Williams, N. G.	Capt	MC	2/14 Punjab	Lt/Capt	SWS	1939–42
				Capt	TS	1942–3
Williams, S. P.	Lt Col	CIE	2/14 Punjab	Capt	ZM	1921–4
				Major	SWS	1924–8
Woods, D. L. O.	Lt Col	OBE	2/13 FF Rif	Capt/Major	SWS	1937–44
Youngman, H. C. L.	Lt Col	MC	1/4 Bombay Grenadiers	Lt	TS	1930–2
				Capt	CS	1932–5
				Major	TS	1938–41
Yusuf Khan, Mohamad	Lt Col	MC	6/13 FF Rif	Lt/Capt	SWS Pol	1937–43

Bibliography

Official Histories published by Government of India Press

The Third Afghan War 1919
Operations in Waziristan 1919–20
Operations on the North-West Frontier of India 1921–35
Operations on the North-West Frontier of India 1936–7
Annual Reports, Baluchistan 1919–39
Annual Reports, North-West Frontier Province 1919–39

Non-official Publications

'The Attack on the Convoy at Shahur Tangi', *United Services of India Institution Journal*, April 1937
Sir Olaf Caroe, *The Pathans*, London, 1965
Sir Evelyn Howell, *Mizh: A Monograph on Government's Relations with the Mahsud Tribe*, Government of India Press, 1931
'Iblanka. The Advance to the Sham Plain', *United Services of India Institution Journal*, April 1938
Edward Lydall, *Enough of Action*, London, 1949
Lieutenant General Sir George McMunn, 'A Study in Martyrdom', *Blackwood's Magazine*, February 1930
John Masters, *Bugles and a Tiger*, London, 1956
Colonel H. R. C. Pettigrew, *Frontier Scouts*, Privately printed
Brigadier J. H. Prendergast, *Prender's Progress: A Soldier in India*, London, 1979
General Sir Andrew Skene, *Passing It On*, Aldershot, 1930
Colonel Sir Robert Warburton, *Eighteen Years in the Khyber*, London, 1900

In India Office Library and Records

L/P & S/12/3144   Report of the Committee on the Civil Armed Forces of the North-West Frontier Province (1926)
L/P & S/13/1860/451/47   Papers on recent events in the Gilgit Agency
Eur MSS C 308   Lieut-Colonel Bolam 'The Ambush in the Shahur Tangi'
Eur MSS D 879   Letters of R. H. D. Lowis

Index